Approaches to Modern Chinese History

EDITED BY
ALBERT FEUERWERKER
RHOADS MURPHEY
MARY C. WRIGHT

Approaches to Modern Chinese History

UNIVERSITY OF CALIFORNIA PRESS
BERKELEY AND LOS ANGELES 1967

University of California Press
Berkeley and Los Angeles, California

Cambridge University Press
London, England

Copyright © 1967, by
The Regents of the University of California

Library of Congress Catalog Card Number: 67–15640
Printed in the United States of America

Designed by David Pauly

FOR JOHN KING FAIRBANK

From his students
on his sixtieth birthday, May 24, 1967
—a modest token of our admiration,
affection, and gratitude.

CONTRIBUTORS

Harold L. Kahn, Lecturer in Far Eastern History, School of Oriental and African Studies, University of London

E-tu Zen Sun, Associate Professor of History and Research Associate in Mineral Economics, The Pennsylvania State University

Kwang-ching Liu, Professor of History, University of California, Davis

John L. Rawlinson, Associate Professor of History, Hofstra University

Paul A. Cohen, Associate Professor of History, Wellesley College

Marius B. Jansen, Professor of History, Princeton University

Robert A. Scalapino, Professor of Political Science, University of California, Berkeley

Akira Iriye, Assistant Professor of History, University of California, Santa Cruz

Ernest P. Young, Assistant Professor of History, Dartmouth College

Joseph R. Levenson, Sather Professor of History, University of California, Berkeley

John Israel, Assistant Professor of History, Claremont Men's College

Albert Feuerwerker, Professor of History, The University of Michigan

Rhoads Murphey, Professor of Geography, The University of Michigan

Mary C. Wright, Professor of History, Yale University

Contents

Introduction

ARLY study of the modern history of China in Europe and America concentrated heavily upon the foreign relations of that country—its relations with the Western powers whose intrusion upon it, so to speak, marked the beginning of its modern history. Magisterial works were produced by the first scholars who, shunning both the minutiae of contemporary sinology and the inevitable condescension of treaty-port journalism, turned to look as historians at the last century of the Manchu empire. H. B. Morse's *The International Relations of the Chinese Empire* (3 vols. London, 1910–1918) was a landmark in English-language writing on modern China, although perhaps only the first of its three volumes may still be read with profit today; so, too, was Henri Cordier's *Historie des relations de la Chine avec les puissances occidentales, 1860–1902* (3 vols., Paris, 1901–1902) a landmark in French. Morse was never able to escape completely the typically superior tone of the treaty-port critic of mandarin behavior. But his detailed, documented history represented a major qualitative advance beyond the writings of contemporary "old China hands," who first postulated and then deplored for a foreign audience the inscrutability of Chinese ways and the utter hopelessness of the Middle Kingdom's situation.

While Morse and Cordier made good use respectively of English and French documents, including unpublished materials, their lengthy accounts were almost barren of documentation from the Chinese side. In part this omission reflected the nonavailability of Chinese archival materials even on the relatively restricted subject of diplomatic relations with the Western powers to which Morse and Cordier confined themselves. The major collections of published Chinese diplomatic documents began to appear only in the 1930's (e.g., *Ch'ou-pan i-wu shih-mo*

[A Complete Account of the Management of Barbarian Affairs], 260 *chüan,* Peiping, 1930; *Ch'ing-chi wai-chiao shih-liao* [Historical Materials on Foreign Relations in the Latter Part of the Ch'ing Dynasty] 243 *chüan,* Peiping, 1932–1935). Although some parts of the vast archives of the Manchu dynasty were available to scholars in the 1920's and 1930's, they were never organized for the purposes of research. Indeed, in 1921 the impoverished Historical Museum sold some 8,000 sacks of Nei Ko (Grand Secretariat) documents for pulping to a Peking paper manufacturer. A considerable portion of what was sold was fortunately recovered through the intercession of the eminent antiquarian Lo Chen-yü, and some of this was eventually sold back to the Historical Museum. But the remainder was scattered into the hands of private collectors.

More was involved, however, than the nonavailability of Chinese materials. Even at the time Morse wrote, in 1908–1917, he could have used Chinese-language documents—if he had been able to read them, and more important if he had thought it essential to do so. One of the characteristics of the first Western scholars of modern Chinese history—a fact to which their successors still respond ambiguously—was their separation from the tradition of sinological learning which had developed in the West from the time of the Jesuits in the seventeenth century until it came under attack by Chavannes and Pelliot in the first part of the twentieth. It was less true of Cordier than of Morse, but true enough of both that neither was deeply committed to the literati-official self-image of Chinese civilization which, as Arthur Wright has shown, dominated Western sinology during this entire period. Cordier founded *T'oung Pao,* the premier European sinological journal of the first half of the twentieth century, and was one of its editors until his death in 1925. But the immense corpus of his writing over half a century was not based on the use of original Chinese sources. While Paul Pelliot reviewed Morse's *Chronicles of the East India Company Trading to China* favorably, Morse's death in 1934 did not even merit a *nécrologie* in *T'oung Pao* such as Pelliot and others had produced over the years for numerous minor European sinologues. Cordier's seven years in China, from 1869 to 1876, had been spent in the employ of the American trading firm of Russell and Co. Morse served in the Imperial Maritime Customs from 1874 to 1908, rising to the post of Statistical Secretary before his retirement. Neither was by academic training a sinologue. In writing about the China of his immediate past, each, undoubtedly in part because of his firsthand experience with the trade and new commercial institutions which had recently been forced upon China by the West, was little prone to acknowledge the timeless, changeless civilization of the traditional sinologues, a concept which even as Cordier and Morse wrote was being challenged by the new departures in French sinology. The gain for their accounts was one of substantive relevance; the loss was an ignorance, more probably a slighting, of the potential value of the immense body of indigenous sources even for the problems which they sought to examine.

In general, Morse and Cordier also abstained, as already noted, from the usual carping tone of the treaty-port voices which surrounded them. The gain here was manifestly one of objectivity. There was paradoxically also a loss, but one which is only apparent now and which could have been neither apprehended nor repaired in 1902 or 1918. For all the meretricious words about "mandarins" and their behavior produced by nineteenth-century China hands, perhaps one may at this remove suggest that treaty-port discourses also contained the first attempts—largely implicit and inadvertent to be sure—to grapple with the central problem of the nature of China's response to the Western impact. The efforts, if one excepts such genius as that of Thomas Taylor Meadows, were crude, unfinished, unsystematic, and often misleading. But time and again they touched upon themes of cultural values, social integration, political ideology, and economic organization which in the past decade have become the principal concerns of historians and other social scientists attempting to explain the modern history not only of China but of the entire non-Western world. Inasmuch as we ourselves in the 1960's have barely begun to sound these themes and to elaborate the theory and the body of data with which to investigate them with objectivity, we do not expect to find them developed by Morse and Cordier. Their objectivity at the turn of the century was achieved at the price of restricting themselves mainly to the diplomatic record, to the relative impersonality of the documents shuffled by company and crown, minister and consul.

Research and writing in the West on China's modern history that exploited in depth the Chinese sources, as well as the immense outpourings of Japanese brushes and pens—in the twentieth century it is the Japanese who, primarily because of their vision of Japan's special role on mainland China, have quantitatively surpassed all other nations in their study of China—is a very recent development. This new history of modern China has other equally important dimensions. It has abandoned the restrictions of traditional diplomatic history, and has begun to explore the problems of Chinese society, intellectual life, political structure and dynamics, and economic development, as well as the public and private careers of the men whose actions constitute the history of each of these spheres. It attempts to be firmly grounded in a knowledge of traditional Chinese civilization, having profited from the critical work of Chavannes, Pelliot, and Maspero and from the myth-breaking of a brilliant generation of Chinese scholars who applied Western methods to the critical study of their hoary tradition. It is aware of the rapid development of theory and data in the social sciences in the twentieth century and tries, if only in the historian's eclectic way, to apply these findings to its own research problems. It demands high standards of historical technique and exposition, and by so doing seeks to place the study of the history of modern China within the mainstream of historiography in Europe and America, on an equal footing with the study of any other country.

In the United States, the first prototypes of this new history began to appear only in the 1930's, but although these were exemplary works, they numbered barely a handful. The real burgeoning followed the end of World War II—a conflagration that brought to an end centuries of European domination of Asia, unleashed a civil war in China that radically altered the fate of that vast nation, and awakened in some Americans at least an awareness of their ignorance of the source and probable future course of these transformations and an ambition to comprehend both the massive past and the importunate present of China.

Through the 1930's, during and after World War II, and up to the present, the study of China, including modern China, has been nurtured in the United States by many institutions and dedicated individuals. We have assembled this volume of *Approaches to Modern Chinese History* because we believe that the development of modern Chinese historical studies is to a very large degree the result of the inspiration, the training, and the example provided by John King Fairbank, now Francis Lee Higginson Professor of History and Director of the East Asian Research Center at Harvard University. His students and colleagues (and most of his colleagues were once his students) know the debt they owe him, and yet even they seldom have occasion to step back and observe the dimensions of his achievement. The traditional Chinese custom of honoring all good men on their sixtieth birthdays, and of greatly honoring great men, provides us with a ritual occasion to try to say something which goes beyond ritual.

When Fairbank became an instructor in history at Harvard in 1936, modern Chinese history scarcely existed as a field of scholarship. In China itself a handful of pioneers had just begun to explore the record of the past two centuries. Japanese scholars in that era of military adventure on the Asian mainland generally sought safe subjects. The great French sinological tradition continued to ignore modern China, as did other centers of sinology in western and central Europe. In the Soviet Union, study of modern China was either operationally-oriented intelligence research (and minimal at that) or part of a tortuous debate over general principles of Marxism and Leninism. British writing on modern China was in the main amateur reminiscence in which the tumultuous Chinese scene was tidily framed in the window of an Anglican mission or a treaty port consulate general. Work in the United States was generally a rough version of the British model with occasional enclaves of continental influence. With a few notable exceptions, the Chinese intellectuals among us joined our amateur tradition.

Over the past three decades, Fairbank has transformed the study of modern China. In his own research he has set standards that would have been inconceivable earlier: sustained investigation at once microscopic and comprehensive, imaginative analysis, and publication of the results in clear and witty prose of understated elegance. He has also taken the lead and has done much of the work in the essential but arduous task of producing tools for the development of the field: bibliographies, textbooks, and research guides.

Each of us can testify to the patience, insight, and kindness with which Fairbank encourages students to come into the modern Chinese field, and to the unstinting support he gives them not only in graduate school but throughout their careers. The program of training which he developed now shows a multiplier effect as his former students assume responsibility for instruction in several dozen colleges and universities throughout the United States.

Fairbank's concern has not been to build Harvard to the detriment of other universities but to use Harvard's strength in the modern Chinese field—largely a strength of his making—to develop this field of scholarship wherever an interest can be germinated. Quietly and unobtrusively he has been able to help young Chinese and Japanese scholars extend their training and to help their institutions solve some of the problems involved in developing research on modern China. Increasingly in recent years he has worked towards more effective scholarly relations among all specialists on modern China, East and West, on both sides of the Atlantic and on both sides of the Iron Curtain.

Fairbank's concern with heightened awareness and understanding of modern China has spilled from the academic world into broader sections of society, as he has intended. Over the past twenty years, since his return to Harvard after wartime service in China, his has been an eloquent, moderate, and judicious voice. He has used every channel that our society provides for public enlightenment, not in search of headlines but despite the headlines, out of a sense of responsibility for using all his extraordinary talents to good purpose. But he returns to his study and his students as quickly as possible.

From among these many students, the editors have selected what we hope is a representative group of essays which in technique and theme illustrate the progress that modern Chinese historical studies have made from the time of Cordier and Morse to that of Fairbank. Chronologically their subject matter ranges from the eighteenth century to the early twentieth, concentrating on the late Ch'ing period in which John Fairbank's influence has been most strongly felt. We acknowledge the genial acceptance by our colleagues of our editorial decision to omit several manuscripts which we had originally solicited for this volume in order that the resulting product not only be broadly representative of the work now going on in this field but have substantial thematic coherence as well. We have also, for reasons of space, decided not to include any essays on post-1949 China, although in the past several years study of Communist China has advanced notably—again in considerable measure due to the efforts of John Fairbank.

The twelve essays in this volume play upon four major motifs which if they were present at all in the first stage of Western study of modern China were muted: modern China's internal political-institutional history; the texture of intellectual life; the nature of the traditional and semi-modern economy; and China's foreign relations interpreted as something more than conventional diplomatic history. Each effort to strike the notes of one of these themes, as the reader will readily see, produces overtones which reverberate to one or more of the others. Mr. Kahn, for example, in his study of the education of the future Ch'ien-lung emperor, has produced for the first time an adequate description of the institutional arrangements through which a Ch'ing dynasty ruler was trained for the throne of universal empire. But deeply imbedded in the Palace School and its curriculum was a particular version of the Confucian ideology that established the "values and expectations which defined the ideals and limits of imperial action." Institutional and intellectual history are here inseparably intertwined; and if those latter-day monarchs, the T'ung-chih and Kuang-hsü emperors, were gifted with neither the personal qualities of Ch'ien-lung nor the security of a China which had not yet been challenged by the West, the ideal of imperial action against which their reigns were measured provides indispensable background for the elaboration of the late nineteenth-century policy of "self-strengthening" which Mr. Liu examines in his study of Li Hung-chang's first years as governor-general in Chihli.

The transformation of the content and context of China's internal history from the time of Ch'ien-lung to that of the Kuomintang Nanking government can be traced in the five essays which focus primarily upon domestic political-institutional developments. As Mr. Kahn notes in his concluding remarks, the ethical and historical lessons which had been Ch'ien-lung's preparation for rule would for the last time in China's modern history be relevant to the realities which an emperor faced. The personal and political standards by which imperial success was measured, as we have noted, continued inertially to be part of the intellectual baggage of the time of Li Hung-chang, Chang Chih-tung, and even K'ang Yu-wei, although in the Kuang-hsü era this was in a sense unrealistic. Mr. Liu argues with considerable point that Li Hung-chang, even with the power of the Anhwei Army behind him, was less a proto-warlord foreshadowing Chinese politics in the twentieth century than a loyal official of the Peking court seconded to command the metropolitan province. In his several diplomatic efforts for the court in the early 1870's Li had been able to count on full support and approval. When, however, he challenged the dynasty's fundamental strategic concept—that the reconquest of Sinkiang had precedence over improved coastal defenses and "self-strengthening" innovations—Li ran up against a quixotic reluctance to "abandon territories acquired by an imperial ancestor." It was Ch'ien-lung who had first incorporated Sinkiang into the Manchu empire, and his heirs dutifully demonstrated both their filiality and the persistence of a phylogenetic concern for the territory beyond settled agricultural China in part of which the Manchus themselves had arisen and whence, from other parts, in the days of K'ang-hsi and to a lesser extent of Ch'ien-lung, had come the most serious challenges to the consolidation of the Ch'ing empire. Li Hung-chang, even more dependent on the court than it was on him, found that few of his proposals for military reforms—not to speak of railroad, telegraph, and textile mill projects—were adopted.

Li Hung-chang in Chihli did not have the resources, most importantly the political resources, to go it alone. "The court's support was plainly still the key to the success of any new policy." The failure to tender that support was not simply a failure on the part of the reigning emperor as an individual, as it might have been judged in the days of Ch'ien-lung. When the demands on the imperial office had changed so radically, as they had in China after the Opium Wars and the Taiping Rebellion, the quality of the incumbent while not a trivial matter became definitely a secondary one. The imperial system itself—phenomenal form of the Confucian noumenon, inextricably joined—showed undisguised signs of cracking. But Tso Tsung-t'ang did reconquer Sinkiang, and some of what Li Hung-chang had urged in the early 1870's was accomplished in the 1880's, including the assembly of a modern navy. Mr. Rawlinson notes that by the time of the Sino-French War in 1884 the Chinese side had some fifty modern steam warships, of which more than half were Chinese-built. The problem was that these vessels were parceled out among four quasi-autonomous fleets. The ships of the Foochow dockyard flotilla fought the French unaided in 1884; by and large, Li Hung-chang's Peiyang fleet met the Japanese alone in 1894. Li Hung-chang, who might have wanted to command the entire navy, was unable to do so; but he had no ambition to overthrow the dynasty whose increasing debility was a major reason for the failure of central direction.

One might suggest that the Ch'ing dynasty survived as long as it did precisely because it was weak. If, for example, in 1900 Tz'u-hsi had been able to impel Chang Chih-tung and Liu K'un-i, who commanded the Yangtze provinces, to join the Boxer madness, could the Boxer Protocol fiction of rebellion which preserved the dynasty have been accepted by the Western powers? By the end of the first decade of the twentieth century even the constitutional monarchist Liang Ch'i-ch'ao had abandoned the Ch'ing dynasty. Mr. Young's close analysis of Liang's writings and activities after 1908 make it plain that his commitment to the dynasty, "such as it was, was complicated and conditional." The Manchu mandate to rule China was beginning to crumble after decades of foreign assault and inadequate Ch'ing response. Nationalist sentiment had been nurtured by the writings of Liang himself as much as by those of any other man. For reasons both personal and political, Liang Ch'i-ch'ao became increasingly "radical," drawing closer to the position of the specifically revolutionary organizations. He actually called for a violent uprising against the central government in 1911, and secretly planned a *coup d'état*. If Liang clung for a moment more to the notion of a figurehead monarchy under a constitution, resisting the advice of his colleagues to declare for the republic, he and the republicans were joined in a belief that the Manchu government was totally inadequate to its job, especially in regard to meeting the foreign threat to China.

Was the Nationalist government of the Kuomintang any more adequate? Mr. Israel's study of Kuomintang policy toward the student movement indicates how important a catalyst of student radicalism Japanese aggression was. Ironically, the Kuomintang had become "a prisoner of its own chauvinism. Having risen to power on slogans of national unity and having promoted a stridently nationalistic education through the school system, the ruling party had created a Frankenstein monster: a younger generation that demanded resistance at all costs." While the Manchus toward the end of their reign had at their disposal at least the remnants of a once powerful ideology with which to contain the intellectuals, the Kuomintang had nothing—little *yung* and no *t'i*. Its eleventh-hour efforts at authoritarian control were even less successful than the late Ch'ing attempts at recentralization. The circumstances were too demanding for either to be able to muddle through.

The transformation in Chinese intellectual life traced by Messrs. Cohen, Scalapino, and Levenson both reflected and affected the political changes we have outlined. Wang T'ao, perhaps modern China's first professional journalist, was as Mr. Cohen notes, "acutely alive to the critical issues of his day;" at the same time he "remained profoundly steeped in traditional Chinese culture and learning." Operating through a new medium, the daily newspaper, Wang attacked tradition more directly than his predecessors. Yet his writings imply that there were "certain aspects of Chinese tradition, those which were not inherently unmodern or uniquely Chinese," that were better suited than others to survival in the modern world. Wang was manifestly a transitional figure. Mr. Cohen suggests that the subtle balance between voluntarism and determinism in contemporary Maoism, as well as the notion that "moral agencies must be in cooperation with power," had their roots as much in the Chinese past as evoked by Wang T'ao as in modern Western thought, including its Leninist variety.

If one agrees with Mr. Cohen that there are possible intellectual continuities between Chinese tradition and Chinese Communism, one is prepared to accept Mr. Scalapino's summary of student writings in Japan in the decade before the 1911 revolution. The strident nationalism built upon a strong racial consciousness which he finds a pervasive theme is still a "powerful force in shaping the policies and attitudes of the Chinese elite, the egalitarian universalistic tenets of Marxism notwithstanding." Similarly, a romantic commitment to revolution, a "mirror to the future," characterized a majority of the student writers. Yet the values and goals to which these young men of early twentieth-century China were committed were strongly liberal; Western-style parliamentarism was their passion. If there were already shadows of doubt about the transplantation of Western values and institutions to Chinese society, the student radicals in Japan did not yet have at their disposal the "huge advances in the science of power, centering around organizational and mass media techniques," that truly distinguishes the radicals of today, including the Chinese Marxist-Leninists, from those of an earlier generation.

Into however many small transitions one divides a cataclysmic national transformation, one does not easily remove the dislocation of the conscious individual actors in this drama. Mr. Levenson's effort is to assess the changing content of Chinese identity in the process of transformation from the Ch'ing empire and world to the republican nation. The central role of province and provincialism—once hostile foe of nationalism, under the Communist regime conceived in class terms and as a possible mediator between nationalism and internationalism—is examined in this excursion into the intellectual texture of modern Chinese history. Wang T'ao, who had already begun to abandon the Empire's cosmopolitanism, and the early Chinese nationalists described by Mr. Scalapino—these give way on center stage to the "people" (*jen-min*), a "collectivist abstraction," "provincials," but with "supranational not subnational associations."

If modern China's political and intellectual life was radically metamorphosed in the past century, the economy, while bruised in some sectors, was not fundamentally altered before 1949. Mrs. Sun's survey of mining labor in the Ch'ing period and Mr. Feuerwerker's account of China's premier cement manufacturer touch at opposite ends of the pole of modernization in the industrial sector of the economy. Mrs. Sun's description of the mining industry under the Ch'ing suggests the very profound technical and organizational gap which separated traditional China from the modern West. The conditions of mining labor in early modern China were not merely inhumane; they were both an effect and a cause of very low productivity. Here was certainly one of the important sources of the drive for modernization in recent Chinese history. Mr. Feuerwerker, on the other hand, has examined the history of a Chinese manufacturing firm undertaken at the turn of the century which, unlike many of its contemporaries, turned out to be a success. The particular economic parameters of the cement industry in China contributing to Chee Hsin's growing output and profitability cannot be ignored. But Mr. Feuerwerker is equally concerned with demonstrating the critical importance of political support and a generally favorable political context for the success of modern industrial enterprise in a society whose economy remained essentially traditional. When only a handful of firms were needed to satisfy existing demand and the economy had not been reshuffled so as to induce a rapid growth in demand, the substantial advantage to any firm of having been established first and with strategic political backing cannot be gainsaid.

After 1842, most decisions on Chinese domestic policy had to be taken with a view to the foreigner's reaction. While the largest part of intellectual life continued among traditional ways without reference to the West, there were few departures from the indigenous mainstream that were not either inspired by or a reaction against the new international situation in which China found herself under the treaty system. Similarly, although the largest part of the Chinese economy remained unaffected by the Western intrusion, the economic impact of the foreigner could not be ignored in the treaty ports and their hinterlands. While British trade and the British political role were dominant among the powers in ninteenth-century China, from the perspective of the 1960's one cannot doubt that it was the presence and policies of the Japanese in the late nineteenth and twentieth centuries which made the fundamental difference for the history of modern China. Mr. Jansen's study of Meiji views of China illustrates the range of motivation which led to increasing Japanese involvement on the mainland. The shadings between idealism and self-interest upon which Mr. Jansen focuses are a commentary not only on the intellectual history of Meiji Japan but also on the political condition of China, the object of Japanese attention. A "breathtaking shift of attitudes toward China" took place in Japan after the victory of 1894–1895, reflecting the exposure to the world that Li Hung-chang's Peiyang army and navy were only paper tigers. "China as a political entity capable of will and regeneration all but disappeared from Japanese minds for over a decade." When Chinese students flocked to Tokyo in the first years of the new century, they encountered this new attitude of disrespect; here was the feeding ground of anti-Manchu nationalism.

Mr. Iriye's treatment of the interrelationship between imperialism and public opinion in the formation of late Ch'ing foreign policy makes it clear that the imperialist powers, including late Meiji Japan, "failed to respond consistently and adequately to the emergence of public opinion in China." A radical nationalism was emerging, the first sign of which was the growth of a public opinion—spurred by imperialist diplomacy—which the court could not totally ignore; but the court's response was inadequate too. Both the Ch'ing state and the diplomacy of imperialism were anachronisms, which had to go. This interplay between modern China's domestic history and its international relations, as Mr. Iriye describes it, brings us full circle to the brink of a new, more sophisticated analysis of China's foreign relations—the subject with which Morse and Cordier began the study of modern Chinese history.

HAROLD L. KAHN

The Education of a Prince: The Emperor Learns His Roles

THE Chinese emperor, it has been observed, was the supreme executive in history: "He was conqueror and patriarch, theocratic ritualist, ethical exemplar, lawgiver and judge, commander-in-chief and patron of arts and letters, and all the time administrator of the empire. . . ." [1] He was, to put it mildly, a man of many parts and his office one of heroic complexity. It is surprising then that so little attention has been given to his preparation for the throne. The emperor, after all, did not spring full grown from some miraculous mechanism of omnicompetence. He was not born to rule. He was taught to. As a prince he was taught a set of values and expectations which defined the ideals and limits of imperial action and which were meant to prepare him, however imperfectly, for the realities of the power that he would one day wield.

The imperial ground was carefully laid, the self-image seriously cultivated. There was nothing particularly glamorous or mysterious about the process. It was a hard, demanding, comprehensive course of indoctrination, a blend of classroom lessons, court manners, familial obligations, ritual responsibilities, and straightforward administrative assignments. It catered neither to that larger-than-life creature, the *wunderkind* of traditional Chi-

[1] John K. Fairbank, "Proleptical Prolegomena on the Emperor of China, Etc." (unpublished conference paper [Laconia, N.H., 1959]), p. 6.

nese emperor lore, nor to that abstraction of more recent analytical literature, the Confucianist-Legalist despot. These were the *personae* of a mythmaking process that began in earnest, at least in the Ch'ing period, only after the prince assumed the throne. Before that he still had an unvarnished job to do—lessons to learn, others to obey, and a workable image of the emperorship to form. If the history of the monarchy is ever to move beyond stereotypes to a real emperor, historians will have to take that job seriously. Even exceptional sovereigns, after all, rarely had more than modest beginnings. The Ch'ien-lung emperor (1711–1799; r.1736–1795) is a case in point.

Two Brothers: Lessons in the Public Life

Ch'ien-lung [2] did not know that he was going to be emperor; he knew only that he was eligible for consideration. For starting in the late K'ang-hsi reign, after that monarch's disastrous attempt to nominate an heir, Ch'ing monarchs selected their successors in secret, and, in theory at least, revealed the names only on their death beds. Educated guesses were of course made in circles close to the court [3] and signs of imperial prejudice or preference carefully noted. There is no concrete evidence, however, that the naming of Ch'ien-lung as heir apparent in September, 1723, was ever prematurely revealed or obviously flaunted by the emperor. For thirteen years Ch'ien-lung shared the honors and responsibilities of an untitled heir with the only other possible candidate, his half-brother and junior by three months, Hung-chou (1712–1770). Two other brothers, Hung-shih (1704–1727) and Hung-yen (1733–1765), were not in any real sense eligible. The first had been read out of the family for dissolute behavior; the second was born too late to count. And so it fell to the two favorites to prepare themselves for public life.

---

[2] I prefer, and use throughout, the convenient, if incorrect label, Ch'ien-lung, to the technically more accurate Kao-tsung, Hung-li, or Fourth Imperial Son.
[3] See, for example, the "stakes" placed on Chia-ch'ing and his half-brother, Yung-hsing, by the ex-Jesuits in Peking in 1790, five years before the former was officially proclaimed heir. E. H. Pritchard, "Letters from Missionaries at Peking Relating to the Macartney Embassy (1793–1803)," *T'oung Pao*, XXXI, 1–2 (1934), 5.

Hung-chou and Ch'ien-lung, it must be emphasized, were not rivals for power; they were equals before it. In fact the only major public note of discrimination between them during the entire course of their princedom occurred before their father took the throne. In the last year of his reign, the aged K'ang-hsi emperor had personally bade Ch'ien-lung, then only ten and a half years old, to come live and be educated at court. It was a mark of high esteem, to be sure, and one that traditional historians insisted was prophetic of Ch'ien-lung's inevitable rise to fame. Yung-cheng, of course, may have been influenced in his choice of an heir by this act of favoritism, but there is no proof of this nor any indication of bias on his own part once he succeeded K'ang-hsi.

The two princes were raised as companions and friends. From the start they shared their meals, their lessons, and their beds,[4] and later, in his will, Yung-cheng congratulated them on the close fraternal bonds that they had developed over the years and that he himself had so consciously fostered.[5] They received the same instruction from the same sources, made their literary debuts simultaneously,[6] were awarded equal honors on the same date— being created first-degree princes together on March 22, 1733 [7] —and were given similar duties in their introduction to the public life of ritual and administrative responsibility. They expressed equally ardent fraternal affection for each other, which, despite the demands of good taste, seems to have been both genuine and sincere.[8] Even after they parted ways, Ch'ien-lung to

[4] *Lo-shan t'ang ch'üan-chi* [Collected Writings from the Lo-shan Hall], 40 *chüan*, by Ch'ien-lung (1737 ed.; hereafter cited as *LSTCC*), prefaces, pp. 12–13b; 8. 1–3.

[5] *Ta-Ch'ing li-ch'ao shih-lu* [Veritable Records of the Ch'ing Dynasty], 4485 *chüan* (Tokyo, 1937–1938; hereafter cited as *CSL:STJ* for the K'ang-hsi reign, *CSL:STH* for the Yung-cheng reign, and *CSL:KTC* for the Ch'ien-lung reign), *CSL:STH*, 159. 23b.

[6] In October–November, 1730, Ch'ien-lung with the *Lo-shan t'ang wen-ch'ao* [Selections from the Lo-shan Hall], 14 *chüan*, forerunner of *LSTCC*, and Hung-chou with *Chi-ku chai wen-ch'ao* [Selections from the Chi-ku Studio], forerunner of *Chi-ku chai ch'üan-chi* [Collected Writings from the Chi-ku Studio], 8 *chüan* (printed 1746).

[7] *CSL:STH*, 128. 3b.

[8] See, for example, *LSTCC*, prefaces, pp. 12–13b, and *Chi-ku chai ch'üan-chi*, prefaces, pp. 32–33b, both by Hung-chou; and *LSTCC*, 7. 10–11; 8. 1–3; 21. 4–4b, 7b–8; 27. 11; 30. 18b; 37. 9, all reminiscences by Ch'ien-lung of his companionship with Hung-chou.

the throne and Hung-chou to a life of wonderful eccentricity where he rehearsed his own funeral rites, Hamlet-like, at home, appalled dinner guests with idiosyncratic and thoroughly irreverent renditions of classical opera, and struck the august person of a grand secretary at court, the brothers remained on excellent, if not always intimate, terms.[9]

The radical divergence of their later careers, in fact, tends to obscure their earlier parity as princes. Privately they discovered the world of the gentleman-aesthete, learning apparently with equal facility to ride and shoot, compose, exchange and match verses, paint, and write. Publicly they learned to serve and second their father. Yung-cheng trained and assigned both brothers to perform rites and eventually to plan policy. With few exceptions, the public duties executed by the princes were sacerdotal in nature rather than political. Ch'ien-lung and Hung-chou were commissioned to perform, sometimes in conjunction with but more often in place of the emperor, some of the ritual and ceremonial acts associated with the sovereign as head of state and head of the imperial family. These included mourning rites, sacrifices at imperial and subimperial tombs, holiday rites and celebrations, and sacrifices to culture heroes and select deities whose propitiation was meant to assure dynastic equanimity.[10] As princes, in other words, they were trained first in the charismatic functions of the throne. Only later were they asked to participate in its administrative functions too.

In the last year of Yung-cheng's reign, Ch'ien-lung and Hung-

[9] See Chi-hsiu chu-jen [Chao-lien], *Hsiao-t'ing tsa-lu* [Miscellaneous Notes from the Hsiao Pavilion], 10 *chüan* (preface, 1880; hereafter cited as *HTTL*), 6. 37b–38; *Ch'ing shih* [The Ch'ing History], 8 vols. (Taipei, 1961), V, 3565; Arthur W. Hummel, ed., *Eminent Chinese of the Ch'ing Period, 1644–1912,* 2 vols. (Washington, D.C., 1943, 1944), II, 99. Cf. also Ch'ien-lung's laudatory second preface, dated June 3, 1746, to *Chi-ku chai ch'üan-chi.*

[10] For Ch'ien-lung's services, see *CSL:STH,* 13. 11–11b; 26. 11b; 44. 47b; 50. 20; 51. 13b–14b, 19b–20; 54. 19b; 109. 19; 114. 1b; 128. 9b; 134. 9; 138. 17; 139. 4b; 142. 1–1b, 9b–10; 143. 8b; 151. 2; 153. 6b; 154. 1b; 156. 1b; 159. 1b. For Hung-chou's, see *CSL:STH,* 99. 24; 109. 4b; 115. 14b–15; 122. 2b; 142. 9b–10; 146. 4; 159. 1–1b. This count is based on a cursory survey which necessarily favors Ch'ien-lung as his tabooed personal name, Hung-li, is conveniently and obviously shaded in the text. A more careful count might redress the balance. In any case it would be unwise to take the discrepancy as evidence in itself of paternal favoritism and Ch'ien-lung's prior selection as heir.

chou finally entered active administrative service. They began at the top. On July 15, 1735, together with the two most powerful ministers in the realm, the grand secretaries O-er-t'ai (1680–1745) and Chang T'ing-yü (1672–1755), and nine other high officials, they were appointed to the newly created Council of Miao Control (Pan-li Miao-chiang shih-wu wang ta-ch'en), a high level military policy-planning board in charge of the south-west border areas.[11] This council was specifically established in the summer of 1735 to undertake the suppression of a serious Miao uprising in Kweichow province, the latest in a series of such disorders which had plagued the southwest on and off for ten years. It operated only for several months and was abolished by Ch'ien-lung shortly after he ascended the throne, its functions and those of the Grand Council being subsumed in another specially created office, the General Control Council (Tsung-li shih-wu wang ta-ch'en), the empire's highest policy-planning board during the mourning period for Yung-cheng. During its existence, however, the Council of Miao Control seems to have enjoyed a status equal to that of the nascent Grand Council.

Later in the same year when Ch'ien-lung was himself sovereign, he recalled his service on the council with pride: it had given him the experience necessary to continue the pacification campaign with confidence and purpose and to fulfill his father's posthumous command to put the realm aright. This, on the basis of his prior training, he felt well prepared to do.[12]

SOURCES OF THE SELF-IMAGE: THE INSTITUTIONAL SETTING

In 1737, a year and a half after he took the throne, Ch'ien-lung reminisced about the classroom: "Prior to ascending the throne I had thoroughly got by heart the six classics and the various histories. Since assuming the responsibilities of state I have had

[11] *CSL:STH,* 156. 15–16, 20b–21. This reference and other related information was kindly supplied by Mrs. Lienche Tu Fang. See also the same scholar's *Kuan-yü Chün-chi ch'u ti chien-chih* [On the Establishment of the Chün-chi Ch'u] (Canberra, 1963), pp. 17–19.

[12] *Ta-Ch'ing Kao-tsung ch'un-huang-ti sheng hsün* [Sacred Instructions of the Emperor Kao-tsung], 300 *chüan* (preface, 1807; hereafter cited as *SCSH:KT*), 295. 1.

less free time but have not stopped examining the classics and studying the rites." [13] The first part of this statement was no idle boast. His introduction to classical learning was rigorous and thorough, though not, as noted, exclusive. It began early and continued through his princedom, first at home under his father's tuition, then, from the age of nine *sui*, under the Manchu scholar, Fu-min (1673–1756), specially engaged by Yung-cheng to instruct his sons, and finally, from 1723 on, in the Palace School for Princes (Shang shu-fang) with his peers.

The Palace School was Yung-cheng's invention, inspired by the need to keep the name of the heir unpublicized in the study halls as well as at court. Thus, upon his accession, Yung-cheng created an institution which would provide for the instruction of all the imperial sons, grandsons, and other princes who were of an age for schooling and whose education inside the palace would minimize the threat of factions outside forming around them as potential claimants to the throne.[14] It was in this school that Ch'ien-lung learned the rigors of an orthodox education. Class hours were long, from the 5:00–7:00 A.M. watch to the 3:00–5:00 P.M. watch, and the school operated throughout the year.[15] When the princes were at the Summer Palace they continued their lessons in another study, the Ch'in-cheng Tien, set aside for that purpose. The curriculum was comprehensive, embracing both the civil and military arts, and protocol was strict. As their tutors entered the classroom the princes faced north and bowed to them, thus reversing the roles which status alone would have prescribed and giving expression thereby to the superior claim of ideological over institutional and hereditary authority.[16]

To educate the emperor's offspring was an honor, no doubt,

---

[13] *SCSH:KT*, 13. 1–1b.

[14] Hummel, II, 917; *LSTCC*, 8. 21b.

[15] For this and the following data, see Chi-hsiu chu-jen [Chao-lien], *Hsiao-t'ing hsü-lu* [Additional Notes from the Hsiao Pavilion], 3 *chüan* (preface, 1880; hereafter cited as *HTHL*), 1. 13–13b, and *Ch'ing-pai lei-ch'ao* [Unofficial Sources on the Ch'ing Arranged by Categories], 48 *ts'e* (Shanghai, last preface 1917), *li-chih lei* [Ritual], p. 2.

[16] This was also standard practice in T'ang times. See Robert des Rotours, transl. *Traité des Fonctionnaires et Traité de l'Armée*, 2 vols. (Leiden, 1947–1948), II, 570–571. Cf. also James T. C. Liu, "An Early Sung Reformer: Fan Chung-yen" in *Chinese Thought and Institutions,* ed. John K. Fairbank (Chicago, 1957), p. 123.

but it was still a working honor—a bureaucrat's job, not his titular reward. It was not necessarily assigned to the most highly placed or the most intellectually gifted. Intellectual conservatism, competence, and promise had something to do with the choice. So did imperial preference and favor. Thus one of Ch'ien-lung's tutors, Ku Ch'eng-t'ien, about whom little else is known, was selected for service in the school on the basis of an investigation originally intended to prove him a subversive. A poem by Ku, deemed insulting to the throne, came to light in 1729, and during the investigation another of Ku's verses, a lament on the death of K'ang-hsi, was discovered and passed on to Yung-cheng. The emperor was reportedly so moved that he quashed the charge of *lèse majesté* and brought Ku into the Hanlin Academy as a compiler and into the Palace School as a tutor.[17] Before that Ku had languished for twelve years as an unemployed *chü-jen*. Quite obviously, in this case academic and bureaucratic qualifications took second place to the imperial whim, and Ch'ien-lung got an untried, if poetically agile, teacher.

Ku Ch'eng-t'ien's success story is admittedly exceptional. Of the fourteen others [18] that I have been able to identify as having had either functional or formal roles in Ch'ien-lung's education, all but two, both members of the imperial family, had some prior claim to scholarly experience, either as expositors or compilers in the Hanlin, as editors or consultants in the Imperial Study (Nan shu-fang), the emperor's personal literary advisorate,[19] as writers in their own right, or simply as instructors or directors in private academies. And the royal tutors, uncles of the prince, had little need for such claims. They were teachers not in the school but in the field, Yin-lu, a mathematician and musicologist, being desig-

---

[17] *Kuo-ch'ao ch'i-hsien lei-cheng* [Biographies of Ch'ing Venerables and Worthies Arranged by Categories], 720 *chüan*, comp. Li Huan (Hsiang-yin Li-shih ed., 1890), 126. 8–9. Also, *LSTCC*, prefaces, p. 46.

[18] Yin-lu (1695–1767), Yin-hsi (1711–1758), O-er-t'ai, Chang T'ing-yü, Chu Shih (1665–1736), Chiang T'ing-hsi (1699–1732), Fu-min, Ts'ai Shih-yüan (1682–1734), Shao Chi (d. 1737), Hu Hsü (1655–1736)—for whom see *LSTCC*, prefaces, pp. 3–5, 8–11, 18–45; and Liang Shih-cheng (1697–1763), Chi Tseng-yün (1671–1739), Hsü-yüan-meng (1655–1741), and Wang Mou-hung (1668–1741), for whom see, respectively, *LSTCC*, colophons, p. 16; *SCSH:KT*, 58. 1–1b; and *Ch'ing-shih lieh-chuan* [Biographies for the Ch'ing History], 80 *chüan* (Shanghai, 1928), 14. 10b–11 and 67. 21b.

[19] Established as a palace office by K'ang-hsi. See Hummel, I, 64.

nated Ch'ien-lung's instructor in firearms, and Yin-hsi, a classmate and exact contemporary of his nephew, his archery master.[20] Neither, however, had any discernible qualification as
experts in arms, and their functions appear to have been largely
nominal: to personify through their appointments the imperial
family's direct concern and involvement with the indoctrination
of a potential heir. The sovereign's brothers were tied by a formal
martial curriculum to the sovereign's sons: it bespoke unity,
caution, and familial pride in the fading memory that once upon
a time all the princes—brothers and sons alike—had to know as
a matter of course how to ride, shoot, and kill.

Whatever their qualifications, all of the tutors were caught in a
common dilemma. As instructors they were expected to set high
scholarly and ethical standards for the princes; as fallible and
ambitious officials they often failed to meet those standards
themselves. Through their teaching they provided the future emperor (as well as the current one) with the scriptural arguments
and principles on which he could act to control them and, when
necessary, to condemn them. They were vulnerable before their
own lessons—honored but not privileged characters. Thus O-er-
t'ai posthumously and Chang T'ing-yü at the end of his career
were punished by their former pupil for the excesses of their
power; Hsü-yüan-meng and Hu Hsü were reprimanded
and demoted by their patron, Yung-cheng, for minor bureaucratic offenses after they had already become tutors to his sons;
Shao Chi was rebuked for the more serious crime of favoritism
and official toadying to the mighty; even Fu-min, the favorite
tutor of all and later remembered as a perfect paragon, was not
above reproach and twice under Yung-cheng was reprimanded
or degraded for minor administrative infractions.

Of Ch'ien-lung's fifteen tutors, five were Manchu, ten Chinese,
but, with the exception of the two members of the imperial
family, the distinction was irrelevant. They were officials first and
representatives of their races second. There is no indication that
the Manchus were engaged exclusively as linguists, and O-er-t'ai,
Hsü-yüan-meng, and Fu-min were all capable of holding their
own against any of the others as claimants to the Confucian

[20] *Ch'ing-shih,* I, 128.

heritage. Likewise, geographical distinctions were meaningless. Of the non-banner tutors, four were from Kiangsu, two from Chekiang, and one each from Anhwei, Kiangsi, Fukien, and Honan, a distribution which spoke more of the normal mid-Ch'ing examination quotas than of cliques. There was, in fact, no discernible political or scholastic clique in the Palace School. Several lines of the Chu Hsi tradition were represented, from the more conservative school of Chang Po-hsing as represented by Ts'ai Shih-yüan, to the more sceptical and pragmatic approach of the Yen-Li school as represented briefly by Wang Mou-hung.[21] There was nothing experimental about the palace curriculum or its manipulators. Reliability, not eccentricity or experimentalism, was most prized and in the characters and careers of these men was most apparent. And, with the exception of Liang Shih-cheng, who in 1734 was appointed to the school at the age of thirty-seven long after the prince's lessons had been learned, and Yin-lu and Yin-hsi, who were anomalies at best and anyway marginal to Ch'ien-lung's education, there were no tyros among the schoolmasters. The average age in 1730 of those for whom the dates are available (excluding those mentioned above) was sixty-one, a good safe distance from youthful and quixotic dreams. Ch'ien-lung was unquestionably in dependable and venerable hands.

SOURCES OF THE SELF-IMAGE: THE CURRICULUM

It is neither possible nor necessary here to enumerate and analyze all of the books to which Ch'ien-lung was exposed as a student prince. Rather, a brief selection of titles should adequately suggest the range of interests imposed upon him and the strength of expectations held for him.

Ch'ien-lung's encounter with the Confucian canon appears to

[21] On Ts'ai's connection with Chang Po-hsing's Ao-feng academy, see *Ch'ing-shih,* V, 4049–4050; *Ch'ing-shih lieh-chuan,* 14. 5b–6b; *Kuo-ch'ao pei-chuan chi* [Ch'ing Epitaphs and Biographies], 160 *chüan,* comp. Ch'ien I-chi (1893 ed.), 23. 15–17b; Hummel, I, 51–52. On Wang's career and adherence to the work of Yen Yüan (1635–1704) and Li Kung (1659–1733), see *Ch'ing-pai lei-ch'ao, chüeh-chih lei* [Rank], p. 42; *Ch'ing-shih,* VII, 5153–5154; Hummel, II, 914.

have been correct but decidedly perfunctory. It was sufficient to make him, appropriately, not a philosopher but an ideologue perfectly capable of drawing on the philosophers for the sanctions he needed to operate effectively as monarch. Like all schoolboys he began by knowing his classics before understanding them. By the time he entered the Palace School he was familiar with the texts and had memorized large portions of the *Four Books* and *Five Classics*. This was an exercise in discipline, not interpretation. Interpretation, that is, orthodox understanding, rested on a knowledge of neo-Confucian exegetics and this he got in packaged form, largely through the well-known anthology *Hsing-li ching-i*, [*The Essential Metaphysics*], a work compiled during the K'ang-hsi reign and printed in 1715 as a manageable digest of the massive and disorderly *Hsing-li ta-ch'üan-shu*, a scissors-and-paste symposium of Sung neo-Confucian doctrines compiled in the Ming dynasty. The *Ching-i* represented the ultimate distillation of Sung Confucianist wisdom as sanctioned and approved by the "later sage," K'ang-hsi, and apparently proofread in final draft by him.[22] It comprised summary versions of the seminal texts of the Sung school and anthologized writings grouped under such headings as "spirits," "sages," "Confucians," "the prince's way," and the like, and gave Ch'ien-lung his first and probably only close brush with the writings of Chou Tun-i (1017–1073), Shao Yung (1011–1077), Chang Tsai (1021–1077), and Ts'ai Yüan-ting (1135–1198), all of whose works he singled out for special mention in a colophon on the *Ching-i*.[23]

There were other doctrinal texts as well—the *Ta-hsüeh yen-i*, for example, a forty-three *chüan* cautionary guide for rulers to the ethical imperatives of the *Great Learning* as interpreted by a late Sung adherent of the Chu Hsi school, Chen Te-hsiu (1178–1235);[24] or the writings of Chu Hsi himself;[25] or the *Ku-wen yüan-chien,* a collection of annotated essays in sixty-four

[22] See *LSTCC*, 9. 8b–10; *Ssu-k'u ch'üan-shu tsung-mu t'i-yao* [Summaries of the Contents of the *Ssu-k'u ch'üan-shu*], 4 vols. (Shanghai: Commercial Press, 1933; hereafter cited as *SKCS*), p. 1925; Hummel, I, 474, II, 913.

[23] *LSTCC*, 9. 7b–10.

[24] See *SKCS*, pp. 1912–1913, 1926–1927; *LSTCC*, 9. 12–13, 7. 8b–9b.

[25] See, for example, *LSTCC*, 9. 10–12.

chüan, ordered compiled and personally selected by K'ang-hsi and running the gamut of literature from the *Ch'un-ch'iu* and *Tso-chuan* to the writings of the Sung period.[26] Metaphysics and classical literature, however, were not Ch'ien-lung's strong points, and he seems to have been content at this stage to make the requisite polite noises about them and then run for cover to history, a subject he both loved and understood.

Ch'ien-lung's readings in history were both extensive and intensive, covering the broad spectrum of Chinese history in the great synthetic works for which Chinese historiography is famous and probing more specific problems or persons in lesser works and selected excerpts and documents which focused on a specific time or a concrete question. For him, as for most post-Sung students of the past, history was a cumulative, though rarely integrated, chronicle of moral signposts indicating the good and the bad, the praiseworthy and blameworthy. It was a veritable mirror of revealed truth, reflecting past choices as measures for current actions.

It was the chronicle form of history, best exemplified by the *Ch'un-ch'iu, Tzu-chih t'ung-chien,* and Chu Hsi's abridgement, *T'ung-chien kang-mu,* that most appealed to the prince. Bare fact, he argued, was enshrined in this form as moral judgement. Bad men and wicked trembled before the accusing thrust of the chronicler's brush; they thought twice about their reputations and gave up their usurpations and rebellions as a bad thing. History, that is, became a preventive weapon against the future, as well as a corrective one against the past. In Ch'ien-lung's eyes, however, the weaponry was dulled after the fall of the Chou dynasty and not again honed to perfection until the appearance of the *T'ung-chien kang-mu.* Then Chu Hsi took up where Confucius left off, sorted out the good from the bad, the right from the wrong, judged the past, and warned the future. The would-be regicide and power-seeker, the self-seeking official who would serve two dynastic houses—all were given notice: desist or live in history forever condemned. They desisted. And thus, he argued, was worked a qualitative change in post-Sung political history, marked by the expression of new and stronger dynastic loyalties.

[26] See Hummel, I, 310–311; *SKCS,* pp. 4216–4217.

It was a didactic triumph for the *Kang-mu.* Chu Hsi had, as it were, polished the *Mirror* until it no longer could be ignored.[27]

A prince's job was to know all of Chinese history, but this did not prevent him from developing particular interests. For Ch'ien-lung, the history of the T'ang dynasty held an almost irresistible attraction. Time and again, both as prince and sovereign, he turned back to the high years of the T'ang and its archetypal dynastic accomplishments. The reign of T'ai-tsung (r. 627–649) became almost an obsession with him, as if the very act of reading its record would enhance his own with some of the heroic qualities of that remote age.

A text of signal importance in this respect was the *Chen-kuan cheng-yao* or *Important Deliberations on Government of the Chen-kuan [T'ai-tsung] Period,* written less than a century after the T'ai-tsung era by the censor and state historiographer, Wu Ching (d. 749).[28] The book, comprising some forty pieces in ten *chüan,* is still extant. Annotations to the text were added during the Yuan dynasty and additional comments by twenty-two noted T'ang experts appended. Thus by the time Ch'ien-lung had the text it was a repository of highly reputable observations on early T'ang government and politics, and in the eyes of later critics it remained one of the most reliable early expositions of T'ai-tsung's greatness. This surely was its appeal for Ch'ien-lung. To him it portrayed the quintessential T'ai-tsung, the model king whose record was required reading for all who aspired to rule. And if we can believe his expression of youthful ardor, reading it was an intensely moving experience, transporting him back into a heroic age and filling him with admiration for the abundance of a truly great reign.

Immediately relevant to the T'ang, as well as to the interregnum between the T'ang and Sung, were the writings of Ou-yang Hsiu, compiler of the *New T'ang History* and author of the *History of the Five Dynasties.* Ch'ien-lung was exposed to these

[27] *LSTCC,* 7. 7–8b.

[28] For this and the following, see *LSTCC,* 7. 1–2b; *SKCS,* pp. 1129–1130; E. G. Pulleyblank, "Chinese Historical Criticism: Liu Chih-chi and Ssu-ma Kuang" in *Historians of China and Japan,* ed. W. G. Beasley and E. G. Pulleyblank (London, 1961), p. 139; and Robert des Rotours, transl., *Le Traité des Examens* (Paris, 1932), pp. 261–262.

and wrote an essay, "On Reading the Collected Works of Ou-yang Hsiu." [29] In it he expressed a commonly held historiographical principle that the state of literature is directly related to the state of the nation. The quality and abundance of the first followed the vitality and fortunes of the second; letters were circumscribed perfectly by politics. Thus in periods of instability the "civilizing lessons of learning" (*wen-chiao*) went unspoken and unheeded. They had to wait for the reappearance of a literary savior who could restate them again boldly and clearly in an age amenable to the task. Thus the literary-moral vacuum of the Six Dynasties period was filled finally in the T'ang by Han Yü and that of the Five Dynasties period by Ou-yang Hsiu some seventy years after the founding of the Sung. Not only did they revive learning but through their inspiration assured its continuance. Their contemporaries and disciples carried forward the good work in a kind of intellectual chain reaction, and in doing so added lustre to their times.

As a prince Ch'ien-lung was required to learn more than the contents of history. He was also expected to be familiar with the methods of state historiography over which he might some day preside. Specifically, he was introduced to the mechanics of the self-glorifying compilation. On January 17, 1732 he witnessed the devout and solemn reception by the throne of the *Veritable Records* and *Sacred Instructions* of the K'ang-hsi reign. In a poem commemorating the occasion, he showed his familiarity with the suprahistorical or ideological function of such literature and with the process of compilation, from the day-to-day diarial notations to the final, revised, and perfected edition which was to stand forever as the embodiment of the imperial accomplishment and will.[30]

It is uncertain whether Ch'ien-lung actually had access to these collections during his princehood. While it is reasonable to as-

[29] *LSTCC*, 10. 14–15. The following remarks are based on this essay. For a relevant discussion of dynastic and cultural correlation, see Lien-sheng Yang, "Toward a Study of Dynastic Configurations in Chinese History" in the same author's *Studies in Chinese Institutional History* (Cambridge, Mass., 1961), pp. 7–10.

[30] *LSTCC*, 31. 15b–17b; also *CSL:STH*, 113. 17–18. Cf. Harold L. Kahn, "Some Mid-Ch'ing Views of the Monarchy," *Journal of Asian Studies*, XXIV, 2 (February, 1965), 232.

sume he did—as testaments of dynastic continuity they were meant above all for the eyes of the royal heirs—the record is mute, and we cannot legitimately assign to his curriculum a course in Ch'ing documents. Later, of course, as emperor, he did make use of them, supposedly reading one *chüan* of the *Veritable Records* daily, before bathing, except when on tour, at the hunt, or fasting.[31]

If Ch'ien-lung learned something about the methodology and a great deal about the ideals of history, he also learned about the practical politics and personalities of the past. He read, for example, Yang Lien's (1571–1625) celebrated memorial enumerating the "twenty-four crimes of Wei Chung-hsien" (1568–1627), the infamous eunuch of late Ming times, and was well acquainted with the details of Wei's reign of terror.[32] He also read the brief collected writings of another courageous Ming official, Yang Chi-sheng (1516–1555), best known for his dogged opposition to the establishment of horse markets on the Ming frontier and for his courageous criticism of the powerful grand secretary, Yen Sung (1480–1568), one of the "Six Wicked Ministers" of the Ming, which led ultimately to his imprisonment and murder.[33]

Thus by the time Ch'ien-lung came to the throne he was well versed in the record of the darker side of court politics. Long before the advent of Ho-shen, he was aware of the crude facts of favoritism and clique machinations. If old age dulled that awareness in the end, during most of his career he was hypersensitive to these problems and their precedents and accordingly kept a tight rein on his court. His lessons in history had prepared him well.

This being so, it is surprising to note one glaring omission in Ch'ien-lung's early writings. There is no single essay or poem devoted expressly to the problem of political cliques. As noted,

[31] *HTHL*, 1. 11.
[32] *LSTCC*, 10. 16–17.
[33] *LSTCC*, 31. 9b–10; Hummel, I, 398, II, 864; E-tu Zen Sun and John de Francis, eds. and transls., *Chinese Social History* (Washington, D.C., 1956), pp. 315–318; and Nelson I. Wu, "Tung Ch'i-ch'ang (1555–1636): Apathy in Government and Fervor in Art" in *Confucian Personalities*, eds. Arthur F. Wright and Denis Twitchett (Stanford, 1962), pp. 264–266.

he was familiar with the works of Ou-yang Hsiu and thus can be presumed to have seen the famous memorial, "On Parties." And recently his father had launched a virulent public attack on this classic justification for group politics with a similarly entitled essay of his own specifically aimed at quashing any bureaucratic notions that factions, however dedicated to the good of the realm, would be tolerated.[34] Certainly Ch'ien-lung was familiar with Yung-cheng's arguments, for this was a major issue of the day and one that could hardly escape the notice of a prince being tutored daily in the principles of power. Moreover, since Yung-cheng's essay was made required reading in all government schools, it surely must also have found its way into the curriculum of the Palace School. Yet Ch'ien-lung did not join the debate. He praised Ou-yang Hsiu for his history while his father was damning him for his politics. He was content to recount the orthodox horror tales of baneful cliques and factions rather than to synthesize his views in a princely echo of the emperor's words. Only after he inherited the throne did he speak out, and then it was to reiterate and to reinforce what Yung-cheng had said so emphatically in 1724.[35]

Two other aspects of the prince's curriculum must be briefly treated—his training in the arts and in warfare. There is no need at this remove to disturb Ch'ien-lung's very secure reputation as an indifferent painter, poet, and calligrapher, and I intend simply to point to the origins of his later image of himself as a universal patron and connoisseur.

Ch'ien-lung began to paint in earnest in 1729 at the age of nineteen *sui*; presumably his training in calligraphy began earlier, when he began his lessons in composition at the age of fourteen *sui*.[36] His models in both were impeccable—the great

---

[34] David S. Nivison, "Ho-shen and His Accusers" in *Confucianism in Action,* eds. David S. Nivison and Arthur F. Wright (Stanford, 1959), pp. 225–228. For a translation of Ou-yang's memorial, see Wm. Theodore DeBary, Wing-tsit Chan, and Burton Watson, comps., *Sources of Chinese Tradition* (New York, 1960), pp. 446–448.

[35] Nivison, "Ho-shen and his Accusers," pp. 228–232. Hummel, II, 917, gives the date as 1725.

[36] See, respectively, Sugimura Yūzō, *Ken-ryū kōtei* [The Ch'ien-lung Emperor] (Tokyo, 1961), p. 27, and *LSTCC*, prefaces, p. 1. The following, on his models, is from Sugimura, pp. 26–27.

masters of bird and flower painting, Pien Luan (fl. ca. 785–802), Lin Ch'un (fl. ca. 1174–1189), Huang Ch'üan (ca. 900–965), and Hsü Hsi (d. before 975), and two of history's greatest calligraphers, Wang Hsi-chih (321–379) and the Ming master, Tung Ch'i-ch'ang (1555–1636). Except for Tung's works, however, and possibly some of Wang's, it is unlikely that Ch'ien-lung ever saw an original of any of these artists. Current criticism argues that none of their works survive, and while early eighteenth-century attributions may have convinced the prince of their authenticity, it is almost certain that he was in fact working from copies or later specimens in the same stylistic tradition.[37]

Mediocre talent and false attributions could not combine to stop the prince any more than they could later stop the emperor from putting his skills to work. Long before he became emperor Ch'ien-lung began that practice, so annoying to later critics, of cluttering up palace treasures with his own brush and seals. In his years as a prince he inscribed over forty paintings and album leaves from almost every important period of Chinese painting.[38] It was a well-meaning effort, no doubt, to continue the honored tradition of expressing admiration and pride of ownership directly on the cherished work itself. Yet the incongruity of indifferent calligraphy often tastelessly misplaced on master paintings and the obscuring of works by obtrusive seal imprints have not endeared him to the world of art.[39] And when it is

[37] See Michael Sullivan, *An Introduction to Chinese Art* (London, 1961), pp. 150–151; Laurence Sickman and Alexander Soper, *The Art and Architecture of China* (Baltimore, 1956), p. 125; R. H. van Gulick, *Chinese Pictorial Art, as Viewed by the Connoisseur* (Rome, 1958), pp. 394–395. A more conservative view is Osvald Siren, *Chinese Painting, Leading Masters and Principles,* 7 vols. (London, 1956–1958), II, "Annotated Lists of Paintings . . . ," 20, 27, 28, 66. On the authenticity of Wang's surviving specimens, see Michael Sullivan, *The Birth of Landscape Painting in China* (London, 1962), pp. 85, 197–198, note 35. I am indebted to Sandra Kahn for many of the references here and below in notes 39, 40.

[38] See *LSTCC, chüan* 19–40, under entries beginning with the word, *t'i* (superscription).

[39] See *Chinese Art Treasures, A Selected Group of Objects from the National Palace Museum and the Chinese National Central Museum, Taichung, Taiwan* (Geneva, 1961–1962), p. 18; *Chinese Calligraphy and Painting in the Collection of John M. Crawford, Jr.* (New York, 1962), pp. 24–25; Sullivan, *Introduction,* p. 168; and Roger Goepper, *The Essence of Chinese Painting* (London, 1963), p. 100 and plate 6. Ch'ien-lung was not, of course, always unsuccessful; see Goepper, p. 109.

recalled that he wrote 54 inscriptions on one handscroll alone and eventually possessed at least 195 seals of which he used as many as 13 on a single painting,[40] the charge of bad taste becomes serious.

The charge, however, does not take into consideration the extra-asethetic function of such exercises. It was not so much the royal prerogative as the royal duty to remain at the head of the arts even if, in the process, the art was destroyed. The paintings, after all, were the private possessions of the throne; the imperial script and seals were the possessions of the realm. Their appearance was an assertion not only of artistic sensibility (however warped) but of dynastic grandeur. And since the dynasty consisted of the royal house as a whole, a prince as well as a sovereign could legitimately participate in that simultaneous function of enhancing the imperial ego and enhancing the riches of the realm. It could only be hoped that the prince and emperor had taste; it had, however, to be expected that they would leave their marks—preferably, as in earlier ages, with discretion—on the treasures that defined the glory of their reign.

Ch'ien-lung was educated to be both a scholar and soldier. The emphasis, of course, was on the first, for by mid-dynasty it was more important for the emperor to be a practicing gentleman than a practicing general. After K'ang-hsi, there was little need for a Manchu warrior-king, and now, on the edge of an age of peace, a passing acquaintance with weaponry was enough. That is what Ch'ien-lung got. He received instruction, of a sort, in both archery and firearms and read just enough military history to gain a rudimentary (and idealized) knowledge of the T'ang militia system and through it an understanding of the evanescence of imperfect military institutions.[41]

Ch'ien-lung's expertise with arms is a matter of conjecture. One story, almost certainly apocryphal, puts him in the expert class with a bow. It recounts how, on a balmy morning in 1749, the young emperor picked up a bow in one of those spur-of-the-

[40] Sullivan, *Introduction*, p. 169, note 1; *Chinese Calligraphy and Painting*, p. 28, note 11; and Hsien-chi Tseng, "A Study of the Nine Dragons Scroll," *Archives of the Chinese Art Society of America*, XI (1957), 27–29, 30–31 (nos. 16–28). This scroll is in the Boston Museum of Fine Arts.

[41] *LSTCC*, 9. 17b–19.

moment inspirations so useful to historical fiction and hit the bull's-eye with nineteen of his twenty shots.[42] By making him slightly fallible the story gains in verisimilitude but not necessarily in truth. We simply do not know how good he was. The same may be said about his use of firearms, a more important and more complicated matter by far.

The term "firearms," *huo-ch'i,* was used generically to describe all armaments which employed gunpowder in any form. It thus included the whole range of individual arms, field pieces, and explosives, such as land and water mines, then known in China. In fact, a contemporary mid-Ch'ing illustrated guide shows twenty-three different pieces of ordnance and forty-nine types of musket,[43] but many of these were useless for anything but ceremonial firing, most were already long obsolete, and almost all were difficult if not impossible or dangerous to fire. It would be misleading then to suppose that Ch'ien-lung learned to handle anything larger or more complicated than the standard musket, the *niao-ch'iang* or fowling piece, a derivative of the late Ming long gun and Portuguese snapping matchlock musket, employed both for military and hunting purposes.[44] Until the nineteenth century, the Ch'ing court remained remarkably aloof to the strategic possibilities of modern firepower, and with few exceptions interest in the development and use of arms remained at a minimum in the mid-Ch'ing period. The arsenal was little developed beyond the technical level achieved at the end of the Ming dynasty,[45] and this undoubtedly told on the prince's weapons training. It was confined largely to the single weapon and to the limited tactical context of the hunt.

[42] *HTTL,* 1. 6b.

[43] *Huang-ch'ao li-ch'i t'u-shih* [Illustrated Guide to the Instruments, Utensils, and Paraphernalia of the Ch'ing Dynasty], 18 *chüan* (1759 ed.), 16. 1–75b.

[44] See Chou Wei, *Chung-kuo ping-ch'i shih-kao* [Draft History of Chinese Weapons] (Peking, 1957), pp. 270, 311–312.

[45] Chou, *Ping-ch'i shih-kao,* pp. 311–313, 320. For the few innovations made —under K'ang-hsi, an artillery and musketry division, Huo-ch'i ying, formed within the banner system, and an elite corps of marksmen, Hu-ch'iang ying, equipped with tiger guns; under Ch'ien-lung, a scouts division supplied with firearms—see *Ch'ing-ch'ao t'ung-tien* [Encyclopedia of Ch'ing Statutes], 100 *chüan* (Taipei, 1959 ed.), 69. 2533, and *Ch'ing-ch'ao hsü wen-hsien t'ung-k'ao* [Continuation of the Encyclopedia of the Historical Records of the Ch'ing Dynasty] 400 *chüan* (Taipei, 1959 ed.), 130. 8904; also *HTHL,* 1. 12.

Throughout his career, Ch'ien-lung was to be ruled by a tension between a poetic self and a practical self, and his training in the hunt was no exception. On numerous occasions he joined a mounted hunting party or one bound for archery practice, but for him getting there was half the fun and he has left heroic stanzas describing the beauty of the morning forests, the nobility of the ride, and the heartiness of the companionship.[46] He was enthralled with the romance of the hunt and the garlanded warrior, not with the brutality or practicality of the shot and the kill. Nevertheless, he did learn the paramilitary purposes of these expeditions, often participated in them, and knew the methods of taking game long before he organized his own autumn extravaganzas in Jehol after 1741.

The most common technique in the hunt was that of surrounding (*hsing-wei*), whereby a large number of beaters would form a ring and drive the game into a confined clearing where the royal hunters could shoot at will. On a large scale this had the makings of a military exercise and often served both as imperial sport and martial maneuver. Another method learned by Ch'ien-lung was the use of large game traps or barriers (*hsiao-lieh*). These were constructed of interwoven lengths of wood and placed in the path of the fleeing game. Thus trapped, the animals presented an easy target to the hunter. A third ruse, not specifically mentioned by the prince but later known to him and to succeeding imperial sportsmen and almost certainly learned in his youth, was that known as "calling the deer" (*shao-lu*).[47] This was a stalking procedure of intriguing proportions. A man was clad in deer skins and antlers and sent into the hills with a whistle which imitated the call of an expiring buck. This would apparently lure the does in the area out of the forest in expectation of meeting their stricken mate and thus provide a fair bag to the waiting marksmen. The lure technique was based on dubious zoological

---

[46] See, for example, *LSTCC*, 21. 18–19, 30. 22–22b.

[47] See Yao Yüan-chih, *Chu-yeh t'ing tsa-chi* [Miscellanea from the Bamboo Leaf Pavilion], 18 *chüan* (preface, 1893), 3. 4b, and *HTTL*, 1. 12. Both authors were active in the Chia-ch'ing reign (1796–1820). For a similarly named technique in the Liao dynasty, see Karl A. Wittfogel and Feng Chia-sheng, *History of Chinese Society, Liao (907–1125)* (Philadelphia, 1949), p. 133.

principles. According to the argument, a buck was a virile and libidinous beast who would have at one go up to a hundred of the opposite sex. Thereupon, in understandable exhaustion, he would lie down to die. His last call—that produced by the whistle —supposedly brought to his side his satisfied mates who would attempt to revive him by feeding him grass which they first chewed for him. And so, by attending a fallen buck, they became themselves, as it were, sitting ducks. With this, Ch'ien-lung's education in the field was complete.

THE SELF-IMAGE: PREPARATION FOR REALITY

In 1730 all of this education—in the classroom, in the field, at court—came to a head. Late in the autumn Ch'ien-lung presented to the court the distilled product of seven years of formal learning, the manuscript version of his collected student essays, examination exercises, prefaces and colophons, verse, letters, and historical notes, entitled *Lo-shan t'ang wen-ch'ao* or *A Literary Selection from the Lo-shan Hall.*[48] It was in this work that he began to define his own and his age's understanding of the role of the emperor in history and in politics. It was first printed a year and a half after Ch'ien-lung came to the throne, in 1737, much expanded in forty *chüan,* under the title *Lo-shan t'ang ch'üan-chi* and again in 1758 in a definitive (*ting-pen*) edition of thirty *chüan.*[49]

What we have then is a highly polished version sanctioned by the orthodox considerations of the court and sensitive to the reputation of its imperial author. Nevertheless it remains a useful guide to contemporary opinion. Its views represent the prescribed commitment to what was good and bad in history, to what was admirable and what contemptible. In sum they add up to an impressive accumulation of historical precedent and cliché which serves as the young prince's (and later young emperor's) testament of faith. As he asserts in his 1730 preface, " 'It is not

[48] See *LSTCC,* 1737 facsimile handwritten preface, pp. 2b–3, and prefaces, p. 36. Also note 6 above.

[49] Hummel, I, 370. On the question of its reliability as a source of the self-image, see Kahn, "Some Mid-Ch'ing Views," p. 230.

the knowing that is difficult, but the doing.' I often refer to the words I have written as a mirror for my actions. Were I incapable of self-examination to the point where words and action had no relevance to each other, were I capable of knowing but not of acting—would this not be to my shame?" [50] To insure against such ignominy, he says, he has placed the collection on a table within easy reach for instant reference, consultation, and guidance.

Appended to the *Ch'üan-chi* is a companion volume in four *chüan*, the *Jih-chih hui-shuo* or *Knowledge Accumulated Day by Day,* a collection of 260 study notes compiled in 1736 as a kind of addendum to the *Ch'üan-chi.*[51] The notes appear to be the residue of Ch'ien-lung's apprentice scholarship, the footnotes and italics, as it were, of the lessons learned. Together the *Ch'üan-chi* and *Hui-shuo* constitute the "complete works" of the prince.

After the author became emperor, his private testament became imperial writ: The "Works" were wrapped in the mantle of infallibility and sent on their way to inspire officials and educate students much in the manner of the sacred edicts of K'ang-hsi and Yung-cheng. Palace officials, provincial governors, and former tutors received copies as gifts or on petition to the throne;[52] others urged that they be distributed throughout the realm in the manner of the sanctioned editions of the classics and histories.[53] Ch'ien-lung wondered only briefly about the propriety of this equation of his own words with those of the ancient canon, managed to overcome his modest evaluation of their didactic and sagely value, and delighted in the new popular demand.[54] In time the *Ch'üan-chi* passed into the folklore of imperial erudition; it became a latter-day classic by a later sage. In 1748 a precocious child of seven was discovered in Shantung who had already committed to memory the five classics and the poems from the *Ch'üan-chi.* He was made a *chü-jen* on the spot, was celebrated

---

[50] *LSTCC*, prefaces, p. 2. The quotation is from the *Shu-ching.* See James Legge, transl., *The Chinese Classics,* 5 vols. (Hong Kong, 1960), III, 258.
[51] *Jih-chih hui-shuo* [Knowledge Accumulated Day by Day], 4 *chüan*, by Ch'ien-lung (printed 1736; hereafter cited as *JCHS*), preface, pp. 2–2b.
[52] *SCSH:KT*, 1. 7, 9b; *CSL:KTC*, 64. 6.
[53] *SCSH:KT*, 1. 9.
[54] *SCSH:KT*, 1. 9–9b.

as the "child prodigy," and fortunately died prematurely to carry his reputation unscathed into popular history.[55]

The title of the *Ch'üan-chi,* taken from the name of Ch'ien-lung's private studio, Lo-shan t'ang or Hall of Delight in Doing Good, expressed an ideal of imperial perfection, one that insisted on a leaven of humility in the exercise of ultimate power. It meant, in Ch'ien-lung's eyes, what Mencius meant when he spoke of "the great Shun . . . delighting to learn from others to practice what was good." [56] The critical words here are those that disappear in the *lo-shan* elision—"to learn from others"—for they point to one of the loftiest of the monarchical ideals: modesty. Institutionally this was expressed by the ruler's willingness to accept remonstrance with good grace—with humility and an open mind: *hsü-huai na-chien* or *t'ing-yen na chien*—phrases that, with other variants, occur frequently in Ch'ien-lung's essays on the monarchy.[57]

For a prince who could hope one day to be sovereign, the ideal of imperial modesty stood as an imperative, for without the ability to listen as well as to act, the monarch could be only a despot, never a sage. And the claim to sagehood was the key to imperial as well as intellectual greatness. Without it the ruler would remain just another mark of imperfection in the long line of descent from idealized antiquity; with it he stood a good chance before posterity where, in a world hypersensitive to the judgments of history, the experience of his reign really counted. In a very real sense the genius of the Chinese monarchy was precisely that it held the ruler himself responsible for limiting his essentially unlimited sanction to rule, for putting sagely restraint on despotic tendencies. He might fail to do so in practice, but he knew long before he ascended the throne the consequences of failure. History might admire him as a despot but would not praise him. That it reserved for the sage, or for the man who at least sought to be one.

---

[55] *HTTL,* 9. 47–47b.

[56] *LSTCC,* 8. 18, and Legge, *Chinese Classics,* II, 205.

[57] See for example, *JCHS,* 1. 13b, 4. 6b; *LSTCC,* 2. 2, an entire essay devoted to the subject, and 5. 19b.

Lo-shan, then, was for the prince a practical, concrete formula for success. It was a direct, specific charge to be filial, respectful and submissive, human-hearted, and righteous.[58]

Ch'ien-lung's model ruler, however, was more than modest. He was also "cautious and circumspect, respectful of both heaven and the people, constantly diligent, and never for a moment presumptuous enough to be lax." [59] He was lenient and broad-minded, magnanimous in his treatment of others and indulgent of men's petty faults. In this way he established his own great virtue and thereby inspired gratitude from the people, contentment in their hearts, and submissiveness to his rule. Harsh and impetuous behavior, on the other hand, led inevitably to ruin. He saw in this the reasons for the fate of the short-lived Ch'in and Sui dynasties. Their founders were admittedly diligent administrators: Shih Huang-ti (r. 221–210 B.C.), according to tradition, wading studiously through 120 catties of state documents each day; and Sui Wen-ti (r. A.D. 589–604) personally attending to the details of daily administrative life. "Yet," asked Ch'ien-lung, "to what avail?" Without compassion and tolerance, the minds and hearts of men were lost and with them the dynasties.[60]

Of all the attributes that went to make up the ideal ruler, the most important in Ch'ien-lung's mind was the ability and desire to discover, select, and use ministers of high talent. To get the right man at the right time, to exhaust his talent in the service of the state—this was the most difficult yet most crucial task facing the sovereign. If he succeeded, all else followed: "Though the realm be vast it is not then difficult to regulate." [61] If he failed, either out of jealousy or contempt of the worthy or from an inability or unwillingness to use them fully, his reputation and his reign would be fatally weakened. His human-heartedness, if he possessed it, his frugality, another requisite monarchical virtue, would be wasted, for without an administration staffed by gifted,

[58] *LSTCC,* 8. 18–18b.
[59] *JCHS,* 4. 5.
[60] *LSTCC,* 1. 13–13b.
[61] *JCHS,* 1. 5, 14b–15.

outspoken men, he would be cut off from reality—a king with a kingdom that he neither knew nor could hope even vaguely to understand.[62]

Ch'ien-lung's case for correct ministerial employment was compounded of practical, historical, and moralistic considerations. The argument begins in heaven.[63] There the recipient of the mandate is charged with creating a lustrous reign, a prosperous realm, a reasoned and ordered society; with bestowing benefits and benevolence on all. "But," notes the prince realistically, "man's individual capacity is limited," and even the sage kings, Yao and Shun, accomplished their great works only with the assistance of talented councillors. "How much the more," he adds, "is it imperative for those not equal to Yao and Shun to employ talent." It was precisely such employment that gave to high antiquity its greatness, order, prosperity, and contentment. From the highest minister to the lowest functionary, all were worthy of their posts and were justly and appropriately used. In a rueful, almost modern, aside, however, Ch'ien-lung admits that it was easier then than now: "The difficulty in appreciating men's worth today is ten times greater than in ancient times. The reason is that official positions are daily increasing in number and human nature is becoming more devious." [64]

Ch'ien-lung continues to explore this less perfect world. Like K'ang-hsi before him and modern analysts today,[65] he recognizes several emperor-types. He distinguishes between founding and innovating emperors—those who "sought to establish order" (*yüan-chih chih chün*) or, like Han Kuang-wu (r. A.D. 25–57), reestablished it—and successor emperors—those who "succeeded to the throne" (*chi-shih chih chün*). Each type required councillors whose talents were appropriate to the age. Few in

---

[62] *LSTCC,* 3. 11, 16–16b; 2. 7, 9. Cf. Legge, *Chinese Classics,* III, 41–42, esp. note, p. 42.

[63] Unless otherwise indicated the following represents a summary of his essay, "Proper Rule Lies in the Selection of Talent," *LSTCC,* 3. 9–11b.

[64] *JCHS,* 1. 5b–6.

[65] Cf. *CSL:STJ,* 154.6b; Arthur F. Wright, "Sui Yang-ti: Personality and Stereotype" in *The Confucian Persuasion,* ed. Arthur F. Wright (Stanford, 1960), pp. 59 ff; and James T. C. Liu, "An Administrative Cycle in Chinese History, The Case of Northern Sung Emperors," *Journal of Asian Studies,* XXI, 2 (February, 1962), *passim.*

either group found them, but those that did were marked for greatness: among the founders, Han Kao-tsu (r. 206–195 B.C.), Han Kuang-wu (restorer of the Later Han, legitimately considered a new dynasty), T'ang T'ai-tsung, and Sung T'ai-tsu (r. 960–975); and Han Wen-ti (r. 179–157 B.C.) and Sung Jen-tsung (r. 1023–1065) among the successors.

Even among these most estimable of emperors, however, Ch'ien-lung discerns critical differences in the use of available talent. T'ang T'ai-tsung in this and other respects is the paragon *par excellence,* not without his faults perhaps—notably his inability to soothe the people sufficiently in an age still given to military exploits [66]—but good enough all the same. In his ability to appreciate talent, employ the meritorious, and accept their advice he was without peer. Han Wen-ti, in most other respects a model ruler, was by comparison "insufficient in his appreciation of talent." [67] And Han Kuang-wu, who was comparable to T'ai-tsung in diligence, receptivity to remonstrance, courtesy to the worthy, and sponsorship of learning, nevertheless failed to exploit *fully* the talents of his ministers. Sung Jen-tsung fell short for the same reason. So, outside the list, did Han Wu-ti (r. 140–87 B.C.).[68]

With lesser rulers the shortcomings were more serious. They were guilty not only of a fickle use of competent ministers but of a suffocating reliance on only a few favorites, men whose pettiness and self-interest assured that the emperor would be unable to rule impartially: "He who uses the whole realm as his source of wisdom possesses the public spirit of the sage king; he who uses one or two favorites as his eyes and ears possesses the partial wisdom of the commonplace ruler." Or again: "Since the wisdom in the world is diverse . . . reliance on one man's intelligence as the sum total of wisdom is no match for reliance on the wisdom of many in concert." [69]

Ch'ien-lung cites T'ang Te-tsung (r. A.D. 780–804) as an invidious example. What led to disaster during Te-tsung's reign,

---

[66] *JCHS,* 1. 13b, 21–21b.
[67] *JCHS,* 1. 21.
[68] See, respectively, *JCHS,* 4. 5b–6; *LSTCC,* 2. 9; *JCHS,* 1. 14b.
[69] Respectively, *JCHS,* 1. 11b; *LSTC,* 2. 8. Cf. also *LSTCC,* 3. 10.

he argues, was *not* the three faults historically attributed to him
—excessive lenience, tolerance of eunuchs, and avariciousness—
but rather the use of mean and petty men and the suspicious,
inconsistent use of the accomplished. He wavered between wisdom and foolishness, and his reign wavered accordingly between
brilliance and disaster. It began brilliantly, due to his reliance on
the accomplished Ts'ui Yu-fu (d. 780). It turned to disorder
with his trust in Lu Ch'i (d. 785), a scoundrel. Again it
recovered some lustre with his turn to the counsels of Lu Chih
(754–805), one of the most courageous of his ministers, and
finally it reverted once more to chaos when he withdrew his
support of Lu Chih and fell prey to the slanders of palace courti-
ers and eunuchs. Te-tsung, like Duke Hsiang of Sung in the
Warring States period and Ch'in-tsung (r. 1126), last of the
Northern Sung emperors, failed out of inconsistency. From this,
Ch'ien-lung concluded that all three were capable of heeding
advice in times of crisis but foolishly discarded it and the men
who gave it when crisis seemed past.[70]

The case of the Southern Sung was even more instructive.
There, argues the prince, a whole dynasty, not just a reign, was
doomed by injudicious use of talent. Admittedly this was not the
only reason for failure, but in combination with a dreary succession of pedestrian rulers, a powerful enemy to the north, a debili-
tated army, and an impoverished people, it proved fatal.[71] That it
was able to last as long as it did was due in fact to the presence of
those loyal, upstanding ministers and scholar-officials, filial sons
and chaste wives who, despite the lack of encouragement, still
"loved their ruler and would die for their commanders." [72]

All of this is, to be sure, oversimplified history, but it tells us
something important about Ch'ien-lung's image of the emperorship. Insistently, both here and in many other of his essays, he
emphasizes the personal factor in history. It was *people*—their
perfection or lack of it—rather than institutions and their possible suitability or perfectability which held the key to success or

---

[70] See, respectively, *LSTCC*, 5. 5–6b, 3. 16–16b; *JCHS*, 1. 14b.

[71] See *LSTCC*, 6. 13b–14b, 16–18.

[72] *LSTCC*, 6. 16b, alluding to Mencius. See Legge, *Chinese Classics*, II,
174.

failure. The worthy man made the emperor great by informing him; the wise ruler made the man whole by employing him in his true vocation, politics.

This did not, of course, mean that they were equals. The Confucian canon, and thus the prince paraphrasing it, preserved the emperor's preeminence. Ruler and minister are seen bound in a relationship as fixed and immutable as that between heaven and earth. Just as heaven is high and the earth low, so there is a gulf between sovereign and subject. The ruler is lofty, superior, the minister lowly and inferior. What bridges the gap is their oneness of heart, their mutuality of principle. And the happy result of this mutual interest, meeting like two halves of a tally, is ". . . social harmony; those in high places show favor to the lowly and the lowly and inferior in their turn are well disposed toward the highly placed. There is an end to all feuds." [73] If the gulf is not bridged, however, the results are dire: the ruler is smitten with willfulness and overbearing pride so that the loyal utterances of his ministers fail to reach him; the "great treasure," the State, is abandoned; the mean and petty insinuate themselves around the throne; and toadying and favoritism flourish.

To prevent this, the ruler must treat the lowly according to their merits. In the case of those with superior talent, he should approach them with the respect that he would show a teacher, provide them with generous salaries or emoluments, trust them with sincerity, and concentrate their abilities in suitable posts. In other words, he should give effect to their ministerial vocation and thus assure that their talent will be fully used. In the case of those with only moderate abilities, he was to treat them with propriety, exhort them with sincerity (thus, you trust the best, exhort the second best), and encourage them to exert their utmost efforts in the execution of their duties. Talent thus graded would assure a stable, harmonious reign.[74]

Ch'ien-lung concludes his examination of the ruler-minister relationship with an argument and a suggestion. He argues

---

[73] Richard Wilhelm, transl., *The I Ching or Book of Changes*, one-vol. ed. (New York, 1961), p. 50. This passage provides the inspiration for Ch'ien-lung's essay, *LSTCC*. 1. 20b–23b, from which the summary here is made.

[74] *LSTCC*, 3. 10. The following remarks continue from this, pp. 10b–11b.

strongly against the hypothesis that "it is easy to employ the meritorious but difficult to find them." This, he says, is nonsense. The ruler's influence and power are such that the people will follow his desires as the shadow follows the body. If the ruler wants to obtain precious and rare birds and beasts from far-off lands he will get them. How much simpler is it to obtain the services of the meritorious, who, after all, exist *within* the realm, in the commonplace walks of everyday life. It is up to the emperor to get them: "If you want to build a great house you obviously seek out an artisan; if you want to refine jade from the rough block, you obviously seek out a craftsman; if you want to rule and yet fail to seek out the worthy, this is like trying to go forward by walking backwards." [75]

The suggestion is that talent may be made to beget talent. If, he says, a ruler appreciates the worthy as he thirsts for water, gathers them about him and implicitly trusts them, *and* has them all recommend those of like worth with whom they are acquainted, then all the posts in the administration will be appropriately filled and all the incumbents will emulate one another. A nice balance will be created both at court and in the provinces and then, even if there are some mean and low types who filter into office, their deceit will be changed into directness and honesty. Imperial attractiveness, that is, will breed ministerial attraction; repulsion will breed repugnance. The ruler's role is to consent to be advised. So consenting, he will attract advice: "Good words will nowhere lie hidden." [76] The minister's role, like the artisan's, is to build a wall against heterodoxy, to shore up the fallible structure of the throne.

It is ironic, perhaps, that Ch'ien-lung was reciting these platitudes just at a time when Yung-cheng, from the throne, was making a mockery of them. Later Ch'ien-lung would follow in his father's steps and stress the hierarchical nature of the ruler-minister relationship to the detriment of nicer ethical considerations. But before he could break the rules he had to know them.

---

[75] *LSTCC*, 3. 10b–11.

[76] *LSTCC*, 2. 7, 8. The phrase, from the *Shu-ching,* continues, ". . . no men of virtue and talents will be neglected away from the court." See Legge, *Chinese Classics,* III, 53.

To say that a prince's view of the throne was largely idealistic is not to say that it was either dishonest or wrong. As a prince he could afford the luxury of perfect expectations. As emperor he could not, though even then he just as surely could not ignore them. The monarch might be a realist, but he could not be a Confucianist Jekyll and Legalist Hyde, changing form to suit the needs of the occasion. He was a whole man, imperfect and fallible and hence historical, a prisoner as much of precedent and ideology as of current exigency. This Ch'ien-lung realized even as a prince. He was profoundly aware of the imperfections of the real—the historical—ruler in contrast to the timeless perfections of the ahistorical sage king. In other words, he distinguished between norms and deeds, and while committed of necessity to the former, he was more at home with the latter.

In this world of deeds, one of the most important criteria of excellence was success. All the piety in the world would not help a ruler who failed before reality. Thus Han Wen-ti, moral perfection personified and eminently successful in his own right, took second place in the prince's eyes to T'ang T'ai-tsung, who was even more successful in the immediate matter of making a reign glorious and prosperous.[77] Even in failure Ch'ien-lung discerned priorities. The "hard" ruler—the tyrant—might, in a time of administrative decline, have less consequential effects on dynastic fate than the "soft" ruler—the weakling. The "hard," he argued, might induce swift retribution and restoration by inciting men to assassination or rebellion; the "soft," such as Han Yüan-ti (r. 48–31 B.C.), were less obviously anathema and might live on undisturbed while passing on to their heirs the seeds of doom they sowed.

Imperial success was measureable both by personal and political standards. The emperor could change and so could his historical fortunes; neither was a static quantity. Thus Han Wu-ti moved from tyrant to hero, in Ch'ien-lung's view, by a conscious and highly personal effort to reform his faults. This, he said, was the most difficult and most admirable thing a man could do.

---

[77] For this, and the following on "hard" and "soft" rulers and Han Wu-ti, see, respectively, *LSTCC*, 5. 2, 4. 2–3, 4. 1–1b. Cf. also Kahn, "Some Mid-Ch'ing Views," p. 231.

T'ang Ming-huang (r. 713–755), on the other hand, went from good to bad, broken objectively by rebellion and personally by a loss in self-confidence. He began his long reign with vigorous determination and caution. He burned pearls and jade as a warning against extravagance, conferred upon the barbarians copies of the classics as a gesture of graciousness to the outlander. So peaceful was his rule that punishments were almost completely abolished. His own forcefulness in the planning and execution of policy was in large part responsible for this early success. But he was unable to sustain the spirit and drive of those years. He became less diligent, less committed to the need first to succor the people and only then to consider his own rewards. And so after the year 742, success turned to failure. The people were squeezed dry of their earnings, the great families gorged themselves on meat and wine, the roads were lined with the starving and the dead. Reason gave way to desire, public interest to private acquisitiveness, compassion for the people to a willful fleecing of them.[78]

Human failure, institutional weakness, and deterioration through time: these, Ch'ien-lung learned, were the constituents of real history. They made the image of the emperorship less pleasing to the idealistic eye, but they prepared a prince for reality. Ch'ien-lung came to the throne sensitive both to the lessons of ethics and to those of history. He was ready, ideologically as well as aesthetically and administratively, to rule. The roles had all been learned. And during his reign they would for the last time be played out when they really mattered. For after Ch'ien-lung new realities would render preparations for the old ones obsolete. Never again would a prince be made so thoroughly aware of what, as sovereign, he would have to do. Never again would the emperor, and hence his education, be at the center of Chinese history.

[78] *JCHS,* 4. 9–10.

E-TU ZEN SUN

Mining Labor in the Ch'ing Period

I N most parts of the world before the nineteenth century, mining was a relatively small part of the economy, and those engaged in it tended to exist apart from the rest of the society. This was not only because their work was commonly carried out in locations remote from major population centers, but also because the combination of special skills, special hazards, and unusual working conditions marked miners as a separate group. In an otherwise largely static preindustrial setting, they had often to be mobile, searching for mineral deposits and moving on from exhausted workings to new ones. They were commonly a low-status group, and in any case their incomes and working conditions were poor; mining was often associated with slavery or in varying degrees with individual and group disadvantage.

These generalizations apply to China of the Ch'ing period, and, despite the continuing traditional concern of the bureaucratic state with the management or monopoly of mineral production and sales, mining was a low-status and unrewarding occupation. The Ch'ing administration, perhaps in part as a response to mounting population pressure and to the beginnings of greater demand for mineral products, did attempt to encourage increased mining activity, but the major features of the traditional mining system do not seem to have been much affected until the advent of foreign capital, techniques, and management toward the end of the nineteenth century. While there is a good deal of incidental information about mining practices in the local gazetteers and a few specific reports, mining is not adequately dealt with in the Ch'ing materials and has not been sufficiently studied by subsequent scholars. This reticence may have been partially due to the minor role of mining as a source of government revenue as compared with agriculture, the major industry. It may also be related to the low prestige of miners and mining; many of them were landless, synonomous with low status, some were little better than slaves and were impressed as workers. The necessary mobility of the miners made them an awkward group in that they were often rootless, difficult to control, divorced from consistent local connections, and given to their own particular group associations. Others were part-time slack-season workers whose normal or principal occupation was farming and whose mining activities may therefore have merited less notice.

There is, however, enough material in the Ch'ing sources to put together a useful, if imprecise and incomplete, picture of what was a significant though neglected aspect of late traditional China. Mineral and metal products were an important part of the domestic economy in Ch'ing China, both in the form of consumer goods and as material for the monetary system. They provided livelihood to a sizable portion of the population, and in the statute books there were many regulations and precedents concerning the mineral industries. It would seem to follow that the people who were the basic producers of such goods—mining labor—would occupy a significant place in the economic system. Yet even a cursory study of the source materials leads one to the conclusion that, so far as contemporary institutions went, mining labor as such existed in a veritable legal and economic limbo. It did not properly belong to any of the four traditional general classes of society, and under the Ch'ing it was not assigned to a special census category, as were the salt-makers. Upon hearing the word "miner," a Ch'ing official down to the end of the nineteenth century would have been likely to manifest one of the following reactions: (1) Miners are the unfortunate natives of an area where the agricultural resources are insufficient to support the population, and therefore they are compelled to depend on mining to eke out a living.[1] (2) Miners are people without a proper occupation, often without even a family; they are an impoverished, ignorant, and desperate lot whose dangerous disposition matches their work.[2] (3) Miners are really just local farmers trying to earn additional income in the slack agricultural season.[3] While category 3 carries no onus and this group is usually treated with tolerance or even sympathy, those in categories 1 and 2—especially 2—are generally regarded as potential disrupters of the social order. Much of the official correspondence on mining affairs dealt with the question of the concentration of numerous miners at large or potentially large mine sites, and the possible upheavals that might be caused by these men. The decision as to whether certain mines should be allowed to operate in a given area often depended on this question of the presence of miners. The bureaucrats' attitude toward mining labor, therefore, directly affected government policy with regard to mineral industries.

This ambivalent attitude toward mining labor can be explained by the characteristics of the traditional economy itself. The predominance of agriculture and related interests had set the tone for the institutional framework, under which other eco-

[1] Numerous references can be found that point to this view of the miner: Wang Wen-shao, comp., *Hsü Yün-nan t'ung-chih kao* [Continuation of Draft Yunnan Gazetteer] (hereafter cited as *HYN*), 43. 3, memorial of gov.-gen. Lin Tse-hsü, 1848; Sun Yü-t'ang, ed., *Chung-kuo chin-tai kung-yeh-shih tzu-liao, ti-i-chi, 1840–1895 nien* [Materials on the History of Modern Industry in China, First Collection, 1840–1895], 2 vols. (Peking, 1957; hereafter cited as *CTKY*), II, 613, report of circuit intendant Yang Tao-chia, 1882; *Yang-wu yün-tung* [The "Foreign Matters" Movement], comp. by the Institute of Modern History, Chinese Academy of Sciences, and Bureau of Ming and Ch'ing Archives, Central Archives, 8 vols. (Shanghai, 1957; hereafter cited as *YWYT*), VII, 35, memorial of T'ang Chiung, 1888.

[2] References to miners as social undesirables are even more numerous. E.g., Hsi Yü-fu, comp., *Huang-ch'ao cheng-tien lei-ts'uan* [A Classified Compendium of the Administrative Statutes of the Imperial Dynasty] (Shanghai, 1903; hereafter cited as *Cheng-tien*), 133. 2b, edict of 1727, and 138. 12, edict of 1670; Imabori Seiji, "Shindai ni okeru gōka no kindaika e no keisha" [The Development of Joint Partnerships in the Ch'ing Period], *Tōyōshi kenkyū* [Studies in Oriental History], XVII (1958), 5, shows that in the early nineteenth century miners in Szechuan were put in a class with others who "are without families."

[3] *Cheng-tien*, 133. 5, report of the Board of Revenue on the mines of Hunan and Hupeh, 1743.

nomic activities were held in check and observed with apprehension. Further, the nature of the miner's work tended to isolate him from the surrounding countryside, and since ancient times he had been looked upon with a combination of curiosity, contempt, and fear.[4] Only those who had had firsthand experience with mining labor were able to entertain realistic views, but many of the men who wrote about mining in their official reports appeared to have had little concrete knowledge of it.

It took men of strong character to refute such prevalent conceptions about mining labor. In 1735, for example, O-mi-ta, governor-general of Canton, registered his objections to an imperial order shutting down the mines in Kwangtung and Kwangsi; among other points, he emphasized that laborers who hired themselves out to work in the mines were simply poor people seeking a living, and that such honest workingmen must be distinguished from troublemaking vagabonds.[5] Over a century later, Lin Tse-hsü, in advocating a better policy regarding mining affairs in Yunnan, pointed out that mining laborers were, after all, just human beings who responded to motivations quite common to most men:

Yunnan province is full of mountains, where mining has never been forbidden. The common people care only for material gain: when a mine is productive they will come hither without being summoned, when the ores are exhausted they will go away of their own will. Never has there been a case where people chose to remain at an exhausted mine and court financial loss. Those who maintain that "after large numbers of people have gathered it is difficult to disperse them" speak out of ignorance of the situation at the mines. . . . The present situation indicates that, where a thousand persons have gathered, the production of that mine must be profitable enough to sustain that many

---

[4] This was true of other civilizations as well. For a comparison, see the summary of the miner's legal and social status in the Roman Empire in R. J. Forbes, *Studies in Ancient Technology*, 9 vols. (Leiden, 1955–1964), VII, 223–224, 229.

[5] *Cheng-tien*, 133. 3–4. O-mi-ta had to obey the order, but he could not let the matter pass without putting his views before the Yung-cheng Emperor, who, be it noted, was extremely conservative where the opening of mines was concerned.

persons; where a few hundred have gathered, the production of that must also be enough to sustain that many persons. No one will go to a place where no profit is to be gained. . . .[6]

Yet the gulf between the mine workers and general run of officials and policy-makers remained. As late as 1893, the foremen of a gold mine near Ch'eng-te, Jehol, were amazed when the industrialist Hsü Jun, during a mine inspection tour for the government, insisted on descending to the bottom of the shaft.[7] That anyone of higher standing than a miner or foreman should do such a thing was unheard of. And yet, through nearly all of the Ch'ing period, the decisions of unknowledgeable officials concerning mining labor often determined the fate of a mining enterprise, and thus affected the pattern of livelihood for large numbers of the population in widely scattered localities.

In the following pages an attempt will be made to describe some outstanding features of mining labor in China before the impact of modernization. The emphasis will be on reconstructing the institutional framework rather than on aiming at any statistical conclusions. Given the character of available sources on this subject, it is not possible to arrive at even such a simple quantitative statement as, for instance, approximately how many mine workers there were in the first half of the nineteenth century.[8] However, this much is clear: the mines were of a wide range of sizes, each mine giving employment from a few to "thousands" of mine workers, who came from varying origins in society; mine workers were to be found in all of the provinces of China, and they had their own professional *esprit*, a sort of hierarchy, and

[6] *HYN*, 43. 3–3b, memorial of Lin Tse-hsü, 1848.

[7] *YWYT*, VIII, 156, entry for January 2, 1893, in Hsü Jun's *Chronological Autobiography*.

[8] Among the most useful source materials for this topic are the local gazetteers, followed by various compendia and essays, and special reports as we come toward the last part of Ch'ing. Figures do appear in some of these sources, but in most cases they are either highly localized and too widely scattered to be of statistical validity, or couched in exceedingly broad terms— such as "in the Chia-ch'ing and Tao-kuang periods there were tens of thousands of miners working in this area," or "each mine employs no less than one thousand miners"—to be useful.

their own special customs and semireligious practices. They functioned, as it were, in a world of their own, being at the same time an adjunct of the larger agrarian economy of the country, yet half-detached from it. A view of the life of mining labor will give us some idea of the place the mineral industries occupied in Ch'ing society.

WHO WERE THE MINING LABORERS?

In this study, "mining labor" is understood to mean that category of laborers whose work is related to the extraction of ores from mines (coal mining is dealt with only incidentally). They may do their work underground or in the open air, and their jobs may range from digging, excavating, and manning water pumps to hauling the ore out of the mine and sending it to the smelter. There is, however, a complicating factor in that, as in many preindustrial mineral enterprises in different parts of the world, the smelters were often located right at the mining site. Therefore, in contemporary Ch'ing descriptions of the size of the labor forces in given areas, sometimes both mining and metallurgical workers may be included. However, wherever possible the present paper will focus on the miner himself.

Scattered in all the provinces of Ch'ing China were innumerable small mines producing a variety of minerals, including such basic materials as coal, iron, and copper. A goodly proportion of these small mines—and some of the larger ones—were worked by persons whose regular occupation was farming, but who engaged in mining during the off-season in order to earn additional income. The fact that these "miners" were in reality members of the farming population was an argument often employed by administrators to support their case when advocating the opening or continuation of mining enterprises. In 1738, governor-general O-mi-ta of Canton, in urging the opening of more mines in Kwangtung and Kwangsi, stated that there could not possibly be any danger of the miners in these provinces turning into rebellious mobs, since "they will be recruited from among the local inhabitants, who will come together to work as miners, and return to their farming upon dispersal." [9] Five years later a similar plea was presented by the Board of Revenue in behalf of mining in Hunan and Hupeh. The iron ore of Shao-yang and other districts, for example, was mined entirely by the local farmers, who used the iron to make farm implements; usually the finished products were sold locally, but in at least one district enough implements were manufactured so that there was a surplus sold in neighboring towns. The Board of Revenue proposed that such side activities of the farmers should be allowed to continue.[10] Not only were the farmers' mining activities allowed, but local officials were known to have directly encouraged the populace to take up mining as a means of earning extra income. A clear example of this is found in the late nineteenth century, when a magistrate of Shan-chou, Honan, drew up a program for the promotion of coal mining in that area and urged the local farmers to engage in the mining and transportation of this coal during the winter months.[11]

Not all off-season farmer-miners were self-employed. Many of the larger mines, whether government-operated or privately owned, appeared to have made extensive use of this source of labor in the agricultural off-season. In the last years of the Ch'ing, when the government was exerting a great effort to revive the mines in Yunnan, the farmers were still an important sector of the labor market. T'ang Chiung, who was in charge of the mining administration of Yunnan and Kweichow, reported at one point that as soon as the current busy farming season was over,

[9] *Cheng-tien,* 133. 4b.

[10] *Cheng-tien,* 133. 5. The proposal was approved by the throne. Other factors of a technological nature in the winter also helped to bring about the persistent practice of mining as a seasonal by-employment of farmers; they were: (1) better ventilation in the mines, (2) less possibility of flooding, and (3) better roads. See Leonard G. Ting, "The Coal Industry in China," *Nankai Social and Economic Quarterly,* X, 1 (April, 1937), 65.

[11] P'eng Tse-i, comp., *Chung-kuo chin-tai shou-kung-yeh shih tzu-liao* [Materials on the History of Chinese Modern Handicraft], 4 vols. (Peking, 1957; hereafter cited as *SKYS*), II, 157–158. In the winter of 1890–1891, the farmers in Hsuan-wei, Yunnan, were encouraged by the government to increase their mining enterprises through a policy of subsidies (in the form of food and oil), and it was reported that there was an obvious increase in the number of mines in operation with the coming of winter (*YWYT,* VII, 57).

more miners would be recruited to develop a new and promising lead mine near Wei-ning.[12] This practice persisted into the twentieth century. In early Republican Shansi, for example, miners reportedly returned to farming during approximately six months of the year, primarily because the wages they earned from mining were too low.[13] Whatever the time and place, however, the farmer-miner was considered an inhabitant of the locality in good standing, and his mining work was regarded as a practical supplement to his regular occupation.

The other—and major—category of mining labor consisted of those who had been forced to abandon farming and had taken up mining as their main occupation. Because of their maverick social-legal status, they became the subject of much government attention and concern, expressed in several ways.

First there was the administrator's preoccupation with the issue of livelihood. The "impoverished people" of Kwangtung and Yunnan, for instance, were described as the most important consideration in debates on the opening of mines in these provinces: the opening of lead and tin mines in Kwangtung would provide sustenance for the poor as well as revenue for the government,[14] while gold-washing along the Gold Sand (Yangtze) River in Yunnan and lead and silver mining in Kweichow would keep the very poor at least at a subsistence level.[15] In discussing the advisability of opening more mines in Kwangtung, the provincial authorities assured the throne that the miners to be recruited would definitely not be regular farmers, and that the new mines would therefore provide employment for the landless poor.[16]

Once the miners had gathered to work at a mine, they posed another problem: what would happen to them and to the com-

---

[12] *YWYT*, VII, 54, memorial of T'ang Chiung, May 9, 1890.

[13] Keng Pu-chan and Ch'eng Yüan-chih, comps., *Shan-hsi K'uang-wu chih lueh* [Shansi Mining Gazetteer] (T'ai-yüan, 1920; hereafter cited as *Shansi*), p. 441.

[14] *Cheng-tien*, 133. 1b, memorial from gov.-gen. Kung Yu-hsün, 1724.

[15] Yüan Yüan, comp., *Yün-nan t'ung-chih* [Yunnan Gazetteer] (1835; hereafter cited as *YNTC*), 73. 7; *Cheng-tien*, 133. 7b.

[16] *Cheng-tien*, 133. 5b, memorial of gov.-gen. Na-su-t'u of Canton and others, 1744. This statement also makes clear to the higher authorities that farming would not suffer as a result of the opening of the mines.

munity if this employment had to be discontinued? To the government, the words "miner" or "mining labor" appeared often to have been designations with only an *ad hoc* value: if a mine ceased operation, the miners immediately reverted to being "impoverished people without an occupation." [17] This was the most critical point so far as the administrators were concerned, for were not unemployed riffraff the prime material of which rebellions were made? Often the deterrence of possible social and economic upheaval was considered sufficient reason for maintaining the mines as long as they were productive.[18]

The Ch'ien-lung period, one of economic expansion and prosperity, was also one that witnessed significant progress in the mineral industries. The government not only adopted a more permissive policy toward the opening of new mines in all parts of the country, but it also made an effort to lay down some ground rules concerning the composition and the recruitment of mining labor. The main point reiterated in many imperial orders was that miners should consist of local people only,[19] and at times the workers were required to be placed under bond by their local neighborhood units.[20] Thus the growth of mining was not expected to affect the existing composition of the population; it was further thought that mining labor should be made to fit into the prevailing system of local population control.

However, all evidence points to the conclusion that there were other factors at work, and that the objective of confining mining laborers to their native districts was in actuality seldom realized. Throughout the Ch'ing period, the "professional" mine workers had a habit of roaming the countryside regardless of provincial boundaries, stopping wherever work was available. During the K'ang-hsi period, a magistrate in Kwangtung reported that the

[17] One of the most commonly used phrases in this regard was *wu-yeh p'in-min;* see *HYN,* 43. 1, edict rejecting the proposal to close the mines of Yunnan, Szechuan, and Kweichow, 1794.

[18] *HYN,* 43. 1–1b, edict ordering the continuation of mining operations in Szechuan and the Hu-kuang provinces. A corollary of this line of thought was the government's use of mining to provide work relief for population displaced as a result of either natural or man-made disasters. E.g. in Jehol, 1891, and Hunan, 1896: *YWYT,* VIII, 170, and *Cheng-tien,* 134. 4b, respectively.

[19] *Cheng-tien,* 133. 4b, mining regulations of 1738.

[20] *Cheng-tien,* 138. 2, edict on the coal mines of Shantung, 1740.

miners and smelter workers in Yang-shan district were hired by the owners from other districts or provinces (many smelterers came from Hunan), the sole criterion for employment being professional skill and competence.[21] It appears, therefore, that as soon as mining grew beyond depending upon the part-time farmer-miner and became an industrial enterprise employing hired labor, such considerations as skill, wages, profit, and mobility immediately entered the scene to add new facets to the old modes of control. That professional skill was recognized as a special characteristic of the mining laborer and set him apart from the general run of the rural population was evident in the pronouncements of persons whose work placed them in close contact with mining affairs. While trying to reorganize the mines of Yunnan, T'ang Chiung pointed out in a memorial that "recruiting miners is different from recruiting the militia . . . [for] only those familiar with the excavation work underground can be eligible"; in order to develop the copper mines at Ch'iao-chia and Wei-ning he sent agents to gather workers not only from other districts within Yunnan but from Szechuan as well.[22] Meanwhile, mine workers had been moving about with apparent ease and freedom. In 1744 it was reported that the mines in Kwangtung and various other provinces had been worked largely by the natives of Kiangsi province.[23] This statement is corroborated by the local history of mining in Yunnan, where "professional miners [*tsou-ch'ang-che*, lit. 'persons who go after mines'] from Kiangsi, Hunan, and Szechuan" were employed in the operation of a number of famous mines in the early nineteenth century.[24]

The mobility of the professional miner was not restricted to the limits of China proper. The mineral resources of Sinkiang were opened up by investors and miners from the "interior prov-

[21] Lu Hsiang-jung, *Yang-shan hsien-chih* [Gazetteer of Yang-shan Hsien] (1823; hereafter cited as *Yang-shan*), 5. 48b–49 and 56b, quoting a report by magistrate Wang Yung-ying, 1692.

[22] *YWYT*, VII, 53, T'ang Chiung, January 16, 1890.

[23] *Cheng-tien*, 133. 2, memorial of gov. Ch'en Hung-mou of Kiangsi. In 1899 the magistrate of P'ing-hsiang, Kiangsi, reported that half of the coal miners there were natives of nearby Hunan (*Cheng-tien*, 138. 10).

[24] *HYN*, 43. 28, quoting from T'an Ts'ui, "Yung-chin-ch'ang chi"; cf. Tang Meng, comp., *Hsü-hsiu Shun-ning-fu chih* [Revised Shun-ning Gazetteer] (1904), 13. 29.

inces" even before that territory became a province, and some of these mining areas achieved great prosperity before the Muslim Rebellions of the nineteenth century.[25] According to one account, there was a lack of mining skill on the part of the local population,[26] so that the field was left open for Chinese miners. Further, where the prospects of a high profit were good, Chinese miners in considerable numbers were known to have gone across the border into northern Vietnam and Burma and engaged in silver mining, the products of their labor being carried back to China in the shape of silver bracelets which they wore on their arms. Those who worked in Burma and Vietnam were natives of several provinces in south-central China.[27]

How did the professional miners go about seeking work? By piecing together scattered data, it is possible to get a glimpse of some rather significant features in this aspect of their life. On some occasions the miners were in the market in the form of free labor who went to work for certain mine owners of their choice. Their incentive was the potential earnings, and the miners simply hired themselves out to the most attractive employer.[28] At other times miners traveled in a group under a leader, who not only possessed the capital, but who was also usually an experienced prospector or miner. The group of miners followed the orders of the leader and worked where he decided to start his mine. Often this type of miner worked on a profit-sharing basis.[29] In late Ch'ing, the mines in remote regions then being developed faced a labor problem: in Sinkiang, for example, where neither of the above traditional forms of labor recruitment was practiced and where there was a scarcity of skilled workers, mine owners com-

[25] Yüan Ta-hua, comp., *Hsin-chiang t'u-chih* [Sinkiang Illustrated Gazetteer] (1911, reissued 1923; hereafter cited as *Sinkiang*), 29. 8.

[26] *Sinkiang*, 29. 1b.

[27] The men from Kiangsi, Hunan, and Hupeh generally went to northern Burma, and those from Kwangtung to northern Vietnam; the miners were required to pay a tax to the authorities of these countries. *Cheng-tien*, 135. 6b, quoting Chao I, *Yen p'u tsa-chi* [Miscellaneous Notes of Chao I]; Chao states that he had interviewed some returned miners when he was prefect of Chen-an in Kwangsi (1766–1768, 1769–1770).

[28] *HYN*, 43. 28.

[29] Wu Ch'i-chun, *Tien-nan k'uang-ch'ang t'u-lueh* [Account of Mining in Yunnan] (1845; hereafter cited as Wu), 1. 48b, quoting from Wang Ch'ang, *T'ung-cheng ch'üan-shu* [Administration of the Copper Mines].

plained that they had to pay exorbitant wages in order to attract miners to work there.[30]

Not all hired mining laborers were free professionals, however; from time to time cases of forced labor were reported to the government. In the 1880's, Peking's attention was called to several such instances in different parts of the country, a reflection perhaps of the growing public interest in mining. In I-hsien, Shantung, the smaller, private coal mines, unable to compete successfully against the government mines in both wages and work schedules, were accused of forcibly drafting local men to work as miners.[31] From Hunan came very startling information concerning the practices of certain mines where large numbers of innocent persons—including travelers merely passing through as well as the local poor people—were either tricked or forcibly captured and taken to work in the coal mines; few of these men were ever seen again.[32] While the government tried to punish the offenders whenever a case came to its attention, forced labor among miners was not eliminated for many more decades to come.[33]

One other form of labor "recruitment" deserves mention: the assignment by the government of a certain number of laborers to work in specific mining areas that were deemed important to the national interest. Evidence of this practice first appeared in early Ch'ing and it was still much used in the last decades of the dynasty. It appears that this method was resorted to in the less developed parts of China where the supply of labor was inadequate. In late Ch'ing evidence of the practice shows up nearly always in the semi-frontier regions, from Kansu and Sinkiang to Heilungkiang. This in effect amounted to conscription of mining labor, supplemented at times by men from the regular military

---

[30] *Sinkiang,* 29. 6b.

[31] *YWYT,* VII, 159.

[32] *Kuang-hsü ch'ao tung-hua-lu* [Tung-hua Records of the Kuang-hsü Reign], 5 vols., ed. Chung-hua shu-chü (Shanghai, 1958; hereafter cited as *THL-KH*), II, 1524, memorial of gov. Pien Pao-ti, 1883.

[33] For example, in the "native" (i.e., unmodernized) mines of Shansi forced impressment of miners, who were sometimes lured away or manhandled at wayside inns, among other methods, continued into the 1930's before the provincial government took steps against it. Ting, "The Coal Industry in China," p. 73.

colonies.[34] Judging from the official reports, it was not a satisfactory way to run mining enterprises.

ORGANIZATION AND CONTROL

There are two aspects to the subject of the organization and control of mining labor: that of internal coherence among the mine workers themselves, and that of bureaucratic control achieved through the interlacing of the local administrative structure with the overall organization of the mining enterprise.[35]

At the initial stage of a mine operation, when a group of professional miners arrived at a likely mine site and began to prospect and carry out preliminary excavation, the cohesion and effectiveness of this group depended on the voluntary cooperation of all its members. Hence the predominant characteristic of the internal relationship was one of egalitarianism. In Yunnan, for example, such a group usually numbered no more than a few dozens of persons acting under the direction of the leader who furnished the capital for the enterprise and who was also versed in the techniques of mining; often he had a good deal of knowledge about the locality as well. The leader was called "manager" (*kuan-shih*) and enjoyed a few privileges such as better food. All the rest of the group addressed each other as "brother" (*ti-hsiung*) or "little comrade" (*hsiao-huo-chi*). They lived in hastily constructed shacks in a closely bound, isolated community at the mine site.[36] Unwavering group loyalty was apparently expected of—and rendered by—each member. Local tradition tells how a leader with his "mineurs dévoués" prospected for tin in the Ko-chiu area without success. Eventually they broke up camp and left the mountains. On that same day a straggler in the group finally struck the rich vein. Without a thought of keeping this knowledge to himself, he carried specimens of the ore some thirty

---

[34] Some examples are seen in *Cheng-tien,* 135. 4 (Kansu, 1774), 139. 1–2 (Mo-ho, Heilungkiang, 1887), 136. 5–6b (same place, 1892), 133. 12 (Ili, Sinkiang, 1773); and *Sinkiang,* 29. 8b.

[35] In instances where both mining and smelting were conducted at the same place as parts of an integrated operation, both the miners and metallurgical workers would then be included in any scheme for their organization and supervision.

[36] Wu, 1. 28b; see also *YNTC,* 73. 15b.

or forty *li* until he caught up with the group and told them the good news.[37] The uncertainties about the outcome of a mining venture made it obviously impractical either for the investor-leader to throw his weight around and thereby possibly arouse resentment among the workers, or for an individual of the group to try to strike out on his own. Actually, the miners often did not receive a regular wage before the vein was discovered. A prevalent practice was for the investor to gather a group of miners on a share-profit basis (their proportion could be as high as forty percent of the production), thereby assuring himself of their single-minded labors. The workers who had thus participated in the setting up of the enterprise were called "close brothers" (*ch'in-shen ti-hsiung*). They were distinguished from the hired laborers who probably arrived after the mine had begun operating when more labor was needed and who were known simply as "hired miners" (*chao-mu sha-ting*).[38]

Once a large mine had grown beyond the initial stage, other factors would begin to modify the egalitarian relationship within the group.[39] First, the augmented size of the mining community required a more formal system of organization for the effective carrying out of the tasks of production. Second, whenever large numbers of mining laborers gathered, the attention of the local

[37] According to Emile Rocher, *La Province Chinoise du Yün-nan*, 2 vols. (Paris, 1880), II, 230–231, this was the beginning of the famous Ko-chiu tin works in the eighteenth century. The account indicates that the leader lived with the miners, permitted them to express their opinions (although he alone had the power to make the decisions), and when funds were running low, his diet was no better than that of the miners.

[38] Wu, 1. 48b–49. Thus, the basis of this sort of organization was entirely personal and specific. Smaller mines sometimes presented a variation of the "close brothers" system; e.g., in Kweichow, relatives and friends might form a group to open a mine and, if successful, the profits would be shared (*Cheng-tien*, 133. 7b, memorial of gov. Ho Ch'ang-ling, 1799).

[39] A typical description of the transformation of a mining camp reads as follows: "At a mine site at first there would be no more than a few score people, who carried their own provisions and built huts for shelter. When the mine proves to be productive a multitude would gather from near and far, including merchants, artisans, traveling showmen of all sorts, until increasing day by day the population number over ten thousand." *Kuo-ch'ao ch'i-hsien lei-cheng* [Biographies of Ch'ing Venerables and Worthies Arranged by Categories] (First Series, 1884), 204. 13, memorial of Yün-kuei gov.-gen. Kuei-liang, 1844.

and provincial authorities was aroused because of the issues of civil administration involved. The need for official surveillance of the mining community, as seen by the authorities, brought about a pattern of organization and control that dovetailed local bureaucracy with the workings of the mines, a pattern that was based on the premise of authoritarian hierarchy.

In 1689 a plan was outlined by the magistrate of Yang-shan district in Kwangtung, who held that the owners of iron mines and smelteries ought to organize their labor force (which included many "outsiders") into squads of ten men, each squad to be headed by a "foreman" (*chiang-t'ou*), who would be held responsible for recruiting the workers and for their actions; the magistrate pointed out that in this way the task of the local officials would be greatly facilitated.[40] This idea of letting a foreman (in some areas called "headman" [*t'ou-jen*]), who was accountable to the local authorities, have direct control over the workers served as the general pattern of control in different parts of the country.[41]

Under the supervision of the local officials, each mine that employed wage workers was required to establish a series of self-governing officers. In nineteenth-century Yunnan the most common ones were the "mine foreman" (*tung-chang*), in charge of the miners; the "overseer" (*k'o-chang*), in charge of checking on the business establishments at the mining camp; the "furnace chief" (*lu-chang* or *lu-t'ou*), in charge of the smelter workers; the "street head" (*chieh-chang*), in charge of checking on transient visitors; and the "tax man" (*k'o-chang*), who collected the mining duties in behalf of the authorities. In addition there were the "mess chief" (*kuo-t'ou*), responsible for provisions and feeding the workers; the "timber chief" (*hsiang-t'ou*), in charge of the timbering material in the underground tunnels; and the "charcoal chief" (*t'an-chang*), in charge of the fuel for the smelters. All fulfilled their duties under general supervision of a "mine superintendent" (*ch'ang-yüan* or *ch'ang-chu*), who was an official

[40] *Yang-shan*, 5. 48–49, 51–52.
[41] *HYN*, 43. 5, Lin Tse-hsü's 1848 memorial on the Yunnan mines, where the headman was to recruit the miners as well as supervise their conduct.

appointed from either the local district or the subprefecture.[42] The entire population of the mining camp or town was duly recorded in the local registries and incorporated into the *pao-chia* system.[43]

Further examples of the merging of government administrative procedures with the business structure of the mine can be found in varying forms in other parts of the country. In Shensi there were iron mines where the operators were required to report periodically to the local officials the name, age, native district, and date of employment of each miner; it was also necessary to report any changes in the roster. In gold mines in the same province, however, the practice was to combine labor surveillance with the collection of the mine tax: every fifty gold miners constituted one "certificate unit" (*p'iao*), and each unit was taxed a daily duty of 0.025 *liang* of gold.[44] This method was also used in the late Ch'ing in the gold mines of Kansu and Sinkiang, which the government had farmed out for development. The *Hu-pu tse-li* (Regulations of the Ministry of Finance) shows that at each gold mine in Sinkiang the most experienced and able of the miners were selected to be the "tax men" (*k'o-chang*), each in charge of fifty miners; and in Kansu a "head miner" (*fu-t'ou*) was appointed the leader of each fifty-man unit. It was the duty of the tax men and the head miners to keep the men in their own groups under discipline and to collect the stipulated mining duties (set at 0.03 *liang* of refined gold per person per month) from the miners and turn it over to the local government. They were also required to present for inspection all the gold left after taxation and to obtain a license in order to sell the gold legally on the market.[45] Thus, the power of the local administration was

---

[42] Wu, 1. 49; *YNTC*, 73. 15b–16; Ch'en Tsung-hai, comp., *P'u-erh-fu chih* [P'u-erh Fu Gazeteer] (1900; hereafter cited as *P'u-erh*), 20. 30. It should be noted that the use of these terms was far from consistent even within the same province. The discrepancies that existed as to the exact functions of these officers, or their exact titles, could be attributed to one or more causes: (a) local variations, (b) differences that appeared with the passage of time, and (c) misinterpretation by some of the authors of the source materials.

[43] *P'u-erh*, 20. 30b.

[44] *Cheng-tien*, 132. 3 and 7b.

[45] *Cheng-tien*, 132. 2–2b. It is notable that the *k'o-chang* (tax man) system was most evidently in use in Sinkiang, where the miners were Chinese migrants from other provinces (*k'o-min*). Where non-Han local people were used as

exercised through the outwardly self-governing devices among the miners which were, in reality, extensions of the civil bureaucracy.

MINING AS A WAY OF LIFE

In theory, all hired laborers at the mines were paid regular wages. Wages were calculated in terms of the legal tender copper coins, the major exchange medium among the common people. Copper, however, had a fluctuating rate of exchange relative to silver and gold, in which the bulk of the mining duties were paid. The actual buying power of the copper coins depended on the locality and the time. It is necessary to keep these qualifications in mind as we examine the following facets of a miner's life.

It seems that by and large wages were paid with reasonable regularity, but there were some highly inequitable situations. The wage payments appeared to be closely related to the organization and control mechanisms in force. From late seventeenth-century Kwangtung came the report that some mine owners and metalworks employers were cheating their laborers out of their wages,[46] while in other localities the power of the foreman class appeared to have grown to such an extent that they were able to exact an assortment of irregular levies from the workers.[47] In the latter case, it seems possible that the expanding power of the foremen was linked to the practice of contract labor that began to assume an important role toward the last years of the Ch'ing, whether at the smaller mines in Jehol or at such notable undertakings as the P'ing-hsiang coal mines in Kiangsi.[48]

The wage level was low. The P'ing-hsiang coal mines at the turn of the twentieth century employed a total of some 2,000

---

miners, a modified method was applied: in Yü-t'ien, for instance, the government designated some well-to-do local Muslims to be "mine chiefs" (*ch'ang-t'ou*), each of whom had under him fifty miners who were conscripted from among the agricultural population; this in time created severe problems, and the practice was discontinued in 1887 (*Sinkiang*, 29. 6b–7).

[46] *Yang-shan*, 5. 53.

[47] *HYN*, 43. 7. In Yunnan in the 1840's the additional levies presumably added by the *t'ou-jen* included such items as "transportation fee," "mine owner's share," "cost of thanksgiving service at Hsi-yueh Temple," and the like.

[48] *YWYT*, VIII, 156, 199.

workers, the majority being contract laborers under the control of, and paid through, the labor contractor. Of the 2,000-odd workers, 250 were operators of modern-type machines and machinists, whose wages ranged from C$7.00 or C$8.00 per month up to C$40.00 or C$50.00. The ordinary miner and other less skilled workers could be expected to earn considerably less than the minimum for the machinists.[49] If the data for the first years of the Republic are taken as reflecting the conditions of late Ch'ing (and this is a valid approach inasmuch as little significant change had occurred in the traditional sector of the mining industry), then the wage situation can be seen as precarious. The coal miners of Chü-yung, Kiangsu, were contract laborers paid a piece rate that averaged C$1.00 to C$1.50 per ton of coal excavated. This sum was presumably paid to the labor contractor and distributed by him to the miners under him. When mining operations had to stop during the rainy season, the miners simply ceased earning. At the Chia-wang coal mine in the same province the wages were also based on a piece rate of 70 copper coins per 160 catties coal produced, which means 735 coppers or C$0.56 per ton. These miners worked in twenty-four-hour shifts, and the average production was something less than one ton per man per day.[50]

Many cases indicate that the wages were not always paid as stipulated. The previously mentioned magistrate of Yang-shan reported in 1689 that among the unethical practices of the mine owners in that district was the forcing of miners and smelter workers to buy their daily necessities from the employer's own store, usually at inflated prices and very often on credit that carried a high interest. All such sums would then be deducted from the workers' wages. Any worker who tried to avoid this burden by trading with a local store would be charged with breaking the contract and punished.[51] Although this is the only written record discovered so far which mentions the existence of

---

[49] *YWYT,* VIII, 199.

[50] *Su-che-wan k'uang-chih* [Mining Gazetteer of Kiangsu, Chekiang, and Anhwei], comp. the Mine Superintendent's Office of the Third Region (1914; hereafter cited as *SCW*), 3b, 12–12b. The conversion of cash to dollar value is based on figures given in the book. In nearby Nanking, Chia-wang coal was selling at C$11.00 per ton after high transportation costs were added. In 1892 Hsü Jun reported from Jehol that the gold miners were earning approximately 100 coppers per day, which he considered extremely low. *YWYT,* VIII, 170.

[51] *Yang-shan,* 5. 54b–55.

a "company store" in Ch'ing China, it is possible that variations of this practice might also have existed in other mining areas. Even in the late nineteenth century, mining labor working in government-sponsored projects could still find wage payments subject to built-in hazards. The copper miners of Pai-ch'eng, Sinkiang, for example, often did not receive their monthly wages because the regulations called for the delivery of 160 catties of concentrated copper ore before the wages (Tls. 3 per month) could be paid in full, and yet it usually took a miner two and a half months to produce that much concentrated ore.[52]

The physical aspects of working conditions for the miner were broadly similar to those in other countries before the advent of modern technology. All the stages in the productive process were accomplished by human labor with the help of simple mechanical devices.[53] One who observed mining at firsthand said of the gold miners of Jehol: "They work all day in the midst of danger; underground work is like eating human food and doing the work of the nether world." [54] And in any case the earnings of the local poor, who turned to mining and worked with little more than their own hands, were only enough to give the men a hand-to-mouth existence.[55]

For mining that required extensive excavation, the technical difficulties and the costs of solving them most often determined the environment in which the miners worked. One of the most serious and perennial problems was that of flooding. The existing techniques for the elimination of water from deep mines were so inefficient that in many cases entire mines had to be abandoned because of the presence of water.[56] The urgency of the problem

---

[52] *Sinkiang,* 29. 9b–10.

[53] The introduction of some modern methods did not essentially change the general labor picture at most smaller mines. Usually it was a matter of short-run costs, human labor being cheaper than imported machinery. In Hunan, for example, dynamite was used at the P'ing-chiang gold mine, but everything else was done by hand: the blasted ore was picked up by workers and handed up to the surface in bamboo baskets passed from hand to hand in a relay of laborers stationed at close intervals. Li Chien-te, *Chung-kuo k'uang-yeh tiao-ch'a chi* [Report on China's Mining Industry] (Peking, 1914), p. 123.

[54] Meaning they were living on borrowed time. *YWYT,* VIII, 170.

[55] For descriptions of Kweichow and Jehol miners of this sort, see *YWYT,* VII, 36 and VIII, 153–154, respectively.

[56] *CTKY,* II, 615–618, gives a mid-nineteenth century description of the water problem at the K'ai-p'ing coal field before modernization.

of flooding gave rise to some of the most horrid cases of labor atrocities that have appeared in the history of mining anywhere. As mentioned before, in 1881 the government's attention was called to the situation in Lei-yang, Hunan, where ordinary citizens were lured or forced into working in the local coal mines. The mine owners allied themselves with local gangsters, who established gambling joints, restaurants, and wine shops, and got the poor people into debt; when the latter were unable to pay these debts they were "sold" to the mine. Once at the mine the captives, now called "water frogs," were incarcerated in dark and damp earthen cubicles known as "drums," where the victims were practically sealed in with only one small opening for ingress and egress. There they were set to work manning the water pumps in alternating shifts day and night. To prevent their escape the mine owners took their clothes from them, and the entire complex of cubicles was surrounded by a wooden fence guarded by their foreman—a post, as the official report stated, that was filled by the worst elements of the local population. Those who attempted to escape had their feet slashed. No respite from labor was allowed and no medication given when the "water frogs" fell ill. Depending on his original state of health, a man usually died between a fortnight and a few months after his capture. Those who remained alive in the spring, when mining operations were suspended, were kept in the "drums" through the summer, to be used again as water pumpers in the next season. It was estimated that at each mine where such a practice prevailed, up to several hundred persons perished every year in these circumstances.[57]

While the above is an extreme example of the intentional maltreatment of mine workers, there were other instances that are almost as appalling. The old-style coal mines of I-hsien, Shantung, were reported not only to have relied on forced labor, but to have worked these men to death with no relief in case of

---

[57] *THL-KH*, II, 1524, memorial of Hunan governor Pien Pao-ti, May 23, 1883; *YWYT*, VII, 405–406. The local authorities arrested the mine owners and the foremen of the water pumpers, and liberated about 140 "water frogs"; the provincial government then prosecuted the offenders on separate criminal counts, and Peking backed up the authorities' decision to mete out severe penalties as a warning to others.

illness.[58] Even in the best of premodern mines miserable conditions prevailed. The men employed to pump the water from the copper mines in Yunnan, for example, worked stark naked in the mud and mire at the bottom of the pit, "looking like so many clay figures that could move." The regular miners, who had to descend narrow, near-perpendicular steps down the side of the mine shafts, were hemmed in by earth and rocks on all sides, and, notwithstanding the small oil lamps that were used for illumination, their underground environs "resembled the Hell as depicted by the Buddhists." [59]

There were other sources of physical danger to the miner. The most feared disasters were collapse of the mine tunnel, and fire; lack of proper ventilation also became a matter of concern as the knowledge of modern mining techniques increased.[60] In north China, as well as in Yunnan, the miners who died as a result of the collapse of mine tunnels were left where they were; in fact, several old diggings at K'ai-p'ing were abandoned after an accident claimed twenty-eight lives in the mid-nineteenth century.[61]

Mining laborers were known for their tendency to form cliques, factions, or brotherhoods, leading to clannish behavior and feuds. The forming of semireligious brotherhods, complete with incense-burning rituals, probably helped to establish a sense of solidarity among the miners and provided mutual help when needed. At the same time, this was exactly the sort of activity that set the officials' nerves on edge. Disciplinary measures dealt out to miners were as a rule brutal and severe; this was thought to be necessary for keeping public order. Some of the ways of correcting delinquent behavior were the use of the whip, and hanging up a man by the thumbs with rattan strips.[62]

Considering all the hazards, vicissitudes, and the stark severity of life that made up the mining laborer's lot, it is not surprising to find that he tended to be extremely superstitious. His prime

[58] *YWYT*, VII, 157, Chu Ts'ai's report, 1882.

[59] Wu, 1. 29.

[60] *CTKY*, II, 618; *SCW*, 11–11b.

[61] *CTKY*, II, 615. The miners in Yunnan believed that those who died inside the mine would turn into ghouls, who would ask for food and drink when the tunnel was reentered, and that they could be stilled only by being spit upon (Wu, 1. 29b).

[62] Wu, 1. 37; *YNTC*, 73. 16b; *HYN*, 43. 7.

preoccupation was with the presence of the sought-after ore, and this was expressed in many of his taboos. For example, in the miner's daily speech certain sounds must be avoided: "stone" (*shih*) was called *hsia*, because *shih* was the phonym of the word meaning "to lose"; "earth" was called *huang* and not *t'u*, because the latter sounded like "to spit out"; and to say "to lose" or "to spit out" might presage losing the ore body.[63] The mining laborer also believed that those who carried metal weapons or had an official position should not be allowed to go into a mine, because the vein of the ore deposit was a divine dragon who would forsake the locality if exposed to the presence of officials.[64] Old-timers maintained that once a productive mine was closed down and sealed, the remaining deposit would disappear forever; consequently the word "to seal" (*feng*) was forbidden at mining camps, and the character *feng* for "plentiful" was used in its place.[65] At the same time, supernatural help was invoked for the success of the mines. The first prosperous tin miners in Ko-chiu erected two "magnificent temples" as a gesture of thanksgiving to mountain spirits in the district.[66]

With all its drawbacks and risks, mining remained a profession and a way of life among thousands of people in all parts of China. A mining town began as a mere collection of huts, while the first prospectors dug tentatively into the surrounding hills. When a rich vein was struck, the area was immediately transformed into a lively town, with merchants and artisans gathering from afar to provide the goods and services needed by the mining community. "At a mine there are many ways to come into wealth: some do it through mining, some through refining the ore, some through craftsmanship, some through sheer labor, some even through gambling, and some too through thievery."[67] The rise and decline of a mining town is graphically depicted in a mid-Ch'ing treatise on mining in Yunnan: An investor in a mine

[63] Wu, 1. 30b.

[64] Wu, 1. 31. One may wonder a bit, however, whether this particular taboo was entirely a matter of superstition, or whether it might not have been a way for the mine workers to keep the officials at a distance.

[65] *HYN*, 43. 28b.

[66] Rocher, II, 232; cf. Western traditions about the godesses of mines in T. A. Rickard, *The Romance of Mining* (Toronto, 1945), p. 2.

[67] *YNTC*, 73. 16b.

might change overnight from a destitute near-failure into a wealthy magnate if the ore was discovered in time. How the people crowded around him then, how he lavished every extravagance on himself; the presents piled up his house, smart servants and handsome horses were his to order about. But the resources of the mine were not inexhaustible, and just as quickly prosperity might become poverty again. "One day there are carriages and crowds in the streets, lights shine from ten thousand houses; in a flash it all reverts back into a wilderness, where birds build their nests and wild beasts have their lairs, and nothing is visible but nettles covering ruins in the valley. Only woodcutters or herdboys will occasionally come here, to pick up some leftover pieces of ore from the former mine." [68]

Such a view was clearly a foreshortened one emanating from a literary mind. But whether the ordinary mine worker had taken part in such a dramatic cycle of events, or whether he had merely plodded through his assigned tasks at a less spectacular mining community—perhaps at times mixing farming with mining—he was nonetheless a part of the economy that sustained traditional China, and the special features of his place in that society may be regarded as symbolic of the problems to be overcome in the era that followed.

Even so necessarily incomplete a survey may suggest one of the important contributing factors to the drive for modernization in China: the traditional system was not merely inhumane; it was also one of very low productivity. The low status and poor rewards associated with mining were perhaps a reflection of the relatively small role which it played in the age-old agrarian civilization. To the extent that modernization and industrialization depended on massive increases in mineral production and use, traditional mining was grossly inappropriate to China's needs. An examination of the nature and conditions of mining labor under the Ch'ing may suggest, therefore, something of the overall technical and organizational gap which separated traditional China from the demands of the modern world.

[68] *YNTC*, 73. 16b–17.

KWANG-CHING LIU

Li Hung-chang in Chihli: The Emergence of a Policy, 1870-1875

THE year 1870, which saw the unification of Germany and the consolidation of a revolution from above in Japan, saw a major event in China—the appointment of Li Hung-chang (1823–1901) as governor-general of Chihli and as imperial commissioner for the northern ports. Even while he was absorbed in the task of suppressing internal rebellion in the 1860's, Li had been the foremost advocate of "self-strengthening" (*tzu-ch'iang*)—the policy of building up China's military potential, chiefly by adopting Western technology, so as to meet the challenge of external aggression.[1] In his new position of influence, close to Peking, Li worked to continue and expand this policy.

A reassessment of the self-strengthening movement must include an inquiry into its ideological implications. Did men like Li (there were very few of them) aim merely at the adoption of Western technology, or did they also propose reform? Did they modify the Confucian emphasis on moral government, which relied chiefly on virtue and culture as the sources of power?

---

[1] I have dealt with Li's early advocacy of *tzu-ch'iang* in a forthcoming article, "Li Hung-chang and 'Self-strengthening': The Origins of a Policy, 1862–1867."

Inquiry must also be made into the complex factors that frustrated the success of the movement—the institutional and intellectual milieu, and the weakness of the new military and economic forces that had arisen after a generation of contact with the West. But first of all, it is necessary to consider the political context. Was the self-strengthening movement initiated by the central government or by the provinces? Was it a matter of sporadic efforts by a governor-general here, by a governor there, or was it a part of Ch'ing national policy?

The self-strengthening movement began in the early T'ung-chih period, originating chiefly in the provinces but enjoying the strong support of the court. It was Li Hung-chang who first proposed the teaching of mathematics and the sciences at a government "interpreter's college," and who founded China's earliest modern arsenals; it was Tso Tsung-t'ang who planned a large shipbuilding program. Li and Tso were stoutly backed, however, by the Tsungli Yamen at a time when Prince Kung was at the height of his power and when Wen-hsiang was still in good health. The development of "regionalism"—the administrative leeway which the governors-general and governors enjoyed regarding the temporary imperial armies (*yung*) and the likin—did not handicap the cooperation between Peking and provinces in the new projects.

In 1870, a new page was turned in the history of the self-strengthening movement. Li Hung-chang, in moving so close to Peking, became in effect a metropolitan official. Li performed many central government functions in the fields of diplomacy and military planning, and he made an attempt to coordinate self-strengthening efforts not only in Chihli but in other parts of the empire. It remained to be seen, however, whether on the one hand Li—and for that matter Prince Kung and Wen-hsiang (before his death in 1876)—would continue to have an effective voice in the councils around the throne, and whether on the other hand the measures they proposed could be carried out in the provinces, particularly in the militarily and financially vital area of the lower Yangtze.

This paper presents aspects of Li's first five years in Tientsin—his functions in the imperial government, his ideas regarding self-strengthening, and the manner in which his proposals were received in Peking and in the provinces. As a senior official who had occupied key positions during the campaigns for the suppression of the Taipings and the Niens, Li had formed many friendships among governors-general, governors, and lesser officials. As the acknowledged but untitled leader of the Anhwei Army, Li also developed a degree of influence in provinces where units of that army were stationed.[2] But in the last analysis, it was the specific imperial sanction for each of Li's proposals, as well as his position as imperial commissioner, that accounted for his role as coordinator of policy. In the early 1870's, we find him taking remarkable initiative in shaping policy, and for a time it appeared that his programs might, at least in part, be carried out on a national scale.

Lɪ's Central Government Functions

It was a crisis in China's foreign relations that brought Li to Chihli. Under the pressure of the harsh French demands that followed the Tientsin Massacre of June 21, the court on July 26 ordered Li, who had been engaged in operations against the Moslem rebels in Shensi, to move his forces to Chihli and join the twenty-eight battalions of the Anhwei Army (*Huai-chün*) previously brought there by Tseng Kuo-fan. A month later, on August 29, when Li and an army of about 25,000 men arrived at the border of Chihli, he was appointed its governor-general, replacing the ailing Tseng.[3] It was the court's wish that the Anhwei Army, which had proved so effective in fighting the Taipings and the Niens, should now be used for the defense of the metropolitan province against possible invaders.

For one who thinks in terms of twentieth-century Chinese politics it is possible to imagine Li as a proto-warlord, henceforth dominating the area where the capital was situated. This is completely misleading, for although Li's role as leader of the Anhwei

[2] See Stanley Spector, *Li Hung-chang and the Huai Army: A Study in Nineteenth-Century Regionalism* (Seattle, 1964).

[3] Li Hung-chang, *Li Wen-chung kung ch'üan-chi* [Complete Works of Li Hung-chang], 100 *ts'e* (Nanking, 1908; hereafter cited as *LWCK*), *Tsou-kao* (hereafter cited as *Memorials*), 16. 34, 48, 50.

Army certainly accounted for his being brought to Chihli, the Anhwei Army itself was by this time an integral part of the dynasty's armed forces. While its status continued to be that of *yung*, or temporary imperial army, Peking had control over the appointment of its higher officers and over its finances. The commanders (*t'ung-ling*) of the Anhwei Army, although normally recommended by Li, were appointed by imperial edict and all had the title of general-in-chief (*t'i-tu*) or brigade general (*tsung-ping*) under the Green Standard system. The subordinate officers, although chosen by the commanders, were also given the titles of Green Standard officers by the Board of War—colonel (*fu-chiang*), lieutenant-colonel (*ts'an-chiang*), and the rest, usually in an "expectant" (*hou-pu*) capacity.[4] There is no question that the troops and officers of the Anhwei Army regarded themselves as serving the dynasty. It was, moreover, from imperially authorized sources that the Anhwei Army was financed—the maritime customs of Shanghai and Hankow, the likin from Kiangsu and Kiangsi, and in smaller amounts the treasuries of Liang-chiang, Hupeh, Chekiang, Shantung, Szechuan, and Shansi. While Li enjoyed close personal relationships with the governors-general of Liang-chiang (Tseng) and of Hu-kuang (Li Han-chang) and was friendly with several governors, the court had the authority and influence to see that the funds were continued or withheld and, indeed, to change the governors-general or governors.[5] Ever since 1864, units of the Anhwei Army had been frequently moved by imperial edict from one province to another. In summoning Anhwei troops to Chihli, the throne was merely calling upon the services of one of its best forces.

On the other hand, thanks to his role as the leader of the Anhwei Army, Li gained a trusted position near the capital itself and was relied on to perform duties that belonged to a central government official. On November 12, 1870, less than three months after his designation as governor-general, he was given

---

[4] In 1870, Liu Ming-ch'uan and Kuo Sung-lin had the title of *t'i-tu,* while Wu Ch'ang-ch'ing was a *chi-ming* (designated) *t'i-tu,* and Chou Sheng-ch'uan a *tsung-ping.* See, for example, *LWCK Memorials,* 17. 6b–7, 12; Chou Sheng-ch'uan, *Chou Wu-chuang kung i-shu* [Works of Chou Sheng-ch'uan], 10 *ts'e* (Nanking, 1905), 2 *hsia*, 1–9.

[5] *LWCK Memorials,* 17. 8 and 21. 30–31.

the further appointment of imperial commissioner (*ch'in-ch'ai ta-ch'en*), vested with duties even broader than those of the former commissioner of trade for the three northern ports (*san-k'ou t'ung-shang ta-ch'en*).[6] Li was instructed to reside at the strategic port of Tientsin and not at the provincial capital of Paoting. The edict stipulated that Li was to go to Paoting only in the winter months when the port of Tientsin was closed; it was not until December, 1871, that he first visited Paoting. Beginning in 1872, he also went to Peking about once a year for audiences with the throne and consultation with the ministers. Li's letters of 1872–1875 mention his discussions with Prince Kung, Wen-hsiang, Shen Kuei-fen, Pao-yün, and Li Hung-tsao—all five being grand councillors and, except for the last, ministers of the Tsungli Yamen.[7]

Li was responsible, of course, for Chihli provincial affairs. The provincial treasurer at Paoting was authorized to act for him on routine petitions, but important matters were brought to his yamen at Tientsin.[8] Among provincial matters to which Li gave his personal attention was internal policing, for which he used the so-called Trained Troops (*lien-chün*), an army of about 6,000 men selected from the Green Standard forces by previous governors-general.[9] Among questions of civil administration brought up by Li in memorials to the throne were local government finance (particularly the question of how to reduce the burden on *chou* and *hsien* magistrates), the province's financial obligations to Peking, the salt monopoly, and the transmission of tribute rice to T'ung-chou. Li's most pressing and difficult pro-

---

[6] *LWCK Memorials*, 17. 10. When Ch'ung-hou was appointed *san-k'ou t'ung-shang ta-ch'en* in 1861, the edict specifically stated that he was not given the title *ch'in-ch'ai*. However, the commissioner of trade for the southern ports (*nan-yang t'ung-shang ta-ch'en*) had been given the title *ch'in-ch'ai* in the early 1860's. Li's office of imperial commissioner at Tientsin was often referred to later as commissioner of trade for the northern ports. See *Ch'ou-pan i-wu shih-mo* [The Complete Account of Our Management of Barbarian Affairs], 260 *chüan* (Peiping, 1930; hereafter cited as *IWSM*), Hsien-feng, 72. 1b–2; T'ung-chih, 18. 25b.

[7] *LWCK Memorials*, 18. 76 and 19. 83. *P'eng-liao han-kao* (hereafter cited as *Letters*), 12. 26; 13. 3–4, 6b–8, 32b; 15. 16.

[8] *LWCK Memorials*, 17. 29b and 18. 76.

[9] *LWCK Memorials*, 19. 31b and 20. 46. *Letters*, 11. 12. For the figures on the Green Standard forces in Chihli, see *Memorials*, 20. 39b.

vincial problems, however, were those created by the breaches in the dikes of the Yün-ting River. Northern Chihli saw one of its worst floods of the century in the summer of 1871, followed by a more moderate one in 1873. It was Li's responsibility to raise funds for relief and to revive agriculture in the areas affected. He also had to supervise repairs on the dikes—work that was to continue for several years.[10]

Meanwhile, Li was increasingly involved in his duties as imperial commissioner. These entailed first of all the supervision of foreign trade at the ports of Tientsin, Chefoo, and Newchwang through the superintendents of customs at the three ports—the one at Tientsin being a new post created at Li's recommendation.[11] But Li was also relied on by the Tsungli Yamen in questions concerning foreign trade in the empire as a whole. The Yamen often asked Li to study the proposals made to it by Robert Hart—for example, the latter's draft regulations, submitted in the spring of 1872, concerning the customs declaration form, the re-export certificate, and the transit pass. On his authority as imperial commissioner, Li sent "instructions by letter" (*cha-ch'ih*) to the superintendents of customs at Tientsin, Shanghai, and Hankow for their comments. Li added his own ideas and recommended to the Yamen that revisions be made in Hart's draft to make it more difficult for Chinese merchants to evade duties and likin. The final draft was worked out at Tientsin between Li and Hart.[12]

As imperial commissioner, Li had the responsibility of dealing with foreign representatives on local issues—for example, ironing out the final details of the Sino-French settlement regarding the Tientsin Massacre and determining the Russian and British claims.[13] Li's diplomatic activity soon included, however, national issues which the Tsungli Yamen considered it would be more convenient for him to handle at Tientsin. Moreover, the

---

[10] *LWCK Memorials, chüan* 17–26, especially 17. 41–43; 18. 88–89, 92–93; 19. 5–6, 20–21, 40; 20. 10–11b, 67; 21. 7–8, 12–13, 51–52; 22. 10–11, 39–41; 24. 36. *Letters,* 10. 33; 11. 6b, 13b–18, 20b–23; 12. 2, 9–10b; 13. 18.

[11] *LWCK Memorials,* 17. 10, 14.

[12] *LWCK, I-shu han-kao* (hereafter cited as *Tsungli Yamen Letters*), 1. 32–33b; *Letters,* 12. 23b.

[13] *LWCK Tsungli Yamen Letters,* 1. 2b–8b, 14–15b, 17b–19, 24b–25b; *Memorials,* 18. 57.

Yamen frequently sought Li's advice on policy and sometimes would entrust policy-making to him.

The first important national issue Li handled was the treaty with Japan. As early as October, 1870, after his first meeting with the Japanese representative who came to China to request a treaty, Li advised the Yamen that it was in the Ch'ing interest to form such ties. Li was impressed by Japan's comparative success in dealing with the West (for example, their ability to manage maritime customs without employing foreigners and to regulate missionary activity) and by the large funds which Japan was reported to have raised for arsenals and steamships. Li felt that China should befriend Japan, perhaps even send officials to reside in that country, with a view to preventing her from siding with the Western nations. On the Yamen's recommendation, the throne entrusted Li and Tseng Kuo-fan, who was the commissioner of trade for the southern ports, with formulating a policy for the treaty. Subsequently, Li was given full powers for the negotiations. The talks took place in the summer of 1871, China being represented by two officials of lower rank under Li's supervision. Eight months later, when the Japanese representative came to China to demand changes in the draft of the treaty, he was again dealt with at Tientsin. In May, 1873, Li was the plenipotentiary who exchanged the ratified texts with the Japanese foreign minister, who came to Tientsin for the purpose. Li discussed various matters with him, including China's concern about Korea.[14]

Similarly, Li was given the authority to meet with the representative of Peru who requested a treaty in October, 1873. Through the intermittent negotiations that lasted until June, 1874, Li's objective was to have the Peruvian representative accept a Chinese mission to investigate the conditions of Chinese labor in that country. The upshot was the Yung Wing mission to Peru in August, 1874.[15]

[14] *LWCK Tsungli Yamen Letters*, 1. 3b–4, 10–13, 22–24b, 28b–30, 34–35, 40–46, 48b–50. *Memorials*, 17. 53–54b; 18. 11–13, 28, 36, 42–52b; 19. 24, 57–59; 20. 73–74b; 21. 18–19. Cf. T. F. Tsiang, "Sino-Japanese Diplomatic Relations, 1870–1894," *Chinese Social and Political Science Review*, XVII (1933), 4–16.

[15] *LWCK Tsungli Yamen Letters*, 1. 51–52; 2. 1–7, 29b, 31–33, 34–35. *Memorials*, 23. 23–25b; 25. 24–25.

Beginning in 1872, the Yamen often enlisted Li's assistance in vital matters with which the Yamen itself was dealing. In September of that year, Li took the opportunity of the Russian and German ministers' passing through Tientsin to discuss with them, on the Yamen's behalf, aspects of the "audience question." In April, 1873, when Li himself was in Peking, he supported the compromise solution proposed by Wen-hsiang against those who insisted on kowtow. Li's intervention is said to have been important among the factors that "smoothed away all difficulties," resulting in the modified ceremony adopted at the audience held on June 14.[16]

In May and June, 1874, during the crisis created by the Japanese landing of troops on Taiwan to seek redress for ship-wrecked Ryūkyū sailors murdered by the aborigines, Li participated in the search for a solution. Li advised the Yamen on the military measures which would strengthen China's hand in the negotiations—"to prepare for war secretly so that peace may be achieved quickly and be lasting."[17] When the Japanese minister to China arrived in June, 1874, the Yamen hoped that he could remain at Tientsin to negotiate with Li. However, he proceeded immediately to Peking, as did Ōkubo, the special commissioner who came in August. A settlement which involved China paying Tls. 500,000 to Japan was reached on October 31, with Sir Thomas Wade acting as intermediary. But meanwhile Li had been active in seeking the mediation of Benjamin P. Avery, the new American minister who had just come from Japan and was at that moment in Tientsin.[18]

If Li was serving as a central government official in his diplomatic activities, the same may be said of his role in the Ch'ing government's military planning—despite the fact that he played but little part in the great Ch'ing military achievement of the period, namely the suppression of the Moslem rebels in Kansu in 1873 and the reconquest of Sinkiang that followed three years later. It was on Li however, that the court relied for the defense

[16] *LWCK Tsungli Yamen Letters,* 1. 35b–38; *Letters,* 13. 4, 10b; Hosea Ballou Morse, *The International Relations of the Chinese Empire,* 3 vols. (London, 1910–1918), II, 267.

[17] *LWCK Tsungli Yamen Letters,* 2. 34; see also 2. 20, 24, 26b–29, 30–31.

[18] *LWCK Tsungli Yamen Letters,* 2.35–40, 51b–57. Cf. Tsiang, "Sino-Japanese Diplomatic Relations," pp. 16–34.

of the capital area and for coordination of military preparations in the coastal and Yangtze provinces. It has been shown above that as the Chihli governor-general, Li had control over the 6,000 Trained Troops used primarily for local policing. As imperial commissioner, he had the further duty of supervising the coastal defense of the metropolitan area, including the safeguarding of the Taku estuary and points halfway between Tientsin and Peking.[19] Similar responsibility was formerly borne by the Mongol prince Seng-k'o-lin-ch'in, who was imperial commissioner during the crisis of 1857–1860, and by the Manchu grandee Ch'ung-hou between 1861and 1870, when he served as commissioner of trade for the three northern ports. Ch'ung-hou had built fortifications in the Taku area and had organized the Foreign Arms and Cannon Corps (*yang ch'iang-p'ao tui*), which grew to 3,200 men, under the command of the Tientsin brigade general.[20] Li was authorized to take charge of the forts and the corps, although his predecessors as governor-general, including Tseng Kuo-fan, were never given this authority. In November, 1870, Li appointed Lo Jung-kuang, the famous Anhwei Army artillery officer, as the Taku regiment colonel in charge of the forts. The Anhwei Army's best artillery, as well as new cannon built at the Nanking Arsenal, was brought to Taku, and new Krupp guns were ordered. Li put the Foreign Arms and Cannon Corps through retraining, particularly in the Anhwei Army's favorite technique of constructing fortified encampments.[21]

In November, 1870, the court directed that the twenty-eight battalions (about 14,000 men) of the Anhwei Army originally under Liu Ming-ch'uan be moved from Chihli to join the nine battalions of the Anhwei Army which Li had left in Shensi. At Li's recommendation, ten battalions of the Anhwei Army under Kuo Sung-lin also went to Shensi and Kuo himself was to bring ten battalions to Hupeh, to help guard against the secret societies of the Hunan-Hupeh area. However, two battalions of Liu's best troops were retained at Paoting, together with two battalions of the Anhwei Army cavalry. Two battalions of Li's personal

[19] *LWCK Memorials*, 17. 10b.
[20] *LWCK Memorials*, 17. 50b; 21. 40–41. Cf. *IWSM*, T'ung-chih, 10. 16; 61. 22.
[21] *LWCK Letters*, 10. 30b, 34b, 35b; 11. 5b; 13. 14b. *Memorials*, 17. 50b; 18. 20, 66, 67b; 20. 36–37; 21. 40–41.

guards were stationed at Tientsin. In addition, twenty-three battalions (about 11,500 men) under Chou Sheng-ch'uan were
stationed in the area south of Tientsin, particularly at Ma-ch'ang,
a base which Chou was to build up. In 1873, Chou's troops were
used to construct a fortified town between Taku and Tientsin,
and later they were put to work repairing dikes and reclaiming
salt marshes for farmland. But they were also drilled and given
training in the latest types of rifles and artillery. Li described
them as a "mobile force for the defense of the metropolitan
territory." [22]

Due chiefly to Li's relationship with the Anhwei Army, he
also participated at times in the court's military planning for
other parts of the empire. His role was passive with regard to the
northwest. In 1870–1872, he sent two contingents of 1,000
men each from the Trained Troops of Chihli to Urga, to help
guard against possible Russian encroachment on Outer Mongo-
lia. [23] On September 1, 1871, apprized of the Russian occupation of Ili, the court ordered Liu Ming-ch'uan, who had requested a leave of absence on the ground of illness, to take his
forces from Shensi to Kansu and thence to Sinkiang. Liu again
pleaded illness, and on September 21 the court revised its orders,
requiring him only to advance to Su-chou in Kansu. Although Li
was not convinced of the value of Sinkiang in China's total
strategic picture, he wrote Liu to urge him to comply. Without
consulting Li, however, Liu once more begged the throne for a
leave and recommended that Ts'ao K'e-chung, a general not of
Anhwei Army background replace him and lead his forces to
attack Su-chou. The request was granted. Ts'ao was summoned
to Peking for an audience in November, 1871, and appointed to
the command. Li pledged himself to support Ts'ao with Anhwei
Army funds but recommended that only twenty-two of Liu's
thirty-seven battalions be transferred to him. [24] In August, 1872,
mutiny occurred in certain units of Ts'ao's forces; the throne
referred the matter to Li, who recommended that Liu Sheng-

---

[22] *LWCK Memorials*, 16. 42; 17. 1, 6b, 12b, 51; 20. 37; 23. 27b. *Letters*, 11.
2b. Chou Sheng-ch'uan, *Chou Wu-chuang Kung i-shu, chüan-shou*, 32–40.
[23] *LWCK Memorials*, 17. 27b; 18. 32, 63.
[24] *Tung-hua hsü-lu* [Continuation of the Tung-hua Records] (Taipei reprint,
1963), T'ung-chih, 91. 53, 55–56, 61b, 62b; 92. 1. *LWCK Letters*, 11. 19,
22–25.

tsao, Liu Ming-ch'uan's nephew and a former Anhwei Army officer, should take over. Liu Sheng-tsao came to Tientsin for consultations with Li and was given the appointment by the throne. Li had hoped to suggest that Liu move all the Anhwei forces in Shensi back to the coastal area, but the twenty-two battalions were retained in Shensi at the request of its governor.[25]

Li's own conviction was that the coast, particularly with a restless Japan quickly arming, was far more in need of protection. Ever since the end of the Nien Rebellion, eight battalions of the Anhwei Army, under Wu Ch'ang-ch'ing, had been stationed at several points in Kiangsu; at Li's recommendation, the throne in November, 1870, approved their remaining there. These forces were under the direction of Tseng Kuo-fan, the governor-general of Liang-chiang, but Li often wrote to him to make suggestions on such subjects as the training needed by the artillery corps or the strategic places where troops should be quartered. Tseng, on his part, would inform Li when he ordered the transfer of units from one location to another. In November, 1871, Li took the opportunity of the Anhwei Army in Shensi being transferred to Ts'ao K'e-chung's command to recommend to the throne that fifteen of the thirty-seven battalions be moved to Hsü-chou in northern Kiangsu. In approving the idea, the throne directed that these battalions (led by an Anhwei Army officer named T'ang Ting-k'uei) be put at the disposal of Tseng.[26] After Tseng died in March, 1872, Li continued to give his successors in the Liang-chiang post advice on military affairs —including the organization of a small navy with gunboats built by the Kiangnan Arsenal. Though Tseng's successors were free to direct the Anhwei Army in Kiangsu, they developed the practice of informing Li of their decisions whenever units were reassigned to new locations.[27]

[25] *LWCK Memorials,* 19. 80–82b; 20. 16. *Letters,* 12. 20, 23; 13. 31b. *Tunghua hsü-lu,* T'ung-chih, 95. 37, 45.

[26] *LWCK Memorials,* 17. 7. *Letters,* 10. 27b, 30b; 11. 7b, 12b–13, 23b. *Tunghua hsü-lu,* T'ung-chih, 92. 7.

[27] *LWCK Letters,* 12. 12b–13, 24; 13. 7, 10b–11, 14b, 27b, 31b, 14. 2b. Tseng's successors as governor-general of Liang-chiang up to early 1875 were Ho Ching (acting, March-November, 1872), Chang Shu-sheng (acting, November, 1872–February, 1873), and Li Tsung-hsi (February, 1873–January, 1875).

In the summer of 1874, during the crisis created by the Japanese invasion of Taiwan, Li extended his concern to the Fukien-Taiwan area. It was upon Li's advice that the Tsungli Yamen recommended to the throne that Shen Pao-chen, the director-general of the Foochow Navy Yard, be appointed imperial commissioner for the defense of Taiwan. In June, Li suggested to Shen and to the Yamen that thirteen battalions (6,500 men) of the Anhwei Army at Hsü-chou, under T'ang Ting-k'uei, be dispatched to Taiwan to be put under Shen's control. This was approved by the throne in late July, as was Li's further recommendation that the twenty-two battalions of the Anhwei Army in Shensi be transferred to Kiangsu and Shantung, to meet the contingency of a Sino-Japanese conflict.[28]

Meanwhile, Li kept in touch by correspondence with Shen, with Li Tsung-hsi, the governor-general of Liang-chiang, and with Chang Shu-sheng, the governor of Kiangsu, arranging to ship munitions from Kiangsu and Chihli to Taiwan. On July 13, Li was instructed by the throne to "make a general plan for the entire situation" and to "deliberate jointly" (*hui-shang*) with officials in the provinces concerned regarding defense preparations.[29] Li advised Shen that clashes with the Japanese were to be avoided, while preparations for war must be hastened. Li arranged to have three ships of the China Merchants' Steam Navigation Company and three Foochow-built steamships transport the troops in Kiangsu to Taiwan. Since the six vessels had to make three voyages to complete the shipping of 6,500 men, the last contingents did not reach their destination until October, although the first arrived in mid-August. Li corresponded with officials in Fukien and in Liang-chiang on defense measures. Alarmed by rumors of Japanese intentions, Li Tsung-hsi and Chang Shu-sheng requested that the twenty-two battalions of the Anhwei Army from Shensi come to southern Kiangsu. Li decided, however, that only five should go there, and that the remaining seventeen (including five cavalry battalions) should

---

[28] *LWCK Tsungli Yamen Letters*, 2. 24b, 34b; *Letters*, 14. 6b–7, 9b; *Tung-hua hsü-lu*, T'ung-chih, 98. 39b–40.

[29] *LWCK Memorials*, 23. 28b; *Letters*, 14. 7b, 8, 11, 14b–15, 18b, 19b, 24, 31.

be stationed at Chi-ning, Shantung, where they could easily be moved either north or south. Li assured his colleagues that even should there be war, given the resources of the Japanese, action was not likely to spread to the coast for a few months. There was, therefore, time to plan coastal fortifications carefully and to order foreign-made guns and rifles.[30] It is difficult to say whether these defense efforts had any actual bearing on Japan's accepting a peaceful settlement in late October. But Li had clearly emerged during the episode as the coordinator of Ch'ing military preparations on Taiwan and on the coast.

The crisis also revealed that Li depended on the throne's support for the continued financing of the Anhwei Army. Beginning in 1872, such provinces as Shantung, Chekiang, Szechuan, and Shansi had been reducing their annual contributions (*hsieh-hsiang*) to the Anhwei Army, if not defaulting entirely, due to Peking's pressure on them to supply funds for other purposes. In 1872, the Anhwei Army still received large sums from the Shanghai and Hankow maritime customs and from Liang-chiang sources (especially from Kiangsu likin and Kiangsi salt likin), but in the eighteen months following January 29, 1873, the annual average received from Kiangsu likin (which was the largest single source of Anhwei Army funds) dropped from Tls. 1,000,-019 to Tls. 873,332.[31] There was danger that the trend might continue, for we find Li frequently writing to the governor of Kiangsu and governor-general of Liang-chiang, urging them to see that payments were made promptly. Li had to remind these officials that the appropriations were backed by the throne itself. He warned Li Tsung-hsi not to withhold the Anhwei Army funds "so that I do not have to appeal to the throne." To Chang Shu-sheng, who had formerly been an Anhwei Army commander but whose interests were now not necessarily identical with its interests, Li wrote bluntly: "I will certainly fight for the funds. Let me swear it by smearing my mouth with blood." [32] On at least one occasion, Li actually did appeal to the throne regarding the Anhwei Army appropriations. He requested in a memorial dated

---

[30] *LWCK Letters,* 14. 12–13, 16–18, 20b–23.
[31] *LWCK Memorials,* 21. 30–31b; 25. 40–41b; 27. 16–17.
[32] *LWCK Letters,* 14. 16b, 22. See also 13. 8.

September 1, 1874, that Szechuan province be instructed to pay its arrears of more than Tls. 200,000. In his letters to the governor-general of Szechuan and others, Li stressed that the Anhwei Army was in the service of the state and should be supported by it.[33]

SELF-STRENGTHENING—THE EMERGENCE OF A POLICY

Li's service to the state was not limited to diplomatic work or to advising the throne on the use of the Anhwei Army. As he himself conceived it, his role in the dynasty's military planning should include the enhancement of China's military capability— which alone could insure peaceful relations with the powers. Li assumed that the aim of the Western maritime powers in China was commerce and not aggrandizement. Nevertheless, he feared that an occasion might arise when one or more powers would use force. Moreover, a real threat existed in a rising Japan. "It is only when we can strengthen ourselves every moment," Li exhorted his colleagues, "that peace can be maintained and trouble prevented." [34]

Li found that he had to redefine as well as to expand his program for self-strengthening. While his primary objective continued to be the building up of an armament industry, experience had shown that arsenals and shipyards were by no means easy to operate. Moreover, innovations in these fields were constantly being made in Western countries, and it was impossible to catch up quickly. To meet China's needs for some time to come, it was necessary to purchase foreign-made weapons of the latest types and to create a navy of foreign-built ships. Li further realized that the capacity of Chinese arsenals and shipyards had been severely restricted by lack of competent personnel and of revenue —the two Chinese words both pronounced *ts'ai*.[35] While seeking a gradual expansion of the armament industry, it was necessary to support new programs of personnel training and to devise means for enlarging the income of the state.

[33] *LWCK Memorials,* 23. 37–38; *Letters,* 14. 24b, 26.
[34] *LWCK Letters,* 11. 10. See also 10. 22b, 25, 27b–28; 11. 6, 21, 27; 12. 14; 13. 8.
[35] *LWCK Letters,* 12. 3b; 14. 28b, 32.

How then could the state best encourage technical personnel or increase its revenue? Although perhaps he was aware that they were not all feasible, Li nevertheless advocated certain institutional reforms—which he had been considering since the mid-1860's. The Taiwan crisis and the discussion on coastal defense that followed gave him the opportunity to present his views to the throne, along with his proposal for a fundamental change in the dynasty's strategic concept: to abandon the plans for reconquering Sinkiang and instead to concentrate the available resources on defense and self-strengthening programs on the coast.

While Li could usually count on the court's approval of his conduct of diplomacy or his advice regarding the disposition of the Anhwei Army, it was not as easy to persuade the throne to accept self-strengthening measures involving innovation. The Tsungli Yamen enthusiastically supported some of Li's recommendations, but it was either indifferent or unable to give support to some others. There was, moreover, the need for coordinated efforts at the provincial level. After Tseng Kuo-fan's death in 1872, Li felt increasingly the need for allies in Liang-chiang and other parts of south China, and we find him using his influence on the court to see that such men as Shen Pao-chen and Ting Jih-ch'ang were appointed to key posts.

Li's Efforts up to November, 1874.   Since the mid-1860's, four modern arsenals had been founded, two of them being shipyards as well: the Nanking Arsenal (moved from Soochow to that city in 1865), the Kiangnan Arsenal in Shanghai (founded in 1865), the Foochow Navy Yard (1866), and the Tientsin Arsenal (1867). Except for the Nanking Arsenal which was financed by Anhwei Army funds,[36] all had been authorized by imperial edict. The Nanking and the Kiangnan arsenals had been founded by Li himself, but he was disappointed by

---

[36] Sun Yü-t'ang, ed. *Chung-kuo chin-tai kung-yeh shih tzu-liao, ti-i-chi, 1840–1895 nien* [Materials on the History of Modern Industry in China, First Collection, 1840–1895], 2 vols. (Peking, 1957), I, 263; *LWCK Memorials*, 21. 31b; *Yang-wu yün-tung* [The "Foreign Matters" Movement], comp. by the Institute of Modern History, Chinese Academy of Sciences, and Bureau of Ming and Ch'ing Archives, Central Archives, 8 vols. (Shanghai, 1961), IV, 127.

the results. The Nanking plant, which was operated by the Scotsman Halliday Macartney, could produce bronze cannon as well as percussion caps and shells. The Kiangnan Arsenal, a much larger establishment, had spent about Tls. 2,500,000 in five years, principally from the Shanghai maritime customs revenue. It did contribute to the Anhwei Army's campaign against the Niens with muskets and carbines, bronze cannon, percussion caps, and shells, but it was not until about 1868 that it succeeded for the first time in producing a rifle—the outdated muzzle-loading type.[37] Li regarded the Kiangnan and Nanking arsenals as no more than "the first beginning." Between 1867 and 1870, the shipyard attached to the Kiangnan Arsenal constructed four small steamships, described by Li as "neither merchant steamers nor warships," and as "useful for warfare on the river but not at sea."[38]

One of Li's earliest acts in Chihli was to expand the Tientsin Arsenal, founded by Ch'ung-hou three years before. Li recommended to the throne that a former manager of the Kiangnan Arsenal be appointed its head and that its equipment be increased. Since Li was, at that juncture, planning to equip his army in Chihli with foreign-made breechloading rifles and Krupp guns, he decided that the best contribution the Tientsin Arsenal could make was to supply the ammunition required by these weapons. Between 1871 and 1874, the arsenal received nearly a million taels allocated by the throne from the maritime customs revenue of Tientsin and Chefoo. Three new plants were added to the one originally in existence, so that by 1874 more than a ton of powder was produced daily, as well as a large quantity of cartridges and shells. Li also planned, however, to manufacture the breechloading rifle itself. Machinery for the production of rifles of the Remington type was ordered and installed in 1874–1875.[39]

[37] Demetrius C. Boulger, *The Life of Sir Halliday Macartney, K.C.M.G.* (London, 1908), pp. 148–150, 177; *North-China Herald*, August 16, 1867; *Chiang-nan chih-tsao-chü chi* [Records of the Kiangnan Arsenal], 11 *chüan*, comp. Wei Yün-kung (Shanghai, 1905), 3. 2, 58; *Chi-ch'i chü* [Arsenals], 2 vols., in *Hai-fang tang* [Files on Maritime Defense], ed. Kuo T'ing-yi et al. (Taiwan, 1957), I, 27–28, 41.

[38] *LWCK Letters*, 11. 7b, 23b, 13. 14b. See also 11. 6b, 27b.

[39] *LWCK Memorials*, 17. 16–17, 36; 20. 12–15; 23. 19–22; 24. 16; 28. 1–4.

Li hoped that the Kiangnan Arsenal, with its larger plant, could devote greater resources to the manufacture of rifles and ordnance. Although the Kiangnan Arsenal was controlled by the governor-general of Liang-chiang, Li often discussed its affairs in his letters to Tseng Kuo-fan. Twice in 1871, Li urged Tseng to check the accuracy of the boastful reports made by Feng Chün-kuang, its chief manager, and to give greater authority to Hsü Shou, the famous mathematician and engineer in the arsenal's service. Li sometimes communicated directly with these managers. It was presumably on his advice that the arsenal acquired additional machinery in 1871 for rifles of the Remington type, some 4,200 of which were produced before the end of 1873.[40] After Tseng died in March, 1872, Li continued to advise his successors regarding the arsenal. He urged that, in addition to breechloading rifles and bronze cannon, it should manufacture cast-iron cannon and torpedoes. The first cast-iron cannon was produced in February, 1874. In the period 1871–1874, 2,000 rifles and 1,100 carbines produced by Kiangnan were sent to Chihli, but the bulk of its products were assigned to the various armies of the Liang-chiang area.[41]

Since the Nanking Arsenal was financed with Anhwei Army funds, Li retained control over its personnel and policies. There was at least one occasion, in 1873, when an order for the change of the arsenal's Chinese director was issued by Li (presumably in his capacity as imperial commissioner for the northern ports), although he acted with the written concurrence of Li Tsung-hsi, the governor-general of Liang-chiang. Until 1874, the bronze mortars built by Macartney were for the exclusive use of the coastal fortifications at Chihli. Beginning in early 1874, however, Li Tsung-hsi ordered the arsenal to make guns and various kinds of ammunition needed by the forces in Kiangsu.[42]

Li's concern for the Chinese armament industry also extended

[40] *LWCK Letters,* 10. 28; 11. 23b, 31b; 12. 3. *Chiang-nan chih-tsao-chü chi,* 3. 2.

[41] *LWCK Letters,* 13. 7, 11, 14; 14. 38b–39; 15. 13b. Sun Yü-t'ang, *Chung-kuo chin-tai kung-yeh shih tzu-liao,* I, 294, 299; *Chiang-nan chih-tsao-chü chi,* 5. 3b–4b.

[42] Boulger, *Life of Sir Halliday Macartney,* pp. 188, 198, 209, 212. *LWCK Letters,* 13. 11b, 27b; 14. 7a, 10. Sun Yü-t'ang, *Chung-kuo chin-tai kung-yeh shih tzu-liao,* I, 327.

to Fukien. Late in 1871, the Foochow Navy Yard was attacked by a sub-chancellor of the Grand Secretariat as wasteful and ineffective. This official, Sung Ching, recommended to the throne that the shipbuilding programs at both Foochow and Shanghai be discontinued. Instructed by the throne to give his views, Li joined Tso Tsung-t'ang and Shen Pao-chen, the founder and the director of the Foochow Navy Yard, in defending it. Li's memorial of June 20, 1872, made the famous statement that China was encountering "the greatest change of situation (*pien-chü*) in three thousand years." Since Western military power was based on rifles, cannon, and steamships, China must master the secrets of such equipment so as to insure her survival in the long run. Li warned that Japan was ahead of China in these matters and was "viewing China in a threatening manner." Supporting a suggestion made earlier by the Tsungli Yamen, Li proposed that the Foochow and Shanghai shipyards might build freighters as well as gunboats and make the former available for purchase or hire by Chinese merchants. Li added a proposal of his own involving reform of institutions. Since the government-built gunboats could be used for coastal and river patrol by the coast and Yangtze provinces, should they not be financed by the appropriations from the provinces devoted to the old-style navy? Li suggested that the court should issue an edict to the effect that the construction of war junks be discontinued altogether.[43] He was greatly disappointed when this last proposal was not supported by the Tsungli Yamen, although at its recommendation the throne decided to continue shipbuilding at Foochow and Shanghai.[44]

Li attached great importance to the Foochow Navy Yard and its training programs and took it upon himself to assist Shen Pao-chen's work. Li had formed the opinion by 1872 that Shen (who happened to be a *chin-shih* classmate of Li) was one of the very few high officials of the time who had a clear understanding of what self-strengthening required. Several times Li used his influence with Li Ho-nien, governor-general of Fukien and Chekiang, to persuade the latter not to obstruct Shen's work. In May,

[43] *IWSM*, T'ung-chih, 84. 35; *LWCK Memorials*, 19. 44–49.
[44] *LWCK Letters*, 12. 21, 26b.

1874, during a visit to Peking, Li spoke on Shen Pao-chen's behalf with Shen Kuei-fen, grand councillor and president of the Board of War (who also happened to be a *chin-shih* classmate) and obtained his promise and that of Prince Kung that they would make favorable recommendations on Shen's future requests about the financing of the Foochow yard.[45]

Li realized, more acutely than he had in the early T'ung-chih period, that successful operation of arsenals and shipyards depended on trained technical personnel. The school Li founded in 1863, the Shanghai T'ung-wen Kuan (which was combined with a new translator's school of the Kiangnan Arsenal in 1867 and renamed Kuang Fang-yen Kuan) had been giving instruction in English, mathematics, and sciences to classes of about forty students still in their teens. But few outstanding graduates had been produced; the results, as in the case of the Peking T'ung-wen Kuan, were disappointing.[46] In 1864, Li had suggested to the Tsungli Yamen that a new category (*k'o*) be created under the examination system to accommodate men who specialized in technology. The little interest which the Shanghai and Peking schools had aroused among the literati convinced Li that only some such change could provide the incentive for the pursuit of "Western learning." [47]

Li supported a proposal to send Chinese youths to the United States for education. He was persuaded that a prolonged period of study abroad was the best way to train Chinese who, upon their return to China, could become instructors in the Shanghai and Peking schools or serve in the arsenals and shipyards. The proposal originated with Yung Wing and Ch'en Lan-pin and was brought to the court's attention in a memorial from Tseng Kuo-fan in October, 1870. However, Tseng merely mentioned the idea casually in connection with another matter, and Li, in a letter dated December 13, 1870, urged him to draft concrete plans to be submitted to the court. "It can never be expected," Li wrote, "that the matter be initiated by the court." [48] Li also sug-

---

[45] *LWCK Letters*, 12. 25b; 13. 2, 13, 28–29, 32b–33.

[46] Knight Biggerstaff, *The Earliest Modern Government Schools in China* (Ithaca, 1961), pp. 156–176; *LWCK Letters*, 10. 34.

[47] *IWSM*, T'ung-chih, 25. 9–10b; *LWCK Memorials*, 24. 23b; *Letters*, 15. 4.

[48] *LWCK Letters*, 10. 28.

gested that the draft regulations include a provision that the students be awarded *chien-sheng* status before going abroad and that upon their return they be assigned official ranks, after being given an examination by the Tsungli Yamen. Li was later satisfied that the regulations merely promised official positions for the returning students. In August, 1871, he joined Tseng in submitting a memorial to the throne on the subject, after having corresponded with the Tsungli Yamen and obtained its concurrence, particularly on the proposal that Tls. 1,200,000 be allocated over a twenty-year period from the Shanghai maritime customs revenue.[49] As authorized by an imperial edict, a bureau was established in Shanghai in 1872 to select students, and the first group of thirty left Shanghai that summer, to be followed by a similar number annually for three years. The boys selected were between eleven and sixteen *sui*. A tutor went along to teach them Chinese subjects, but each student was to spend fifteen years abroad, travelling during the last two years. Since the plan authorized was based on a joint memorial from Tseng and Li, it was regarded as under the supervision of the two commissioners at Nanking and Tientsin. The officials in charge in the United States reported to Li and to the governor-general of Liang-chiang.[50]

In June, 1871, Li had briefly considered sending students to Britain also. His more urgent problem, however, was to find mature personnel in China who could serve at once in managerial or technical capacities in the arsenals, the shipyards, or the customs administration. Li often wrote to colleagues in other provinces inviting nominations of such personnel.[51] In January, 1874, when Shen Pao-chen consulted him about a plan to send the graduates of the Foochow Navy Yard School to Britain and France, Li responded with enthusiasm. He wrote to the Yamen about the plan and brought it to Prince Kung's attention when he

[49] *LWCK Letters,* 10. 32b; 11. 1b, 4b, 7b, 11; 12. 3. *Tsungli Yamen Letters,* 1. 19b–22. *Memorials,* 19. 7–10. *IWSM,* T'ung-chih, 82. 46b–52.

[50] *IWSM,* T'ung-chih, 86. 13–14b. Hsü Jun, *Hsü Yü-chai tzu-hsü nien-p'u* [Chronological Autobiography] (preface dated 1927), pp. 17–23. *LWCK Letters,* 12. 15, 17b; 13. 12; 14. 1b, 8b–9; 15. 12. *Yang-wu yün-tung,* II, 165.

[51] *LWCK Tsungli Yamen Letters,* 1. 22. *Letters,* 11. 12, 31b; 13. 6b, 7, 28, 30; 14. 31, 38b; 15. 14b, 16b.

was in Peking in May, 1874. Li also considered sending the sons of the Tientsin Arsenal's Chinese technicians to Germany for study.[52] The Taiwan crisis intervened, and it was not until 1876 that further action was taken.

Li was increasingly convinced that Western technology could be used to augment the wealth of the Ch'ing state as well as its military strength. In Kiangsu, in the early T'ung-chih period, he had been impressed by the successful invasion of the carrying trade in Chinese waters by Western steamships, although at that time he was anxious to protect the seagoing junks which carried the tribute rice to Chihli. As early as 1864, Li had proposed to the Tsungli Yamen that Chinese merchants be permitted to own and operate steamships and foreign-style sailing vessels, in competition with Western ships.[53] In the two years after he came to Tientsin, a series of events prompted him to make immediate plans for a Chinese steamship company. During the flood and famine in Chihli in 1871, he deeply resented the exorbitant rates foreign ships demanded for the transport of relief grain. New breaches of the Yellow River dikes that winter convinced him that the Grand Canal was to become useless. He was against investing enormous sums to restore the former course of the Yellow River so as to improve the Grand Canal's navigability. He saw in a fleet of Chinese-owned coastal steamships the solution to the ancient problem of how to carry tribute rice from the south to the north.[54] It was at this juncture that the Tsungli Yamen suggested that ships built by the Foochow Navy Yard might be hired out to Chinese merchants. Li was asked by the Yamen to make arrangements to this purpose, and through the summer of 1872 we find him corresponding on the subject with such officials as the superintendent of customs at Shanghai and the head of the Liang-chiang administration's new naval fleet (which consisted chiefly of Kiangnan-built ships.)[55]

Li found that the Foochow- and Shanghai-built ships were not

[52] *LWCK Letters,* 13. 28b, 32b–33.

[53] *Chi-ch'i chü,* I, 3–5. *LWCK Memorials,* 8. 30–31; 9. 67–68.

[54] *LWCK Letters,* 11. 22, 30b; 12. 1b–2, 9, 22b; 13. 15b, 17b–18, 22. *Memorials,* 22. 9–18.

[55] *Kou-mai ch'uan-p'ao* [Purchase of Ships and Weapons], 3 vols. in *Hai-fang tang,* III, 903–910. *LWCK Letters,* 11. 31b; 12. 2b, 4, 9b.

suitable for the freighting trade, since they were costly to operate and drew too much water for some harbors. Following the advice of Chu Ch'i-ang, a Chekiang official in charge of the junk transport of that province's tribute rice, Li decided that the best plan was for a group of Chinese merchants to buy foreign-built steamships and to operate them for the general carrying trade as well as for the transport of tribute rice; presumably Chinese-built ships could be added to the fleet later. Li approved Chu's plan to establish a bureau (*chü*) in Shanghai and to "invite merchants" (*chao-shang*) to operate steamships. It was understood that the enterprise was to be "supervised by the government and undertaken by the merchants" (*kuan-tu shang-pan*). Li arranged a loan of Tls.136,000 to the enterprise from Chihli military funds, making it clear, however, that "profits and loss are entirely the responsibility of the merchants and do not involve the government." [56] While the availability of government appropriations for tribute rice transport made the project particularly feasible, Li undoubtedly regarded it as part of a general policy for China's self-strengthening. "The use of the steamship for the transport of tribute rice is but a minor consideration," Li wrote the governor of Kiangsu in December, 1872. "The project will open up new prospects for the dignity of the state (*kuo-t'i*), for commerce, for revenue, for military strength—for the China of centuries to come." Li was also interested in reports of Japan's effort to develop commercial shipping. He wrote in early January to an official whom he had recommended to be a secretary of the Tsungli Yamen: "We let other people move about at will in Chinese waters. Why do we deny the Chinese merchants alone a foothold? Even Japan has sixty or seventy [merchant] steamships of her own; we alone do not have any. How does this look?" [57]

To obtain the tribute rice cargo for the steamships, Li had to enlist the cooperation of officials in the lower Yangtze area. Siding with the vested interests of the junk owners, the Kiangsu officials initially opposed Li's plan. In October, 1871, Shen Ping-ch'eng, the superintendent of customs at Shanghai, and

---

[56] *Kou-mai ch'uan-p'ao*, III, 910–923: *LWCK Tsungli Yamen Letters*, 1. 38–40; *Memorials*, 20. 32–33b.

[57] *LWCK Letters*, 12. 31, 34b. See also 12. 36b.

Feng Chün-kuang, the head of the Kiangnan Arsenal, joined in a petition of protest to Ho Ching, the governor-general of Liang-chiang, and their views were supported by Chang Shu-sheng, the Kiangsu governor. Invoking Peking's authority, Li reminded Ho that the proposed steamship company eventually would purchase and hire Chinese-built ships and was in line with the Tsungli Yamen's original proposal which had been approved by the throne in June, 1872; it was therefore a matter with which Ho, as acting commissioner of trade for the southern ports, should be properly concerned. To governor Chang, Li exploded: "I have worked together with you for nearly twenty years. Did you ever see anything I am determined to do discontinued because of unjustified criticism?" [58] Ho and Chang eventually allowed twenty percent of the Kiangsu tribute rice to be shipped annually by steamer. Together with a similar quota from Chekiang, this assured the new enterprise an annual tribute rice freight of 200,-000 piculs, or a payment of Tls. 112,000. In December, Li memorialized to request imperial sanction of the entire plan. The memorial was approved on December 26, and on January 14, the Bureau for Inviting Merchants to Operate Steamships (Lunch'uan chao-shang chü; known in English as the China Merchants' Steam Navigation Company) was inaugurated in Shanghai.[59] Since it was on the basis of Li's memorial that the project was approved, the Bureau was regarded as under the jurisdiction of the imperial commissioner for the northern ports. Li retained firm control of its personnel and policies. In July, 1873, when two Cantonese compradors, Tong King-sing and Hsü Jun, became the directors (*tsung-pan*) of the new company, it was Li who issued the appointment. Li found it necessary, however, to appeal to the Kiangsu governor and the Liang-chiang governor-general to help by giving the enterprise larger tribute-rice consignments and by providing it with loans from provincial funds. Thanks to such assistance, as well as to the efforts of its ex-comprador managers, the company's fleet grew to thirteen ships

[58] *LWCK Letters,* 12. 28b–29, 30b.

[59] *Kou-mai ch'uan-p'ao,* III, 925; *Han-cheng pien* [Section on Shipping], 6 vols. in *Chiao-t'ung shih* [History of Communications in China], comp. Ministries of Communications and Railroads (Nanking, 1930 ff.), I, 142.

(8,546 net tons) by 1875 and services were developed on the Yangtze River and on several coastal routes.[60]

The purpose of the Chinese merchant steamers, as Li told the Tsungli Yamen, was to compete with foreign enterprise and restore China's "control of profit" (*li-ch'üan*).[61] But Li was particularly intrigued by the possibility of opening up a new source of revenue to the state by working mines with Western methods. Early in 1868, when he was still involved in the war against the Niens, Li had proposed in connection with the question of treaty revision that foreign engineers be allowed to work Chinese coal and iron mines. After coming to Chihli, Li became increasingly convinced that the use of pumps and other machines in mining pits not only would provide the Chinese arsenals and shipyards with vital materials and fuel but would profit the state financially. Li was also aware of the fact that the Japanese had been working their mines with Western techniques. In his memorial of June 20, 1872, concerning the Foochow shipyard, he proposed projects "supervised by the government and undertaken by merchants" to work mines with machinery. He also recommended using Western foundry techniques to produce cast iron and steel. Li emphasized that coal and iron could be marketed for profit and were "of great importance to the policy of enriching the state and strengthening military power." [62]

Li was disappointed when the Tsungli Yamen, while favoring the continuation of the Foochow shipyard, failed to make a recommendation to the throne regarding mining projects. He wrote Wang K'ai-t'ai, the governor of Fukien, that the failure indicated that the Yamen thought only of the present and not the future: "What will become of us a few decades hence?" [63] On his own initiative, Li encouraged Feng Chün-kuang, the director of

---

[60] Hsü Jun, *Hsü Yü-chai tzu-hsü nien-p'u*, p. 18. *LWCK Letters,* 13. 13b, 23–24; 14. 1b–2. Kwang-Ching Liu, "British-Chinese Steamship Rivalry in China, 1873–1885," in C. D. Cowan, ed., *Economic Development of China and Japan* (London, 1964), pp. 55–58.

[61] *LWCK Tsungli Yamen Letters,* 1. 40; *Memorials,* 20. 33b.

[62] *IWSM,* T'ung-chih, 55. 15b–16; Knight Biggerstaff, "The Secret Correspondence of 1867–1868: The Views of Leading Chinese Statesmen Regarding the Further Opening of China to Western Influence," *Journal of Modern History,* XXII (1950), 132; *LWCK Memorials,* 19. 49b–50.

[63] *LWCK Letters,* 12. 21, 26b.

the Kiangnan Arsenal, and others to make plans for working coal and iron mines at Tz'u-chou, in southern Chihli. In 1874, an English merchant, James Henderson, was sent to Britain to buy machinery and hire workmen.[64] Li was not, however, merely concerned with the opportunities for such projects in Chihli. He wrote the governor of Shansi, Pao Yüan-shen, in November, 1873, urging him to open up the rich mineral deposits of that province with new methods. "The earth is not stingy with its treasure," Li wrote,"but few in China are aware of this truth; please give this matter your attention and not worry all the time about poverty." Early in 1874, Li asked Li Tsung-hsi, the governor-general of Liang-chiang, to try to persuade Liu K'un-i, the governor of Kiangsi, to introduce machinery in the coal fields at Lo-p'ing, Kiangsi. Liu refused, however. In August, 1874, at the height of the Taiwan crisis, Li advised Shen Pao-chen to try to work the mines of that island. Assisted by H. E. Hobson, the commissioner of customs at Tamsui, Shen succeeded in 1875 in making arrangements for a coal mine near Keelung.[65]

Li's Proposals of December, 1874.   Since the Tientsin Massacre, the initiative for self-strengthening had come chiefly from Li, with some cooperation from the Tsungli Yamen and from Tseng Kuo-fan and Shen Pao-chen in the provinces. The Taiwan affair further stimulated attention to the problem of military preparedness. On November 5, 1874, the Tsungli Yamen, in which the ailing Wen-hsiang was still the dominant spirit, memorialized on the lessons of the incident. The Yamen lamented that although there had been much talk of self-strengthening since 1860, little had actually been done. The Yamen recommended that governors-general, governors, and Manchu commanders-in-chief of the coastal and Yangtze provinces be invited to submit their views on the needs of coastal defense (*hai-fang*) under five headings: military training, weapons, shipbuilding, revenue, and personnel. In a personal memorial submitted a month later, Wen-hsiang (who had risen from his sickbed to take charge of

[64] *LWCK Letters*, 14. 30b, 34b; 15. 14b. Ellsworth C. Carlson, *The Kaiping Mines, 1877–1912* (Cambridge, Mass., 1957), p. 7.

[65] *LWCK Letters*, 13. 21b; 14. 2, 19, 30b. *Yang-wu yün-tung*, VII, 70. Morse, *International Relations*, II. 263.

the negotiations with the Japanese on the Taiwan incident) reminded the throne that there was a real possibility that Japan, "accustomed to break her word," would allow her rebels at home to seek adventure in China. Wen-hsiang recommended that military preparations on Taiwan be continued and that plans be made immediately to buy ironclads and gunboats from abroad.[66]

While it was the Yamen that initiated the policy debate in 1874, Li put forward the boldest proposals. "What is urgently needed today is to abandon established notions and seek practical results," he urged in his memorial of December 10.[67] The two essentials for a successful coastal defense program were, in his view, "the change of institutions (*pien-fa*) and the proper use of personnel (*yung-jen*)." Li wrote Wen-hsiang that he was aware that not all his proposals could be adopted, but he had to make them, since "the responsibility is on my shoulders." [68]

Li proposed general military reform for the coastal and Yangtze provinces. In the early T'ung-chih period, when he worked with the British and French forces in Shanghai and with the Ever Victorious Army, he had formed the conviction that the number of troops in the Chinese armies could be much reduced; funds saved thereby could provide better equipment and pay for selected and efficient units. Soon after he became imperial commissioner in 1870, Li had drawn the throne's attention to the uselessness of the Green Standard Army, including the so-called Trained Troops.[69] He now went further and pleaded that "Rather than having a large number that are useless, it is better to have fewer of high quality." Li proposed that all "weak and exhausted" army units, whether Green Standard, Trained Troops, or *yung* forces, should be disbanded altogether, while the best troops, fewer than 100,000 for all the coastal and Yangtze provinces, should be converted into "foreign-arms and cannon corps." Equipped with rifles and cannon of recent model and reinforced by coastal fortifications, the comparatively small number of troops could be relied on at least to defend the two vital

---

[66] *IWSM*, T'ung-chih, 98. 19–21, 40–42.
[67] *LWCK Memorials*, 24. 10–25. See also 24. 26–28; *Letters*, 15. 12–15b.
[68] *LWCK Letters*, 14. 32; *Tsungli Yamen Letters*, 2. 57b–59.
[69] *LWCK Letters*, 3. 16b–17; 5. 28b, 32, 34–35. *Memorials*, 7. 29; 17. 12.

areas, Chihli and the lower Yangtze Valley. Li suggested that orders be placed immediately for firearms such as the Martini-Henry and the Snider and for cannon produced by Krupp, Wool-wich, Armstrong, and Gatling. China's own arsenals, however, must also be expanded. They must aim at making breechloading rifles and cannon, as well as torpedoes, while further plans could await the day when a steel industry was developed, along with the coal and iron mines. The manufacture of powder, cartridges, and shells needed to be expanded and new plants for this purpose should be established at inland places like Soochow and in the interior provinces.

Li supported Wen-hsiang's proposal for a Chinese naval fleet of foreign-built vessels. Li felt that the navy was not quite as important as the army, but agreed that effective defense required ironclads for the open seas and floating gun-carriages as well as torpedoes for the harbors. He recommended that six ironclads be ordered immediately, two to be stationed in north China (prob-ably at Chefoo and Port Arthur), two close to the Yangtze estuary, and two at Amoy or Canton. In addition, twenty floating gun-carriages should be ordered for use at the various ports. Li suggested that Chinese students should be sent abroad to the shipyards where the vessels were to be built, to learn shipbuilding and navigation techniques. Meanwhile, the building programs at the Foochow and Kiangnan yards should be strengthened. Li visualized a Chinese naval fleet consisting eventually of sixty vessels.

To finance the new army and navy, Li suggested, first of all, that revenue be saved by disbanding worthless troops and by discontinuing the construction of war junks. The new army and navy were expected, however, to cost more than Tls. 10,000,-000, and additional appropriations must be arranged. The most reliable source, Li emphasized, was the "four-tenths quota of the maritime customs revenue" (*ssu-ch'eng yang-shui*).[70] This fund had been allocated at some ports for the use of arsenals and for the Anhwei Army, but a considerable portion remained, particu-larly if the part reserved for the Board of Revenue at Peking was

[70] See C. John Stanley, *Late Ch'ing Finance: Hu Kuang-yung as an Innova-tor* (Cambridge, Mass., 1961), pp. 81–84.

included. Li proposed that some Tls. 3,000,000 which had been saved by the Board from this source should also be used for coastal defense. He also suggested that loans could be obtained from foreign firms, to be paid in installments out of the four-tenths quota. Li recommended that likin on imported opium could be raised somewhat, while taxes could be levied on native opium, which might as well be legalized until such time as the drug's importation could be stopped altogether. To insure larger revenue for coastal defense, Li proposed, for the first time explicitly, that preparations in coastal provinces be accorded priority over the recovery of Sinkiang. He pointed out that Sinkiang had come under Ch'ing rule only in the Ch'ien-lung reign, and that it was very difficult to defend, particularly now that the Moslem chieftain at Kashgar had Russian and British support and the Russians had occupied Ili. Given the limited revenue available, the court would have to make a choice between adequate preparations in the coastal area and the recovery of the "wasteland" in the far northwest. Li would draw the defense line at the Kansu border and guard it with military colonies into which some of the present armies there could be converted, while the Moslem leaders at Ili, Urumchi, and Kashgar might be accorded the status of native chieftains (*t'u-ssu*) or tributaries. Presumably a balance between Russian and British influences would help to insure stability in Sinkiang. Funds saved by cancelling the expedition could be diverted immediately to the coastal provinces.

Undoubtedly with Li in mind, the Tsungli Yamen had proposed in its memorial of November 5, 1874, that there should be a single commander-in-chief (*t'ung-shuai*) in charge of the coastal and Yangtze provinces, and that under him there should be a system of newly chosen generals-in-chief and brigade generals, to be stationed in different provinces. Li regarded the idea as impractical. Given the existing authority of the governors-general and governors in financial and military affairs, a single command for all the provinces concerned was hardly feasible, particularly since the lack of telegraph and railway prevented rapid communication. Moreover, mere "consultation" (*hui-t'ung shang-ch'ou*) between the commander-in-chief and the provinces was not likely to lead to effective action. Li, therefore, favored more than one command for the coastal and Yangtze areas—perhaps three "high officials" (*ta yüan*) exercising supervision over such new projects as the naval fleet. For the supervisory positions in south China, Li recommended Shen Pao-chen and Ting Jih-ch'ang. From Li's correspondence, we know that he had been using his influence with Wen-hsiang and other ministers at court to get Shen appointed as the governor-general of Liang-chiang and Ting to a responsible post in south China.[71] Li obviously hoped that with himself at Tientsin and Shen at Nanking, a high degree of coordination could be achieved in carrying out new programs.

While Li was concerned with the immediate financial and political arrangements, he also put forth proposals of long-range significance. He brought up, for the first time directly to the throne, the need for a change in the examination and civil service systems. Li lamented the continuing apathy among the literati toward Western methods (*yang-fa*) and pointed out that neither the T'ung-wen Kuan type of school nor sending students abroad would arouse sufficient interest if the criteria for the selection and the advancement of officials remained unchanged. Li attacked the literary examinations, which emphasized calligraphy and the eight-legged essay, as "hollow and ornamental." He pleaded that while this kind of examination could not be "abolished immediately," it was necessary to create "another basis (*k'o*) of advancement through government activity concerning foreign relations (*yang-wu*)." Li proposed that a Bureau of Foreign Learning (*yang-hsüeh chü*) be created in each province involved in coastal defense, where science and technology (including such subjects as chemistry, electricity, and gunnery) would be taught by carefully chosen Western instructors, as well as by qualified Chinese, such as those being trained in the United States. Advanced students were to be "tested through performance" and were to be assigned posts in arsenals, shipyards, and the armed forces. Moreover, such personnel were to be allowed opportunities for rapid promotion, comparable to those for persons possessing military merits, and were to be awarded "substan-

[71] *LWCK Memorials,* 12. 26; 13. 2; 14. 32; 15. 2b, 6b–7. See also 14. 38; 15. 17.

tive posts, in the same way as officials who advanced through regular channels." Li predicted such a new personnel policy would result in an appreciable advance in armament-making in China in about twenty years.

Li urged the use of Western technology in transport, mining, and manufacturing. He drew the throne's attention to the military and commercial advantages of the railway, and to the military value of the telegraph. Pointing out that British textile imports into China amounted to more than Tls. 30,000,000 per year and were harmful to Chinese handicrafts, Li suggested that the Chinese themselves should establish machine-operated textile mills. He particularly stressed the opportunity that lay in opening up mines—not only coal and iron, but also copper, lead, mercury, and the precious metals. Li compared the failure to exploit such resources to keeping family treasures permanently sealed up while worrying about starvation and cold. He recommended that foreign geologists be invited to prospect the mines in the provinces and that Chinese merchants be encouraged to form companies (*kung-ssu*) to work mines with machines; the government could help the companies with initial loans and thereafter receive ten or twenty percent of their profits. Li expected the benefits from the mines to be apparent in ten years. He realized that new mining projects were opposed by the gentry and the people on grounds of geomancy and by "incompetent officials" who feared that the concentration of miners might lead to disorderly conduct. Li described such objections as "ridiculous," for the Western nations and Japan were all developing mines: "Why is it that they do not suffer from them and on the contrary have achieved wealth and strength (*fu-ch'iang*) through them?"

Li had thus proposed programs for self-strengthening which were broader and more far-reaching than those presented by him or by others in the 1860's. The question was, of course, whether any or all of the proposals might be accepted. Li received scant help from the governors-general, governors, and Manchu commanders-in-chief who also gave their views on the Tsungli Yamen's original memorial. Stimulated by the recent Taiwan crisis, all the memorialists agreed that coastal defense needed to be strengthened. But, in the view of the Tsungli Yamen, except for

Li and Shen Pao-chen (who also made a strong plea for a navy which included foreign-built ironclads and for the development of mines), none put forward proposals that were "concrete and practical." By early January, 1875, replies had been received from twelve officials, in addition to Li and Shen.[72] While all twelve favored new training for the army, only one suggested that the particularly weak units of the Green Standard forces should be disbanded. Six favored forming a new navy with foreign-built ironclads, but only one or two had useful suggestions on how they were to be financed. All twelve assumed that war was to be carried into Sinkiang; two in particular argued eloquently that the Russian threat to the land frontier posed an even more urgent problem than coastal defense. Four favored making some exception in the rules of civil or military service to place competent men where they were needed, but only two vaguely suggested that Western studies should be encouraged. Four realized the importance of mineral resources, but only one (Li's brother Han-chang) supported without reservation the use of machines in mines. Only one (the governor of Kiangsi, Liu K'un-i) agreed with the Tsungli Yamen that there should be a single commander-in-chief for coastal defense, but he qualified the proposal by suggesting that the generals-in-chief and brigade generals chosen by the commander-in-chief should be under the direction of the governors-general and the governors of the provinces concerned. Three recommended that the command of coastal defense be divided between the two commissioners at Tientsin and Nanking—two mentioned Li by name for the supervisory responsibility in north China.

Decision rested, of course, with the court. A meeting of the ministers was to consider the matter on January 2, but it was postponed due to the T'ung-chih emperor's illness and his death on the 12th. In late January, Li went to Peking and was summoned three times to audiences with the dowager empresses. He also talked with Wen-hsiang and Li Wen-tsao and urged that Shen Pao-chen be appointed governor-general of Liang-chiang, a post which had been vacated by Li Tsung-hsi (who was taken ill) and temporarily filled by Liu K'un-i as acting governor-general.

[72] *IWSM,* T'ung-chih, 98. 31–100. 44.

Wen-hsiang arranged to have Robert Hart, who had obtained price quotations on British-built gunboats through his agent in London, go to Tientsin and discuss the details with Li.[73]

While in Peking, Li personally urged the court to reconsider the expedition into Sinkiang, and according to Li there were people at court who agreed with him.[74] But due chiefly to reluctance to "abandon territories acquired by an imperial ancestor," the throne abided by its decision (made as early as February, 1874) to encourage Tso Tsung-t'ang to proceed. On March 10, Tso was instructed to formulate plans for the expedition, including arrangements for the supply line. On May 3, Tso was appointed imperial commissioner for military operations in Sinkiang.[75] This effort to reconquer the far northwest was bound to cut into the revenue for the proposed coastal defense plans, although as of 1875 it was still uncertain whether Tso or the dynasty would really persevere in the long and arduous task of recovering Kashgar and Ili.

The court did not entirely neglect coastal defense, however. The Taiwan affair was fresh in its memory and in April, 1875, the murder of A. R. Margary, an interpreter entering Yunnan from Burma, raised the possibility of a threat from the British. The court was willing to see Li in a position to coordinate military preparations on the coast. On May 30, 1875, Shen Pao-chen was appointed governor-general of Liang-chiang and commissioner of trade for the southern ports. At the same time, Li was appointed commissioner of coastal defense for north China and Shen, commissioner of coastal defense for south China, both charged with the responsibility of training troops, establishing

---

[73] *LWCK Letters,* 14. 34, 38b–39; 15. 1b. *Tung-hua hsü-lu,* T'ung-chih, 100. 47–48.

[74] *LWCK Letters,* 15. 2b. Strangely enough, Prince Ch'un, who had urged a belligerent stand during the crisis created by the Tientsin Massacre, agreed with Li on Sinkiang; see 16. 17.

[75] *LWCK Letters,* 15. 2, 10b; *Ch'ing-chi wai-chiao shih-liao* [Historical Materials on Foreign Relations in the Latter Part of the Ch'ing Dynasty], 243 *chüan* (Peiping, 1932–1935), Kuang-hsü, 1. 4–5; *Tung-hua hsü-lu,* T'ung-chih, 98. 30, 32; Kuang-hsü, 1. 35. Cf. Immanuel C. Y. Hsü, "The Great Policy Debate in China, 1874: Maritime Defense vs. Frontier Defense," *Harvard Journal of Asiatic Studies,* XXV (1965), 217–227; Wen-djang Chu, "Tso Tsung-T'ang's Role in the Recovery of Sinkiang," *Tsing Hua Journal of Chinese Studies,* New Series I, No. 3, pp. 136–145.

"bureaus" (meaning, probably, chiefly arsenals), reorganizing taxes, and other tasks necessary to defense. An edict of the same day declared: "Coastal defense is vitally important, and it is urgently necessary to make preparation before the coming of trouble, so as to strengthen ourselves." The throne noted that ironclads were extremely costly, but authorized Li and Shen to order "one or two to begin with." [76] The Board of Revenue and the Tsungli Yamen subsequently recommended that beginning in August, 1875, an annual appropriation of Tls. 4,000,000 be made for coastal defense, to be expended by the two commissioners. It was specified that the yearly sum was to come from the "four-tenths quota of the maritime customs revenue" at the coastal ports and from the likin revenue of coastal and Yangtze provinces. Since the Board of Revenue did not want to give up that portion of the four-tenths quota reserved for itself (or the sums it had received in the past from this source), and since the board plainly was not giving coastal defense priority over other imperially sanctioned claims on the four-tenths quota, Li feared that only a fraction of this annual fund would be left for him and Shen. Moreover, Li was certain that with the pressure from Peking to raise large sums (at least two or three million taels annually) for the construction of imperial mausoleums and palaces and with the Sinkiang campaign being given priority, probably only one or two coastal and Yangtze provinces would have any surplus in their likin revenue, which was also relied on by the provinces themselves for their own financial needs. Li foresaw that the Tls. 4,000,000 appropriated was to become largely nominal, although he hoped that at least some small portion might be available. [77]

Predictably, the court did not heed Li's counsel concerning the reform of institutions. Admitting the weaknesses of the Green Standard Army, the court, also on May 30, instructed all governors-general and governors concerned with coastal defense to complete, within a year, the reorganization and consolidation of the Green Standard "outposts" (*hsün*) and to provide the troops

---

[76] *Tung-hua hsü-lu,* Kuang-hsü, 1. 33, 56–57.
[77] *LWCK Letters,* 15. 19b, 20b, 21b, 22b, 26b, 30b–31, 33b–35. *Tsungli Yamen Letters,* 3. 18; 5. 40.

with uniform training. No mention was made, however, of disbanding the inferior units. The throne also passed over the proposed "bureaus of Western learning" and the new civil service category for persons versed in this learning. One of the May 30 edicts states that both proposals had been referred to Prince Li (Shih-to) and to Prince Ch'un (the new child-emperor's father), along with the Tsungli Yamen's recommendation that diplomatic envoys be sent to Japan and the West. While the two princes favored the latter idea, they did not comment on the proposals regarding Western learning. So as to avoid "disagreement," the throne would, therefore, defer decision on these proposals until the diplomatic missions abroad proved successful! In another edict of the same day, the throne encouraged Li and Shen to recommend to it men who were versed in *yang-wu,* including those qualified to serve as envoys abroad. None of the edicts mentioned Li's proposals regarding railways, telegraphs, and textile mills, but one gave Li and Shen authorization to proceed with the specific mining projects they had mentioned in their memorials—the coal and iron mines in Tz'u-chou, Chihli, and on Taiwan.[78]

Thus only a few of the proposals Li put forward were adopted by the throne, and, in view of the priority it gave to Sinkiang and to the increasing financial needs of the court itself, a major new start in coastal defense and in self-strengthening was hardly to be expected. Yet it may be said that new ground had been broken in Ch'ing policy. Not being able to compete with the arsenals and shipyards of the West, China, it was decided, would have to acquire Western-made armaments through purchase. In the next few years, a spate of orders came from Tientsin and elsewhere for Remingtons, Sniders, Krupp, and Gatling guns.[79] As early as

[78] *Tung-hua hsü-lu,* Kuang-hsü, 1. 56–57. According to Li's information, when the officials at court held a meeting to discuss the proposals on coastal defense, Wen-hsiang was sympathetically inclined toward Li's recommendations on "bureaus of foreign learning," railways, telegraph, and mines, but two Chinese officials strongly condemned them, and others at the meeting were indifferent. *LWCK Letters,* 17. 13.

[79] In a letter to C. Hannen dated October 25, 1875, Robert Hart commented on the Chinese purchase of foreign arms and on the arrangements being made for a modern coal mine on Taiwan: "Forts are bristling all round Tientsin and in many other places, and official talk loves to dwell on the sweet syllables the Chinese mouth makes of the word 'Krupp.' Torpedoes are toys in all the houses, and, as for an 80-ton gun creating astonishment, the wonder is that

April, 1875, with the Tsungli Yamen's support, Li ordered four gunboats from Armstrong & Co., through Robert Hart's London agent—two 330-ton ships, each carrying a 26.5-ton rifle gun, and two 440-ton ones, each equipped with a 38-ton gun. The ordering of more gunboats and of an ironclad was contemplated, pending the availability of funds. It was planned during 1875–1876 to send graduates of the Foochow Navy Yard School to Britain and France.[80] Both Li and Shen interpreted the imperial sanction for the mines in Chihli and on Taiwan as general approval covering such projects elsewhere. Within the year following May, 1875, Li wrote to the governors of Hupeh, Kiangsi, Fukien, and Shantung, urging them to work mines with machines. Coal and iron fields were planned in Kuang-chi and Hsing-kuo, Hupeh, in late 1875 under the sponsorship of the commissioners at Tientsin and Nanking as well as the Hupeh governor; a similar project was initiated in Kiangsi in 1876, the same year that prospecting was done at K'ai-p'ing, Chihli. During that year, Li and Shen Pao-chen also considered the establishment of a cotton textile mill at Shanghai.[81]

What was particularly gratifying to Li was the fact that at least two like-minded colleagues had been brought, partly on his recommendation, to positions of influence. Shen Pao-chen arrived at his new post in Nanking in November, 1875. In September, Ting Jih-ch'ang, on Li's recommendation, had been appointed director-general of the Foochow Navy Yard, and in January, 1876, he became governor of Fukien with authority over Taiwan.[82] In Chihli, Li pressed forward with plans of long-range significance—the sending of five young officers of the Anhwei

---

thousand-tonners have not yet been devised for the Chinese and sent out in cases, and as numerously, as needles and matches! The big giant is really waking up, but what a time it takes to yawn and rub his eyes!" Quoted in Morse, *International Relations,* II, 263. See also *LWCK Tsungli Yamen Letters,* 3. 17–19; Chou Sheng-ch'uan, *Chou Wu-chuang kung i-shu, chüan-shou.* 40b.

[80] *LWCK Tsungli Yamen Letters,* 3. 6–14, 16; 4. 26; 5. 40b; 6. 28–29b. *Letters,* 15. 21b, 31, 33b, 36; 16. 3, 12, 14b, 21b–22, 26b–27. Stanley F. Wright, *Hart and the Chinese Customs* (Belfast, 1950), pp. 469–474.

[81] *LWCK Letters,* 15. 14, 16, 22, 24, 27b, 29b–30, 31, 36; 16. 3b, 20. *Yang-wu yün-tung,* VII, 103–106, 113.

[82] *LWCK Letters,* 15. 29, 30b, 33, 35; *Memorials,* 29. 1–2; *Tung-hua hsü-lu,* Kuang-hsü, 1. 115, 140.

Army to German military academies, further expansion of the Tientsin Arsenal, the establishment of a school of Western sciences in connection with the Arsenal's new plant for manufacturing torpedoes.[83] Similar work was being carried on by Shen and Ting in south China. In early 1877, thirty students of the Foochow Navy Yard School were sent to Europe. Meanwhile, Shen did much to strengthen the Nanking and Kiangnan arsenals, adding to the former a torpedo plant and acquiring for the latter machinery for making cast-iron rifle guns of the Armstrong type, the first of which was produced in 1878. A school was set up at the Nanking Arsenal, and an effort was made to improve the school and the translation department at the Kiangnan Arsenal. Although the plan for a textile mill was found not to be immediately feasible, in late 1876 Shen Pao-chen arranged large loans from the Liang-chiang provinces to the China Merchants' Steam Navigation Company, enabling it to buy sixteen ships from the American firm of Russell and Co. and thereby increase its fleet to thirty-one vessels (22,168 net tons).[84] For the first time since Tseng Kuo-fan's death in 1872, Li had an ally at the head of the Liang-chiang administration.

We see, therefore, that only a small part of Li's comprehensive program was put into practice. Nevertheless, as compared with its beginnings in the early T'ung-chih period, the self-strengthening movement had certainly expanded. In the new shipping and mining enterprises, the movement had gained another dimension: to the desire for effective armament was added the desire to augment the state's wealth, again by using Western technology. The plan for a navy of foreign-built vessels represented a realistic appraisal of the capacity of China's new shipyards, as well as an awareness of the urgent need for preparedness. The sending of students to Europe, in the wake of the educational mission to the

[83] *LWCK Letters,* 16. 12. *Tsungli Yamen Letters,* 4. 39. *Memorials,* 28. 1–4; 33. 25–29.

[84] *LWCK Letters,* 15. 35–36b; 16. 1b, 3, 5b, 7–9, 14b, 22, 24, 31b, 34b–36. *Tsungli Yamen Letters,* 6. 37b–38. Shen Pao-chen, *Shen Wen-su kung cheng-shu* [Works of Shen Pao-chen], 8 vols. (1880), *chüan* 6–7. Sun Yü-t'ang, *Chung-kuo chin-tai kung-yeh shih tzu-liao,* I, 282, 299–300, 317–319, 328. *Yang-wu yün-tung,* IV, 37–41. Liu, "British-Chinese Steamship Rivalry," p. 60.

United States, was a further acknowledgment of the need for technical personnel. Among the high officials there were very few men who, like Li, wanted to see drastic reform in civil service regulations and in the military system. But under the continued pressure from foreign powers, at least the objective of gaining "wealth and strength" for the state, which Li so eloquently advocated, had won widespread acceptance, if not active support.

With Li as the imperial commissioner at Tientsin, the self-strengthening movement had, moreover, acquired a strategically placed coordinator. It is plain that Li's power was limited. He could get the court to accept only a few of his proposals, and the financial and other resources he needed often lay in provinces beyond his jurisdiction. But it may be said that in the 1870's, Li was at least given a good opportunity to expand his efforts. The Anhwei Army in Chihli and elsewhere enjoyed the throne's support, and imperial approval had been given to his program for the arsenals, for studies abroad, for merchant steamships and mines, and for a new navy. Beginning in 1875, men recommended by Li, Shen Pao-chen and Ting Jih-ch'ang, were in the vital posts in Liang-chiang and Fukien, and with sympathetic officials in other provinces, there was at least a chance that self-strengthening might become an empire-wide effort. If by "regionalism" is meant the administrative leeway enjoyed by the governors-general and governors over the armies and the likin of the provinces, this trend had continued since the early T'ung-chih period. But the imperial authority over armies and revenue anywhere in the empire was never questioned, and Peking's control over provincial appointments, at least at the higher levels, had not diminished. The court's support was plainly still the key to the success of any new policy. To the extent that Li's recommendations on policy and personnel met with imperial approval, he represented, in effect, a centralizing force on behalf of what he considered an urgent national task.

JOHN L. RAWLINSON

China's Failure to Coordinate Her Modern Fleets in the Late Nineteenth Century

H AD China managed in the 1890's to repel the Japanese
attack, the history of the twentieth century might have
been radically different. China's inability to defend herself
on the sea in modern times was part of a larger failure to adjust
her institutions to the Western impact. Although no single explanation for this failure will suffice we may argue that China's
defeat by the French and Japanese navies in the late nineteenth
century was to a large degree the result of her incapacity to concentrate her modern naval strength. In other words, China finally
did manage to obtain relatively modern fighting ships, but she
did not change the traditional organization of her water forces.[1]

THE OLD SYSTEM

At first glance, we might say that the old water force was organized in such a way as to permit centralized direction or routine
concentration of strength—which for this study is the crucial

[1] This paper has been based on material gathered for the author's book,
China's Struggle for Naval Development (Cambridge: Harvard University
Press, 1966). Most of the general problems raised in this paper receive fuller
treatment in that book.

aspect of organization. The Manchu banner units, garrisoned in strategic places in the empire, were subject to central direction by the Board of War. So were the provincially organized Chinese Green Banner troops, the second military arm of the dynasty. The old water force was a subordinate part of the Green Banner land units, although some of the Manchu banner troops also had attached water forces. Manchu garrisons were commanded by Manchu commanders-in-chief, the so-called "tartar generals." Chinese Green Banner land units, organized by province, each had a general, who was subordinated in turn to the governor and governor-general, the latter usually holding authority over a pair of provinces. Although Manchu commanders-in-chief, governors-general, and governors were not consistently related to each other, all were of course subordinate to the emperor. Each provincial water force, with its nine grades of officers from admiral to sub-lieutenant, was organized as a hierarchy of units from brigade down to post, with separate branches in some cases for internal waterways and the high seas.[2] Water force organization and regulations were well established, being based on Ming precedents.[3]

Each of the Green Banner water force posts had an assigned cruising beat, interlocking with those of its neighbors. Although northern partols were suspended during the gales of winter, the coast was nominally screened throughout the commercial season by cruising war junks.[4] There were also arrangements for cooperation among provincial fleets. For example, the Ts'ung-ming command, established in the seventeenth century, drew together 10,000 men from the three Liang-chiang provinces into a naval

[2] Summary based on H. S. Brunnert and V. V. Hagelstrom, *Present Day Political Organization of China*, trans. A. Beltchenko and E. E. Moran (Shanghai, 1912), pp. 128–139, 336–337; Hsieh Pao-chao, *The Government of China* (Baltimore, 1925), pp. 255–260, 291–299; T. F. Wade, "The Army of the Chinese Empire: Its Two Great Divisions, the Bannermen or National Guard, and the Green Standard, or Provincial Troops: Their Organization, Locations, Pay, Conditions, Etc.," *Chinese Repository,* XX (1851), 390–401; and H. B. Morse, *The Trade and Administration of China* (Shanghai, 1913), p. 52.

[3] *Ch'ing-shih kao* [Draft History of the Ch'ing Dynasty], "Ping-chih" [Monograph on Military Affairs], comp. Chao Erh-hsün *et al.* (movable type ed., 1927; hereafter cited as *CSK:Pc*), 6. 1.

[4] *CSK:Pc,* 6. 1a–b, 13b–14; Wade, "Army," pp. 376–377.

garrison on the strategic Ts'ung-ming islands. The Namoa unit was responsible to the governors-general and admirals of two regional systems, the Liang-kuang and the Min-Che. In 1750, three coastal regions, Kwangtung-Kwangsi, Fukien-Chekiang, and the Liang-chiang, were combined for a system of patrols from Namoa to Ts'ung-ming.[5]

In practice, however, nineteenth-century Chinese shippers enjoyed very little protection from the water force. Often merchants hired their own protection against pirates. Not only was interprovincial cooperation usually in default; within the paired-province regions, and even within single provinces, there was only a fitful coordination of water force effort, and that depended largely on the chance presence of such outstanding officials as Shih Lang, who in the late seventeenth century was Fukien admiral and defeated the formidable Koxinga. The explanation for the lack of coordination lay in the details of the command structure. The Board of War did not exercise a single authority. Jurisdiction over imperial clan members in Manchu banner units was in the Clan Court in Peking, and in practice all Manchu soldiers were subject to the captain-general of the Banners. In addition, the Board of War was subordinated in military policy matters to the Grand Council.[6] In the last resort, everything depended on the emperor. A strong emperor could coordinate his forces; a weak one—and the nineteenth century was not distinguished for its imperial leadership—could punish officials who might offend him, but chastisement was not positive leadership.

But it was not strictly true that everything depended on the emperor. The provincial organization of the empire was decentralized, there being, for example, no centrally devised budget including all provincial accounts. The system generated rivalries within the provinces, between them, and between them and the central government.[7] The Manchus added a checks-and-balances

---

[5] *CSK:Pc*, 6. 1; Wade, "Army," p. 373.

[6] Wade, "Army," pp. 252, 310; Morse, *Trade*, p. 44; Hsieh, *Government*, p. 255.

[7] For fuller discussion, see Franz Michael, "Regionalism in the Nineteenth Century," Introduction to Stanley Spector, *Li Hung-chang and the Huai Army* (Seattle, 1964).

system which buttressed their own security vis-à-vis the subject Chinese but hampered military or naval coordination. Manchu commanders-in-chief, governors-general, governors, provincial Green Banner generals and admirals, and even lesser provincial officials such as finance commissioners, were not in a single chain of command. Rather, each was bound to the throne by the right (or obligation) of direct memorial. Manchus and Chinese watched each other, and all provincial officials had to rely on the local gentry to some extent. The whim of the emperor was not everything.

Furthermore, there was no clear-cut system of civilian supremacy over the military. The Manchu commander-in-chief was independent in his garrison and usually outranked the governor-general of the region. But as noted, top civilian provincial officials had concurrent military responsibilities, with powers supposedly superior to those of the provincial Green Banner military men. This system of civilian-military concurrencies reached down to the taotai level, and there were even some assistant taotais for waterways and military affairs whose duties embraced coastal defense.[8] An example of this overlapping of responsibility is seen in the reaction of Chekiang officials to the British advance in 1840. Admiral Chu T'ing-piao led forces to sea; so too, we are told, did Li Shao-fang, the Ning-shao-t'ai taotai.[9]

The foregoing system did not represent an orderly parcelling of responsibility. The underlying irregularity is seen in the old system of commands, which was the real core of China's defenses. Banner forces, Chinese and Manchu, were divided into commands, but not in uniform fashion. For example, there were five in Kwangtung, one each under the governor-general, governor, admiral, general, and Manchu commander-in-chief. The metropolitan province of Chihli, on the other hand, had but two, under the governor-general (who was concurrently the general) and the admiral. The device of the "direct" command further complicated matters. A governor-general's direct or

---

[8] Hsieh, *Government*, pp. 298–299; Morse, *Trade*, p. 52.
[9] *Ch'ou-pan i-wu shih-mo* [The Complete Account of Our Management of Barbarian Affairs], 260 *chüan* (Peiping, 1930; hereafter cited as *IWSM:TK* for the Tao-kuang reign, and *IWSM:TC* for the T'ung-chih reign), *TK,* 11. 7–10b.

personal command stood at his immediate disposal; the other Chinese troops in the province, some of them answering to other direct commands, were not so readily moved by him.[10] Kwangtung in 1851 showed these commands: the Green Banner forces included five battalions of landsmen plus 929 water-force men under the governor-general; a two-battalion brigade waited on the governor; the admiral had twelve battalions; the general, twenty-one. There were eight other Green Banner units in the province, each under a brigadier general, and these subordinate officers deferred to the governor-general rather than the general.[11] At about the same time in Chekiang, the general was nominally under the admiral, but he did not really answer to him, nor to the governor, for the general's rank excluded that; in practice, he followed the governor-general.[12] A little earlier in Chekiang, in 1840, the governor had approached his own governor-general only by way of a direct memorial to the emperor, and a general on special wartime assignment to the province bypassed both of these superior civilian officials—in both cases requesting military assistance which was to come in part from the paired province of Fukien.[13] In some cases, troops had no "direct" commanders and, in others, an officer might correspond with three or four chiefs. A senior post captain on Taiwan, for example, with three land and fifteen water battalions, corresponded with the Board of War about the Taiwanese aborigines and was responsible as well to the Manchu commander-in-chief, the admiral at Foochow, *and* to the governor-general of Fukien and Chekiang. Most of the commands were practically independent of each other.[14] In times of dynastic decline, local forces were unofficially organized; if the local officials approved, such forces were regarded as official; if not, they were called bandit gangs.[15]

China's naval disorganization was reflected also in the variety of coastal fortifications, which during the Opium War ranged

[10] Wade, "Army," p. 365; Hsieh, *Government,* pp. 258–259.
[11] T. T. Meadows, in *Chinese Repository,* XX (1851), 53–54.
[12] Wade, "Army," p. 375.
[13] For reports and edict, see *IWSM:TK,* 11. 7–10b; 12. 15a–b, 23a–b; 13. 23b–25b; 14. 3b–4, 8b–9.
[14] Wade, "Army," pp. 255, 373–374; Hsieh, *Government,* pp. 258–259.
[15] Michael, "Regionalism in the Nineteenth Century," p. xxxvi.

e massive granite emplacements in Canton and Amoy to
f mud or upturned fishing junks whose slimy bottoms
)posed to make cannonballs slither harmlessly aside.[16]

kind of disarray appeared in the names of war-junk
types, which varied from province to province with nothing like
the system of rating used in the British navy. Many type designations were known only locally—proof of the old compartmentali-
zation of the coast.[17] As it was organized the old water force in
the nineteenth century was at best an anti-pirate force. Even if its
fleets had been entirely made of war steamers, it was not ready
for coordinated action, or for any action that demanded con-
forming to an agreed-upon strategy.

\ At no time during the Opium War was there any coordination
or concentration of war junks capable of making even a token
resistance. A Chinese war junk was of course no match for an
armed steamer like the *Nemesis*. For that matter, there was even
no comparison between a war junk and the seventy-four-gun
third-rate sailing ships which the British used.\ Furthermore, the
Opium War did not serve as a stimulus to innovation, either in
the design of war vessels in China or in their organization. Nor
were any basic changes made in naval technology or organization during the Second China War—although we should note
that the old weapons system scored an important victory at Taku
in June, 1859. Some modernization of ships and arms did begin
in the 1860's, sponsored by Tseng Kuo-fan, Li Hung-chang,
and Tso Tsung-t'ang. Why it took some Chinese so long to
conclude that China needed naval modernization, or, better, why
it took so long for China's official system to accommodate such
projects, is a study in itself.

Even the tentative beginnings made at the Kiangnan Arsenal
in Shanghai or at the dockyard near Foochow came only in
military technology and were not matched by any corresponding
changes in naval organization or in the political compartmentali-
zation of the empire. We may speak of "corresponding changes"
here, for the speed of modern steam vessels in itself would facili-

[16] On crude fortifications, see memorial by Ch'i Chun-tsao and others,
IWSM:TK, 10. 19b–23, May 16, 1840.

[17] For romanized names, see Wade, "Army," p. 379; for another list, in
Chinese, see *CSK:Pc*, 6. 10–11b.

tate centralization. But such organizational changes would have been beset with an official opposition far greater than that which the decrepit old water force might offer to piecemeal technological change. The discrepancy between technological and institutional change is nicely illustrated by the Lay-Osborn flotilla fiasco of the early 1860's.[18]

CHANGES AND IMPERFECTIONS

The allies in the Second China War in 1860 forced the Peking government to set up a new agency, the Tsungli Yamen, to handle foreign affairs. In 1861 this unprecedented agency was under the direction of Prince Kung, concurrently chief of the Grand Council. After the T'ung-chih coup of 1861, key court personnel were relatively progressive. In June, 1861, Robert Hart of the newly organized Chinese Imperial Maritime Customs, which came under the control of the Tsungli Yamen, approached Prince Kung with the suggestion that China purchase war steamers to speed the attack on the Taiping rebels. The Tsungli Yamen had attracted earlier foreign offers of military aid, which had been suspiciously rejected, but since this one came from a foreign employee of the government it was cautiously approved. In time, eight war steamers were purchased for China in England, the largest of them displacing about 1,000 tons and showing eighteen knots on her trails—"one of the fastest vessels afloat," said the London *Times* of May 8, 1863.

The actual purchasing was done by Horatio Nelson Lay, the Inspector-General of Customs and Hart's immediate chief, who was then on leave in England. Lay, who handled everything with a supreme conviction that he knew what was best for China (he even designed a flag with a dragon on it for the new Chinese navy), drew a secret agreement with Captain Sherard Osborn of the Royal Navy, which provided that the new fleet should be manned by English tars under Osborn's command; that *all* modern ships in China should be under Osborn's command; that

---

[18] Based on author's paper "The Lay-Osborn Flotilla," *Papers on China,* IV (Harvard University, Committee on International and Regional Studies, 1950).

Osborn was to take his orders from Lay alone; and that Lay would take *his* orders only from the emperor himself—*if Lay concurred in those orders*. Lay, then about thirty, saw himself as an admiralissimo.

Sir Frederick Bruce, Her Majesty's Minister to China under the Tientsin treaties, who did not know of the Lay-Osborn agreement until the whole scheme had collapsed, had his own strong if sober interest in fostering political centralization in China. Only a strong central regime could meet the new treaty obligations. Like most of his foreign colleagues, Bruce distrusted provincial officials; his writings refer to their "caprice and jealousy," [19] which he wished to offset with a strengthened "Chinese Executive." [20] He supported the flotilla scheme, as he knew it, as a lever for this broad policy.

But of course the Lay-Osborn agreement was beyond the pale to Prince Kung, who throughout had been consulting with Liang-chiang governor-general Tseng Kuo-fan. Tseng was to man the boats with his own Hunan "braves" (although Peking preferred mixed crews not exclusively loyal to Tseng) and use them as he saw fit, with no upstart foreign hindrance. Prince Kung was adamant about putting the ships under Tseng's control, and remained so even when Lay abandoned his agreement with Osborn and sought only to ensure that the fleet would be at the disposal of the Tsungli Yamen itself. Late in 1863, the ships had to be returned to England.

The point is not that centralization might have been effected by a Lay-Osborn tour de force, but that throughout this sorry episode the Tsungli Yamen, while handling all of the negotiations, had no intention of "standing forth" as a director of foreign policy or of naval development. Technical innovation was started, for during these years Tseng Kuo-fan bought two

[19] British Parliamentary Papers: "Correspondence Respecting the Fitting Out, Dispatching to China, and Ultimate Withdrawal, of the Anglo-Chinese Fleet under the Command of Captain Sherard Osborn; and the Dismissal of Mr. Lay from the Chief Inspectorate of Customs" (1864), p. 21, Bruce to Russell, November 19, 1863.

[20] British Parliamentary Papers: "Further Papers Relating to the Rebellion in China" (1863), p. 146. Bruce to Kuper, November 22, 1862; "Extract of a Despatch from Sir Frederick Bruce Respecting Maintenance of Treaty Rights in China" (1864), Bruce to Russell, June 12, 1863.

steamers and even had a small one built by his own men. But the "ancient system of thrusting the responsibility upon the provincial authorities" (the phrase is from Osborn's fretful summary) [21] was, if anything, strengthened after the Taiping Rebellion, for, in relying on men like Tseng to put it down, the dynasty was forced to allow them to adjoin high provincial office with a kind of personal military power which had no regular precedent. Angry though some Englishmen might be about it, it was to be these "fat mandarins" who were to see to things. [22]

Men like Tseng, Tso, and Li undertook military innovations in order to protect the Confucian system, which they had just saved from the loathsome pseudo-Christianity of the Taipings. In 1866 Tso Tsung-t'ang founded the Foochow (Ma-wei) Navy Yard, and by 1874, when the yard's French director had fulfilled his contract, fifteen steam warships had been built. These wooden steamers ranged from the 1,393-ton, twelve-gun *Yang Wu* to the 515-ton, three-gun *Mei Yün*. This modern fleet was under the direction of Shen Pao-chen, the dockyard's first superintendent, who held the rank of imperial commissioner.

But the modern Foochow ships were not joined in a single squadron for long. As they were built, maintenance bills grew apace, and some of the ships were sent to other provinces to distribute these daily costs. In a differently organized polity, this dispersal would not have affected the integrity of the fleet. But Shen Pao-chen encountered peculiar problems. For example, in 1873 he felt that two of the young Chinese naval officers just trained at the English-run naval academy at the dockyard were ready for command. Heretofore China's few modern ships had been captained by men imported from the old water forces. Now he assigned the newly graduated cadets Chang Ch'eng and Lü Han respectively to the *Hai Tung Yün,* a ship purchased by a Fukien official in 1869, and the *Ch'ang Sheng,* another old steamer purchased by Tso Tsung-t'ang in 1865 when he was in Fukien. Still preferring water force captains for his newer Foochow-built ships, Shen planned at the time to give the 1,200-ton *Chi An,* then building, to Wu Shih-chung, master of the just-

---

[21] "Anglo-Chinese Fleet," p. 16, Osborn to Admiralty, November 20, 1863.
[22] Phrase used in editorial in London *Times,* March 5, 1863.

launched *Fei Yün*. Wu's berth in *Fei Yün* was to be filled by his first officer, Lin Wen-ho, also ex-water force. But it was more easily planned than done. The *Fei Yün* had been sent to Shantung to distribute maintenance costs, and that province refused to allow the change in command. Shen then sought the captain of the Foochow-built *An Lan*, Lü Wen-ch'ing, formerly of the water force, for the *Chi An*. But the *An Lan*, by the same token, was claimed by Kwangtung, and Shen was frustrated again. At last for the *Chi An* he took yet another water force man, Cheng Yu, from the much smaller Foochow-built ship *Ching Yüan;* Shen gave this last ship, still under his own direct command, to Chang Ch'eng, although she had been launched only the year before and was much newer than the *Hai Tung Yün*, which Chang captained only briefly. The *Hai Tung Yün* then passed to Yeh Fu, another graduated cadet. Evidently Lü Han took the *Ch'ang Sheng*.[23] Only in the assignment of Lü Han was Shen able to exercise his judgment as to the optimum use of the scanty naval manpower available to him. There was a shortage of men, but the bigger obstruction was the way in which the fleet had been broken up.

The crippling contradiction between potential modern naval strength and actual fleet organization may clearly be seen in the crisis between China and Japan in the early 1870's. The dispute concerned whether some Ryūkyū islanders, killed by Taiwanese aborigines in 1871, were Japanese or Chinese subjects, and, indeed, whether or not China was responsible for the Taiwanese miscreants. Japan claimed the Ryūkyūs and demanded compensation. In 1874, tiring of Chinese vacillation (and seeking an outlet for restless dispossessed samurai), the Japanese launched an expedition to Taiwan to punish the aborigines themselves. Lo Ta-ch'un, the Fukien general, reported "twenty-six or twenty-seven" Japanese steam warships.[24] In fact, however, Japan had two ironclads, rather than the nine or ten imagined by Lo; according to a report of July 5, 1874, in the *North China Daily News*, one was "old and completely unseaworthy" and the other

[23] Reports by Shen in *IWSM:TC*, 91. 33b–35b; *Ch'uan-cheng tsou-yi hui-pien* [Memorials on the Foochow Dockyard], comp. in part by Tso Tsung-t'ang, 54 *chüan* in 22 *ts'e* (last entry dated 1902; hereafter cited as *CCTY*), 9. 20a–b.
[24] *IWSM:TC*, 95. 14b–19.

was laid up for boiler repairs. Japan's total modern navy, no older than China's, numbered only seventeen ships with a gross tonnage of about 14,000. For the Formosa venture the Japanese used three steamers carrying about 3,600 men. Shen himself at one point doubted if these steamers were a match for Chinese ships.[25] The newspaper account cited above counted twenty-one modern ships for China, most of them built at the Foochow yard and in the 1,000-ton class. The correspondent was convinced that "the Chinese Navy is probably well able to cope with the Japanese." Quite probably it was.

But there was one error in these calculations: China's ships could not be added up in a single column. There were several fleets. China's modern naval ships, whether built at the Foochow yard or the Kiangnan Arsenal, or purchased, were partly at the disposal of Shen Pao-chen, partly in the fleet of the Canton governor-general, and partly in that of the southern commissioner at Nanking, Li Tsung-hsi. Li's opposite number, the northern commissioner at Tientsin, Li Hung-chang, had some steam merchantmen. We might expect that the Taiwan crisis would have fallen under the see of the southern commissioner, but it was Li Hung-chang who recommended in May, 1874, that Shen Pao-chen be given special authority to gather a fleet and repel the Japanese invaders of Formosa. Shen was given power to requisition ships from neighboring provinces and started to collect a fleet.

In several communications to Peking Shen spoke of nineteen ships scattered from Amoy to Newchwang. He planned to use sixteen of them, including two from the Nanking fleet, and some of Li Hung-chang's carriers. He recommended that two ironclads be purchased as well. Yet only late in September was he able to report that seven steamers had lifted some 6,500 of Li Hung-chang's Anhwei Army troops to the Pescadores and that another battalion of Hupeh men was enroute. By November, 10,000 Chinese troops had landed,[26] but nearly six months had intervened

[25] Statement in report of June 4, 1874, *CCTY*, 10. 1–5.
[26] Reports in September and October, 1874: *CCTY*, 10. 17a–b; *IWSM:TC*, 97. 19–24; *Fu-chou ch'uan-ch'ang* [The Foochow Dockyard], 2 vols., in *Hai-fang tang* [Files on Maritime Defense], ed. Kuo T'ing-yi *et al.* (Taiwan, 1957; hereafter cited as *HFT:FCCC*), I, 525–527.

between Shen's assignment and this muster, and by that time the negotiators in Peking had settled the matter. Although a recent study concludes that China won a diplomatic victory over Japan in 1874, Article III of the October 31 agreement obligated China to pay "a certain sum to compensate the families of the shipwrecked Japanese who were murdered." It would thus appear that China conceded one major substantive matter in the protracted dispute. It is true that Japan did not take Taiwan, but this was due more to the wiliness of Wen-hsiang, coupled with foreign reluctance to see the crisis go too far, than to Shen's show of force.[27] At least the following contemporary comment is, in retrospect, misleading: "The possession of a respectable fleet of war steamers enabled the Chinese government to act with becoming dignity in the difficult affair of Formosa. . . ."[28]

To say that by the mid-1870's nothing had changed in the organization of the empire would be untrue. The growth in the power of Li Hung-chang cannot be ignored.[29] That he held one of his principal posts, that of northern commissioner, for twenty-five years is proof of his unprecedented sway. After 1875, his interest in naval reform was heightened, and he began to buy foreign-built warships. Li, whose political rivals included the court itself, interested himself after the Taiwan crisis in naval reorganization. In 1874 Ting Jih-ch'ang, a partisan of Li's, proposed a three-way division of the coast, with three sixteen-ship fleets based respectively on Tientsin, Woosung, and Amoy. Each fleet would have its own admiral and would meet with the other fleets for regular joint maneuvers. The governor of Shantung proposed that Li Hung-chang, P'eng Yü-lin, and Shen Pao-chen be the three admirals.[30] Li also backed the idea. To divide the coast into three parts rather than two would suit him, for he held office in the north and yet still enjoyed great influence in the

[27] Sophia Su-fei Yen, *Taiwan in China's Foreign Relations, 1836–1874* (Shoe String Press, 1965), p. 282 (on October 31 settlement); p. 303 (on China's victory over Japan).

[28] Cyprian A. G. Bridge (Capt., R. N.), "The Revival of the Warlike Powers of China," *Frazer's Magazine* (June, 1879), p. 788.

[29] Spector, *Li Hung-chang,* is a detailed study devoted entirely to Li's political and military power.

[30] Memorial of Chang Chao-tung, governor of Kwangtung, enclosing Ting's suggestion, *IWSM:TC,* 98. 23b–27; for Wen Ping, governor of Shantung, see *IWSM:TC,* 98. 31–34.

Liang-chiang region, where he had been governor-general and where he still kept units of his Anhwei Army; thus he might in fact control both the Tientsin and the Woosung admiralships.[31] But the court in 1875 confirmed the older northern-southern commissioner system, although it did assign to Li Hung-chang the concurrent responsibility for the defense of the northern coast. The two-way system was further buttressed in 1875 when Peking established a sea defense fund, to be based on customs remissions from the maritime provinces and divided annually between the southern and northern commissioners. Late in the 1870's Shen Pao-chen proposed that the northern commissioner be given the whole fund until he had built up a sufficient fleet; then the southern commissioner should receive the entire fund in his turn. The request was denied.[32] In 1879, the court proposed that Robert Hart be made naval chief, but Li and Shen blocked the move. In 1883, Hart was again offered such a post; again nothing came of it, although Hart did approve of the idea of setting up a central naval directorate and proposed that Prince Ch'un, the father of the Kuang-hsü emperor, be placed at its head.[33] In 1884, Li himself once again urged the Tsungli Yamen to set up a one-man naval command, and, while acknowledging the political difficulties involved, Li nonetheless stated that he would be available.[34] Shortly thereafter Chang P'ei-lun (Li's former personal secretary) proposed naval unification, undoubtedly

[31] For fuller discussion, see Spector, *Li Hung-chang,* pp. 178–181.

[32] Hsien Yu-ch'ing, "Ch'ing-chi hai-chün chih hui-su" [A Retrospect on the Ch'ing Navy], *Tung-fang tsa-chih* [Eastern Miscellany], XXXVIII, 11 (June 15, 1941), 29–33, discusses the fund; for later comments, confirming that it was drawn from the forty per cent of customs funds remitted to Peking, see memorials by Wen Yü and Shen Pao-chen, January and March, 1877, *HFT:FCCC,* II, 724, 785. For Shen's suggestion, see Ch'ih Chung-yu, "Hai-chün ta-shih chi" [A Record of Important Naval Events], in Tso Shun-sheng, ed., *Chung-kuo chin-pai-nien-shih tzu-liao hsü-pien* [Additional Materials on the History of China in the Last One Hundred Years], 2 vols. (Shanghai, 1933), II, 327–328.

[33] On the blocking of Hart in 1879, see letters of Li-Hung-chang to Shen Pao-chen, Li Feng-pao, Tseng Chi-tse, in October–November, 1879, *P'eng-liao han-kao* [Letters to Friends], 24 *chüan,* in *Li Wen-chung-kung han-kao* [The Letters of Li Hung-chang], ed. Wu Ju-lun (Shanghai?, 1902; hereafter cited as *LWCK:PLHK*), 21. 9–10b, 11, 13b–14, 20b–21. On the 1883 offer, see S. F. Wright, *Hart and the Chinese Customs* (Belfast, 1950), p. 481, and note 72, p. 496.

[34] Spector, *Li Hung-chang,* pp. 186–187, for an interesting discussion of Li's circuitous argument.

thinking of his old chief, and Prince Kung favored the idea, supporting Li for the chief office.[35] But Prince Kung was cashiered in the spring of 1884 on the grounds that he had been unsuccessful in negotiations with France. China entered her naval war with France in 1884 with her fleets still in the old disarray.

With no coordination, provincial authorities had bought ships and arms as the occasion offered for a decade. Arms huckstering by foreign agents was enormously profitable; a London commission agent in 1875 bemoaned an order for 30,000 rifles which had gone to other dealers who had not refused to bribe the buyers and so made £50,000 on the transaction.[36] Hart wanted to bring all provincial orders into a single system, for they were all secured on customs receipts. He amassed information on the costs of rifles, naval guns, and men-of-war (British goods) and did serve as agent for a number of Li Hung-chang's warship purchases without commission, but he was never able to rationalize the haphazard provincial purchases. Li, too, wanted to systematize provincial purchases, and although he tried to arrange that all provincial gunboat purchases would be placed through him, he was unsuccessful.[37] Perhaps it would have benefited China if either of these men, rivals themselves, had monopolized arms ordering, for as it was huge sums were wasted in purchasing, for example, antiquated gunpowder or offsize ammunition.[38]

Another result of this disorganization was that even in China's four modern war fleets—those of the northern and southern commissioners, the Foochow dockyard, and the Canton governor-general—there was a variety of equipment that obviated any thinking about a common naval mission. This was true even in Li Hung-chang's single fleet. In 1882, he had about a dozen modern ships. Six were "unique" gunboats of British design, with

[35] S. Y. Teng and J. K. Fairbank, *China's Response to the West* (Cambridge, Mass., 1954), Doc. 34, pp. 124–145; and Li Chien-nung, *The Political History of China, 1840–1928* (Van Nostrand, 1956), p. 124.

[36] Wright, *Hart*, pp. 467–468.

[37] For Li's correspondence on such purchases, see *LWCK:PLHK*, 21. 18, 18b–19, 19b–20, 21; 22. 6–7, 9a–b, 9b–10, 11–12, March through June, 1880. Wright, *Hart*, p. 475, mentions purchases for Shantung.

[38] On duds, see edict in *Ch'ing-chi wai-chiao shih-liao* [Historical Materials on Foreign Relations in the Latter Part of the Ch'ing Dynasty], 243 *chüan* (Peiping, 1932–1935; hereafter cited as *CCWCSL*), 48. 16; comments on the problem by Tseng Chi-tse are in *CCWCSL*, 49. 12.

"guns of large calibre and high velocity, moved by hydraulic power, machine guns, electric lights, torpedoes and torpedo boats, engines with twin screws, steel rams, etc." [39] There were also two British ironclad ram cruisers, and four Foochow-built composite gunboats, with French guns. The cruisers were rated at sixteen knots; the gunboats, at nine—perhaps sufficient for harbor craft; the Foochow ships were given a maximum of ten knots, from which we might subtract two or three to allow for hard use and indifferent maintenance. Li also kept traditional water force units, although he probably did not envisage them as part of his modern naval team. The foreign observer quoted above ended his note on Li's fleet by saying: "Indeed, the material of this squadron is really complete, yet it is evident that in order to be really effective it needs an intelligent personnel and a thorough organization." [40] He might have added the word "standardization" to his list of requirements.

As for interfleet standardization and the condition of coastal preparedness, a memorial of the governor of Kwangsi written late in 1883 is instructive. He asked to have the Foochow yard send ten large steamers to defend the southern coasts. The steamers of Liu Ming-ch'uan, governor of Fukien, were "small and weak" (the province did have a few ships which were not part of the dockyard fleet); those of Kwangtung were fit for enclosed waters only (being mostly torpedo boats, which Chang Chih-tung favored). The complaining governor spoke of fire-raft defenses as well. [41] The literature of those years is cluttered with references to old war junks, decorated with calico for dress occasions, whose crews drilled with cutlasses and sword sticks or by "swimming about in bamboo lifebelts and howling." [42] This

---

[39] P. H. Clyde, *United States Policy Toward China* (New York, 1940), Item XXIII, "Shuffeldt's Indictment of China, 1882."

[40] *Ibid.*

[41] Memorial of Governor Hsü T'ing-hsü, *CCWCSL,* 38. 23b–24b.

[42] The calico-tied guns were noted by a British navy man, H. N. Shore, in the 1870's; see his *The Flight of the Lapwing* (London, 1881), pp. 60–61. E. H. Parker, *John Chinaman, and a Few Others* (New York and London, 1902), pp. 118–119, discusses naval incidents in the mid-1880's, including the cutlasses and sword sticks; the water drill is mentioned by a British consul at Ningpo in Great Britain, *Accounts and Papers,* "Commercial Reports of Her Majesty's Consuls in China" (Ningpo, 1873), p. 87.

brief catalogue of the absurd points again to the lack of central direction in China's maritime defenses.

An organizational shift of sorts was taking place. Although all of the coastal provinces had at least a steamer or two—Shantung, for example, had two gunboats purchased for it by Li Hung-chang—by the time of the Sino-French War, there were only those four modern fleets mentioned above which were worthy of the name. This limitation was a by-product of the high cost of steamers. The growing power of Li Hung-chang has been noted above, but this, hardly the product of rational administrative reform, sufficed only to protect what he considered to be his interests, rather than to advance some sort of "national" policy. By way of illustration, let us turn to China's failure to assemble a national fleet during the naval war with France, 1884–1885.

THE FRENCH AT FOOCHOW

French aggression in Annam started in the Taiping period. Although Annam sent tribute to Peking in 1880, it was clear that France intended to end the tributary relationship. There had been land fighting in Tongking between French and Chinese forces in the early 1880's. A Chinese victory (she was not always defeated) in June, 1884, led to a renewed French insistence on an indemnity, a demand which China had previously rejected. A French naval buildup on the China coast reinforced their negotiations.

In 1884, China had about fifty modern steam warships. Over half were Chinese-built. Of the ships bought abroad, fifteen were British gunboats with heavy ordnance; two were Armstrong cruisers, and another pair were German steel corvettes of about 2,200 tons displacement. Two of the last-mentioned four modern ships were in the fleet of Li Hung-chang, and two were in that of the southern commissioner at Nanking, Tseng Kuo-ch'üan. The Foochow fleet had thirteen ships, all at least nine years old, and, save for the two small American gunboats bought by Shen Pao-chen in the 1870's, all built at the Foochow yard. Coastal fortifications had been irregularly improved. Some showed torpedoes and mines as well as forts and sunken junks. Along the Min River, on the approach to the Foochow dockyard, were many forts, some repaired as late as July, 1884.[43] The twelve-mile channel showed concrete forts, some with steel armor and British and German ordnance, nearly impassable—but, thanks to Chinese indecision and disorganization, the French did pass it all, and the disastrous battle of August 23, 1884, was fought in the dockyard anchorage, *behind* most of the forts.

The Tsungli Yamen, after the dismissal of Prince Kung, took no lead. Local officials had wide freedom of action. Chang Chih-tung, governor-general at Canton, blocked his river approaches without Peking's authorization; Chang P'ei-lun, in charge of defenses in Fukien, preferred to wait for such authorization for a similar defense in the Min River, and never got it.[44] There were too many leaders. At or near the Foochow dockyard there were five men with overlapping authority: the Min-Che governor-general, Ho Ching; the governor of Fukien, Liu Ming-ch'uan; the Manchu commander-in-chief Mu T'u-shan, with his headquarters at the Ch'ang-men fort at the Min entrance; the dockyard superintendent, Ho Ju-chang; and Chang P'ei-lun, who was sent to the province as deputy for Fukien coastal defense.

The French intended to take the dockyard as a surety for their indemnity demand, and Li Hung-chang advised the court accordingly on July 11. On July 13, a slightly damaged French warship came upriver to the dockyard, seeking assistance. The "Army people" (Mu T'u-shan?) wanted to block the channel after this, but nothing was done. On July 17, Admiral Courbet came upriver in his flagship *Volta* and was followed in two days by three more French ships. They came up under cover of an international agreement allowing two nonbelligerent war vessels to make visits of this kind. France had not declared war. When

---

[43] *IWSM:TC*, 96. 22b–25b, memorial from Min-Che governor-general and others giving data on fortified places; Chang P'ei-lun report, about the same time, *CCWCSL*, 44. 1–3b; see also Capt. Chabaud-Arnault, "Combats on the Min River," transl. Lt. E. B. Barry, *U.S. Naval Institute Proceedings*, XI, 2 (1885), for other details as seen by the attackers.

[44] On Chang Chih-tung at Canton, see Young to Frelinghuysen, No. 38, February 11, 1884, *Foreign Relations of the United States* (1884; hereafter cited as *FRUS*), pp. 67–69, and No. 44, April 18, 1884, p. 96. On the attitude of Chang P'ei-lun, see *CCWCSL*, 44. 1–3b, August 13, 1884.

Mu T'u-shan insisted that the two-ship rule had been broken and that China should eject the "visitors," the governor-general disagreed.[45]

Dockyard superintendent Ho Ju-chang made his own plans. Nominally, the dockyard fleet answered to him, and he ordered the captains to prepare for war on July 22. Chang P'ei-lun on the other hand received a wire from the Tsungli Yamen saying that a "little defeat" at that time might later be recouped.[46] On July 20, Mu T'u-shan was ordered to resist if the French struck; around August 14, Chang P'ei-lun was authorized to destroy the dockyard if necessary, to keep it from the French.[47] About a week later Ho Ju-chang urged a policy of firmness, by which he meant delay in destroying the dockyard in the hope that help would come from elsewhere in China.[48] In the many communications which kept the wires hot between the first French arrival and the destruction of the dockyard on August 23, the several leaders were variously involved, sometimes reporting individually, sometimes joining one or more of their fellows. Chang P'ei-lun, Ho Ju-chang, and Mu T'u-shan were most vocal, but they did not pull together. We can see here a modernized version of the old system of personal commands, involving modern ships, war junks, troops ashore, and even a contingent of "swimming braves." Chang P'ei-lun later lamented: "In one province to have four military leaders isn't as good as having an army under one's self, when things can be done quickly, and without irregularity and delay."[49]

If the men on the scene were often at loggerheads, there was no intermediate authority empowered to pull them into line. Li Hung-chang was influential, but neither he nor Tseng Kuoch'üan at Nanking served as a regular channel for reports from the scene or edicts from the court—even though both of them

---

[45] For reports on these early arrivals, see Ho Ju-chang, July 19, 1884, *CCTY*, 25. 10. 11b; Chang P'ei-lun, August 13, 1884, *CCWCSL*, 44. 1–3b.

[46] Report by Ho, *CCTY*, 26. 12–14; for other details, see report by Chang P'ei-lun, rec'd. August 14, 1884, *CCWCSL*, 44. 9b–12.

[47] Order to Mu T'u-shan, *CCWCSL*, 42. 11, July 20, 1884; to Chang P'ei-lun, *CCWCSL*, 44. 4.

[48] *CCWCSL*, 45. 4, 5a–b.

[49] Ch'ih, "Hai-chün," p. 365, mentions the swimmers. Chang's lament in *CCWCSL*, 46. 12b.

were given special authority to effect defenses against the French or negotiate with them. The relationship of these two high officials to the court, to each other, and to the tense confrontation in the Min River is shown in the sequence of attempts made by the several local officials in Fukien to get naval reinforcements from other fleets in China to offset the French buildup, which was known to be directed at taking the dockyard.

The court assured the Foochow authorities on July 16 that if an emergency arose Li and Tseng would send ships.[50] Superintendent Ho Ju-chang assured his captains about a week later that the Nanyang and Peiyang fleets would send ships and asked "the Empress Dowager and the Emperor" to see to it. The reply was that no help could now be sent by Li and Tseng. On July 24, Ho and Chang P'ei-lun again asked the court for Nanyang and Peiyang aid.[51]

On the same day, the court received a report from the governor of Chekiang, saying that he could not spare a ship for the dockyard; he had only two. Peking then ordered Li Hung-chang to send two ships south. Here was the first direct order to Li. He evaded it, arguing his own need for defense against three French ships off Chefoo; Port Arthur, "hanging alone in the outer seas," needed cover as well. His gunboats were good only for harbor work and were, in any case, occupied. To Li, the north was more important than the south. Chang P'ei-lun then turned his sights on the southern commissioner, but the court replied that negotiations were still in progress, and that instructions would be sent when needed.[52] It was not until August 14 that the court ordered Tseng Kuo-ch'üan to send the ship *K'ai Chi* from his fleet to the dockyard, but Tseng in reply raised a smoke screen about morale problems and did not send the ship.[53] On August 18, the court

[50] Edict July 16, 1884, *CCWCSL*, 42. 4b–5.
[51] Request by Ho, *CCTY*, 26. 12–14; court reply, *CCWCSL*, 42. 11; renewed request of Ho and Chang, *CCWCSL*, 42. 19b–20.
[52] Report from gov. of Chekiang, *CCWCSL*, 42. 20; edict to Li, *CCWCSL*, 42. 20b, July 25, 1884; Li reply, *CCWCSL*, 42. 21b, July 26, 1884; Chang request for aid from Nanking, *CCWCSL*, 42 30a-b; court reply, *Chung-Fa chan-cheng* [The Sino-French War], ed. Shao Hsün-cheng *et al.*, 7 vols. (Shanghai, 1955; cited hereafter as *CFCC*), V, 447–448, July 29, 1884.
[53] Tseng report, *CCWCSL*, 44. 19a-b; court reply, *CCWCSL*, 44. 21, August 15, 1884.

predicted war and gave all officials involved the freedom to attack as they saw fit.[54] But another plea for ships, in which the governor of Fukien conjured up the spectre of rebellion if China were defeated in the war, elicited only a query from the court to Li and Tseng on the advisability of raising more troops. Chang was told that talks were still going on and that he should continue his "secret preparations." On August 21, Tseng Kuo-ch'üan was given sole responsibility for the defense of the Liang-chiang region. Li Hung-chang was told to order German guns, and finally, after another cry from Ho Ju-chang, Li was "firmly ordered" to send two ships. A like order went to Tseng Kuo-ch'üan, with the remonstration that these officials were not to be "province-minded." [55] Similar orders over the past month had produced nothing, and this one was too late, for the French attacked on August 23.

Chang Chih-tung did send in two Foochow-built ships which had for a time been maintained by him,[56] but his gesture does not change the fact that the dockyard battle was fought by the Foochow flotilla unaided—and that the flotilla was almost totally obliterated in about fifteen minutes and the dockyard destroyed. Some have argued that the telegraph served to centralize the empire,[57] but evidently more than technology was needed.

The eleven Chinese ships at the Foochow dockyard faced eight French ships. France had the advantage, for China had nothing like the 4,727-ton *Triomphante*. But actual fire power stood only in a ratio of about three to two, which was not an overwhelming advantage for France. Moreover, given the way in which the hostile ships were clustered, the fact that harbor depths limited the movements of the heavier French ships, and the speed of the tide which moved at about four knots, there was a chance that if the Chinese had seized the last-minute initiative the Foochow

[54] *CFCC*, V, 502.

[55] Appeal from Foochow authorities, August 19, 1884, *CCWCSL*, 44. 29b; court inquiry about troops, *CCWCSL*, 44.30; instructions to Chang P'ei-lun, *CCWCSL*, 45. 1b; appointment of Tseng and order to Li, *CCWCSL*, 45. 2b; Ho report *CCWCSL*, 45.4; new appeal for help and court acknowledgment, *CCWCSL*, 45. 5a-b.

[56] Report by Chang Shu-sheng, *CCWCSL*, 45. 28.

[57] Morse, *Trade*, pp. 41–42, holds that the telegraph tended to aid in the centralization of power.

flotilla alone might have won the day. Admiral Courbet, whose battle plans revolved around the tide bringing the lightened *Triomphante* upriver on the 23rd, was quite aware of his temporary vulnerability and counted on Chinese indecision to give him the initiative.[58] That it came about in the way he wished was due to the confusion in the local command.

There are several accounts, immediate and retrospective, of the last day or so before the French fired the torpedo which in twenty seconds sank the Foochow flagship *Yang Wu*. Perhaps the story will never be finally told. One reconstruction has it that Ho Ju-chang on August 21 was warned of French attack plans, but he kept the information to himself.[59] In another, it appears that local gentry sought out Chang P'ei-lun on August 22, but that he ignored them. Wei Han (a former construction student at the dockyard and then on its staff) was advised that the French were only biding their time before attacking.[60] Chang P'ei-lun, who noted bad weather on the 21st and 22nd, told Chinese captains that action would come on the 23rd.[61] We are told that on that fateful day, at ten in the morning, a Roman Catholic priest was sent by the French to governor-general Ho Ching with a declaration, but that Ho kept the information back and delayed informing the dockyard by telegraph in the face of gentry insistence that he do so. Chang P'ei-lun had only the starting gun as his warning. Ho Ju-chang had reassured Wei Han that Li Hung-chang still had hopes of the negotiations. Chang P'ei-lun sent Wei Han to the French fleet with a request to delay action—but the action started on French initiative when the tide turned in their favor and while Wei Han was in transit.[62] After the battle, it was reported that Ho Ju-chang had been told at noon on August 23 of a battle which would start at 2 P.M. (a reference to the tide), and that he informed Chang P'ei-lun, Ho Ching, and others, but argued that China was not ready and so sent Wei Han on his

[58] See *CFCC*, III, 548–549, for partial translation of Loir's *L'Escadre de L'Amiral Courbet,* in which the admiral made this point.

[59] Ch'ih, "Hai-chün," p. 366.

[60] Chang Tsu-keng, *Min-hsien hsiang-t'u chih* [Gazetteer of Foochow] (1903 ed.), p. 78b. Ch'ih's account is generally similar to this.

[61] *CFCC*, V, 523–525.

[62] Ch'ih, "Hai-chün," pp. 331–332.

futile mission.[63] Ho Ju-chang acknowledged the noon warning and reported himself that he tried to wire Mu T'u-shan at Ch'ang-men but that the wire was down.[64] Ho Ching also reported the noon warning, adding that as soon as the dockyard and Ch'ang-men had been advised the fighting started.[65] (Was the wire down?)

Apart from reading a roll call of most of the officials involved, we note certain contradictions, and charges by later historians of suppressed warnings. It is hard enough to get a single account of any crisis, but had there been a single local leader responsible for what went on, some of the contradictions might never have appeared; there would also have been a smaller likelihood of information held back. And the Foochow fleet might have seized that initiative which Admiral Courbet so desired. As for the French, they were surprised by their victory. Let the following eyewitness account say it:

When one reads attentively Admiral Courbet's report on the Min River fight, one thing more perhaps than anything strikes one—the enormity of the task accomplished from the 22nd to the 29th of August by the 1800 sailors of our squadron, and the amount of perilous hard work endured by this handful of men in such a short space of time. They were, indeed, at the extremity of an impassable road, before a hostile arsenal, surrounded by men-of-war, fire-ships, torpedo launches, batteries, and armed men; having behind them a narrow channel twelve miles long, lined with other batteries, commanded by heights where were encamped soldiers ten times their superior in point of numbers, and terminating in a much narrower funnel-shaped mouth, for the closing of which their adversaries had prepared everything. Well! After six days not only had our little squadron come forth safe and sound from this impassable barrier, but it had destroyed nearly everything: arsenal, men-of-war, fire-ships, torpedo launches, barriers, cannon of the batteries. The struggle carried on by it comprehended all kinds of operations likely to be undertaken by a number of men-of-war: naval action with cannon, against fire-ships and torpedo launches; bombardment of an arsenal; fights with batteries and against infantry; debarkations; shore fights against

[63] *CFCC*, V, 132–133.
[64] *CCWCSL*, 47. 1–4.
[65] *CFCC*, V, 512.

batteries and against infantry; destruction of barriers, and dragging of a pass—nothing is wanting.[66]

Li was ordered to send ships to a Nanyang flotilla being made up after the Foochow debacle to relieve the blockade of Formosa, and under threat of punishment he did send two ships (he was ordered to send five). But before his ships joined the fleet at Shanghai he redeployed them to Korea, where there was trouble. Li was saved by events, and by his power; his insubordination went unpunished.[67] The fleet which was sent after the French blockaders—it was really the pursuers who were pursued—was made up of Nanyang ships entirely.

LI HUNG-CHANG'S EFFORTS

The modern historian Li Chien-nung, in summing up the Sino-French war, writes that China lost it through "indecision" and the French won it by "sheer luck." [68] Certainly much of the indecision and the luck were products of the vagaries of China's organizational scheme. In this context, we might expect that the creation of a *Hai-chün yamen,* or Navy Board, which came in 1885 as a response to China's defeat, would have little real meaning. Tso Tsung-t'ang called for such an agency in his vale-dictory memorial, and several others added their support to this familiar project.[69] Accordingly, Prince Ch'un was placed over all coastal defense, to be assisted by two Manchus and two Chinese, the last being Li Hung-chang and Tseng Chi-tse.[70] Robert Hart

[66] Chabaud-Arnault, "Combats," p. 308.

[67] Edicts, including threat of punishment, October–November, 1884, *CCWCSL*, 48. 7b–8, 22; Li's report on his readying of the ships, *CCWCSL*, 48. 24a-b; arrival of Li's ships at Shanghai reported by Tseng Kuo-ch'üan, December 6, 1884, *CCWCSL*, 49. 22; Li reports on the withdrawal of his two ships, December 14–15, 1884, *CCWCSL*, 50. 9b, 10.

[68] Li, *Political History*, p. 121.

[69] Tso's recommendations are translated in Denby to Bayard, No. 119, October 16, 1884, *FRUS* (1885), pp. 178–180. See also *Huang-ch'ao cheng-tien lei-tsuan* [A Classified Compendium of the Administrative Statutes of the Imperial Dynasty], 500 *chüan* (preface, 1903; hereafter cited as *HCCTLT*), 342. 4a–6b, for Tso's memorial and one making similar suggestions by Chang P'ei-lun.

[70] *HCCTLT*, 342. 7.

was elated, seeing here a culmination of pressures of his own; even his old candidate was made chief, so that he exulted, "I kept the Navy in English hands." [71] The Navy Board was given charge of the sea-defense fund of 1875, supposedly four millions annually. But provincial organization was not touched. The new board soon degenerated into an agency for the collection of funds for the refurbishment of the Summer Palace, to which the Empress Dowager was soon to retire.

Li Chien-nung gives Li Hung-chang the credit for the formation of the board.[72] But as the board degenerated, Li, whatever his hopes for his new position in the capital, found that the board was increasingly a rival for the sea-defense funds, half of which he previously had expended himself for Peiyang coastal defense. The contretemps was partially resolved by the provision in the board's charter edict, which gave Li sole charge of the reorganization of naval affairs on the northern coast. Since Li in fact dominated the board, we shall follow Li rather than the ineffectual "admiralty."

In 1888, Li reorganized the Peiyang fleet, which then numbered twenty-five modern ships. His admiral had entire control, and no land official was to have any authority over a Peiyang ship wherever it might be. The fleet was divided into British-type functional units; this and other aspects of the regulations were to be emulated by other fleets. Provision was made for joint north-south maneuvers. If Peiyang participation in a Nanyang cruise were inconvenient, the northern commissioner would so advise his opposite number through naval channels; but apart from this exception the southern commissioner was enjoined not to avoid drilling his ships just because he was far away. Southern ships in northern waters would be under orders of the northern commissioner, and he would distribute rewards or punishments among them, while charging their maintenance to Nanking. The northern commissioner checked the itineraries of Peiyang ships. If a ship were to be sent to a treaty power or on a commerce-protecting mission, the northern commissioner would inform the Navy

[71] Hart to Pauncefote (Foreign Office), October 17, 1885, cited in Wright, *Hart*, p. 480.

[72] Li, *Political History*, pp. 125–126.

Board in a "communication" (the term signified equality between correspondents). Protocol was carefully delineated. If a
mission bore an imperial commissioner, the northern commissioner would report to the Navy Board and its parent Tsungli
Yamen, while bearing the expense of such "national" missions on
Peiyang accounts.[73]

The foregoing highly selective collection of Li's regulations
shows that Li wanted a nonreciprocal relationship between the
Nanyang and Peiyang fleets. The northern commissioner had
rights not matched by his southern counterpart; in time, the
disparity could be telling. Li could apparently send a ship from
any part of China, either in his own right or in that of a Navy
Board member, and yet for certain missions he could bear the
expense on his own regional account. This provision and that
whereby he could give rewards to southern captains and crews in
his own waters were hardly based on altruism. We can see how
Li planned to use the regulations to enhance his own power,
primarily as a regional official.[74]

In 1890, joint maneuvers were held in northern waters in
which Peiyang, Nanyang, and Kwangtung ships participated. In
1894, another similarly constituted review took place.[75] Although
Liu K'un-i complained in the early 1890's of Li's unprecedented
tenure of a single high office which gave him the opportunity
to build China's greatest fleet,[76] China was fortunate that it was
this fleet, rather than, say, that of Kwangtung, which met the
Japanese by and large alone in 1894.

There was some interfleet cooperation in 1894–1895. The
governor of Taiwan got two ships from the Nanyang fleet.[77]
Shortly thereafter Li was engaged in an undeclared naval war
with Japan over Korea. Three Kwangtung ships which had sailed
in the 1894 joint maneuvers were caught in the fighting, as was
one Nanyang ship. These few and small ships did not fare well in

[73] *Pei-yang hai-chün chang-ch'eng* [Regulations of the Peiyang Navy], 2
chüan (Tientsin, 1888); see in particular "Officer System" and "Ship System"
in *chüan* 1, and "Chain of Command" and "Inspections" in *chüan* 2.

[74] Spector, *Li Hung-chang*, p. 233, also argues that Li thought of himself
primarily as a regional official.

[75] Ch'ih, "Hai-chün." p. 336.

[76] *CCWCSL*, 84. 25–27, July 28, 1891.

[77] Reports by Shao Yu-lien in July, 1894, *CCWCSL*, 93. 2b–3b, 17a–b.

the crucial Yalu action of September 14, 1894. Two of them, we are told, fled; one of these, because her captain "kept such a keen eye aft," was driven to disaster on a reef.[78] After the Yalu battle, in a flurry of personnel changes and the creation of a new supreme war board, help was sought from the south. Liu K'un-i could spare no ships, although later he himself was brought north on a special military mission. Chang Chih-tung replaced him at Nanking, and he was ordered to send ships north.[79] Some ships did come north; the record is unclear, but, since they were returned to their fleets, they must have been dispatched *after* the Weihaiwei surrender in February, 1895, for all of the ships there passed into Japanese possession. Since the orders for help came in October, 1894, we can hardly take this as proof of a heightened naval coordination.[80]

That naval assistance to Li Hung-chang was largely inadvertent, and regretted, is shown by an anecdote taken from the sad end of the Peiyang fleet, after the fall of Weihaiwei and the suicide of Admiral Ting in February, 1895. The victors confiscated all remaining Chinese ships but one, the gunboat *Kwang Keng* of the Kwangtung flotilla. She was spared for the solemn duty of bearing away in state the remains of Admiral Ting. The captain of the *Kwang Ping*, another of the Kwangtung contingent unhappily present at Weihaiwei, went to the Japanese commander and pled that he too be allowed to take his ship away, as it belonged to another squadron which had taken no part in the war.[81] Comment would be superfluous.

We cannot argue here that centralized direction—or, more to the point, a concentration of fleets—would necessarily have won the war against Japan. Li's fleet off the Yalu was about evenly matched with the Japanese ships present; in fact, foreign observ-

---

[78] Inouye Jukichi, *The Japan-China War* (Shanghai, n. d.), sec. I, p. 42, citing *North China Daily News* despatch on the captain of the *Kwang Chia*. The phrase suggests journalistic license.

[79] *CCWCSL*, 97. 4, 17, correspondence in October and November, 1884.

[80] Ch'ih, "Hai-chün," p. 342, lists five ships which came north in 1895, but none of them were in the surrender of Weihaiwei.

[81] "Vladimir" (Zenone Volpicelli), *The China-Japan War* (New York, 1896), p. 300, mentions the incident; so too does Yuan Tao-feng, "Li Hung-chang and the Sino-Japanese War," *T'ien Hsia Monthly*, III, 1 (August, 1936), 9–16.

ers tended to favor Li. However, other variables were at work: morale, tactics, training, supplies, and so on. But certainly we may argue that an organizational scheme suited to the needs of a modern navy would have increased China's chances for a successful defense.

CONCLUSION

China's failure to concentrate her modern ships was not just the work of Li Hung-chang, or of some cabal determined to keep Li in his place. The problem lay with China's institutions. In this time of dynastic decline, regional forces challenged the central Manchu regime. But even a man like Li never gained the power to direct; he could only withhold. Had the relatively progressive Li overthrown the Manchus, many of his projects might have enjoyed a greater longevity and so, in time, may have partially reshaped the institutional structure. But Li, although not the ideal sort of Confucian we see in Tseng Kuo-fan, entertained no such ambition; he and his fellows had just defended the dynasty from the pseudo-Christianity of the Taiping rebels, and the dynasty stood foursquare for the Confucian tradition. Li would not have changed fundamental institutions, for all of his piecemeal innovations. And the political structure which he and his colleagues sought to defend with Western means was itself inimical to the effective use of those means.

We might hazard this seemingly contradictory proposition: the weaker the dynasty became, the stronger those inhibiting institutions became. Perhaps this was due partly to the peculiar ambivalence of Confucianism, which in a time of public decay could justify an exclusive concern with family and an indifference to the commonweal. Confucianism as a system never was threatened in its entirety. It was a system of public rectitude which provided for its own perpetuation in times of crisis by prescribed political action. Hence, the dynastic cycle.

The dynastic cycle, as understood by the Chinese, was powerfully suggestive. In its phase of decline, it generated the mood of "restoration," which was precisely wrong for China's unprecedented problems in the nineteenth century. Just when an experimental mood was needed, the rigidity long inherent in the intellectual tradition was strengthened. Apart from a few isolated people like Wang T'ao, no one called for institutional change as a remedy for China's numerous problems which were seen as part of something well understood—the decline of a dynasty.

The contradiction may be made all the more confounding if we add that even in a time of dynastic vigor it is unlikely that the Confucian system could have made the corrective adjustments demanded by the modern world. The proposition cannot be proved. But certainly China's officials at the end of the Ch'ing period were enmeshed in a hopeless dilemma, and we can see it much more clearly than they could.

PAUL A. COHEN

Wang T'ao's Perspective on a Changing World

ITH the unprecedented intensification of Sino-Western intercourse from the mid-nineteenth century on, a growing number of Chinese found themselves involved in radically new kinds of situations. Such involvement often carried with it a sharp challenge to earlier attitudes and assumptions, and the story of what happened to these over time is one of the most intriguing chapters of modern Chinese history.

In dealing with this transitional process, however, we must be mindful of certain pitfalls. For example, the urge to establish a point of departure which is clear and unambiguous may tempt us into taking an oversimplified view of Chinese tradition. It is possible, especially in light of the fact that harmony was a prized Confucian virtue, that the culture of traditional China was more harmonious than most. But it also had its share of rough edges and unresolved tensions, and in our efforts to trace the tortuous relationship between the past and a shifting present these too must be taken into account. As we move toward a more complex view of the traditional culture, we may discover, among other things, that not all of it was irretrievably traditional. Here and there, in one realm or another, strands may turn up which cannot meaningfully be characterized as either "traditional" or "modern," and we are likely to find that such strands, if they exist, have been less vulnerable than others to the pressures of time.

We Westerners are the beneficiaries of a seductive tradition of romantic exoticism which often draws us to those aspects of another culture which are most different from our own. For students of the Sino-Western confrontation of the last century, this hypnotic power of the unfamiliar is greatly reinforced by historical reality. For what, in fact, could be more different from modern Western civilization than the civilization of traditional China? Given this heavily weighted situation, we are obliged to make a special effort not to overlook those less visible aspects of the two civilizations which, without in any sense being identical, do nonetheless converge or overlap. Such points of convergence between cultures which in other respects are so far apart may be significant in at least two ways. For one thing, there is always the possibility that in them we have a reflection of basic human responses to inherently human—and hence to a degree supracultural—predicaments. For another, we are doubtless safe in assuming that, in areas in which the cultures of traditional China and the modern West have tended to overlap, the pressure on modern Chinese to abandon earlier habits of thinking has been weaker and the predisposition toward continuity (or possibly revival) stronger.

Wang T'ao (1828–1897), the subject of the present paper, was one of modern China's earliest transitional figures. As an individual who was acutely alive to the critical issues of his day and wrote prolifically about them, Wang can be studied from any number of vantage points. My chief concern here will be with his views on "foreign matters" (*yang-wu*), in particular interstate relations and contemporary history. A tentative effort will also be made to describe Wang's perception of the larger changes going on about him and his response to these changes. Lastly, with a view to exploring further the possibilities suggested in the foregoing paragraphs, I shall try to place some of the strains of Wang T'ao's thought in a larger temporal and spatial context.

WANG T'AO'S LIFE AND WRITINGS

Wang T'ao's career was unprecedented in Chinese terms. His failure to pass the *chü-jen* examinations in 1846 closed off, at least temporarily, the possibility of a post in the bureaucracy. Then, with the sudden death a few years later of his father, on whom the family relied for support, he was prevailed upon to take up work as an editorial assistant at the London Missionary Society's press (Mo-hai shu-kuan) in Shanghai.[1] In the winter of 1861–1862, after working in Shanghai for more than a decade, Wang was accused of furnishing gratuitous advice to the Taiping rebels who were then threatening the city and henceforth became *persona non grata* to the Manchu regime.[2] On escaping to Hong Kong (with British help) he found employment aiding James Legge in the translation of the Chinese classics. When Legge went to Europe, Wang followed him in late 1867 and remained there (mostly in Scotland) for over two years. Shortly after his return to Hong Kong early in 1870, Wang, now in his mid-forties, began a career as a professional newspaperman,[3] using his daily editorials to advocate far-reaching reforms in Chinese society and government and to stimulate discussion of Chinese and European foreign relations. Though much of his time from 1876 on was spent in other forms of writing, Wang's associations with the world of journalism in China and Japan (which he visited in 1879) remained extensive.[4]

[1] During his career, Wang T'ao worked closely with the following missionaries, among others: Walter Henry Medhurst, William Muirhead, James Legge, John Chalmers, Joseph Edkins, Alexander Wylie, and John Fryer. This group (all Protestant) includes some of the most active transmitters of Western secular knowledge to the Chinese in the late Ch'ing.

[2] Although Wang always insisted on his innocence, most Taiping scholars contend that he did indeed betray the Ch'ing cause at this time. See, e.g., Hsieh Hsing-yao, "Wang T'ao shang-shu T'ai-p'ing t'ien-kuo shih-k'ao" [An Inquiry into the Matter of Wang T'ao's Letter to the Taipings], *Kuo-hsüeh chi-k'an* [Journal of Sinological Studies], IV (March, 1934), 31–49, reprinted with minor changes in the same author's *T'ai-p'ing t'ien-kuo shih-shih lun-ts'ung* [Essays on Taiping History] (Shanghai, 1935), pp. 186–211.

[3] See Ko Kung-chen, *Chung-kuo pao-hsüeh shih* [A History of Journalism in China] (Peking, 1955), pp. 119–120.

[4] On Wang's Japan sojourn, see Sanetō Keishū, "Ō Tō no raiyū to Nihon bunjin" [Wang T'ao's Visit to Japan and Japanese Men of Letters], in Sanetō Keishū, *Kindai Nisshi bunka ron* [On Modern Sino-Japanese Culture] (Tokyo, 1941), pp. 52–100. The fullest and best-researched account of Wang's life is Wu Ching-shan, "Wang T'ao shih-chi k'ao-lüeh" [A Brief Examination into the Life of Wang T'ao], in *Shang-hai yen-chiu tzu-liao* [Materials for the Study of Shanghai] (Shanghai, 1936), pp. 671–691. In English, see Arthur W. Hummel, ed., *Eminent Chinese of the Ch'ing Period, 1644–1912*, 2 vols. (Washington, D.C., 1943, 1944), II, 836–839, and H. McAleavy, *Wang T'ao: The Life and Writings of a Displaced Person* (London, 1953).

Even a cursory glance over the corpus of Wang T'ao's writings reveals a staggering range of interests and talents. In addition to doing lengthy commentaries for Legge on a number of the classics—Legge thought that he "far [excelled] in classical lore any of his countrymen whom the Author had previously known . . ." [5] —Wang published a volume of poetry, two volumes of letters, a compendium of tales about "singing girls," diaries of his trips to Europe and Japan, a collection of his newspaper editorials and one of miscellaneous short pieces, a contemporary account of life in Shanghai, and three large volumes of short stories which brought him considerable renown in his day.[6] He also wrote essays on Western learning, firearms, trade, and a variety of scientific subjects—some of these in collaboration with the Protestant missionaries Joseph Edkins and Alexander Wylie.[7] Finally, in the realm of foreign affairs and history, apart from his editorials and some scattered brief pieces, he compiled a detailed account of the Franco-Prussian War of 1870–1871, and also wrote histories of France, the United States, and Russia.[8]

[5] James Legge, transl., *The Chinese Classics,* 5 vols. (Hong Kong, 1960), III (The Shoo King), viii. See also IV (The She King), 176 ("Prolegomena"); V (The Ch'un Ts'ew with The Tso Chuen), 145–146 ("Prolegomena"). The original drafts of Wang's commentaries upon the *Classic of Songs* ("Mao-shih chi-shih," 30 *chüan*), the *Record of Rituals* ("Li-chi chi-shih"), and the *Classic of Changes* ("Chou-i chi-shih") are in the New York Public Library. None of the three was ever published. Wang's treatises on the calendar and eclipses of the Spring and Autumn period have been assessed by modern Chinese and Japanese scholars as a major advance in classical scholarship. See Tseng Tz'u-liang's introduction to the recent reprint of three of these treatises under the composite title, *Ch'un-ch'iu li-hsüeh san-chung* [Three Works on the Chronology of the Spring and Autumn Period] (Peking, 1959).

[6] For the titles and dates of most of these works (many of which came out in more than one edition) see Hummel, II, 836–839. Quite a few of Wang's writings appear never to have been published (see Wu Ching-shan, pp. 686–689).

[7] The work on firearms is entitled *Huo-ch'i lüeh-shuo* [An Introductory Treatise on Firearms] (1 *chüan*). Wang collaborated with Edkins in the translation of two Western works into Chinese under the titles *Ko-chih Hsi-hsüeh t'i-yao* [The Essentials of Science and Western Learning] (1853) and *Ko-chih hsin-hsüeh t'i-yao* [The Essentials of Science and the New Learning] (1858). With Wylie he compiled *Hsi-hsüeh chi-ts'un liu-chung* [Six Works on Western Learning] (1889–1890).

[8] The choicest of Wang's editorials were gathered together in *T'ao-yüan wen-lu wai-pien* [Supplement to *T'ao-yüan wen-lu*], 10 *chüan* (Hong Kong, 1883; hereafter cited as *WLWP*). Some pieces on foreign matters may also be found in *Weng-yu yü-t'an* [Gossip from a Poor Man's Window] (8 *chüan*), first published in Shanghai in 1875. The work on the Franco-Prussian War, *P'u-Fa*

A perusal of Wang T'ao's life and writings evokes the image of a man who, despite many novel interests and experiences, remained profoundly steeped in traditional Chinese culture and learning. Indeed it could be argued that it was this very immersion in tradition that permitted Wang to entertain certain highly untraditional notions without experiencing the shock of cultural dislocation. It was one thing to advocate change, even of a far-reaching kind; this had been done by Chinese reformers through the ages. But it was something else again to direct a concerted attack on tradition itself, a phenomenon that was not to take place in China until the present century.

Yet Wang T'ao does represent something new on the Chinese scene, and we must not overstate the parallel between his situation and that of earlier generations of Chinese intellectuals. The life crises which he faced—failure in the examinations, the abrupt death of a father, the charge of *lèse majesté*—were crises which could have been encountered by Chinese in any age. But the means by which Wang worked his way out of these crises were available only after the mid-nineteenth century.[9] Similarly, although there were Chinese in all ages who were critical of dynastic policy, their capacity to give vent to this criticism was usually strictly limited. Wang T'ao, operating through a new

---

chan-chi [An Account of the Franco-Prussian War], compiled with the help of Chang Tsung-liang, was first published in 14 *chüan* in 1873 (although it had been widely circulated in manuscript form prior to this). It was reprinted in Japan in 1878 by the Army Department and again in 1887 (Osaka). In China it appeared in expanded 20-*chüan* editions in 1886 and 1895 (unless otherwise noted, this is the edition I have used, hereafter cited as *PFCC*) and in a 4-*chüan* edition (abridged by Li Kuang-t'ing) in 1898. The histories of the United States and Russia seem never to have been published (see Wu Ching-shan, pp. 686–689). The history of France, *Fa-kuo chih-lüeh* (which I have still not been able to examine), apparently came out in a number of editions. Hung Shen claimed to have seen a revised lead-type edition in 6 *chüan* ("Shen-pao tsung-pien-tsuan 'Ch'ang-mao chuang-yüan' Wang T'ao k'ao-cheng" [An Examination of the Evidence on Wang T'ao, Editor-in-Chief of *Shen-pao* and "First-Ranking Metropolitan Graduate of the Taiping Rebels"], *Wen-hsüeh* [Literature], II [June, 1934], 1042). *Ch'ing-shih-kao* [Draft History of the Ch'ing] lists a 24-*chüan* edition (see Lo Hsiang-lin, "Wang T'ao tsai Kang yü Chung-Hsi wen-hua chiao-liu chih kuan-hsi" [The Significance of Wang T'ao in the Interchange of the Western and Eastern Cultures], *Tsing Hua Journal of Chinese Studies*, New Series II, No. 2 [June, 1961], p. 54, n. 46).

[9] This career pattern seems to have become increasingly common in the late Ch'ing. See Benjamin Schwartz, *In Search of Wealth and Power: Yen Fu and the West* (Cambridge, Mass., 1964), pp. 25–26, 32.

medium, the daily newspaper, and protected (whether in Shanghai or Hong Kong) by a new institution, foreign law, was limited in his criticisms only by his own cultural presuppositions. Finally, Wang's extensive exposure to the West and to Westerners, while it did not serve to uproot him, did serve to give him a perspective that was not accessible to Chinese of earlier epochs or, for that matter, to most of his contemporaries. The uncertain equilibrium which he maintained between this new perspective and the older Chinese assumptions that continued to exercise their sway is plainly revealed in Wang's writings on contemporary European history and the international scene.

Wang T'ao's observations in these areas, in so far as they are available to us, fall largely within the period from the early 1870's (when he first took up journalistic work and wrote the compendium on the Franco-Prussian War) to the late 1880's, his published letters terminating in 1888. Although none of Wang's editorials, essays, or letters is dated, in many instances approximate dates can be assigned from internal evidence. Nevertheless, in what follows I shall for the most part make no attempt to trace the shifts in Wang's positions over time. For my impression is that during the 1870's and 1880's, though he certainly embraced new positions at various points, he rarely discarded *in toto* the old ones, however contradictory the two might be in any given instance.[10]

MIGHT AND RIGHT IN INTERSTATE RELATIONS

The question of the relationship between morality and power was always an important one for Confucian thinkers. Mencius made a distinction between two kinds of power: (1) power which was derived from virtue and exercised in just ways (*wang-tao*), and (2) power which was grounded in brute force and exercised without reference to moral considerations (*pa-tao*). Both kinds of power could exist. But only the former, in Men-

[10] For a somewhat different approach, see Leong Sow-theng, "Wang T'ao and the Movement for Self-strengthening and Reform in the Late Ch'ing Period," *Papers on China,* XVII (Harvard University, East Asian Research Center, 1963), 101–130.

cius' view, was capable of providing the basis for a stable and lasting social order.

The Mencian view left a deep mark on Chinese attitudes toward power. But Confucian monarchs, for all their lip service to the ideal of government by virtue, knew full well the value of force. The resulting commitment to a Mencian idealism tempered by hardheaded appreciation of practical political realities found expression not only in the domestic arena but also in China's relations with other countries. The tributary system, within which these relations were generally conducted, was built around the Mencian belief that if the Son of Heaven were demonstrably virtuous, the countries on China's peripheries would spontaneously assent to Chinese primacy. But real power also played an essential part in the system's operation.

In the nineteenth century the tributary system disintegrated. This had happened before in Chinese history. But now for the first time China was confronted with an entirely different mode of handling interstate relations. In certain respects—for example the Western notion of a world of legally equal nation-states— Chinese adjustment to the new order proved exceedingly difficult. In other areas, the adjustment could be made rather easily because there simply was not that great a disparity between Western and Chinese conceptions to begin with. An example of this was the common ability of China and the West to appreciate the part played by sheer power in the *actual* ordering of world affairs ("world" of course being taken in a relative sense), despite the very radical differences between Chinese and Western conceptions of the basis on which the world *ought* to be arranged. Thus Western countries in modern times have abided by international law when it has been in their interests to do so, but have ignored or defied it when it has conflicted with national goals. Similarly, the Chinese worked through the tributary system when it yielded results but reverted to other means, such as war, when their political objectives could best be achieved outside of the system.

This dual strain in the Chinese view of power comes through with great sharpness in the analyses of the international scene periodically penned by Wang T'ao. The basic framework through which Wang views power is grounded solidly in the Mencian tradition. Yet running as a counterpoise to this idealism is a high degree of sensitivity to the operation of "real power factors" in the shaping of world affairs. This is revealed in his newspaper editorials, where he draws sometimes elaborate parallels between the political situation in Europe and that of the Spring and Autumn (722–481 B.C.) and Warring States (403–221 B.C.) periods in ancient China. For example, in arguing against the advisability of a Franco-Russian alliance against Germany, Wang writes (around 1873–1874):

The general situation in Europe today is no different from that which prevailed in earlier times in the Spring and Autumn and Warring States periods. Russia corresponds to Ch'in, France to Ch'i, England to Ch'u, and Germany [which Wang still refers to as Prussia, P'u] and Austria to Han and Wei. If Germany and Austria are strong, Russia cannot advance a step into Western Europe. Similarly, if Han and Wei had been strong, Ch'in would have had to be content with making a lot of noise in her own backyard . . . Thus the failure of the Six States [Chao, Wei, Han, Ch'i, Yen, Ch'u] consisted in their inability to strengthen Han and Wei in order to keep Ch'in in check. As respects the peace of Europe, formerly it rested on England and France helping Turkey to fight Russia [in the Crimean War], but today it depends upon Germany and Austria combining to withstand Russia. If France were to ally with Russia to attack Germany, would she not be sacrificing the very means of her protection? [11]

The wisdom or lack thereof of Wang T'ao's specific proposals in these editorials does not concern me. The really important thing is that in his combing of Chinese history for analogies he should fasten upon the late Chou rather than some other period. Although we have long been accustomed to think of China as a single country, a nation, there was a time, from the late Spring and Autumn period until the Ch'in unification in 221 B.C., when the Chinese culture area was not coterminous with any-

---

[11] *PFCC*, 19. 15b–16a. For other examples of comparisons between late Chou and contemporary European interstate politics, see *PFCC*, 17. 28a–b, 20. 36b; *WLWP*, 4. 6a, 24a, 26b, 27b–29b, 5. 13a; Wang T'ao, *T'ao-yüan ch'ih-tu* [Letters of Wang T'ao] (Peking, 1959; hereafter cited as *CT*), pp. 143, 232.

thing that could properly be called a Chinese state but was divided up into a number of independent political units, much as has been the case with the European culture area in the modern era.[12] The concept of a unified Chinese state did exist during these centuries, but the reality was one of a plurality of competing states with sovereign attributes whose relations with one another were expressed in terms of treaties, alliances, exchanges of envoys, and war.[13] Little wonder then that, upon observing the contemporary European scene, Wang T'ao was reminded of this early period.

And it was not just the existence of a multitude of sovereign states in the late Chou that made a comparison natural. It was also the fact that in this period there was no effective "supranational" restraint upon the behavior of the individual sovereign units. As Richard Walker has put it: "The moral code of the former Chou feudal age had meaning only when it added to the power and prestige of the state which claimed to adhere to it. The ritual framework of the feudal tradition could at times serve as a code of conduct for the individual states, but this code carried little weight unless power considerations argued in favor of adherence." [14] In short, might was the ultimate arbiter in interstate relations, not right.

Keeping this situation in mind, let us examine Wang T'ao's attitude toward the role of international law and treaties in his own day. At times Wang seems to attribute to international law a modicum of usefulness, as a means of justifying certain kinds of actions and inhibiting others. In the mid-1870's, for example, during the embroilment over the Ryūkyū Islands affair, he urges the Tsungli Yamen to use international law to apply pressure on Japan.[15] But there is every indication that Wang's underlying view of international law is one of extreme cynicism. Thus,

[12] See, e.g., the treaty of September 26, 1815, which set up the Holy Alliance and in which the signatories (the kings of Austria, Prussia, and Russia) refer to themselves as "members of one and the same Christian nation" called upon by Providence to govern "three branches of the One family. . . ." In E. Hertslet, ed., *The Map of Europe by Treaty*, 4 vols. (London, 1875–1891), I, 318.

[13] See Richard L. Walker, *The Multi-State System of Ancient China* (Hamden, Conn., 1953).

[14] *Ibid.*, p. 99.

[15] *CT*, p. 118. See also *WLWP*, 6. 6b–7b; *PFCC*, 5. 1b.

prefacing a criticism of the Western powers for not speaking out in favor of justice in connection with the Ryūkyū question, Wang editorializes: "Alas, the countries beyond the seas, as numerous as the stars in the heavens or the pieces on a checkerboard, all scheme to realize their private interests. The great dominate the small, the strong coerce the weak, the countries of others are annexed and their rulers mistreated. This goes on all over. Though there is international law, it exists on paper only." [16]

Wang's comments on the effectiveness of international law in intra-European relations reflect the same mistrust. Using the example of Russia's helplessness in the face of England's refusal to participate in a general conference on matters pertaining to the conduct of war, he generalizes: "When a country is strong it can dispense with international law or promote it, but when a country is weak, though it may wish to use international law, international law remains inaccessible to it. Alas, the world of today may be summed up in two words: profit [*li*] and power [*ch'iang*]." [17]

A similar pattern of thinking is evidenced in Wang T'ao's stand on the value of treaty agreements. These may be of some use in some circumstances, but at bottom they are distinctly untrustworthy. For "if one country is strong and the other is weak the first will not be willing to adhere to a treaty agreement forever, while if the first is weak and the other is strong the first will not be able to adhere to it over the long run. In the case in which both countries are strong and the treaty is not to the first's advantage, again the first country will certainly not be inclined to adhere to it indefinitely." Wang documents his point by referring to Russia's unilateral repudiation in October, 1870, of the Black Sea clauses of the Treaty of Paris (1856). These clauses, which forbade Russia to maintain a fleet or construct fortifications in the Black Sea, had been imposed on her after her defeat in the

[16] *WLWP*, 6. la.

[17] *WLWP*, 2. 3a. For another example of Wang's position that before a country can make effective use of international law it must become wealthy and powerful, see *WLWP*, 2. 5b. For a Communist assessment of Wang's views on international law, see Wang Wei-ch'eng, "Wang T'ao ti ssu-hsiang" [Wang T'ao's Thought], *Chung-kuo chin-tai ssu-hsiang shih lun-wen chi* [Essays on the History of Modern Thought in China] (Shanghai, 1958), pp. 43–44.

Crimean War. But that was a weak Russia. Now, Wang T'ao observes, Russia has become wealthier and stronger, enabling her to act with impunity.[18]

Wang T'ao's intense skepticism over the capacity of a "moral code" or "ritual framework" to act as a restraining force in a world of power-hungry sovereign states is one reason why he saw the interstate relations of his day, to some extent at least, through late Chou eyes. But I think there is another. We must be wary of focusing on Wang T'ao the "detached" foreign-affairs analyst at the expense of Wang T'ao the man. It is possible to argue that the analogy with the late Chou represents something more than just a cool perception of two seemingly parallel historical realities, that it is also, at least implicitly, a moral judgment against the West by a Chinese who is incensed over the injustices perpetrated against China in recent times.

It must not be forgotten that for the Confucian historian, as indeed for Confucius and Mencius themselves, the latter part of the Chou period stood condemned as a degenerate and politically immoral age, an age in which the *tao* did not prevail. This was the period which, through the shortsightedness and turpitude of its rulers, had rejected Confucius and Mencius and all that they represented. It was a period in which brute power was worshiped and moral power ridiculed, in which kings augmented their territories not through humane government but through military conquest. The general character of the age was expressed quintessentially in the rise to dominance of the geographically peripheral state of Ch'in, a state which, because of its militant anti-Confucianism and its glorification of war, came to be viewed by Confucians of subsequent ages as something very near to a moral monstrosity.

Given this highly negative image of late Chou political life, it seems fair to infer that, in suggesting certain similarities between the late Chou and contemporary Europe, Wang T'ao is passing

---

[18] *WLWP*, 5. 7b–9a. Compare Wang's position on international law and treaties with that of Fukuzawa Yukichi (as of 1878): "A few cannons are worth more than a hundred volumes of international law. A case of ammunition is of more use than innumerable treaties of friendship." Quoted in Carmen Blacker, *The Japanese Enlightenment: A Study of the Writings of Fukuzawa Yukichi* (Cambridge, 1964), p. 129.

judgment on the latter. This inference would be less supportable
if nineteenth-century China were included, along with the states
of Europe, in Wang's analogies. But it is not. Wang is of course
vitally concerned with the implications for China of the policies
and actions of the world's states. But these states remain in a
separate world, subject to separate rules. Like the late Chou, it is
a world which has been tendered the opportunity to operate
according to Confucian canons of political behavior and has
rejected the offer hands down.

One other point seems worth mentioning in this connection.
This is Wang T'ao's practice almost invariably of equating Ch'in
with Russia.[19] For if Ch'in was the supreme ogre in the Warring
States period, it was Russia which more than any other country,
in Wang's view, loomed as a dark shadow over the future of Asia
in the 1870's and 1880's.[20] There were of course real grounds
for making this analogy in that Russia also was situated on
China's periphery and had demonstrated for some time a distinct
and growing greed for Asian real estate. At the same time, one
cannot discount the possibility that Wang T'ao's view of Russia
was also influenced by associations of a less tangible and justified
sort, derived from an apparently long-standing Chinese tradition
of viewing the Russians as semibarbarous "man-eating
demons." [21]

The vision of the world which can be pieced together from
Wang T'ao's commentaries on contemporary interstate relations

---

[19] See *PFCC*, 19. 15b–16a; *WLWP*, 4. 6a, 24a, 27b–29a; *CT*, pp. 143, 153
(Wang states here that the countries of Europe also imagine Russia as a
"predatory Ch'in devoid of moral principles" [*wu-tao chih hu-lang Ch'in*]).

[20] See, e.g., *PFCC*, 20. 36a–37b (argues that England and France should, for
the sake of their own interests, help to make China strong so that China can
withstand Russian encroachments in Asia); *WLWP*, 4. 21a–23a, 23a–25a
(argues that China, England, and Japan—the three Asian powers—should
form an alliance against Russia), 25a–27b, 5. 11b–13a (discusses the English
policy of strengthening China to check Russian expansion in Asia); *CT*, pp.
232, 243 (proposes an intensive thirty-year program of "Russian studies"; in
regard to this, see also *WLWP*, 4. 25a–27b). A similar view of Russia was
conveyed to Wang by his Japanese friend Oka Shikamon in 1879 (see Sanetō,
p. 98).

[21] See T. A. Hsia, "Demons of Paradise: The Chinese Images of Russia,"
The Annals of the American Academy of Political and Social Science, Vol. 349
(September, 1963), p. 28.

is one in which justice counts for little and power for a great deal. What are the implications of this vision for China? Wang T'ao's answer to this question may seem at first to be contradictory. In the foreseeable future, China has no choice but to respond to the West on the West's own terms. She can try, through such dubious expedients as international law, to stave off further depredations at the hands of Europe and Japan. But this can at best be a holding operation. Ultimately she, like the West, must become wealthy and strong.[22]

Yet for a Chinese this could hardly be a satisfying solution in the long run, for how would China then differ from the West? Pertinent here is the double-edged nature of Mencian logic. The West, according to this logic, was unvirtuous because it had used force to expand. But, in a world so manifestly unresponsive to Chinese monarchical virtue, there was the nagging inference, in terms of the same logic, that the Chinese monarchy might also be unvirtuous. Wang T'ao, if one excepts his flirtation with the Taipings, never to my knowledge openly advanced this suggestion. (In his mature years he was usually much too busy professing his loyalty to the Ch'ing in order to counter the earlier charges of treachery.) [23] But his persistent advocacy of rather sweeping changes in Chinese governmental policies and practices amounted to such a suggestion in fact. Here, it would seem, we have a clue to the question of how China would ultimately differ from the West. A thoroughly renovated China would be strong— as was the West. But it would also be virtuous—as the West was not. And this combination would enable China, which had started out by responding to the West on Western terms, to end up by compelling the West to respond to China on Chinese terms.

THE PATTERN AND MOTIVE FORCE OF HISTORY

Wang T'ao's image of a future world shaped by China is supported by his perspective on history. This perspective is complex.

---

[22] Wang's writings teem with references to wealth and power (*fu-ch'iang*) as China's proper goals. But, as a Confucian, he is careful to dissociate himself from the Legalist implications of these goals (see *CT*, pp. 111–112).

[23] See, e.g., *WLWP*, 5. 19b–21a, where he sings the praises of the reigning dynasty and condemns the Taiping, Nien, and other rebellious movements.

But I suspect that its complexity is conditioned as much by the problematic nature of traditional Chinese attitudes towards history as by the unprecedented problems which faced a man like Wang T'ao in the late nineteenth century.

The question of the pattern of history may be taken as an illustration. As was perhaps natural in an agrarian society, strongly conditioned by the seasonal rhythm of growth and decay, Confucian historians often viewed history in cyclical terms. The rise-and-fall concept was deeply embedded in the Chinese outlook, embracing virtually everything human. Change, from this viewpoint, did not consist in becoming, but rather in "an endless round of alternating, recurrent conditions." The concept of progress was alien. In a sense, the overriding purpose of civilized society was to arrest decay.[24]

The notion of arresting decay suggests a second view of change that had considerable currency among Confucian historians. This was the concept of history as a process of decline from a utopian age in the past. Logically considered, the cyclical and devolutionary views can be construed to be mutually contradictory, for the former denies the possibility of "upward" or "downward" movement except in relative terms, while the latter seems to imply a steady, nonrepetitive, "downward" flow of change. There were all sorts of ways in which these two views of history could be rendered less incompatible. Confucian historians, for example, might choose to see the world not as *progressively* degenerating, but merely as having suffered an initial fall in remote antiquity.[25] Nevertheless it appears that most Chinese did not pay too much attention to these scholastic niceties and were quite willing to entertain potentially inconsistent views without being greatly disturbed.

[24] John T. Marcus, "Time and the Sense of History: West and East," *Comparative Studies in Society and History,* III (1960–1961), 134. See also Mircea Eliade, *Cosmos and History: The Myth of the Eternal Return* (New York, 1959), esp. pp. 87–90. There were a few Chinese thinkers in the traditional era, such as Wang Fu-chih, who did enunciate theories of progress, but these were highly atypical.

[25] Blacker, pp. 158–159. Another possibility was to extend the time limit of the cycles and view all of history since the "golden age" as part of the downward swing of one long cycle. See Derk Bodde, "Harmony and Conflict in Chinese Philosophy," in Arthur Wright, ed., *Studies in Chinese Thought* (Chicago, 1953), pp. 27, 30–31, 36.

Another issue in regard to which traditional Chinese attitudes were far from consistent is the related question of how historical change occurs. Many, in the Confucian-Mencian tradition, would have agreed with the famous historiographer Liu Chih-chi (661–721) that man is the primary shaper of his own destiny and "if one must bring fate into one's discourse . . . reason is outraged." [26] Good actions, for those who took such a stand, produced desirable consequences, while bad actions produced results which were undesirable. The extent of a man's capacity to influence events varied directly with his standing in society. Hence the rulers of society were in a particularly strategic position. Virtuous rulers, by the sheer power of their example and by the enlightened policies which their humaneness prompted them to formulate and promote, would succeed in fostering social harmony and well-being, while conflict and disorder would ensue when the throne was occupied by men of inferior moral stature.

Here again we find a potential inconsistency. For if history is part of a larger cosmic process and if this cosmic process operates according to fixed, determined patterns—as most Chinese views of the universe seem to presuppose [27]—then there would appear to be little room for human beings to influence the course of historical change. This is not the place to enter into a discussion of this dilemma, which, though it has taken different forms, has been no less prominent in the West. The main point to be made, as before, is that numerous Chinese thinkers seem to have been either unaware of its existence or, in any event, quite capable psychologically of embracing both of its horns, at times assigning a large role in historical causation to man, at times laying almost everything at the foot of fate (*t'ien*).

Strains and stresses similar to these are also to be found in Wang T'ao's perception of history. But, while these may be perfectly plain to us, there is no indication that Wang himself felt them. Here I believe it is essential to make a distinction between the way (or ways) in which a man looks at history intellectually

[26] E. G. Pulleyblank, "Chinese Historical Criticism: Liu Chih-chi and Ssu-ma Kuang," in W. G. Beasley and E. G. Pulleyblank, eds., *Historians of China and Japan* (London, 1961), p. 145.

[27] Bodde, p. 21.

—his understanding of it—and the way in which, as it were, he wants history to go. If the former concern is the primary one, inconsistencies will presumably generate strains; but if the latter dominates, there is no reason why views of the past which are incompatible by themselves cannot be harmoniously pressed into the service of a vision of the future which is utterly consistent. Chinese society in the last decades of the nineteenth century was in the throes of a general crisis of unprecedented dimensions. Unlike many of his contemporaries, Wang T'ao sensed this crisis acutely, and it was extremely important for him, from a psychological standpoint, to be able to visualize a time when the crisis would be surmounted to China's advantage. Faced with such a transcendent goal, it is little wonder that he at times took up one position, at times another, clutching at every straw that could give some comfort for the future.

The natural starting place for a perusal of Wang T'ao's picture of history is his *Account of the Franco-Prussian War* (*P'u-Fa chan-chi*), based largely on Western newspaper accounts and written with the help of a Chinese colleague skilled in English. Initially published in 1873 in fourteen *chüan* and later expanded to twenty *chüan,* this was the work which first brought Wang fame as a foreign affairs expert. It was reissued periodically in the last decades of the nineteenth century in China and Japan and won the praise of Tseng Kuo-fan, Li Hung-chang, Ting Jih-ch'ang, Liang Ch'i-ch'ao, and a host of lesser contemporaries.[28] *P'u-Fa chan-chi*, as one of its prefacers points out, represented a radical departure from previous Chinese accounts of the West. The best of these, the works for example of Wei Yüan and Hsü Chi-yü, tended to be extremely broad in coverage and general in nature.[29] Wang's book was the first to subject to close scrutiny a single major event in recent European history. It was also noteworthy for being written under the explicit assumption that, in the wake of the events of recent years, the histories of China and Europe were now, for better or for worse, inextricably woven

---

[28] See n. 8 above. For Chinese praise of *PFCC,* see Lo Hsiang-lin, p. 47, and the prefaces to the 1873 ed. of *PFCC*. For laudatory Japanese comment, see Sanetō, pp. 61–62.

[29] For Wang's own evaluation of the works of Wei and Hsü, see *CT,* p. 105.

together, so that a major turning point in the European situation would necessarily have consequences for China.[30] To come to such a position in the China of the early 1870's took not only insight but courage.

Operating with this new assumption, Wang T'ao did not have to make constant reference to China in *P'u-Fa chan-chi*. The important thing was to present information about Europe, which, having entered the stream of world (Chinese) history, could now be regarded as a useful subject of study in its own right. The resulting product undeniably has something of the character of an "amateurish hotch-potch." [31] But in terms of its expressed purpose it was a resounding success. It literally teems with information—however ill-digested and disorganized— about the histories and national customs of France and Germany (including a translation of "La Marseillaise"), European political institutions and their day-to-day operation, the latest advances in military technology and tactics (such as the extensive use of charts and maps by the Prussian armies, the besieged Parisians' use of balloons outfitted with cameras for air reconnaissance, the military advantages of the telegraph and railroad), the conduct of European diplomacy, the events of the war itself, and so forth.

If this were all, *P'u-Fa chan-chi* would be of little more than passing interest to us. But Wang goes further and, particularly in his two prefaces (dated August, 1871), places the Franco-Prussian War in the framework of a more generalized perspective on history. In format this perspective is cyclical pure and simple. The war is viewed as yet another chapter in the unending saga of the rise and fall of states,[32] Prussia having risen from a condition of extreme weakness to send France plummeting from her accustomed position of strength. Nor was this the end of the matter: "Those who are good at probing the fortunes of nations [*kuo-yün*] do not take victory as an auspicious sign or defeat as an omen of doom. [They know that] upon reaching its most flourishing point [a country] begins to decline and that upon

[30] Wang constantly berates his contemporaries for not appreciating this. See, e.g., *WLWP*, 5. 14b–16b.

[31] McAleavy, p. 25.

[32] *PFCC*, first preface, p. 2b (also in *WLWP*, 8. 15b); *PFCC*, second preface, *passim* (also in *WLWP*, 8. 17b–21a).

attaining a point of maximum weakness it gradually gains in strength." [33] France in short would rise again and Prussia would once more fall.

With cyclical change in the political arena elevated virtually to the status of a natural law, does this mean that there is no room for man to shape developments? No. Here Wang T'ao implies a kind of division of jurisdictions. General problems of historical timing appear to be within the jurisdiction of Heaven and therefore beyond man's control. Thus the reason why hostilities between France and Prussia broke out just when they did was that Heaven did not wish France, because of a private grievance, to bring harm to China (*t'ien-hsia*).[34] (Presumably Wang is referring here to the Tientsin Massacre of June, 1870, which might have led to war between France and China had not the European outbreak intervened.) [35] The mind (or course) of Heaven (*t'ien-hsin, t'ien-tao*) also dictates the overall pattern of history and the basic ground rules of causation, in this respect superseding national fortune (*kuo-yün*) as an influencing agent in history. On the other hand, in the actual operation of the cause-and-effect nexus man's role looms large. For example, Heaven establishes the iron rule that immoral actions have untoward consequences, but whether to act morally or immorally in any given situation is up to man.[36]

The influence that the "actions of men" (*jen-shih*) can have on the outcome of historical events is best seen in Wang's analysis of the reasons for Prussia's victory and France's defeat. It was understandable that Wang should be intrigued by this question. Only a few months before the outbreak of the war he himself had passed through France and had been sufficiently impressed to write a history of the country on his return to Hong Kong. Prussia by contrast was an unknown quantity in China and certainly was not viewed as one of the major European powers.

[33] *PFCC*, first preface, p. 4a (also in *WLWP*, 8. 17a–b).

[34] *PFCC*, first preface, p. 4a (also in *WLWP*, 8. 17a).

[35] See Paul A. Cohen, *China and Christianity: The Missionary Movement and the Growth of Chinese Antiforeignism, 1860–1870* (Cambridge, Mass., 1963), ch. IX.

[36] *PFCC*, first preface, pp. 4a–b (also in *WLWP*, 8. 17a–b); *PFCC*, 20. 36a.

Consequently, when in the early weeks of the war Prussia rode roughshod over the French colossus, Wang T'ao was both puzzled and fascinated.[37]

In sorting out the many causes for the sudden collapse of French power, Wang of course gives extensive attention to the strictly military side—tactics, weapons, training, and the rest. Also—perhaps with the contemporary Chinese situation in mind —he reveals a profound appreciation for the political strength which Prussia derived from the unification process.[38] One senses, nevertheless, that more fundamental than any of these immediate power factors in determining the war's outcome was the moral element, power *per se* being less crucial for Wang than the manner of its employment. "Only through right," he states, "can [a country] exert control over world developments. How can it value might alone? When [a country] uses might to coerce people it is rare for it not to be destroyed." The fate met by France, Wang adds, is clear evidence of the truth of these words.[39] For France had relied on her preeminent strength to act so tyrannically that the countries of Europe came to look upon her virtually as "a predatory Ch'in devoid of moral principles" (*wu-tao hu-lang Ch'in*).[40]

Wang again touches on the question of the proper use of power in his examination of the internal policies of the French and Prussian governments in the period leading up to the war. It is here that the human factor assumes for him a place of overriding importance. For example, in discussing the Prussian government's effective utilization of Prussia's human resources,

[37] *CT*, p. 105.

[38] See, e.g., *PFCC*, 1. 24b–25b, 3. 18a, 6. 16a, 15. 13a–14a. Wang appears also to have been greatly impressed with German patriotism and the active identification of all classes with the national war aims. He cites, for example, instances in which groups of German merchants in such faraway places as Jakarta and India voluntarily raised funds to help the war effort (see *PFCC*, 2. 9b–12a).

[39] *PFCC*, second preface, p. 7b (also in *WLWP*, 8. 20a). For a similar Japanese viewpoint, see Donald H. Shively, "Nishimura Shigeki: A Confucian View of Modernization," in Marius Jansen, ed., *Changing Japanese Attitudes Toward Modernization* (Princeton, 1965), p. 223 n.

[40] *PFCC*, first preface, p. 2b (also in *WLWP*, 8. 16a). See also *PFCC*, 6. 16a. The application of the Ch'in symbol to France in this instance marks an exception to Wang's general tendency to reserve it for Russia.

he remarks: "If in the world something uncommon is to be accomplished there must be men who are uncommon to assist. Hence if a country is to rise it must recruit courageous military leaders to defend it and officials of undivided loyalty to shoulder the heavy burdens of state. In recent times the outstanding quality of Prussian leadership has been quite without match among the countries of Europe." Wang goes on to present biographical profiles of Bismarck, Moltke, and others, and concludes: "With talent of this order Prussia's rise as a nation was predictable. Even without her successes in battle, informed people could see that her national situation was steadily improving. Alas! The connection between men of ability [*jen-ts'ai*] and national fortune [*kuo-yün*] is no thing of chance." [41]

Was France then devoid of talented leaders? Not at all. Though she may not have been blessed with a Bismarck or a Moltke, she certainly had men of outstanding caliber (Wang particularly admired Thiers). The trouble was that Napoleon III either failed to use these men or, in using them, too often ignored their counsel.[42]

Napoleon III in fact comes in for a very large share of the blame for the French debacle. Wang recognizes him to have been a ruler of some ability. But he had one fatal flaw, that of loving to wage war, and this brought on "the depletion of [French] territory, the surrender of his army, the loss of his throne, and the weakening of his country." This flair for war however was not the sole cause of France's defeat. Deep divisions within the French body politic were equally to blame. Mencius had once asserted: "A state sows the seeds of its own destruction before others finally destroy it. It first occasions an attack upon itself before others finally attack it." In Wang's view these words were fully borne out by the situation in France on the eve of the war— a situation marked by growing popular discontent with Napoleonic policies and increasing dissension between ruler and ruled.[43] What a contrast to the steady increase in strength and

[41] *PFCC*, 2. 16b–20a; see also 4. 24b–25b.
[42] *PFCC*, 14. 7b–13b, 20. 36a.
[43] *PFCC*, 6. 20b–21b.

prosperity that had distinguished Prussia's development ever since the accession of William I in 1861! [44]

In *P'u-Fa chan-chi* Wang T'ao is to a very large extent concerned with the West as a world unto itself. Therefore it is quite possible for him to identify France as a declining power and Prussia as a state on the rise, Napoleon III as a predatory and oppressive monarch, William I as an enlightened and just one. As long as Wang stays within the bounds of an intra-Western context he can also be reasonably detached. Whether a war is won by France or Prussia, whether any given nation is strong or weak, is ultimately unimportant to him. Yet, as soon as Wang's concern shifts back to the world as a whole, as soon as the lines of battle are again drawn between China and the West, Wang's desires as a Chinese begin to shape his judgments as a historian. The West as a whole cannot be in the right, and Wang is sublimely confident that China in the future will reassert her supremacy in the world.

Two potentially incompatible elements in Wang T'ao's view of history are readily summoned to the support of this vision: the tacitly determinist cyclical conception and the voluntarist notion that man's fate (history) is dictated by his conduct. His position is better understood through an editorial, "Chung-kuo tzu yu ch'ang-tsun" (which may be freely rendered "China's Enduring Superiority"). In this piece Wang argues that the world primacy of China (by which he apparently means Chinese civilization) is a constant element in history. This primacy cannot always be asserted, for China is subject to the general cyclical alternation of strength and weakness, and, when weak, has been prey to the depredations of non-Chinese peoples. But a review of the long history of Chinese-"barbarian" relations which he provides reveals one fact which is supremely comforting. One foreign people after another has used its momentary strength to intimidate a momentarily weak China. But sooner or later foreign aggressors, like the waters of a flood, have receded into the

[44] *PFCC*, 2. 20b. Compare this with Fukuzawa Yukichi's interpretation of the outcome of the war (Blacker, p. 96).

oblivion of time, while China, imperturbable and timeless—a mountain periodically submerged beneath the torrent—has always endured. In the future, as in the past, wise rulers and worthy ministers may be counted on to come to the fore and renovate the country, at which point "the strong will again lose their strength, and the distinction between superior and inferior will be made clear." [45]

The latest representative of "the strong" (which, needless to say, has negative connotations in this context) is the West, and Wang T'ao never tires of pointing out that Western strength is doomed to destruction. This is so on general cyclical grounds because military technology is rapidly approaching the point where the total destruction of the human race could result. Since "every phenomenon upon arriving at its limit enters upon a return course" [46] and Western military science is obviously nearing such a limit, its development will of necessity be arrested and reversed.

Another reason why Western power is doomed—and this is the reason most often cited by Wang—is that, as we have already seen, it is used in immoral ways. Relevant in this connection is Wang's attitude toward war as a principal manifestation of power. As a patriotic Chinese reformer, Wang sees clearly that China must pull abreast of the West in general military capability and his writings are full of information on military matters.[47] But as a Confucian moralist—and, one might venture, as a human being—he regards all war as evil and is particularly horrified at the potentialities for mass destruction inherent in modern warfare.[48] Nevertheless, people being what they are, they have always engaged in wars—even sage kings have been forced to take

---

[45] *WLWP*, 5. 18b–19b; many of these same themes are also found in 5. 16b–18a. See also *CT*, p. 216.

[46] *PFCC*, second preface, pp. 5a–8b (also in *WLWP*, 8. 17b–21a). See also *WLWP*, 3. 17b–19a.

[47] Aside from *PFCC* and numerous editorials, see his treatise on Western firearms, *Huo-ch'i lüeh-shuo*.

[48] See, e.g., *PFCC*, second preface, pp. 5a–8b (also in *WLWP*, 8. 17b–21a); *WLWP*, 3. 17b–19a, 4. 10a, 5. 6a, 13a–14b, 16a. Wang's attitude toward war is well within the mainstream of traditional Chinese thought on the subject (see Bodde, pp. 51–52).

up arms [49]—and the problem ultimately comes down to one of distinguishing between just and unjust wars. In Wang's words:

When [a ruler] is bent on extending his territory and increasing his wealth, with only his own gain in view, it is in the interest of one party but not of all. . . . Even if his might is unrivaled, at length there will surely be an uprising of the people and he will be killed. When [a ruler] is on good terms with large countries and protects small states, with a view to remaining at peace with the one and to preserving the other from destruction, this is in the interest of all parties rather than only one. And if at length he encounters an external threat, even though his might is not great enough to repulse the enemy, he can vanquish it with right. For where right is followed the masses will spontaneously come to [a ruler's] aid. . . . Then, will he still have to worry about his army being too small? [50]

Clearly the selfish application of a state's power for purposes of extending its territory or increasing its wealth is not moral. Hence the whole process of Western expansion in modern times has been by definition an immoral one.[51] It is equally plain that, in Wang's view, history is on the side of the angels. Consequently the trend of domination of the world by Western power will have to be reversed if history is to continue to have meaning. Will the world of the future, then, be the same as that of the past? Is the Western intrusion *simply* the latest manifestation of an age-old cyclical pattern of "barbarian" invasion? Yes and no. The Western intrusion is similar to previous "barbarian" assaults in that its instrument is force and the intruder is insensitive to the Chinese view of things. But it is also significantly different from earlier intrusions because of the West's high and constantly rising technological level. It is, after all, Western technology which forms

[49] *PFCC*, second preface. p. 5a (also in *WLWP*, 8. 17b); *WLWP*, 3. 17b.

[50] *PFCC*, second preface, pp. 7b–8a (also in *WLWP*, 8. 20a–b).

[51] In one of his editorials Wang gives, as examples of recent European wars fought for unjust purposes, the Crimean War and Prussia's successive conquests of Denmark, Austria, and France; he compares these to the essentially just "wars" of the Ch'ing government against the rebels. Note that in this context Prussia in her war with France is judged to have acted unjustly. See *WLWP*, 3. 17b–19a. For a sampling of Wang's critical attitude toward Western (and Japanese) expansionist activities in Asia, see *WLWP*, 5. 14b–16b (the West in general), 6. 1a–3a (Japan and the Ryūkyū Islands), 6. 7b–9a (France and Annam); *CT*, pp. 121, 150–151, 153–154, 199, 232, *et passim*.

the essential underpinning of the West's great military power, and it is this technology which has for the first time in Chinese history made massive foreign intrusion by sea possible.[52]

Here we also have a hint as to what the future world will look like. In a certain sense it will be very different from the world of the past, for China and other countries, if they are to defend themselves against the encroachments of Western power, must accept the West's technology. (Wang, as is well known, was also an admirer of British political life, but he saw it essentially as an embodiment of the ancient Chinese ideal. Thus, if certain British governmental institutions were to be introduced into China, it would represent less a departure from than a return to the past.) [53] Wang T'ao is fully committed to technological revolution, arguing that China has undergone sweeping changes before (witness the Ch'in-Han unification)[54] and that Confucius himself, were he alive, would certainly "not cling rigidly to antiquity and oppose making the changes required by circumstances." [55] It may be difficult for us to reconcile this view of change with the simple cyclical view taken by Wang on other occasions. Yet I find no indication of his ever having explicitly abandoned the latter. In fact, in some of his writings the two views can be found side by side.[56]

Technological development thus plays the ambiguous role of being at once the cause of Western political ascendancy in the world and the means by which this ascendancy will eventually be ended. It also serves the related function of providing the material basis for the establishment of a single universal world order. Wang T'ao uses the term *ta-t'ung* to describe this order and has sometimes, because of this, been viewed as a forerunner of K'ang Yu-wei. But his "*ta-t'ung* thought," compared with K'ang's, is

[52] For a discussion of some of the differences between the Western and earlier foreign intrusions, see *CT*, p. 215.

[53] See Wang's note on the British government in *WLWP*, 4. 16b–18b (partly translated in S. Y. Teng and J. K. Fairbank, *China's Response to the West: A Documentary Survey, 1839–1923* [Cambridge, Mass., 1954], pp. 139–140).

[54] See *WLWP*, 1. 10a, 12b, 5. 17a.

[55] *WLWP*, 1. 13a (see also 1. 10a). For a fuller discussion of the variety of arguments used by Wang to justify change, see Leong, pp. 118 ff.

[56] See, e.g., *WLWP*, 5. 16b–18a.

extremely rudimentary; the fully developed concept of human progress found in K'ang's utopia, for example, has little or no parallel in Wang's writings.[57]

Since Wang T'ao is apparently unable to conceive of a stable and just world order in which there is a plurality of legally equal sources of authority, his *ta-t'ung* has a pronounced hierarchical orientation.[58] When the technological gap has been closed and the Westerners have lost their military and economic advantage, "by land and by sea, in fear and trembling, they will hasten in droves to come and share with us universal peace" (*t'ai-p'ing*).[59] Or, in a somewhat more bellicose mood, upon losing their superiority in strength, the Western countries will "all bow their heads in submission to [our] authority" (*fu-shou i t'ing-ming*).[60]

What is the philosophical basis for this China-centered world of the future? Clearly not technology. Technology (*ch'i*) can conquer geography and draw the world together, but "it cannot be regarded as the basis for the governing of a state or the setting in order of all under Heaven." An object of such grand dimensions can be accomplished only by *tao*, a concept which for Wang T'ao signifies the code of conduct natural and proper to all human beings. This code is unchanging in character and in a sense therefore lies beyond the pale of history. Yet it is coterminous with history in that "beyond man there is no *tao* and beyond *tao* there is no man." *Tao* is universal: "There is but one *tao* in the world. How could there be two?" Nevertheless, since the beginning of human history men have given their loyalties to many imperfect copies of the one true *tao*. And if there is any sense in which Wang T'ao may be said to hold to an idea of human (as distinguished from technological) "progress," it is in

---

[57] Wang's vision of a world unified by man's technological achievements appears in his writings at least as early as 1873. See *PFCC*, second preface, pp. 6a–b, 8a (also in *WLWP*, 8. 19a, 20b–21a); *WLWP*, 1. 2a–b, 11b, 12b, 2. 1b, 4. 23b–24a, 5. 16b–18a; *CT*, p. 208. On K'ang, see L. G. Thompson, *Ta T'ung Shu: The One-World Philosophy of K'ang Yu-wei* (London, 1958).

[58] As Wang puts it at one point: "If, in the affairs of the world, a supreme source of authority is not established, there will be chaos without end" (*WLWP*, 5. 7b).

[59] *WLWP*, 5. 18a.

[60] *CT*, p. 216.

his very un-Condorcetian vision of the gradual extension to all men of a standard of perfection which has already been grasped by some.[61]

Given this conception of *tao,* the political implications are fairly straightforward. Since *tao* embodies the loftiest ethical precepts, the world will be properly and justly ordered only when supreme authority emanates from *tao* or from that person or "country" most conversant with it. The term "country" is not entirely appropriate in this context, because the sphere of *tao's* operation could conceivably—and should ideally—be coextensive with the whole world of man. But however one chooses to define its limits, its center of gravity is in China. For *tao,* though necessarily prior in time to Confucius, finds its clearest historical expression in the teachings of China's Sage. Indeed it is identical with these teachings (*K'ung chih tao jen tao yeh*).[62]

If we return now to our earlier question concerning the character of the future world, Wang's *ta-t'ung,* our answer must necessarily be in the nature of a paradox. Plainly, in the lower, more mundane realm, where change has always occurred, the world of the future will be different—and radically so. But in the higher realm, the home of the changeless, where ultimate human values reside, it will still be a world which Wang T'ao can inhabit comfortably. For there the past will live on. And it will be a familiar past, a Chinese past.

BETWEEN CHINESE TRADITION AND THE MODERN WEST

In my opening comments I suggested two potential danger areas to be kept in mind as we reassess the fate of traditional Chinese attitudes and beliefs in modern times. One had to do with the nature of Chinese tradition in and of itself, the other with its nature relative to modern Western culture. In raising these considerations, I did not intend to imply that a good part of Chinese

---

[61] Condorcet considered the human race to be capable of "indefinite perfectibility" in all of its aspects (moral, intellectual, and the like). His view of progress, if one may speak metaphorically, is a vertical one; Wang T'ao's is horizontal. See *Sketch for a Historical Picture of the Progress of the Human Mind,* transl. June Barraclough (New York, 1955), pp. 173–202.

[62] *WLWP,* 1. 1a–2b, 11a, 5. 11a–b.

tradition may have survived the upheavals of the past century. I only wished to suggest that certain aspects of Chinese tradition, those which were not inherently unmodern or uniquely Chinese, have probably been better suited to survival than others and that in our search for continuities we should look first to these aspects.

This may be illustrated by a comparison of some of the "traditional" attitudes toward history found in Wang T'ao's thought with more recent Chinese views. If, focusing on the *pattern* of history, we conclude that formerly the Chinese tended to view history in cyclical terms, we can say with assurance that here is one area in which present-day Chinese attitudes are radically different. Perhaps in the deepest recesses of the Chinese peasant's mind, history continues to be viewed in such terms,[63] but China's leadership appears to be fully imbued with the faith of our fathers in progress. On the other hand, if we turn our attention to the question of historical causation, a fascinating study in parallelism suggests itself. Compare the following two statements, the first by Hellmut Wilhelm on the concept of change in the *Classic of Changes* (not far from Wang T'ao's view), the second by a Chinese Communist:

. . . man is in the center of events; the individual who is conscious of responsibility is on a par with the cosmic forces of heaven and earth. This is what is meant by the idea that change can be influenced. . . . such an influence is only possible by going with the direction of change, not against it. . . . No small role is thus assigned to man. Within set limits he is not merely master of his own fate, he is also in a position to intervene in the course of events considerably beyond his own sphere. But it is his task to recognize these limits and remain within them.[64]

Men are not slaves to objective reality. Provided only that men's consciousness be in conformity with the objective laws of the development of things, the subjective activity of the popular masses can mani-

---

[63] See, e.g., Hsia Hsiang, "Hsieh ch'ün-chung ti li-shih, wei ch'ün-chung hsieh li-shih" [Writing the History of the Masses and Writing History for the Masses], *Li-shih yen-chiu* [Historical Research], No. 5 (1965), p. 5.

[64] Hellmut Wilhelm, *Change: Eight Lectures on the I Ching*, transl. Cary F. Baynes (New York, 1960), p. 22.

fest itself in full measure, overcome all difficulties, create the necessary conditions, and carry forward the revolution. In this sense, the subjective creates the objective.[65]

My object is not to argue the case for the equivalence of these two views. Rather it is to suggest that their overlap is sufficient in certain respects to warrant further examination. The strong voluntarist strain in Chinese Communism may, as a recent writer has suggested, be partly inherited from Lenin, partly due to the impatience of an underdeveloped country to transform the environment overnight, and partly influenced by Mao Tse-tung's own love of struggle and drama.[66] But the predisposition to accept the subtle balance between voluntarism and determinism found in Marxism-Leninism may also have been encouraged by a similar polarity in traditional Chinese views of history.

Another current of traditional Chinese thinking found in the writings of Wang T'ao and frequently echoed in Communist pronouncements is what might be called the Mencian view of power: the notion, first, that true power emanates from just or right action and, second, that history is on the side of the truly just (the truly powerful). There is a prominent, if latent, note of "populism" in this view. For Mencius, Wang T'ao, and Mao, right wins out in the end not merely because it is right in some abstract sense (though Mencius sometimes seems to come close to such a position), but because just policies and causes command popular support and a ruler with popular support is invincible. Of course, the Chinese Communists, in proclaiming that they "believe in the people" and that "it is the people who will determine the destiny of mankind," go far beyond the populism —if such it may be called—of their forebears. Mao is no Mencian. But when he and his colleagues argue that ultimately "atomic bombs are just paper tigers," that it is "the people, and not one or two new-type weapons, who are really strong," [67] we

---

[65] Quoted in Stuart R. Schram, *The Political Thought of Mao Tse-tung* (New York, 1963), p. 80 (Schram's italics omitted).

[66] *Ibid.,* pp. 80, 194.

[67] *Peking Review,* October 16, 1964 (No. 42), p. iii; January 1, 1965 (No. 1), pp. 20, 22. For similar statements see the extract from Mao's interview with Anna Louise Strong, August, 1946, quoted in Schram, p. 279.

need not conclude that their thoughts are conditioned only by the Communist military experience of the past few decades or by the propaganda imperatives of the present. This whole strain of thinking, emphasizing people over things, right over might, and so forth, though revealed today in a more militant guise than ever before, has deep roots in the Mencian tradition.[68]

A noteworthy feature of the continuities or parallels referred to above, and very possibly a primary reason for their existence in the first place, is that they all pertain to realms in which—unlike, say, that of technology—the impact of the West in modern times has *not* meant an uncompromising assault on Chinese tradition. Views of history embracing both voluntarist and determinist elements in varying combinations pervade modern Western thought (including the Christian theology brought to China by missionaries); they have by no means been limited to Marxism-Leninism. Similarly, the notion that power must be exercised in cooperation with moral agencies if it is to retain history's backing is scarcely one that is unfamiliar to the modern West. Whether it be the Franco-Prussian War of the last century or the two World Wars of this one, it has been an easy matter to persuade the victor that victory was due not to force alone but also to the intrinsic rightness of his cause.[69]

There is no reason in principle why cross-cultural overlap, where it occurs, cannot be attributed to sheer coincidence. But I do not think that is the case here. I would argue that these points of convergence reflect a basic (and possibly universal) psychological need of human beings to have their history intelligible and bearable. In any event, whether or not one agrees with such an interpretation, it must be granted that the existence of overlap between the modern West and traditional China in so critical an area is likely to have had an important bearing on the chances of continuity between traditional and modern China in this area.

There are, on the other hand, certain traditional cultural patterns which seem to have survived in the modern Chinese synthe-

[68] For similar themes in the writings of Sun Yat-sen, see *San Min Chu I: The Three Principles of the People* (Shanghai, 1927), pp. 20–21, 76, 84–85, 99; Teng and Fairbank, pp. 264–265.

[69] Herbert Butterfield, *Man on His Past: The Study of the History of Historical Scholarship* (Boston, 1960), pp. 126–127.

sis despite radical incompatibility with Western patterns. Let us not lose sight of the distinction, elaborated with such sensitivity by Joseph Levenson, between the modern and the Western faces of the "modern West." [70] The West has forced China to become modern in order to survive in a modern world. But the degree to which being modern entails becoming Western is still a very open question. Thus one of the major themes of modern Western history has been the rise of nation-states and the corresponding conception of an international order based on equal sovereign units. This conception ran directly counter to the hierarchic-ecumenical traditional Chinese view and constituted a fundamental feature of the Western challenge in the nineteenth century. But with the reemergence of a strong, united China in the mid-twentieth century, there have been signs of the revival—fed by both Chinese nationalism and Marxist universalism—of the older view.[71] Specifically, it appears to be as difficult for China's present leaders as it was for a man like Wang T'ao to visualize a justly ordered world in which more than one standard of truth (*tao*)—and hence more than one source of ultimate authority— prevails. This echo from the past may yet prove to be an anachronism. Cultural monism may be an intrinsically traditional characteristic and, as such, incompatible with a fully modern outlook. But as long as the issue remains unsettled, we must resist the temptation to let our desires as Western moderns color our judgment as to the forms modernity could take in a post-Western world.

[70] See, e.g., Levenson's discussion of the changing character over time of Chinese opposition to Christianity, *Confucian China and Its Modern Fate: The Problem of Intellectual Continuity* (Berkeley, 1958), pp. 117–124.

[71] See Mark Mancall, "The Persistence of Tradition in Chinese Foreign Policy," *The Annals of the American Academy of Political and Social Science,* Vol. 349 (September, 1963), pp. 14–26.

MARIUS B. JANSEN

Japanese Views of China During the Meiji Period

EW areas of Japanese scholarship have undergone more sweeping change than the interpretations of the attitudes toward China held by Japanese in the Meiji period. Until the end of World War II, most Japanese historians saw the Meiji China specialists and adventurers in terms of the title of the Amur Society biographical compilation: as "Pioneers of East Asia," precursors of a future Japanese domination of the mainland. For at least a decade after the Japanese surrender this pride was replaced by unanimous disapproval. The accounts of the China adventurers were regarded as poor sources for history, infected by the dishonesty and self-congratulation that had blighted so much of wartime Japan's estimate of its mission in East Asia.

Within the last decade a new trend has become apparent. Historians are willing to reconsider both stereotypes, and they are able to see the drawbacks of each. A new objectivity makes it possible to see each as a reflection of the self-image of the writers who produced it. A new subtlety of interpretation has been made possible by the voluminous literature devoted to the modern intellectual history of Japan. And a new generation of scholars, largely uninvolved in their fathers' tragedy and increasingly unencumbered by their seniors' Marxist shackles, can treat the recent past without the ritual invocation of remorse and doubt that strained the tolerance even of Japanese sentence structure in the postsurrender decade.

The facts of the matter are more on record than ever before. The foreign office documentation is available for the entire Meiji period.[1] Autobiographical and biographical accounts of Meiji participants return to the publishers' lists. It even becomes possible to find publishers and readers for accounts that begin to resemble the presurrender themes.[2] There are in these writings endless nuances of periodizing and categorizing in an attempt to separate the permissible from the aggressive, the promising from the demonic. Japan is rediscovering itself and is startled to find that its nineteenth-century forbears wrestled with most of the themes of self, country, Asian and world order that have tortured the sensitive thinkers of our own day.

Treated in this comprehensive manner, a discussion of Meiji views of China would require examining the entire world view of a generation in transition between seclusion and expansion. It is possible here to select only a few aspects to indicate the nature of the problem. What follows is interpretive as well as selective; it summarizes less the 1960's view of Meiji views than the author's approach to Meiji in the light of that view.

NATIONAL SECURITY

The Meiji concern with China was first of all a function of its prior concern with Western power. The changing requirements and definitions of national power coincided with new measurements of cultural superiority which were designed to reverse the old Japanese notions of national hierarchies. An early pronouncement of the Meiji government had to warn the Japanese that "the ignorant opinion that foreigners are wild barbarians, dogs and sheep" was to be abandoned; "we must set up new procedures to show that they are to be considered on the same level as Chinese."[3] Within a quarter century, China-firsters

[1] *Nihon gaikō bunsho* [Documents of Japanese Diplomacy], now 47 vols. in 76 books, complete through 1914.

[2] See Ashizu Kazuhiko, *Dai Ajiyashugi to Tōyama Mitsuru* [Asianism and Tōyama Mitsuru] (Tokyo, 1965), p. 212.

[3] Osatake Takeshi, *Kokusai hō yori mitaru Bakumatsu gaikō monogatari* [Accounts of Bakumatsu Diplomacy from the Point of View of International Law] (Tokyo, 1926), p. 73.

like Arao Kiyoshi were fighting an uphill battle to persuade their contemporaries in Japan that China was as important as the West and ought to be treated with as much respect.

The first diplomatic efforts of the modern government were directed toward clarifying the national boundaries. The Kuriles, Sakhalin, the Ryūkyūs all fell within this concern. But the liveliest apprehensions, and the only real threat, lay to the north. Fear of Russia had begun in the eighteenth century when Tsarist moves alarmed Honda Rimmei. In the 1870's the opinions of Western statesmen like Harry Parkes and legal advisers like Boissonade all reinforced the Japanese dread of losing their northern territories to Russia. All the military estimates were directed first at Russia.[4] There were plans for colonizing Sakhalin, calls for immediate war with the Russians, and, in 1873, a readiness to postpone measures against Korea because they would profit chiefly the Russians. It is true that Japan's first negotiated settlement with a European power, Admiral Enomoto Takeaki's Petersburg agreement of 1875 which set the line between the Kuriles and Sakhalin, temporarily created a more favorable climate and even produced suggestions of an alliance with the Russians during the Ili crisis.[5] But for the most part the Russian presence gave rise to fears for northeast Asia, to the insistence on Korean independence from faltering Manchu control, to strategic control of south Manchuria to better secure Korea against Russia, and ultimately to war with Russia before the Trans-Siberian railroad could make permanent Russia's control of Manchuria, north China, and Korea.

If the West, and especially Russia, posed the danger, Japanese attitudes toward China could focus either on a defensive alliance against the West or on a demonstration to Europe that Japan belonged in a different category from the rest of Asia. Modernization at home and expansion abroad could establish Japan as "Western." Talk of an alliance with China began in late Toku-

---

[4] Yasuoka Akio, "Ni-Shin sensō zen no tairiku seisaku" [Continental Policy before the Sino-Japanese War], in Kokusai Seiji Gakkai, ed., *Nihon gaikōshi kenkyū: Ni-Shin, Nichi-Ro sensō* [Studies on the Diplomatic History of Japan: Sino-Japanese, Sino-Russian Wars] (Tokyo, 1961), pp. 18 ff.

[5] *Ibid.*, p. 26. The suggestion was Takezoe Shin'ichirō's.

gawa times. Advocates of opening the country, like Katsu Kaishū, used it with good effect to enlist men like Kido Kōin, Saigō Takamori, and Sakamoto Ryōma for the dream of a modernized Japan with a new mission in East Asia.[6] But tradition as well as changing patterns of thought insured that Japanese interpretations of "alliance" would run into trouble. Traditional thought, developed in a feudally structured, hierarchic society, postulated an order of development in which there could scarcely be true equals. The whole trend of alliance thought was moreover one of mission and meaning for Japan rather than for China. China had met humiliation at the hands of the West, Japan far less. Japan was undertaking her own reform, China and Korea were not. Therefore alliance almost inevitably meant that Japan should lead. Fukuzawa Yukichi in the 1880's coined the term *meishu,* a compound of "blood" and "leader," for Japan's role, and in 1887 Kitamura Saburō made explicit the significance of this by arguing that Sino-Japanese friendship could hardly be developed before a definitive test of strength settled the matter of which country would play the *meishu* role.[7] Only on the basis of this "rectification of names," it would seem, could the East Asian alliance turn to deal with the West.

The social Darwinism that dominated the intellectual climate of Meiji provided congenial grounds for assertions of Japanese superiority and leadership. In late Tokugawa times, Japanese travellers, in letters from Europe, expressed pleasure in European assessments of Japanese advance and Chinese torpor; but it was the ideology of Herbert Spencer with its assurance of the survival of the fit and the inevitable victory of the modern that served to persuade virtually all doubters that Japan, on the side of history and science, would lead. This conviction breathes through the transcripts of the talks which leading Meiji modernizers had with their Chinese counterparts: Mori Arinori with Li Hung-chang in 1875, Itō Hirobumi with Li Hung-chang a dec-

[6] See M. B. Jansen, *Sakamoto Ryōma and the Meiji Restoration* (Princeton, 1961), p. 165.

[7] For Kitamura's argument, see the excerpts in Akiyama Kenzō, *Ni-Shi kōshōshi kenkyū* [Study of the History of Sino-Japanese Relations] (Tokyo, 1941), pp. 642–643. I am indebted for this and for the references in notes 14 and 20 to Miwa Kimitada.

ade later, Itō with Li again at Shimonoseki, and Ōkuma Shigen-obu and Konoe Atsumaro with K'ang Yu-wei in 1898.[8]

Some advocates of alliance believed that a test of strength might have to come first. And all those responsible for national security had to consider the possibility that war with China might prove necessary. The government had all but resigned itself to at least a short campaign at the time of the negotiations that followed the Taiwan expedition. And as China's self-strengtheners began to purchase Western arms and warships and employ European military advisers, the Meiji military leaders turned to investigate the Chinese potential. At Yamagata Aritomo's behest, Katsura Tarō, then chief of the Western section of the General Staff, was assigned the job of surveying Chinese capabilities in 1879. He himself went secretly to north China in the fall of that year, but, more importantly, he saw to it that some ten officers were assigned to travel throughout China. He also saw to it that military men were assigned to diplomatic posts as military attachés. The report on the 1879 survey was prefaced by an introduction by Yamagata. The Japan of today, he noted, was not the Japan of yesterday, nor was its neighbor China. Energetic steps were being taken to reform the Chinese military establishment; English and German methods and advisers were being used, ship and armament manufacture was being speeded, and it was essential that Japan know more about these activities. This was especially so in the contemporary world of imperialism, since the great powers, particularly Russia, built empires with utter disregard for international law.[9] *Military Preparedness of Neighboring Countries* was put out in 1880, augmented and updated in 1882, and again in 1889. Each issue gained in

---

[8] For Ito-Li, see S. Y. Teng and J. K. Fairbank, *China's Response to the West* (Cambridge, Mass., 1954), pp. 126–127; for a transcript of Mori-Li talks, see Kimura Kyō, *Mori sensei den* [Biography of Mori] (Tokyo, 1899), pp. 84–106; for a reference to the Konoe-K'ang talks, see Somura Yasunobu, "Tairiku seisaku ni okeru *imeeji* no tenkai" [Changing Images in Continental Policy], in Shinohara Hajime and Mitani Taichirō, eds., *Kindai Nihon no seiji shidō: Seijika kenkyū II* [Political Leadership in Modern Japan: Studies of Politicians, Part II] (Tokyo, 1965), pp. 260–261.

[9] *Rimpō heibi ryaku*, [Military Preparedness of Neighboring Countries], Introduction, pp. 1, 2.

fullness and thoroughness of reporting. The Chinese banner forces and regular troops, their dispositions, bases, organization, weapons, and standards were reported with meticulous care. The intrepid scouting of officers like Fukushima Naomasa, who ventured alone into Siberia, later became material for romantic hero worship.

Yamagata's initial concern about China's growing strength seems to have been alleviated by the time of the French success over China in 1884. The question of China's strength was a lively subject for discussion in the 1880's, however, and the public press of the time took it up frequently. Thus the *Ōmei zasshi* of April 13, 1880, ran the text of a lecture by Azuma Sadanosuke entitled "There Is No Need to Fear China," which summarized and refuted the arguments of those who cited China's tradition, her size, and her potential strength. Actually, he argued, China was an empire in name only, and it would be more accurate to think of it as a league or federation of largely autonomous areas.[10] This theme persisted: as late as 1894 Fukuzawa editorialized in *Jiji Shimpō* that "there is no need to fear China's size," supporting his statement with a number of the same arguments.[11]

Even so, there was reason to fear that the West might be learning more about China than Japan was. In transmitting the first survey to his superiors, Katsura noted with concern that although officers and officials all wanted to travel to the West (he himself had spent six years in Berlin) no one was enthusiastic about going to China.[12] It is in this context that one can understand the praise for Arao Kiyoshi, who sacrificially chose to go to China in 1882, at a time when everybody wanted to go to the West. At that time Arao was dissuaded from going to China in order to continue his army career, but he went in 1886 after he had been appointed to the general staff. At Hankow he set up an ostensibly mercantile establishment and assigned his men geo-

---

[10] *Ōmei zasshi* [The Ōmei Journal], April 13, 1880, pp. 13, 14.

[11] Quoted in Somura, "Tairiku seisaku," p. 258.

[12] Tokutomi Iichirō, *Kōshaku Katsura Tarō den* [Biography of Prince Katsura Tarō] (Tokyo, 1917), pp. 388–389.

graphic sectors of investigation, thereby collecting information in areas that "even Western missionaries had not penetrated." [13] There was thus an air of urgency, even in the China investigation, that derived from fears of Western primacy.

THE NATIONAL AND SELF-IMAGE

In Meiji Japan there were several factors that strengthened the efforts of those who wanted to affiliate with East Asia. One was the recent emergence of sharply defined national borders. Did men who rushed about trying to promote the "regeneration of Asia" have a sharp image of the distinct national and historic units within that area? Some surely did not. The adventure of Ōi Kentarō in 1885, so implausible and unstructured as to suggest captious frivolity on the part of its chief, shows a failure to conceive of Japan and Korea as distinct units. Even members of the power elite who were doing the most to bring about a sharp national consciousness were capable of grouping Japan and China as "we." Foreign Minister Inoue Kaoru, in instructions to his representative in Peking, could distinguish only between the "we" of East Asia and the *gaikoku* of the West.[14]

Tarui Tōkichi was one of those associated with Ōi in the Osaka Incident. Three years earlier he had been involved in (and imprisoned for) the founding of the Tōyō Shakaitō. For years he hoped to find an unpopulated island near Korea on which a group of partisans might work out some form of socialism. But he was also determined to "revive" Asia, and when the French discomfited the Manchu dynasty in 1884 Tarui made for Hong Kong in hopes of working out a program with the Ko-lao Hui. When Tarui was imprisoned for suspected complicity with Ōi Kentarō, he had with him a manuscript he had just completed. It was seized by the political authorities, but Tarui laboriously

---

[13] Inoue Masaji, *Kyojin Arao Kiyoshi* [Grand Old Arao Kiyoshi] (Tokyo, 1910), p. 31.

[14] *Nihon gaikō bunsho,* XIII (Tokyo, 1950), 370. And, as Mushakoji Kinhide has pointed out, to this day the *Daigenkai* illustrates the usage of *ijin* with the sentence, "That man's not an *ijin:* he's Chinese."

rewrote it in *kambun* in hopes of having it circulate on the mainland. It was published only in 1893.[15]

Tarui's book, *Nikkan gappō ron,* advocated union of Japan and Korea as the most appropriate measure to stabilize the East Asian situation. After ritual recitations of historical relationships, Tarui focused on the state of the contemporary world as his main argument. As separate units, he argued, countries had little hope of preserving their independence. As a union, which he proposed to call Daitō (Great East), Japan and Korea could survive. In discussing the various ways of reaching union, he drew on the experience of Europe and explained that it was Europe that had perfected principles of nationality which had been known earlier in the East but were later abandoned. The successful nations of the West—Great Britain, the United States, Germany—all represented unions of earlier political entities. Not only was Tarui able to cite Western precedent and teaching and to reconcile them with the Eastern tradition and need; but he could identify writers like Mill and Spencer as English *jusha* and Bright as an English *ninjin* (*jen-jen*). Japan, he felt, had already taken the material wisdom, but not yet the political wisdom, of the modern West.[16]

Tarui's proposal was based upon the superiority of Japan's present state forms and policies to those of Korea. He advocated retention of both ruling houses and warned that unless his proposed union was formed Korea, where political conditions were deplorable and where no ideology of divinity and respect existed to moderate political change, would know a disorder worse than that of the French Revolution. The Ch'in dynasty had been able to overcome its enemies in antiquity because they lacked the wisdom to ally against it; the same situation now existed in Asia, where the West would devour countries consecutively if permitted. It followed that the Japan-Korea union was to China's advantage too, and that even a further extension might be possible one day. But Tarui noted the Manchus' tendency to try to

---

[15] Takeuchi Yoshimi, *Ajiya shugi* (*Gendai Nihon shisō taikei*) [Asianism (Outline of Contemporary Japanese Thought)] (Tokyo, 1963), Introduction, pp. 33–37.

[16] Tarui's text reprinted in Takeuchi Yoshimi, *Ajiya shugi,* pp. 106–129.

balance off barbarians and adopted a stern tone of warning; they should remember that they had only a temporary hold over the Chinese people, and that it was the Russians who were to be most feared.

The general tone of Tarui's book suggests an emergency situation. The West is allowing the East very little time. One might almost compare Tarui's suggestion with Churchill's offer to the French in 1940. Tarui's West is a demonic entity of an alien race, material strength, and complete ruthlessness. It is an engine of inevitable, destructive advance. Tarui's response is appropriately intense; he sees a war between the races as a matter of time and takes an expansive view of possible associates in the battle for liberation that lies ahead. Malaysia, the islands to the south, and of course China must ultimately join the stand of the colored races or be destroyed by the white.[17]

Government officials were afraid that Tarui's book might have an inflammatory impact on public opinion, and in any case they were less likely to take such an optimistic view of Korean and Chinese understanding. Ura Keiichi, an associate of Arao Kiyoshi, who although lost in 1890 in the course of making surveys of Russian strength in the Ili area was romantically reported killed in Central Asian and Indian revolutions, spoke of his hopes for a Japanese-Korean and possibly Chinese union to Soejima Taneomi in 1885. Soejima dismissed it as "idle student chatter" and warned that it was all nonsense. "What kind of a world do you think this is? It's a world in which strong countries annex weak countries, develop them and make them serve their purposes, and fight over them. To live in a world of struggle like this, we have to build up our military strength. Nobody without military power can stand in a world like this. No matter how civilized Korea became, do you think that the powers that grab what they want like ravenous wolves would let up? . . . The only way for Japan to preserve its independence for the long future is to acquire territory on the mainland. The only territory it can get on the mainland is in Korea and China. You students spout all kinds of nonsensical teachings about justice and rate the culture of Western countries as number one. The scholars limit

[17] *Ibid.*, pp. 128–129.

themselves to windy rhetoric and arguments about the way Western countries should stop their aggression and fighting. But it's different with responsible political leaders like us. To wage war in order to make one's country strong is the highest justice and loyalty to country and ruler." And war, Soejima went on, would be necessary, for the Manchus considered Manchuria vital to themselves, and Korea vital to Manchuria. There was no slightest chance that they would let it go without a fight.[18]

One solution, of course, was for Japan to acknowledge that Asian governments and leaders were probably selfish and short-sighted and to help their enemies to overturn them. It is striking to see how quickly the small number of Japanese in China and Korea turned to help political malcontents. They could do so with complete confidence that they were helping the people of the country whose government they were trying to subvert. Spencer's gospel of modernity had its own inevitable rationale. Unfortunately such efforts were uniformly unsuccessful. And the discovery that it would take longer and involve more than good will to topple neighboring obscurantist regimes hardened Japanese positions and produced an important shift in the 1880's.

Fukuzawa, as he so often did, gave the signal. He had long been in close touch with Korean reform movements. He was among the first to meet Kim Ok-kiun, and he made the educational facilities of Keiō available to Korean students. But as things went from bad to worse in Korea, Fukuzawa's editorials in *Jiji Shimpō* began calling for Japanese leadership in East Asia. A Chinese war, which he had earlier warned against, now came to seem essential if Japan was to impress upon the Chinese elite its superiority and leadership potential. After the 1884 riots in Seoul, Fukuzawa turned his back on the thankless job of leading and reforming countries that had no interest in leadership or reform. His famous editorial, *Datsu-A ron,* of March 18, 1885, called for Japan to "part with Asia." It was a waste of time to wait for Japan's neighbors to accept civilization. Moreover, he wrote, "If we keep bad company, we cannot avoid getting a bad name." Asia was now bad company; "Oriental" was synonymous

[18] Quoted in Somura, "Tairiku seisaku," pp. 256–257.

with a decadent, weak, and ignorant age from which Japan had escaped.[19] Within a few months Fukuzawa could go so far as to write that a (Korean) government that had done so little for its people should be whistled to its grave with good cheer; "foreseeing the death of this country in the near future, we would first like to sound a note of condolence for its government, and then, looking back upon its people, express our most cordial congratulations." The censors stopped this editorial, but it stands as an important piece.[20]

Fukuzawa's proposal, of course, was that Japan should establish a non-Asian identity in order to be able to treat its neighbors just as the Western powers did. The inclusion of the commercial clauses in the Shimonoseki Treaty was a manifestation of this attitude, and Japan won the rewards of modernity elsewhere in Asia: in the Netherlands Indies, for example, the Japanese were removed from the classification of "Asian and colored" in 1898 and grouped with Westerners. Indeed, as John White shows in his study of the diplomacy of the Russo-Japanese War, Japanese leaders were scrupulously careful to avoid any suggestion of an "Asian" front against Russia, lest the West see the struggle in racial terms.[21] Safety and strength meant playing the game in Western ways, but belief, as well as tactics, was involved. The Spencerian escalator to progress and civilization was accepted as fact by most of the Meiji Japanese, as it was by so many of their Western counterparts. From that perspective there could be no real affiliation with the Asia of today, regardless of how profound one's knowledge of and admiration for the Asia of yesterday.

Takeuchi Minoru's study of the travel diaries of three of the great Meiji sinologues is full of fascinating information on this point and serves to remind us that for *Kangakusha,* as well as for

---

[19] *Datsu-A ron* [On Parting with Asia], which appears in *Fukuzawa Yukichi zenshū* [Complete Works of Fukuzawa Yukichi], 20 vols. to date (Tokyo, 1958–   ), X, 238–240, has in recent years become a standard point of reference for all discussions of this outlook. It is quoted virtually in full in Takeuchi, *Ajiya shugi*, pp. 38–40, and in Somura, "Tairiku seisaku," pp. 290–291.

[20] *Fukuzawa zenshū*, X, 379–380.

[21] John A. White, *The Diplomacy of the Russo-Japanese War* (Princeton, 1964), pp. 120–121.

Western specialists, Meiji brought release from the unfulfilled yearnings for China of Tokugawa days.[22] Takezoe Shin'ichiro traveled in China for 111 days in 1876 and published his account in 1879. His values were still securely those of classical Chinese civilization, which he had studied, and he tended to make little distinction between the China he had studied and the China he visited. Spencer had not yet appeared on his horizon. But when it came to contemporary politics Takezoe was by no means uncritically pro-Chinese. He was later willing to recommend, from a consular post at Tientsin, that Japan take the opportunity presented by the Russo-Chinese confrontation at Ili to land at Taiwan and Pusan,[23] and in 1884, as minister in Seoul, he was one of the architects of that ill-fated plot. But even so Takezoe shared most of the values of his Chinese contemporaries; he thought that China would probably not modernize as Japan had done, but he was not convinced that China would lose greatly because of that.

In 1892 a second sinologue, Oka Senjin, published his account of a 350-day trip made in 1884. Oka's knowledge of China and Chinese was no less thorough than Takezoe's, but his world was that of the Spencerian 1880's. He found China hamstrung by two "poisons": addiction to opium and addiction to the great family. In numerous discussions with Chinese intellectuals he urged on them the importance of change to meet the Western challenge, only to encounter deprecation of Western capacity and immorality. In vain he argued that the way of the sages was to do as the sages would have done; his line of argument, in fact, is reminiscent of Ogyū Sorai's a century and a half earlier. But there is little indication that his talks were successful. He returned inclined to extend his list of "poisons" to include the very classics that were his love, concluding that the Six Classics had

[22] Takeuchi Minoru, "Meiji Kangakusha no Chūgoku kikō" [Meiji Sinologists' Accounts of Travel in China], *Jimbun gakuhō* [Journal of Humanistic Science], No. 36 (August, 1963), pp. 65–97.
[23] Yasuka Akio, "Ni-Shin sensō," p. 26. Biographies of Takezoe are found in Kuzuu Yoshihisa, *Tōa senkaku shishi kiden* [Stories and Biographies of Pioneer East Asian Adventurers], 3 vols. (Tokyo, 1935–1938), III, 302–304, and in Nakajima Masao, ed., *Taishi kaiko roku* [Memoirs About China], 2 vols. (Tokyo, 1936), II, 198–202.

become yet another form of addiction for Chinese intellectuals. His Chinese hosts refuted his assurance of the approval of the sages by countering that the sages would have sought wealth and power by utilizing their own resources, and that Japan, by going to school with the West, had left the proper path.[24]

The third sinologue, Naitō Torajirō, published his diary of an 1899 trip the following year. By this time the political entity that had been China was in deep trouble, and Naitō was among those who warned his countrymen of a possible breakup of the Manchu empire into its ethnic groupings.[25] Naitō felt it was Japan's mission to extend and transmit Western culture to China. Naitō's outlook was in no sense, as Takeuchi points out, Europe-centered, but a fully developed and articulated Japan-centric view of international affairs. Chinese students were coming to Japan, he noted; more should be invited. The proper path for Sino-Japanese relations clearly lay with Japanese leadership in the tasks of modernization.[26]

It is worth noting that China-centered careers of the Meiji period often originated in a sense of "duty." The path to success in government, education, and business lay obviously in the West. Not a few of those who developed a special interest in China did so only after an initial, or an unsuccessful, attempt to make the grade in Western affairs. There were also elements of competition with the West involved in decisions to turn to Asia. It is striking to read Inaba Iwakichi's lament for the dearth of good Japanese coverage of contemporary China of his day; Western sources, he suggests, are more varied and useful, and Westerners less bound to the picture of a China that has ceased to exist. The noted archaeologist Shiratori turned to archaeology because he was determined that Japan should not lag behind the West in its reserves of scholars in East Asian matters. It required Gotō Shimpei to persuade Oda Yorozu to undertake his massive study of the Ch'ing administrative system, and to exhort him and his assistants with the challenge and duty of

[24] Takeuchi Minoru, "Meiji Kangakusha," pp. 80–92. Biographies of Oka are also found in Kuzuu, *Tōa senkaku shishi kiden*, III, 177–178, and in Nakajima, ed., *Taishi kaiko roku*, II, 421–425.

[25] Takeuchi Minoru, "Meiji Kangakusha," pp. 92–97.

[26] *Ibid.*, p. 94.

Japan in China studies.[27] The West thus played a role even in the development of Orientology.

The need to find a role in a world dominated by Western power and science made it natural that "Japanists" of the late 1880's should come to the conclusion that the development of Oriental studies was one of the contributions that Japan might appropriately make to the world civilization of the future. The establishment of the Tōhō Kyōkai in 1891 and publication of *Tōyō Gakuhō* represented implementations of this decision. "East Asia," a lead article announced, "is the place for Japanese progress." [28] Others would argue that Japan could find a mission not only in bringing modernization to East Asia, but also in developing a new, third force between the materialism of the West and the passive spiritualism of the East.[29]

ROMANCE AND REFORM

Meiji attitudes toward Korea and China were characterized by elements of adventure and idealism. That there should have been excitement and stimulation inherent in the thought of overseas activities after the Tokugawa centuries of isolation is natural. By late Tokugawa times many writers were speculating on the possibilities of an overseas role for Japan, one usually phrased in terms of expansion, exploration, or leadership. With the sudden consciousness of Japan's smallness, and with the new-found criteria of progress and vitality drawn from European expansion in Asia, many dreamed of finding uninhabited islands, perhaps near Korea. Iwasaki Yatarō, during his service in Nagasaki in the 1860's for the Tosa domain, thought that Il-lung-do, off Korea's east coast, might qualify as a sort of Hong Kong for trade with the peninsula and mainland. He prepared a signboard in accord-

[27] Inaba is quoted in Somura, "Tairiku seisaku," pp. 266–267. For Gotō and Oda, see Banno Masataka, "Nihonjin no Chūgokukan; Oda Yuzuru no *Shinkoku gyōseihō* o megutte" [Japanese Attitudes Toward China; as Seen in Oda Yuzuru's *Administrative Law in the Chinese Empire*], *Shisō* [Thought], No. 452 (February, 1962), pp. 205–214.

[28] See Kenneth B. Pyle, "The New Generation: Young Japanese in Search of National Identity" (Unpubl. Ph.D. dissertation, The Johns Hopkins University, 1965; forthcoming, Stanford University Press), p. 184.

[29] Chihara Kazan, quoted in Somura, "Tairiku seisaku," pp. 283–284.

ance, he thought, with international law, identifying himself as its "discoverer"—only to find that Koreans had anticipated him there.[30]

For some time in the Meiji period the South Pacific seemed the only possible location for unknown and promising bits of territory. Shiga Shigetaka's travels and account of the South Pacific (*Nanyō Jijō*, 1887) highlighted the importance of the area and warned of what the Europeans were doing to it. And when Miyake Setsurei was permitted to journey to the South Pacific on board a naval vessel in 1891, he went in hopes of finding some spot as yet unclaimed that could be added to the Empire. Some writers refer to the enthusiasms of the period around 1890 as a "South Sea fever." [31]

The same or similar sentiments, frustrated in the islands to the south, had been a factor in the colonization schemes developed around the time of the Taiwan expedition.[32] And these same sentiments inspired talk of aiding and saving the more populous countries across the Japan and China seas. In those countries, however, adventure came to be associated with altruism, and Japanese liberals and reformers saw a future for themselves and for their country in sponsoring reforms and modernization there.

It is true that the earliest continental interests of the nascent liberal movement of Meiji Japan took the form of blatant hostility and rapacity toward Korea in the early 1870's. But before very long increasing sophistication and discernment changed these emphases. As opportunities for political action within Japan grew, the liberals became less eager to exercise their power abroad. During the 1882 crisis with Korea, the Liberal Party's organ criticized advocates of force, arguing that such policies could end only in alienating the Korean people. It was more important to nurture national strength against the West, it argued, and to this end to seek amity in East Asia. The crudities of the first era had, for some, given way to a greater consciousness

---

[30] Jansen, *Sakamoto Ryōma*, p. 277.

[31] Pyle, "The New Generation," p. 184; for Shiga, I have profited from an unpublished paper by Miwa Kimitada, "Shiga Shigetaka: A Meiji Japanist's View of his Country and the World."

[32] Leonard Gordon, "Japan's Abortive Colonial Venture in Taiwan, 1874," *Journal of Modern History*, XXXVII, 2 (June, 1965), 171–185.

of the Koreans as neighbors.[33] It had not done so for all. And as the scope for political activity within Japan narrowed a few years later, energies thwarted at home tended again to be focused abroad.

In the early 1880's Kim Ok-kiun's cause served to bring many of these issues to focus. Kim first came to Japan on a mission of apology for the events of 1882 and formed important contacts with leading publicists, like Fukuzawa Yukichi, and politicians, like Gotō Shōjirō. A few years later Kim's desperate situation in Korea and the frustration of his friends in Japan, where liberal politics were temporarily halted by the dissolution of parties and papers, resulted in the bizarre filibustering expedition that Ōi Kentarō tried to stage in 1885. This experience showed in the most graphic manner the possibilities inherent in talk of political reform, Japanese liberalism, and Asian affinity. "Our spirit of liberty and equality," Ōi told the court, "could not allow us to be indifferent to the fate of a nation so close to us, and we rushed forward to help." [34] But what seemed to Ōi a problem of political and spiritual salvation through fraternal commitment—a turn from indifference and selfishness, and a rededication to the aims of the larger polity—opened the door to interpretations of many sorts, which served many groups and interests. And when Kim's projects failed, men of substance and realism like Fukuzawa disassociated themselves from this revivalist drive and worked out a rationale for becoming, temporarily at least, less Asian and more Japanese.

Yet there always remained an active core of idealists and reformers. In the case of Korea, Tarui Tōkichi's proposal for union rather than annexation remained influential long after his book was published. Even the Kokuryūkai head, Uchida Ryōhei, used Tarui's formulation at the time the Yi dynasty came to an end. Without this element of idealism and commitment, many Japanese would have found it much more difficult to endorse

---

[33] Hatada Takashi, "Nihonjin no Chōsen kan" [Japanese Attitudes Toward Korea], in Hatada Takashi, *Nihon to Chōsen* [Japan and Korea] (Tokyo, 1965), pp. 19–22.

[34] Cf. Takeuchi Yoshimi, *Ajiya shugi*, pp. 28–32, and M. B. Jansen, "Ōi Kentarō: Radicalism and Chauvinism," *Far Eastern Quarterly*, XI, 3 (May, 1952), 305–316.

what was done in their name, and Uchida himself (who later claimed to disapprove of the way things went) would have found it vastly more difficult to enlist Koreans in his *Il chin hoe.*[35]

The Meiji liberal and reformist movement maintained a consistent Asian orientation. When Nakae Chōmin, Saionji Kimmochi, and others launched their first explicitly egalitarian paper in 1881, they christened it the *Tōyō* (East Asian) *Jiyū Shimbun,* before the Jiyutō itself had been formed.[36] In 1887 Nakae Chōmin, in his *Sansuijin keirin mondō,* argued the case for associating the reform of China with that of Japan in order to silence illiberal Japanese elements. Ueki Emori, another major member of this group, participated in a Rise Asia (Kōa) Society as early as 1881. In those same years Itagaki Taisuke exclaimed that the liberals by no means restricted their aims to Japan, but that they were dedicated to spreading the regenerating ideals of freedom and liberalism throughout Korea and China as well.[37] And even after the mainstream of the liberal movement drew closer to the Meiji establishment by participating in constitutionalism, and after a desire for equality with the West replaced thoughts of Asian solidarity, the radical wing maintained the outlook of their predecessors. It was entirely natural that Nakae's disciple Kōtoku Shūsui and other anarchist and socialist leaders should maintain and extend the earlier assumption of East Asian solidarity. More internationally minded and politically disadvantaged than their predecessors, they were also more successful in spreading their ideas to Asian comrades, less successful in finding recruits within Japan, and less likely to join the twentieth-century establishment in Japan.[38]

[35] Hatada, "Nihonjin no Chōsen kan," pp. 27–28. A reprint of Uchida's *Ni-Kan gappō* can be found in Takeuchi Yoshimi, *Ajiya shugi,* pp. 205–238.
[36] A photographic reprint edited by Nishida Taketoshi appeared in 1964: *Tōyō Jiyū Shimbun* (Tokyo University Press), 164 pp.
[37] For Nakae, see Takeuchi Yoshimi, *Ajiya shugi,* p. 41. Reprint of *Sansuijin keirin mondō* [Three Inebriates' Discussion of Statecraft] is available in Iwanami Bunko. For Ueki and Itagaki, see Ienaga Saburō, *Ueki Emori kenkyū* [A Study of Ueki Emori] (Tokyo, 1960), pp. 200–201.
[38] There are some useful comments in Ishimoda Makoto, "Kōtoku Shūsui to Chūgoku" [Kōtoku Shūsui and China], in Takeuchi Yoshimi, *Ajiya shugi,* pp. 384–410; cf. also Takeuchi's regret that the late Meiji split of the "Asia-firsters," which saw the Uchidas and Kōtokus part company, doomed Asianism to paths of aggression, *ibid.,* p. 55.

By far the most striking example of cooperation among Asian reformers was that of Miyazaki Tōten, Hirayama Shū, Kayano Chōchi, and a few others on the one hand, and Sun Yat-sen and the Chinese revolutionaries on the other. This relationship was heir to all that had gone before. The Japanese found in it high adventure and relief from an increasingly restrictive and organized modern society. They were suffused with the idealism and adventure of breaking out of capitalist as well as feudal patterns and building a new world of Asian brotherhood. Most of them were at some point associated with the democratic, Christian, and socialist traditions of reform. Sun Yat-sen, himself the heir of an Asian social-democratic gospel, was perfectly fitted to work with them. And the Japanese in turn became at times, although not entirely intentionally, the instruments of nonsocial and non-Christian forces of national interest in their work.[39]

These qualities of courage, adventure, and idealism helped make and keep the China adventurers popular. Miyazaki's autobiography receives increasing respect today as one of the great literary and human documents of the Meiji period.[40] The 1960's has seen a rebirth of interest in the Meiji adventurers in popular Japanese journalism.[41] There are many reasons why this should be so. The unhappy terminus of the arguments for cooperation and mutual benefit is farther away, and guilt for aggression less fresh. Once again the mainland is remote, dangerous, and unknown, and again it is experiencing momentous transformations. The thought of courageous and colorful idealists risking much to influence continental developments, convinced that their country's future must somehow lie with mainland Asia and not with the West, carries conviction to many. Perhaps most of all, it is a part of Japan's modern heritage which has been long ignored and which, upon restudy, leaves readers well pleased with their progenitors.

Whatever the attitudes of the 1960's, there can be no doubt

---

[39] Described in M. B. Jansen, *The Japanese and Sun Yat-sen*, (Cambridge, Mass., 1954), *passim*.

[40] Takeuchi Yoshimi, *Ajiya shugi*, p. 48, groups it with the Fukuzawa and Osugi Sakae autobiographies.

[41] For one example, see the special number of *Jimbutsu Orai* (January, 1965), *Tairiku rōnin: Ni-Chū kōshōshi no wakiyakutachi* [Continental Adventurers: Helping Hands in the History of Sino-Japanese Relations].

that the popularity and character of the Meiji adventurers made it easier for their contemporaries to accept and endorse their government's harsh and minatory attitude toward the Korean and Chinese regimes that stood between their Asian friends and success. The results of such actions, including Japan's success in joining the privileged ranks of Western treaty powers, made it possible, after all, to provide effective help and encouragement to the Sun Yat-sens. But at the same time it made for a setting in which idealism inevitably gave way to self-interest.

MISSION AND DUTY

For the first three decades of Meiji, discussions of participation in Asian affairs had been conducted principally in terms of idealism, adventure, and cooperation between neighbors in opposition to the West. Gradually the overtones shift. The historian's subjective impressions of that discussion are that a new phraseology of "mission" and "duty" enters and soon dominates. It would not do to exaggerate this shift. Many of the most important activists, certainly the Miyazakis, never changed their outlook and tended to carry what might be called early Meiji attitudes into late Meiji activities. They were not frauds or dupes of their betters; if they had been, they could scarcely have had the influence they did. Nor had the phrases "duty" and "mission" been totally lacking in earlier periods.

But that there was a shift in emphases seems clear. It derived principally from Japan's "success" in modernization. There was, for one thing, much less talk of reforming Japan (except among confirmed revolutionaries) through Asian activities. Japan's reform was accomplished, her institutional structure perfected and increasingly sacrosanct. The modernized and westernized Japanese were now looking for an area in which they could make a contribution comparable to those the West had made in the underdeveloped world. It seemed clear that that mission lay in nearby Korea and China. But the choice of terminology is revealing in itself. Mission, *tenshoku,* represents a heavenly calling, one which was incumbent upon Japan whether her neighbors saw it that way or not. It represented the acceptance of the responsibilities, tactics, and possibilities of big-power status. It represented policy toward China and Korea, not with them. And duty, *gimu,* was something no responsible citizen or country could avoid.

Undoubtedly the principle milestone on the road to mission was Japan's victory over China in 1895. In the Sino-Japanese War the frustrations, misgivings, and fears of a generation were somehow resolved in glittering victories that won the praise of Europe and reassured the most doubting of the Japanese. A new image of a triumphant Japan began to replace the doubts of purpose and nationality that had assailed many of the liberals in the 1880's. But all of this was achieved at the political and psychological expense of China.

The war precipitated an outburst of chauvinism and self-pride that was expressed as scorn for China. It provided an opportunity to exorcise the Japanese past, the old order that had been abandoned, and to transfer it to China, where it belonged. China and Chinese were pilloried in popular press and song as the epitome of weakness, selfishness, inefficiency, disorganization, and cowardice. The struggle between the two countries was therefore one between right and wrong, modernity and medievalism, light and dark. It is not too much to suggest that this struggle suddenly illuminated the insecurity in which so many Meiji Japanese had lived up to that point. Without this factor, it would be difficult to account for the breathtaking shift of attitudes toward China that was manifested in daily speech and reading. The popular press denounced the Chinese as untrustworthy, slippery scoundrels and demanded nothing less than full submission from Peking. Popular music caught the refrain and marching songs like "On to Peking!" expressed something of the determination to crush the Chinese completely. Donald Keene has recently discussed the startling developments in the prints of the period; they contrast the Western-appearing, rational, orderly, and courageous Japanese with their craven, confused and utterly Oriental opponents. In every way possible, the contrast between modernity and antiquity was brought home to the exulting Japanese.[42]

---

[42] Donald Keene, "The Sino-Japanese War of 1894–1895 and Its Cultural Effects" (prepared for the Fifth Seminar of the Conference on Modern Japan and to be published in the forthcoming *Tradition and Modernization in Japanese Culture,* ed. Donald H. Shively [Princeton University Press]).

The Diet as well as the press was solidly behind the plans of the military for full humiliation and satisfaction from China, making it difficult for wiser statesmen to moderate the peace demands. Throughout Japan so many old samurai wanted to take down their fathers' swords and join the fray that a special imperial rescript was issued telling them to stick to their jobs at home.[43] China as a political entity capable of will and regeneration all but disappeared from Japanese minds for over a decade. It was replaced by a weak, irresolute entity shored up by the great powers as a necessary block to each others' greed. Not that Japan was immediately a great power, for there were new frustrations in the discovery that even victory had not freed Japan fully from second-class membership in the European world order. As the powers turned to prepare for what seemed a probable partition of China, it was evident that continental Asia was incapable of sponsoring its own regeneration, and that Japan would have to hurry if it expected to play any role at all. The Boxer Rebellion further confirmed the Japanese self-image of might and modernity. The twentieth century thus opened with a dramatically new view of China in Meiji Japan. If the Meiji period began with governmental warnings that Westerners were worthy of being treated with the dignity accorded the Chinese, the twentieth century found the government even more hard pressed to assert the opposite side of the case.

The first decade of the new century, the one in which these attitudes were fully hardened and articulated, was also the one in which for the first time Chinese students thronged to Tokyo in search of the secrets of modernization. Inevitably they inherited these attitudes of disrespect, and inevitably they contributed to them through their poverty, disorganization, and general confusion. They seem to have won remarkably little sympathy from the Japanese, who might have been expected to remember their own fathers' student days in late Tokugawa Edo.[44]

Japan had thus to a considerable degree "parted with Asia" in the manner that Fukuzawa had suggested in 1885. It was now

[43] Watanabe Ikujirō, *Ni-Shin, Nichi-Ro sensō shiwa* [Talks on the Sino-Japanese and Sino-Russian Wars] (Tokyo, 1937), p. 197.
[44] The student movement has received definitive treatment at the hands of Saneto Keishū, *Chūgokujin Nihon ryūgakushi* [A History of Chinese Students in Japan] (Tokyo, 1960).

conscious of the need to live by the rules of international society, rules under which it had made its own way. Those rules constituted the criteria of acceptance, and indeed of civilization. Japan's governments, although interested in movements and trends in China, were reluctant to involve themselves deeply in any one. To do so would have meant a greater personal commitment and identification than they were prepared to make, and they might have risked losing the stature that Japan had won in the West. This was particularly the case after the Russo-Japanese War, when the Tokyo government exiled the Chinese revolutionary leaders and preferred to enter a network of treaty relations with the leading imperialist powers.

The modernized Japanese saw their role as one of sponsoring reform from above through governments and enterprises, openly and officially. Itō held to this hope in Korea even after it was clear that others would have their way with annexation. The difficulties he had in persuading army authorities that Japan's rights in Manchuria were limited to what had been Russia's presaged even greater difficulties for his less eminent successors.[45] Japan now lived and profited by the unequal treaties she had resisted for so long. Talk of Asian regeneration and alliance became less common, and Japan's diplomatic and commercial positions led her to join in the efforts to prop up the faltering Manchu regime. But when it collapsed, so too did the western balance of power, the order which Japan had struggled to enter.

TRADE

For most of the Meiji Period considerations of trade with China were a good deal less important to Japan than the political and strategic considerations that have been discussed above. In fact, considerations of trade did not become important until the Treaty of Shimonoseki gave Japan special privileges and the

[45] See the excellent discussion and documentation of Kurihara Ken in "Hayashi Tadasu Gaimudaijin 'Tai Shin seiryaku kanken'" [Foreign Minister Hayashi Tadasu's "Personal View of Policy Toward the Ch'ing"] in Kokusai Seiji Gakkai, ed., *Nihon gaikōshi kenkyū: Meiji jidai* [Studies in Japanese Foreign Relations: The Meiji Period] (Tokyo, 1957), pp. 193–199; Hayashi document, pp. 199–203.

Shimonoseki indemnity helped to develop the industrial sector. It is striking to see what an uphill battle Meiji China trade enthusiasts had to wage before they gained a hearing. In the 1870's early probes of possibilities of trade with China, carried out in connection with the missions headed by Date Masamune and Ōkubo Toshimichi, showed, despite the painstaking enumeration of trade patterns, that they did not amount to very much. Indeed, much of Japan's concern had to do with preventing foreign middlemen from dominating the export of Hokkaido marine products to China.[46] During the 1880's, when treaty revision and institutional reform dominated the stage, Japanese trade was still mostly with the West, and it required individuals of unusual foresight to argue that China should be thought of in terms of future commercial possibilities. Japan's nascent industries were still too weak to be greatly concerned with non-Japanese markets, the need of heavy industry for raw materials was not yet apparent, and trade patterns in China seemed securely in the hands of Western entrepreneurs.

It required the missionary enthusiasm of Arao Kiyoshi and his associates to begin the process of reversing this. Arao utilized the patent medicine establishment of a Kishida Kinkō in Hankow to organize a group of ten young men who, wearing Chinese dress and speaking Chinese, penetrated all parts of the country with the ostensible purpose of salesmenship, but with the actual purpose of compiling intelligence reports on China. Arao interpreted "intelligence" in its broadest sense, for he felt that future Japanese influence in China depended upon the accumulation of information as varied and as accurate as that which Westerners, especially missionaries, had been able to gather. Therefore his little band was told to report the qualities of all categories of local elite in the areas they visited, and they were indoctrinated with inspiring and daring pledges.[47]

---

[46] Study documents prepared in connection with the Date and Ōkubo missions are reprinted in *Ōkuma monjo* [Documents on Ōkuma], 5 vols. to date (Tokyo, 1958–   ), IV, 49–58.

[47] Inoue, *Kyojin Arao Kiyoshi*, pp. 18 ff., gives fascinating details of the group spirit instilled in Arao's agents. Their training consisted of regular meetings for discussion and discipline, a rationalized collective life, and constant indoctrination. Inoue's account of the Hankow School is complete to pledges and school songs, *ibid.*, pp. 49 ff.

This was only the beginning. A few years later Arao resigned his commission to devote all his time to the promotion of Japanese research in Chinese economics and trade. He toured Japan, speaking everywhere on the importance of meeting the West on its own commercial ground in the struggle for influence in China. He argued that Japanese merchants could not hope to compete with their Western contemporaries on the latters' home ground, but that they ought to be able to compete with them in China. What they had to do was study Chinese commercial customs, markets, language, and social structure in order to achieve their purpose. Arao received moral but little financial support from leading Japanese, but he was able to open a Chinese-Japanese Commercial Research Bureau in 1890. Throughout all of this, his biographers insist, the emphasis was on duty and hard work for a long-range, but certainly not immediate, return. One could probably say that until Shimonoseki the main considerations behind the China trade were political, and its principal sponsors the political and military elite. It is not surprising that some of the more romantically inclined China enthusiasts like Miyazaki Torazō, who was briefly associated with Arao in the 1890's, found these commercial ventures less to their liking than their activities in the service of Korean and Chinese revolutionaries.

The Sino-Japanese War of course changed everything. Recent surveys on the background of the war of 1894 make it clear that Japan's commercial relationships with Korea and China at that date were hardly of an order to account for the war decision.[48] But the Shimonoseki indemnity made possible massive beginnings in heavy industry which required raw materials, and for these China soon loomed as an inviting source.[49] The new treaty ports and commercial privileges made it possible for Japanese textile manufacturers to begin to make headway in the China market. And Arao Kiyoshi's shoe-string operations gave way to

[48] Nakatsuka Akira, *Ni-Shin sensō* [Sino-Japanese War], Iwanami kōza Nihon rekishi [Iwanami Lectures on Japanese History], XVII (Tokyo, 1962), p. 133.

[49] For the iron industry, see M. B. Jansen, "Yawata, Hanyehping, and the Twenty-one Demands," *Pacific Historical Review*, XXIII, 1 (February, 1954), 31–48.

the better organized and financed activities of the Tōa Dōbun Shoin.[50]

Many felt that Japanese trade could flourish more in south China than in north, where European interests predominated, and for them political and economic interests never coincided during Meiji. When the 1911 revolution came, spokesmen for the Japanese business interests were among those who warned of the importance of maintaining relations with south China and of the dangers of alienating Chinese public opinion.[51] The preponderance of official attention and concern nevertheless went to north China and Manchuria, and this in itself is evidence of the continued primacy of strategic over commercial concerns. Government leaders like Inoue Kaoru and Gotō Shimpei did all they could to direct the interests of scholars, bureaucrats, and businessmen toward Manchuria and north China. The Twenty-one Demands of 1915 finally made explicit the concerns for territory and raw materials that had taken shape since 1895. And when the Russian colossus, whose threat had so long served to justify concern with the north, collapsed shortly afterward, the Tokyo government inevitably rushed to occupy its place, often with little reference to commercial possibilities which might be sacrificed elsewhere in China.

CONCLUSIONS

A brief review cannot do more than indicate the range of current Japanese work related to Meiji attitudes toward China. The literature grows constantly, and in it one recognizes the awareness of the authors that they are mirroring Japanese images of Japan as well. Perhaps the most important development in this recent work is the treatment and view one gets of the Meiji leaders. They are better documented, liberated from the prewar

[50] Nakajima Masao, ed., *Taishi kaiko roku* and its supplement, *Zoku taishi kaiko roku*, 2 vols. (Tokyo, 1941), contain history and biographies of Dōbunkai leaders.

[51] See Somura, "Tairiku seisaku," pp. 279 ff. In "Shingai kakumei to Nihon" (The 1911 Revolution and Japan), Kokusai Seiji Gakkai, ed., *Nihon gaikoshi kenkyū: Chū-Nichi kankei no tenkai* [Studies in Japanese Diplomatic History: The Development of Sino-Japanese Relations] (Tokyo, 1961), Somura, however, describes the southern trade as hope and not yet fact (p. 53).

official starch and the postwar dirt. They come through as figures
of realism with clarity of thought and expression. Yamagata's
succinct estimates of problems and possibilities take us to the
very center of the Meiji decision process.[52] And the use of documentary sources in determining and analyzing Meiji government
leaders' views is only one example of the increasing fidelity and
skill which characterize the excellent discussions carried on by
organizations such as the Japan Association of International
Relations.

All of this permits a realistic and reasonable appraisal of the
Meiji power structure, one that is not colored by intolerance or
apology. There is a sounder understanding of the considerations
that led Fukuzawa to advocate separation from Asia. A generation of Japanese scholars now coming to maturity is better qualified to respect and sympathize with the Meiji second generation's
struggles for identity and purpose in a world in which the gap
between West and non-West, industrialized and underdeveloped,
seemed to be growing steadily.

The change has, however, not gone so far as to permit
endorsement of the subversion of Meiji idealism by Shōwa ex-
pansionism. There is instead a new understanding of the complexi-
ties of causation and of the irony and tragedy of Japan's twentieth-century course. A new danger that may emerge, and which
is already apparent in popular writing, is that of uncritical praise
for the Meiji founding fathers. Their success not only makes it
easy to overlook the chances they took in furthering continental
interests, but it also confirmed their successors' belief in the
efficacy of force. The Meiji leaders, one suspects, were often
moderate not by choice, but because of Japan's international
handicaps.

It required, for instance, only the excitement of a brief field
command for Yamagata to counsel his emperor from the front in
1895 that Japan would have to dominate, because there was no
force in Korea with which she could ally.[53] And when General
Terauchi raised his cup to toast the Korean annexation in 1910,

---

[52] For some particularly striking documents, printed for the first time, see
Kokusai Seiji Gakkai, ed., *Nihon gaikōshi kenkyū: Meiji jidai*, pp. 183–195.
[53] See Oka Yoshitake, *Yamagata Aritomo* (Tokyo, 1958), p. 61.

he looked around and asked his guests to imagine how Kobaya-
kawa, Katō, and Konishi would have felt on seeing that evening's
moon. "It is as though we see Hideyoshi rise from the ground,"
came the reply, "as the rising sun climbs the high mountains of
Kōrai." [54] These too were authentic Meiji voices, and the con-
straints of the imperialist balance of power undoubtedly prevented their making worse mistakes in China.

[54] Hatada, "Nihonjin no Chōsen kan," p. 10.

ROBERT A. SCALAPINO

Prelude to Marxism:
The Chinese Student Movement
in Japan, 1900-1910

THE Chinese revolutionary movement had no single point of origin nor a specific date of emergence. It sprang from many diverse stimuli and developed out of events greatly separated in time and meaning. As is well known, the abortive revolts and sporadic reform efforts of the nineteenth century were both symbols and agents of the decline of the old China; a fission process was set in motion involving a wide spectrum of institutions and ideas. Westernism served as the catalytic agent. It transformed the energy generated by the unrest in traditional institutions into a rising assault upon the values that underlay those institutions. Ultimately, it was necessary only to add a trigger mechanism, and the stage for a major explosion was set.

There is no need to detail here the significant events that marked the end of the Ch'ing era, but it is helpful to recall some of them in order to provide a setting for our story: the Chinese defeat in the Sino-Japanese War of 1894–1895—a humiliation that made it impossible to hide any longer the truth of China's decadence, and generated the most profound emotions of anger, shame, guilt, and remorse within a "vanguard" element among the younger generation; the Hundred Days' Reform fiasco—the last chance, not merely for reform but for revolution without chaos, for the type of gradual but massive change conducted by a modernizing oligarchy that was taking place in Japan; the Boxer Rebellion—in the tradition of modern primitivist reactions to things foreign and new, and doomed, like all such reactions, to failure in the face of foes superior both in organization and ideas; a rising tempo of foreign incursions upon Chinese sovereignty and the growth of numerous "spheres of influence" on Chinese soil—intensifying xenophobic proclivities and raising the question as to whether China as a political entity would survive; and Ch'ing efforts in the direction of reform, including constitutionalism—proof again that revolution frequently reaches its climatic stage in a period marked not by rigid, unyielding absolutism, but by concessions, divisions, and indecision on the part of those in power.

The students with whom we shall be concerned came to political consciousness while these events, any many others, were taking place. At the outset, however, one basic question should be raised. Is a probe into the student writings of this period worth the effort? Would it not be more fruitful to concern oneself solely with the major figures, the men who dominated intellectual and political trends?

The case for examining these writings cannot rest upon the fame of the authors or the intrinsic merit of their essays. Almost all of the articles in the various Chinese student journals published in Japan were written under a pseudonym, and only a very few of the authors can be positively identified. We may be certain, however, that most of them were destined for relative obscurity, and some were shortly to perish on behalf of the cause to which they had dedicated themselves. Nor do these anonymous writings contain an abundance of original thought, brilliant analysis, or new fact. On the contrary, the mark of immaturity lies heavily upon most of them, and, as is the case with so much contemporary communist literature, one has to stifle yawns brought on by the endless repetition of certain central themes.

It is precisely this element of repetition, however, that offers new perspectives on the Chinese revolutionary movement, for the emphasis as well as the key words and phrases contained in the hundreds of articles written during this period enables us to separate the significant from the trivial. To interpret a major movement like the Chinese revolution correctly, it is not sufficient to analyze the principal actors and their ideas. Such works can be exceedingly valuable, although many must be used with caution because the author's originality is often interwoven with that of his subject, providing problems both of balance and of interpretation. In some measure at least, the writings of this period must be submitted to more precise tests, and this involves some effort at quantification, however crude. This essay makes no attempt to measure or weigh ideas, emotions, or values with any degree of precision. It merely seeks to reach toward the main themes, to cast those themes as faithfully as possible in the terms in which they were originally expressed, and to separate the author's analysis from the subjects with which he is dealing.

First, however, let us set forth briefly the essential details about those Chinese students who were in Japan during the first decade of this century, and particularly during the critical years between 1903 and 1908. Before 1903, the number of Chinese students in Japan was relatively small. One contemporary report suggests that in 1902 there were a total of 270.[1] From this point onward, however, the number rose rapidly. By 1903, there were between 800 and 1000 Chinese students studying in various Japanese schools.[2] In the period 1906–1907, the figures reached between 8,000 and 10,000.[3] It is not difficult to understand why Japan would be a popular place for Chinese students. Travel to and from Japan was relatively easy, and students who could not contemplate lengthy courses could take special short-term courses. Living expenses and tuition, moreover, were much

[1] Hsing-hsin, "New Educational Plans for China," *Hsin-min ts'ung-pao*, No. 3 (1902), p. 6.

[2] Wen-kuei, "No Provincial Boundaries," *Che-chiang ch'ao* No. 2 (April, 1903), pp. 13–32.

[3] Varying estimates have been given. Sanetō Keishū in his *Chūgokujin Nihon ryūgakushi* [A History of Chinese Students in Japan] (Tokyo, 1960), states that the largest number at one time was 8,000. A contemporary article, "The Chinese Students in Japan," in *Kakumei Hyōron* [Revolutionary Review], No. 1 (September 5, 1906), p. 1, states: "There are more than 10,000 Chinese scholars in Tokyo at present." Roger F. Hackett in his article, "Chinese Students in Japan, 1900–1910," *Papers on China*, III, 142 (mimeographed by the Committee on International and Regional Studies, May, 1949), quoting from the *Japan Weekly Mail*, gives a high figure of 13,000 in September, 1906.

cheaper than in the West. In addition, the written Japanese language was more easily acquired than a Western language, and customs—food, living conditions, and patterns of life—were more easily assimilated. Fear of racial discrimination was also less: the Japanese, it was frequently asserted, were of "the same race."

The evidence would indicate that while every province was eventually represented, the largest number of students came from Kwangtung, Hunan, Kiangsu, and Chekiang.[4] The significance of this need scarcely be emphasized. The political and military cadres of the next generation who were now training came from the Yangtze valley—especially the coastal regions around Shanghai—and from the South, a region that was destined to dominate the political fortunes of the revolutionary movement in the decades that lay ahead. The students from each province had their own provincial associations, the idea originating with the Kwangtung students in 1900. The most important of these associations published journals, generally on a somewhat irregular schedule.[5] There are a few other pertinent facts about these students that should be recorded. Three types of students came to Japan: those sponsored by the central government, those sponsored by their province, and those under private sponsor-

[4] Note the following remark in "An Open Letter to the Honorable Elders of Our Country Urging Them to Order the Youth to Study Overseas and to Arrange for the Collection of Public Funds to Send Students Abroad," *Che-chiang ch'ao*, No. 7 (August, 1903), pp. 1–30: "In terms of origin, Kiangsu province has sent the largest number of students abroad." The author goes on to state that Kwangtung province has a considerable number of students, possibly over 60, and Chekiang, Hunan, and Hopeh are reasonably well represented.

[5] This article is based on material from the following student journals: *Che-chiang ch'ao* [The Chekiang Current] (10 issues available; January–November, 1903); *Chiang-su* [Kiangsu] (12 issues available; no dates given but in the 1903–1905 period); *Yu-pao* [Window News] (2 issues available; no dates given but in the 1905–1908 period); *Hu-pei hsüeh-sheng chieh* [The Hupei Student World] (5 issues available; January–May, 1903); *Han sheng* [The Voice of the Han] (2 issues available; no dates given but in the 1904–1905 period); *Erh-shih shih-chi chih chih-na* [20th Century China] (1 issue available; May, 1905); *Ta-chiang* [The Great River] (1 issue available; 1907); *Fu-pao* [The News] (4 issues available; April 15, 1906–January 30, 1907); *Yün-nan* [Yunnan] (1 issue available; August 28, 1906).

In addition, Liang Ch'i-ch'ao's *Hsin-min ts'ung-pao* [New People's Miscellany], Sun Yat-sen's *Min-pao* [The People], *Chung-kuo jih-pao* [The Chinese News] (1907), and *Kakumei Hyōron* [Revolutionary Review] (September 5, 1906–February 25, 1907) have been used.

ship. The second category was the most numerous. A significant number of the students, moreover, were attending military schools. (It was the military students, incidentally, that provided the bulk of support to Sun and his T'ung-meng Hui.) So-called "short courses," whereby a group of Chinese students with an interpreter would receive instruction (with translation provided) in concentrated form were common. Actually, the number of students attending the top three or four institutions of higher learning (i.e., Tokyo Imperial University, Kyoto, Waseda, and Keio) were much smaller than those in other institutions, military academies, and special programs. There were many complaints about the quality of education and also about the discrimination suffered at the hands of some Japanese. Life was not ideal. Indications are strong that the overwhelming number of students came from the middle and upper socio-economic classes.

Initially, the chief political influence on these students was undoubtedly provided by Liang Ch'i-ch'ao. His *Ch'ing-i pao*, which had started publication shortly after his arrival into exile, was later followed by the *Hsin-min ts'ung-pao*, and these were the first organs of the reform-minded students. Liang remained the primary influence upon a number of the top intellectuals from among the student group, especially upon those within "civilian" circles. But increasingly, as the political tide rolled toward revolution and as greater numbers of students came, many of them embarked upon a military training program, and Liang came under fierce attack as an apologist for monarchy, an opponent of the legitimate racial aspirations of the Han people, and a false prophet. After the establishment of Sun's T'ung-meng Hui in 1905, the balance of power within the student movement had clearly swung in favor of a more radical course of action.

CHINA'S PROBLEMS

Let us begin our exploration of student thought with an attempt to capture the dominant mood that characterized those writers who were pouring out their emotions as well as their ideas onto the pages of various journals. There is an interesting interplay of pessimism and hope. The primary source of pessimism, quite naturally, lay in the objective conditions in which China found herself: "enslavement" by the Manchus and threatened parcellation at the hands of various Western powers and Japan; "backwardness" in every field of life and every segment of society; and perhaps most depressing of all, the colossal indifference of the Chinese people to their fate.[6] The central problem was frequently defined as essentially a moral one, and hence a question of how to reshape the basic character of Chinese man. Let us use the words of the student writers:[7] Possessed in the past of a great civilization, the Chinese people had become morally bankrupt. Now they were characterized by lethargy, a profound ignorance of the world in which they lived, and a totally self-centered attitude devoid of any sense of patriotism or public spiritedness. How many Chinese understood or cared about the threat that China as a nation might become extinct in the struggle for survival? How many were prepared to make personal sacrifices for the sake of the whole society? How many had any sense of respect for themselves, and hence any basis from which to resist enslavement at the hands of others? [8]

Brooding over such problems could sometimes lead to despair and bitterness. China is dead, proclaimed more than one young writer, and perhaps nothing can save her. Even less pessimistic authors agreed that immediate action was necessary. The ring of urgency sounded in almost every philippic: It was the last moment to avoid destruction; no more chances would be given.[9] This

---

[6] See, for example, "The Slaughter of Fellow Countrymen," *Fu-pao*, No. 6 (September 25, 1906), pp. 1–8. The author opens with the words, "The country is extinct; the people are enslaved." As he warms to his subject, he decries the lack of initiative among the students, the lack of patriotism among the rich, and the lack of national consciousness among any of the Han. The Han are merely lower-class animals for whom no one has respect—if they are not killed by others, they will be eliminated naturally through the process of evolution, because only the strong survive in the twentieth century.

[7] We have employed the technique of using a colon where we want to reproduce the essence of student thought and vocabulary without the tedium of lengthy direct quotations.

[8] Fei-sheng, "On National Spirit," *Che-chiang ch'ao*, No. 3 (April, 1903), pp. 1–12.

[9] See, for example, the "Opening statement" in *Hu-pei hsüeh-sheng chieh*, No. 1 (January, 1903), pp. 1–16; also, "On Nationalism," *Che-chiang ch'ao*, No. 1 (January, 1903), pp. 19–27.

sense of urgency combined with a feeling of desperation over current conditions to abet the radical mood that steadily gained momentum, no matter what the actions, or inactions, of the government and the more moderate intellectuals.

Even the writings which sounded the most desperate and pessimistic notes, however, usually contained a contrapuntal theme, hope for salvation: Despite their present woes, there was no intrinsic reason why the Chinese people could not move from weakness to power in an unprecendentedly short time. They had proven capable once of developing one of the greatest civilizations known to man. Their territory was vast and rich. Their numbers were much greater than those of any other people, "ten times those of the white population." China was a sleeping lion, and once awakened, she could easily become a dominant force in the world.[10]

This basic theme, with many variations, was often advanced in sharply racial terms. Indeed, one is startled by some of the openly racist doctrines promulgated. The following analysis, for example, is not out of character with many: Four major races were competing in the world. There was little likelihood that victory would got to the brown and black races, since they were inferior in ability. The only meaningful contest was between the white and yellow races, and among the yellow peoples, the Chinese were by far superior in terms of accomplishments. It remained only to mobilize Chinese talents, to produce a national spirit so that the people could unite, ousting all foreigners and taking over their own destiny.[11] Sometimes, racial concepts were presented in more classic form—the *civilized* versus the *barbarian*. Such comparisons did not usually slight white accomplishments. On the contrary, the white race was generally credited with having attained a higher level of "civilization" than other people. What were the attributes of modern civilization? Our young students found them in freedom, popular rights, govern-

[10] See A New Citizen of China, "On Government and Popular Rights," *Hsinmin ts'ung-pao,* No. 9 (1902), pp. 1–8; and for an interesting systhesis between pessimism and optimism, see "The Relation Between Education and Self-Government," *Hu-pei hsüeh-sheng chieh,* No. 4 (April, 1903), pp. 15–23.

[11] See Chung-k'an, "On Self-Government," *Che-chiang ch'ao,* No. 6 (July, 1903), pp. 1–10.

ment under law, and a belief in progress.[12] The Anglo-Saxons were dominant in the world, and a threat to China, because they governed themselves as free men. The brown, black, and red races were uncivilized. Hence, they needed an authoritarian government.[13] But certainly the Chinese people, a superior race in intelligence and character, could shake off the chains of the past, and compete with other civilized societies by gaining control of their own nation and by promoting the doctrines of republicanism and constitutionalism. Fortunately, the Manchus were an uncivilized race. Their barbarism made them relatively inefficient, and hence easily overthrown.[14] Independence became a much more difficult problem when a civilized people, like the British, conquered a people inferior to them, like the Indians.[15]

It is not difficult to uncover the roots of these racial doctrines. The traditional forces of xenophobia and ethnocentrism could interact with racial themes extracted from Darwinist writings. It should not be forgotten that social Darwinism flowed into many channels: ethics, philosophy, economics, and politics, as well as science. Doctrines of racial competition, of a relentless struggle which would result in the survival of the fittest occupied the minds of many of the young students following Western writings. Many other themes, of course, were also avidly pursued: the supreme value of science; the rise of a "modern," scientifically derived ethics; the concept of progress and the inevitability of change; and the importance of both military and industrial power. After surveying the student essays, however, one cannot doubt the presence of a strong racial consciousness among most of the student writers. This consciousness translated itself into brusque dismissals of the potentials of the brown and black peoples, assertions of the superiority of the Chinese among the yellow peoples, and a strongly mixed attitude toward the whites

[12] "Constitutional Theories," *Hu-pei hsüeh-sheng chieh,* No. 2 (February, 1903), pp. 13–21; Szu-hsien, "Disputing the *Hsin-min ts'ung-pao's* Discussion of a Nonracial Revolution," *Fu-pao,* No. 3 (May 25, 1906), no pagination; "The Dangerous State of the Han People's Freedom to Assemble and Speak," *Chung-kuo jih-pao,* March 9 and 11, 1907, p. 2.

[13] A New Citizen of China, "On Government and Popular Rights," p. 4.

[14] Chih-ch'un, "Disputing Liang Ch'i-ch'ao," *Fu-pao,* No. 4 (August 5, 1906), pp. 53–54; see also "On Nationalism," *loc. cit.*

[15] Chih-ch'un, "Disputing Liang Ch'i-ch'ao," p. 53.

—fear and antagonism mingled with admiration for Western accomplishments, and a feeling that a titanic competition lay ahead.

These racial feelings merged into a much broader campaign for the creation of a strong Chinese nation, capable of warding off foreign threats and undertaking massive changes in all facets of the society. Nationalism was the vital student concern, and all other proposals and doctrines advanced by them were derived from or related to this primary goal. Nation-building occupied the first priority as far as the overwhelming majority of student writers was concerned, and many did no go beyond that goal. By what means could a strong nation be constructed? Most of the students argued that a revolution which would oust the Manchus was the essential first step. It was on this point that Liang lost the battle to gain a majority of the students, and Sun won their support. Liang's argument was that if the emperor Kuang-hsü were restored to the throne, China could proceed to advance under a constitutional monarchy, in a manner not dissimilar to Japan. China was not prepared for republicanism, asserted Liang, and dictatorship, not democracy, would be the result of any such experiment. A revolution, moreover, would throw China into chaos, rendering her people easy victims for white conquest and rule. It was upon this point that Liang laid increasing stress as the polemics grew hotter, and he broadened the threat to include the dangers of seeking foreign capital assistance. The Han and Manchus together with the other peoples composing China, could all work together, he insisted, under the framework of a constitutional monarchy, for essentially they were of the same culture. A struggle among the peoples of China could only mean the dismemberment of the nation and subsequent slavery.[16]

For most of the student writers, Liang's words fell upon deaf ears: China belonged to the Han people who were the great majority. There could be no meaning to Manchu constitutionalism, because the Han would continue to be humiliated and enslaved by an alien, barbarian race. Those Han who tried to pro-

[16] "Riots and Foreign Intervention," a commentary by the Master of the Cold Drinks Room, *Hsin-min ts'ung pao*, No. 82 (May 5, 1905), p. 16.

tect Manchu rule were traitors to their people.[17] When some of the young writers talked of revolution, their current frustrations seemed to be released in a flow of heroic, grandiose, and uncompromising language: The old order was totally corrupt, completely decadent. It had to be torn out by the root, with no part left intact. One should not fear such destruction, because only when the old order had vanished could a new civilization be built —witness the enormous destruction of the French Revolution, and the resulting new era for all mankind. The conditions of China required a war in which rivers of blood would flow. Such righteous bloodshed represented a necessary sacrifice so that subsequent generations of Chinese could be free.[18]

Many of the students, no doubt, became revolutionaries after a process of soul-searching and reflection that involved a consideration of alternatives, and used their intellectual facilities in reaching their decision. It cannot be denied, however, that the espousal of revolution was the most logical method of achieving an emotional release, a method with which reformism could not easily compete. To students discouraged and impatient, the commitment to revolution represented a concrete and dramatic personal act through which they could dedicate themselves to the cause wholeheartedly, unselfishly, and with finality. It did not involve them in any of the intricate compromises and potential corruption that reform efforts would inevitably evoke. It was a heroic, simplistic commitment in tune with the psychological needs of the time.

Thus *every* action of the Peking government increased student wrath. By this time, it seems doubtful that the government could have done anything to satisfy the bulk of the students, unless Manchu leaders had been willing to commit suicide collectively. When Peking displayed a coolness toward student attempts to organize an armed force in Japan to resist Russian encroachments in Manchuria, or when genuinely alarmed by increasing revolutionary activities it placed spies in their midst, there were

[17] Hsiao-tzu, "To Correct the Falseness of the Han Thieves, K'ang and Liang," *Ta-chiang,* Nos. 2–3 (1907), pp. 8–13.

[18] "National Heritage," *Han sheng,* Nos. 7–8 (June, 1904?) p. 2. See also Fei-sheng, "On National Spirit," pp. 1–12.

naturally outcries of rage and protest.[19] But the young radicals did not take kindly to the belated reform efforts either: These efforts, including the pledge of constitutionalism, represented a trap, an attempt to poison the minds of the Chinese so that they would be deflected from the revolutionary path.[20] Suppression and radicalism, interacting on an ever increasing scale, dominated the political horizon, crushing the advocates of constitutional monarchy, pushing the moderates onto the defensive.

SOLUTIONS

What should the tactics of revolution be? The influence of the Russian Nihilists, and the general theories of anarcho-syndicalism, were substantial upon the young Chinese revolutionaries of this era. Just as the French Revolution represented to them the great historical model of a righteous and meaningful revolution, so the contemporary acts of the Russian revolutionaries suggested to many of the student writers a pattern to emulate.[21] Indeed, the equation of Russia and China both in terms of problem and solution was a common exercise: Here were two twentieth-century dinosaurs still chained to absolute monarchy and backwardness. Only a revolution could break those chains. One method of striking at the decadent state was to commit one or two heroic acts. Assassination, like a clap of thunder, could arouse a whole people and, providing it reached close to the heart of the system, might set in motion a series of reactions leading to massive revolution.[22]

Other writers, however, seemed to appreciate the fact that a modern revolution, if it were to be successful and lasting, might require methodical planning and an organization: Certainly, one immediate task was to raise the status of the military. For too

[19] See the Student News section, *Hu-pei hsüeh-sheng chieh,* No. 5 (May, 1903).

[20] "Agitation Against Closing Student Associations," *Fu-pao,* No. 2 (April 25, 1906) pp. 34–35.

[21] See "Revolution and Women's Rights," *Fu-pao,* No. 6 (September 25, 1906), pp. 37–39 and "The Ch'ing Court's Proclamation Banning Books and Periodicals," *Chung-kuo jih-pao,* March 19–20, 1907, p. 2, as examples.

[22] "Opening Proclamation," *Che-chiang ch'ao,* No. 1 (January, 1903), pp. 1–6.

long China had depreciated the vital role of the military men in defending the Chinese people at critical junctures in their history. Military heroes of the past had been deliberately hidden. It was now essential to feature them, so that the Chinese people could know the truth about the past, and sense the needs of the times. The first requirement of a modern state was power, and this required a broadly-based, modernized army. It also required a people physically fit, not the white-faced scholars of the past. And it required certain heroes, among whom could be the great Chinese warriors of the past and the student-warriors of the present.[23]

A few writers proceeded to a discussion of appropriate military tactics, a discussion made additionally interesting by subsequent events and doctrines, including those of Maoism. Was it more important to attempt to seize Peking first, or should the initial effort be to take the outlying provinces and surround the capital? Arguments were advanced on both sides.[24] To capture the capital might be of critical importance since if one could seize the seat of authority and hold the emperor hostage, the whole country would be shaken. The Manchus themselves had come to power by concentrating upon the conquest of the capital, and the Taipings, although they had occupied a huge part of China, had ultimately failed because they could not reach Peking. As long as the emperor existed outside the control of revolutionary forces, many would not desert his banners. On the other hand, some student writers were appreciative of the fact that a revolutionary reservoir was slowly being developed in the provinces. Returned students, and many others dissident to some degree, were occupying important military and civilian posts at the provincial level. Moreover, provincial consciousness, despite the rising nationalist tide, was still very strong even among the "enlightened" elements. Might it not be more practical, therefore, to begin the revolution in those provinces which had the best political-military preparations, particularly since the key to

[23] "The Connection Between Military Matters and the State," *Hu-pei hsüeh-sheng chieh,* No. 4 (April, 1903), pp. 49–62.

[24] For this discussion, see "The Rumor that the Revolutionary Party Intends to Take Peking," *Chung-kuo jih-pao,* March 12, 1907, p. 2.

power now lay with certain provincial military forces? Could not the balance of power be decisively altered by seizing a few critical provinces?

For many student writers, however, it was not sufficient merely to espouse Han nationalism and discuss the tactics of revolution. Inevitably, at some point, the question arose, "What should the new China be?" And to this question, most writers had an immediate answer in political terms: The new China should be operated as a constitutional republic. Civilized people had achieved government under law. They had constructed a society in which rights and obligations were clearly specified, and the concept of citizenship made meaningful. This required a fundamental organic law, a constitution.[25] There was almost universal agreement on this proposition among the students and exiles in Japan. While Liang and Sun and their respective supporters could agree upon little else, they could agree upon this, indicating once again how powerful an influence the Western concept of constitutionalism had become by the beginning of the twentieth century. The revolutionaries went further, of course: Monarchy, and particularly the type of absolute monarchy characterizing Russia and China, was completely archaic. What modern, powerful society had not rested ultimate power with its people? An informed, united, participating people—and these alone created a strong nation. Thus, the national capacity to ward off foreign encroachments and maintain independence was intimately related to the acceptance of popular sovereignty and a republican system of government.[26]

And how were these goals to be achieved? Almost invariably, the young writers started with a discussion of education or, as many of them phrased it the necessity of adopting new learning: The power of such nations as Great Britain and the United States, and the rapid rise of Japan, were due in large measure to a new educational program designed for all citizens. Conversely, the fall of nations like India, Egypt, and Poland could be traced

[25] Chih-na-tzu, "The People's Rights of Freedom Under Law," *Che-chiang ch'ao,* No. 10 (November, 1903), pp. 33–40.
[26] Chung-k'an, "On Self-Government," pp. 1–10.

to the backwardness or failure of their educational systems.[27] The purposes of the new education should be fourfold: First, it was essential to develop in the Chinese people a national spirit, a consciousness of their identity as *Chinese,* a spirit of patriotism and of responsibility to society as a whole. Germany, Japan, and the United States were, each in its own way, examples of how education was crucial to the development of a strong and successful nationalism.[28] Second, it was necessary to develop in Chinese youth a new character, a new set of values. Under the traditional educational system, China had been deprived of her youth. From the outset of their educational experiences, young people had been taught the old virtues of submissiveness, dependence, and strict adherence to their seniors' injunctions in accordance with the principles of Confucian ethics; the reading of poetry and the recitation of the classics had been substituted for practical learning. Thus, all youth had been made prematurely old, and China had been prevented from being a youthful nation, capable of tackling with courage, imagination, and vigor the great new challenges confronting her.[29] The modern educational system should inculcate new values: physical fitness (no more white-faced scholars); freedom both for the individual and for the nation; creativity, not the old emphasis upon highly stylistic, ritualized reproductions of the classics; and science, not a reliance upon religion or antiquated myths. The new ethics should thus be built around modernity: the creation of a vigorous, independent, rational man who was capable of and committed to the creation of a strong new China.[30]

It was also important that the new education, in addition to stressing science in general terms, place a heavy premium upon technical training. The new China would need engineers, construction men, chemists, doctors, and modern military men. All of these fields of learning should be emphasized, along with the

[27] "The Citizens' Education," *Hu-pei hsüeh-sheng chieh,* No. 3 (March, 1903), pp. 13–20; "Fundamental Laws," *Chiang-su,* No. 2, pp. 15–22.

[28] A New Citizen of China "The Influence of Academic Knowledge Sways the World," *Hsin-min ts'ung-pao* (1902), p. 4.

[29] "The Relation of Heroes and Civilization," *Ibid.,* p. 6.

[30] I-chiu, "The Education of the Anglo-Saxon Race and the Direction of Today's Chinese Education," *Che-chiang ch'ao,* No. 4 (May, 1903), pp. 41–48.

essential task of training huge numbers of primary and secondary school teachers. China's capacity to compete in the modern world, and her ability to reach the goal of constitutional republicanism, would depend upon success in these respects.[31] Finally, it was necessary that universal primary education be established. The eradication of illiteracy had been one of the factors responsible for the success of nations like Japan, Great Britain, and the United States. A people capable of understanding and following rules—whether of the state or of the factory—were a source of unending strength, whereas ignorance bred poverty and weakness.

It would be difficult to overestimate the emphasis which the young revolutionaries placed upon education. For many, the route to progress was simple; education was a panacea. Educated men became rational men, men capable of operating any political system and equipped to tackle any problem of social or economic development, however complex. Once again, the powerful influence of the contemporary West—and of Japan—is to be discerned. This was an age of enormous faith in the potentialities and promises of the educated man, an age in which thinking about political and social development was relatively simple and uncomplicated. The basic beliefs of many Chinese radicals were little different from those of their more mature Western contemporaries.

MODERNIZATION

The new China should thus be a constitutional republic in which a people, progressively enlightened by "new learning," should be enthroned as sovereigns. Viewed from the standpoint of the Western liberal, these were laudable values, but what operational possibilities existed? To put this question differently, did the students, consciously or unconsciously, grasp the concrete problems of political modernization and show any capacity to deal with them in a systematic, balanced fashion? To approach this question, we must first use the perspective of the 1960's to set forth succinctly the major ingredients of the political moderniza-

---

[31] "The Rise and Decline of the Chinese Race," *Chiang-su,* No. 4, pp. 1–8.

tion process in general as it has operated in our times. Perhaps six primary factors have been involved: a heavy and initial commitment to the creation of a nation-state; the greatly increased centralization of political power, and the eradication or substantial reduction of "private government" and local or regional autonomy; the establishment of a government under law, capped by some type of fundamental law or constitutional system; the movement from an ascriptive, undifferentiated bureaucracy toward a technically trained, scientifically selected, specialized bureaucracy; the shift from legitimization of power and authority via religious myth to legitimization via a secular ideology; and finally, the rise of mass participation in politics, with a corresponding emphasis upon political organization and manipulation.

It would be entirely unfair, of course, to assume that the young Chinese students studying in Japan in the first decade of this century should have acquired the perspective granted to the social scientist of today. Nevertheless, the six basic factors outlined above have underwritten nearly every experiment in political modernization conducted in our times. Thus, they represent suitable yardsticks against which to measure the trends in any particular experiment; we must bear in mind, however, that successful deviations from the normal pattern at one point or another are always possible. To what extent did the above considerations enter into the consciousness of our student rebels? And in those cases where they evidenced concern, how did they propose to initiate the desired change? In sum, how do these revolutionaries relate to their successors and to the more universal patterns of our age?

The first factor, that of nation-building, was clearly regarded as of critical importance by the student writers, as we have already noted. "Why do the foreigners treat us like dogs?" queried one author. Then he proceeded to answer his question, asserting that it was because the Chinese people had no sense of patriotism, no willingness to sacrifice for the whole of the society, no identity as members of a single nation.[32] We Chinese are dead,

[32] "Concerning the Future of China and the Welfare of Our People," *Hu-pei hsüeh-sheng chieh,* No. 3 (March, 1903), pp. 1–12.

mourned another writer, we have no state to give our lives purpose and meaning, protection and consequence.[33] The Japanese term *minzokushugi*, "the principle of a common race," a term frequently used to connote nationalism (with a strong racial tinge) was adopted by scores of student writers. Did nation-building in the student mind involve more than a revolution that would overthrow the Manchus and a new educational program that would stress patriotism and a new morality? It cannot be doubted that these were the two broad themes receiving the greatest attention and emphasis. As we have noted, the racial component in student thought was extraordinarily high, and the insistence that the new China must be a Han China was almost universal. Moreover, with the Japanese model so clearly before them, and with the examples of the "advanced West" also available, the students naturally saw education as the primary means of creating a unified, participating, patriotic people, a people that could serve as the foundation of a powerful modern state.

A number of the student writers, however, advanced other specific measures as necessary if a successful Chinese nation were to be created. Many felt that the first task was that of breaking down certain old patterns of behavior and loyalty that stood as formidable barriers to the development of a modern nation-state. To a few, the chief obstacle was the Chinese family system which had to be frontally assaulted.[34] Others saw the intense local and regional ties as the primary barriers to true nationalism. A number of writers attacked the general "isolationist, self-contented" mentality of the Chinese, and stressed the need to deal broadly and openly with other peoples on a basis of equality and independence, abandoning the intensive hierarchical concept of the world that had nurtured Chinese backwardness.[35] The successful creation of a Chinese nation, in sum, was inextricably connected with basic changes in mental outlook and interpersonal relations ranging from new loyalty priorities for the individual to a radically new approach to international relations.

Coupled with these changes, basic alterations in the traditional

[33] "Opening Statement," *Fu-pao*, No. 1 (April 15, 1906) pp. 1–2.
[34] "An Argument for a Family Revolution," *Chiang-su*, No. 7, pp. 13–22; I-chiu, "The Education of the Anglo-Saxon Race," pp. 41–43.
[35] "The Relation Between Education and Self-Government," pp. 15–23.

class structure would be necessary, argued a number of students. The old China had been completely dominated by the literati; their ways and their prejudices had determined the values and the institutions of Chinese society.[36] Not only had they protected a formalistic, sterile educational system, but they had also exhibited contempt for military men and the entrepreneurial class. But the creation of a modern state was intimately related to the elevation of these two classes. China needed a powerful army based upon universal conscription, modernized in terms of equipment and training, and strengthened in terms of morale.[37] Similarly, it was essential to encourage the development of a new entrepreneurial class, providing it with new incentives and a new status in society.[38] A modern military establishment and modern industry were the two key pillars of a modern state.

While these positions were not taken by a large number of writers, they were expressed with sufficient frequency (particularly the argument relating to the importance of the military class) to indicate that a number of the students were committed to a social revolution of major proportions, recognizing that the nation-building process, if it were to be successful, required drastic changes in traditional Chinese class and social relations. Only those who performed vital functions on behalf of the modern state should be recognized and rewarded. Parasites—whether traditional literati or traditional gentry—should reap neither profits (hence the Single Tax) nor honor. More concrete measures were also proposed. For example, several writers argued that from a nationalist standpoint alone, it was essential that railroads and other means of internal communications be developed. A sense of national identity, as well as a capacity for national action, could be achieved only when the physical barriers to contact had been removed.[39]

[36] "The Problem of Kiangsu Morality," *Chiang-su,* Nos. 11–12, pp. 1–11; Tsung-shih, "On the Responsibility of Yunnanese," *Yün-nan* (1907), no pagination.
[37] "An Open Letter to the Honorable Elders of Our Country," pp. 28–30.
[38] "The Problem of Kiangsu Morality," pp. 10–11; "Causes for the Lack of Development of Chinese Industry," *Hu-pei hsüeh-sheng chieh,* No. 3 (March, 1903), pp. 31–38.
[39] "Opening Statement," *Hu-pei hsüeh-sheng chieh,* No. 1 (January, 1903), pp. 1–16.

Thus, if there were any shortcomings involved in the student approach to nation-building, they did not lie in a failure to appreciate its importance. With respect to the second factor, that of the centralization of political power and the reduction of local authority, the students necessarily displayed some ambivalence. Their personal identification with their own province or locality was still very strong in most cases. The appeal in the Yunnanese journal for *Yunnanese* to save *Yunnan* (not Chinese to save China) was not an untypical approach.[40] But quite apart from this natural localist or provincial legacy, practical considerations abetted a support for strong local action. China was a vast area, greater in size and population than the whole of Europe. A strong case could be made for federalism, and for the emphasis upon *local* self-rule as the first step in the development of *national* democracy. As in the case of the debate over military tactics, one could argue for concentrating first upon the provinces. The crisis was an urgent one, and the most available organizations and institutional facilities were those at the local and provincial levels. For those who thought in terms of stages of development, moreover, the province-by-province development of self-government was the most practical method of reaching constitutionalism and republicanism on a nationwide basis.[41]

It cannot be denied, however, that a certain division existed in the writings between those whom we may call supporters of "instant democracy" and those who were attracted to "developmental democracy." The former tended to emphasize a one-stage thrust toward modernization involving action essentially at the national level, uniform policies, and by implication at least, a high degree of centralized authority. The latter stressed the importance of initiating programs of self-rule at the local and provincial levels, thereby developing the foundations for a national democracy while at the same time revitalizing and strengthening political relations at the grass roots. This conflict, it should be emphasized, was not as clearly spelled out or recognized as our succinct statement of the two positions would suggest. It did

[40] "Opening Statement of the Yunnan Journal," *Yün-nan,* No. 1 (August 28, 1906), pp. 1–9.
[41] "Concerning Local Self-Rule in China," *Han sheng,* Nos. 7–8, pp. 1–8.

exist, however, and in a certain sense it symbolized the curious gap between local and national political institutions that was to plague each successive wave of would-be reformers, including the Communists.

On the issue of a government by law, however, there were few if any divisions. Indeed, as we have noted earlier, constitutionalism was one of the few positions commanding almost universal support. A large number of student writers, moreover, attributed the weakness and backwardness of China to the inadequacies of government by absolutist decree or personal whim. They insisted that only modernized codes, relating to both civil and criminal fields, as well as a constitution fixing the rights and obligations of every citizen on a basis of complete equality before the law, could bring China abreast of civilized states and win her the respect of the advanced world. The impact of Japan upon the student writers in these respects was strongly in evidence.[42] In retrospect, one can discern a fundamental problem that the students were not likely to appreciate. Law, and particularly constitutional law, tends to freeze political institutions in a period of exceedingly rapid socio-economic change. If its operational premises are too far divorced from current realities, it is likely to be little more than a scrap of paper, futuristic possibly, but meaningless. If the premises are more or less even with or only slightly ahead of the socio-political capacities of the society, these capacities are likely to overtake the law quickly, with increasing tension developing as a result. Constitutionalism has been repeatedly challenged in emerging societies because of these problems, and China was to prove no exception. The faith in law at this point, however, was high.

On the other hand, the student writers of this period devoted scant attention to specific issues connected with the recruitment, training, and values of the "new" bureaucracy.[43] A few general principles were usually mentioned, of course: Officials in the new China should be the servants of the people, not their masters. Their training should include the necessary technical courses,

---

[42] "On Sending Shansi Students to Japan," *Yu-pao,* No. 2, p. 115.

[43] "An Open Letter to the Honorable Elders of Our Country" is one of the few articles making any reference to the training of officials.

and as in the case of other civilized nations, they should be selected via a civil service system. On occasion moreover, a student writer would level an attack upon Confucian education as sterile and formalistic. At the same time, however, many of the issues related to the bureaucracy represented another area of political modernization where student attitudes were characterized by some degree of vagueness and ambivalence. This was particularly true of the nonmilitary students. A substantial majority of these students, it must be remembered, came from the upper socio-economic strata and were themselves the products of an essentially classical education. They were largely unfamiliar with the range of technical and specialized materials that could be useful to officials, and the Japanese experience was not always of great help in this respect. In Japan itself, higher education during this period was strongly theoretical or legalistic. Outside the military field, the bureaucracy tended to operate with a minimum of rigorously defined, highly specialized skills. One senses that the Chinese students at this point were far more interested in seeing a spirit of *noblesse oblige* developed within their own class, in the fashion of the British or Japanese tradition, than in the cultivation of a strongly equipped civil service in technical terms.

The commitment to a secular ideology posed no serious problem to the young Chinese revolutionaries, despite the fact that they were in a position to witness in Japan a prominent exception to the general rule: the effective use of a highly primitive religious myth for purposes of nation-building and the legitimization of authority. Their cultural heritage was very different. The essentially secular character of Confucianism made it relatively easy for the Chinese students to dismiss religion as an appropriate or possible base for a meaningful Chinese political ideology. Willing to grant the historic importance of the Judaic-Christian tradition and the church-state struggle to Western liberalism, student writers saw no need or possibility for a similar development in contemporary China.[44] Having firmly established a secular basis for their ideological views, the students, as we have noted, pro-

[44] A New Citizen of China, "Religious Protection Does Not Honor Confucius," *Hsin-min ts'ung-pao*, No. 2 (1902), pp. 4–10.

ceeded to enunciate two basic themes repeatedly: constitution-alism and republicanism. These two themes, of course, were so much in the universal spirit of the times that it would have been surprising had they not been in the forefront of student thought. What is more interesting is the attempt of a few writers to grapple with the problem of how to effectuate these principles rapidly in a backward society. For the first time, a small number of Asian intellectuals began to explore the concrete problems of political modernization in a non-Western society, and their highly tenta-tive and fragmentary conclusions heralded the beginning of a new age.

Any fundamental revolution, argued various student writers, needed heroes—men who could lead their people toward new goals. Given its current condition, however, China needed more than heroes; she needed the sustained tutelage of a dedicated student-intellectual elite.[45] By right, the people were sovereign, but they could assume that role and perform their legitimate function only after they had been educated and instructed in both technology and political values.[46] Guidance of the people would move through several stages, each involving a different institutional requirement. The revolution and its immediate aft-ermath would necessitate military rule. This would be quickly followed, however, by the establishment of civilian tutelage, with a modernizing elite such as the members of the T'ung-meng Hui taking on the burdensome task of preparing the Chinese people for constitutional democracy.[47] This preparation would certainly involve more than political indoctrination, although thought re-form was a factor of signal importance. Social and economic changes of major proportions were also crucial; industrialization, changes in the agrarian system, tax reform, promotion of new learning, alterations in the family system, and the greater equali-zation of wealth and opportunities were among the many policies that had to be advanced.

Thus, in very embryonic form, the Chinese student writers of

[45] "Greeting Fellow Students," *Hu-pei hsüeh-sheng chieh,* No. 5 (May, 1903), pp. 1–16.

[46] "The New Spirit of the Citizens," *Chiang-su,* No. 5, pp. 1–9.

[47] Wei Chung, "Opening Statement of 20th Century China," *Erh-shih shih-chi chih chih-na,* No. 1 (May 1, 1905), pp. 1–14.

this period, stimulated by Sun Yat-sen and countless other sources, set forth the first concept of "guided democracy" to be enunciated in the non-Western world. This concept, to be sure, was advanced by only a few writers, and then often in a very imprecise and casual manner. The outline of ideas presented so concisely above undoubtedly suggests a much sharper and more complete consciousness of the central issues than in fact existed in any one writer's mind. It is enormously important, however, that almost all of the vital issues of the future were raised in some form: the notion of tutelage; the necessity of a "vanguard," a modernizing elite; and the need for specific stages of develop-ment, each involving different authority-institutional patterns. A few decades later, the main stream of political thought through-out the non-Western world would be devoted to these and related issues. The student writers of this period and men like Sun deserve far more recognition than has yet been accorded them for anticipating the great issues of their century. They perceived, however dimly, many of the problems that would soon move to the center of the world stage.

Finally, let us turn to the question of mass participation in politics. The student view of "the people" and their political role was both a part of and distinct from their more general ideologi-cal position. In the most basic sense, as we have noted, the people were by definition the source of all power and all truth. Was this not the essence of democracy? If for the moment they were illiterate, poverty-stricken, and backward, that was the fault of the old system and it could be altered. The first task indeed was to bring to light the true potentialities and real character of the masses. In these respects, as in many others, selected aspects of Chinese tradition could abet the main thrust of contemporary Western thought. This was an age dominated by an almost child-like faith in the rationality of the common man, could he but be liberated from the shackles of backwardness. It was only later that a sadder and wiser generation realized that democracy, and the concept of limited government, could best be defended by admitting the existence of some quotient of irrationality in all men. The Chinese students, however, were not deeply troubled by the thought of any permanent limitations upon all men, only by the conditions in which Chinese men temporarily found themselves.[48] It would be wrong to assume, however, that the avid support for mass participation stemmed only from a fervent belief in the democratic creed. Like the Japanese liberals some years earlier, the student writers of this period saw mass involvement as a source of power for the state: A strong people make a strong nation. An alert, knowledgeable, participating citizenry provide the broad base for modern national power, as the advanced West and Japan so clearly illustrated.[49]

CONCLUSION

How should we summarize the student writings in terms of their content, emphasis, and relationship to the revolutionary path that lay ahead? First, it can be stated with assurance that the most pervasive theme of the times was nationalism, and a nationalism built upon a strong racial consciousness. The support for a Han revolution against Manchu control and white domination was implicit in almost every essay. The constant reference to white, yellow, black, and brown races, and to such ethnic groups as the Jews and the Poles was reflective of the strong racial feelings that characterized the young Chinese intelligentsia of this era. And the method of treating these subjects indicated clearly that prejudice and a penchant for sweeping racial generalization usually accompanied those feelings. Few if any of the writers seemed disposed to set aside racial or ethnic considerations and attempt to deal with human beings as individuals. Almost always, complex feelings of racial superiority intermingled with admiration/disdain, love/hate attitudes toward the white West to provide the psychological base of the nationalist movement. And are these factors still not a powerful force in shaping the policies and attitudes of the Chinese elite, the egalitarian, universalistic tenets of Marxism notwithstanding?

A strong majority of the student writers at this point were also

---

[48] See, for example, Yeh-kuang, "Should China Aspire to Constitutionalism Today?" *Fu-pao*, No. 2 (April 25, 1906), no pagination.

[49] "Mr. Wu Yüeh's Prospectus upon His Personal Sacrifice," *Fu-pao*, No. 2 (April 25, 1906), pp. 1–7.

committed to revolution. Such a a commitment, indeed, became almost a psychological necessity as we have seen—a dramatic, simple act relieving personal tensions, reducing the possibility of being "corrupted," and liberating some of the pure, action-oriented desires among a deeply frustrated group. Blood had to flow. Traditional elites and institutions had to be uprooted. The old had to be levelled before the new could be established. In much of this, one sees romanticism and myth, a defiance of reason, and the espousal of a type of anti-intellectualism that refused to acknowledge complexity, catered only to the simple. For this reason, a number of the most sophisticated intellectuals among the students—Liang Ch'i-ch'ao was never without his supporters—could not follow the revolutionaries. Perhaps it would be more appropriate to consider this a quasi-intellectual movement, rather than one which operated from within the heartland of the Chinese intelligentsia. Once again, cannot we discern in this some mirror to the future, some similarity to the later Marxist-Leninist era?

Like all major movements, however, this one had its paradoxes and contradictions, its elements of insight as well as of naïveté. Revolution for what? The commitments on the part of the student radicals were clearly to the broad values of contemporary Westernism: progress, science, industrialization, and democracy. These were the basic goals. And a constitutional republic was the desired political framework within which to achieve these goals. This was an era, it must be reiterated, when the impact of the classical Western liberal model was at its height—indeed, when this represented the *only* model of political modernization. Already, however, a few student writers had a vague appreciation of the great difficulties that might be involved in transplanting these Western values and institutions to Chinese society. The major conflict between borrowed political institutions and the indigenous proclivities of the society that in some measure was to affect all emerging states during the twentieth century was on the horizon. And this in turn evoked a new pattern of thought. The first tentative experiment with ideas of tutelage, a vanguard elite, and political stages of development began.

In these respects, one must measure carefully the distance between these students and the Chinese Marxist-Leninists of some two decades later. The values, the ultimate goals, of the student radicals were strongly liberal; these were young men thoroughly committed to Western-style parliamentarism as the best system of government known to man. Moreover, while some of the students called themselves socialists, or recognized socialism as the wave of the future, they were, at most, social reformers, not collectivists. Most importantly, perhaps, the radicals of this generation had only very general and simple theories of organization. Huge advances in the science of power, centering around organizational and mass-media techniques, are the factors truly distinguishing the radicals of today from those of an earlier generation. That these techniques flowed in some measure from the discoveries of these students and many others cannot be doubted. Once the significance of the modern nation-state had been realized, once the importance of mass mobilization and commitment had been discovered, once the relation between the people and power had been appreciated, the development of techniques attuned to these facts was only a matter of time—and scientific "progress." The Chinese student radicals of the first years of the twentieth century thus represent a vanguard whose movement was ultimately to diverge from their values and their goals in certain critical respects merely because others pursued with vigor some of the concepts and techniques which they first explored.

AKIRA IRIYE

Public Opinion and Foreign Policy: The Case of Late Ch'ing China

THE relationship between public opinion and foreign policy has long intrigued students of Western, especially American, diplomacy. As Ernest May has said, historians of United States foreign relations "have written more about public opinion than about diplomacy." [1] Not only historians but psychologists, sociologists, and political scientists have tried to examine such questions as how an opinion is developed on a particular foreign affairs issue, how various opinions may be compared and measured, what relations may be seen between a given policy and a set of opinions, and how the government may manipulate public opinion. Many studies have uncovered the irrationality and superficiality of the views of people on political issues, but even these phenomena have seemed worthy of scholarly attention because of the basic assumption that it is the people who constitute the state.

This study attempts to focus on the role of public opinion in the making of foreign policy in the last years of the reign of the Kuang-hsü emperor. It may at once be objected that "public opinion" exists only in a mass society; although there did appear a type of nationalism on a more or less popular basis in late Ch'ing China, it would be misleading to call it public opinion.

[1] Ernest May, "An American Tradition in Foreign Policy: the Role of Public Opinion," in *Theory and Practice in American Politics,* ed. William H. Nelson (Rice University Press, 1964), p. 103.

The term nevertheless seems to be a useful analytical concept for a number of reasons. First of all, Chinese writers themselves began to talk of "public opinion" (*yü-lun*). There was even a journal called *Yü-lun shih-pao* (Public Opinion Daily). What was meant by *yü-lun* may be quite different from public opinion in the West; but the fact is that a number of Chinese writers, notably Liang Ch'i-ch'ao, did talk as if there could be such a thing as public opinion in China. More important, they held there *should* be public opinion as an essential ingredient of modernization, and they believed they were taking the lead in moulding it. Many foreign observers did not hesitate to apply the term "public opinion" when describing the popular nationalistic movement in China. The self-conscious "opinion-makers" of China assumed that they had the right to influence policy; their opinions were not isolated personal views, but they were organized and presented to the government as the voice of the people. Because the emerging "public opinion" was related, in the minds of its moulders, to the broader question of China's political modernization, it seems plausible to discuss it as a new historical phenomenon.

Granted that the nature and content of "public opinion" differ from society to society, the term is still a useful concept in discussing international relations. Assuming that groups of men in a country held specific views on foreign affairs issues and sought to influence the government's policy, one must ask how these views were perceived by policy-makers, how they in the end affected foreign policy, and what impact they had on other countries' policies. These questions have only begun to be studied even by students of American policy. For the historian of late Ch'ing China they seem to offer an opening wedge through which to explore relations between China's domestic politics and foreign relations. This is of particular importance, for the increasing tempo of political change in China coincided with what may be called a climactic stage in the diplomacy of imperialism in the Far East. Imperialist diplomacy, characterized by numerous ententes and understandings among the powers at the expense of China, provided the setting in which Chinese policy operated. It was at this juncture that public opinion became a factor in

Chinese politics. Chinese policy was thus a function both of imperialist diplomacy and of public opinion. How these two factors interacted is the main concern of this study.

DECISION MAKING IN LATE-CH'ING CHINA

Centralization of political power and the "nationalizing of public opinion" have been rightly stressed as two elements of "modernity." In this sense, China after 1901 was definitely becoming modernized. Institutionally, of course, many loci of power remained, and even some new ones were being created. Almost all provinces had their "foreign affairs bureaus," as well as offices dealing with mining, railway, and military affairs. Governors often interfered with affairs in other provinces, as happened during the *Su-pao* case of 1903.[2] They sometimes corresponded directly with Chinese envoys abroad instead of communicating through the Waiwupu (Foreign Affairs Ministry), as for example when the Liang-kuang governor-general telegraphed directly to the Chinese minister in Tokyo during the *Tatsu Maru* crisis of 1908 which involved the seizure of a Japanese freighter suspected of smuggling arms into China.[3] Governors negotiated foreign loans, as Chang Chih-tung did with Hong Kong in 1905 and with Japan in 1906.[4] Powerful provincial figures such as Chang and Yuan Shih-k'ai had to be consulted on many important questions of diplomacy. Most fundamentally, the province could become the basis of nationalism, since the rights recovery movement would often operate at the provincial level and the recovered rights would be put to good use through the official and nonofficial leaders of the province.

At the same time, there was a countercurrent tending toward

[2] *Hsin-hai ko-ming* [The Revolution of 1911], ed. Chung-kuo shih-hsueh hui, 8 vols. (Shanghai, 1957), I, 408–480.

[3] Chang Jen-chün to Waiwupu, rec'd. February 23, 1908, *Ch'ing Kuang-hsü-ch'ao Chung-Jih chiao-she shih-liao* [Documents on Sino-Japanese Relations during the Reign of the Kuang-hsü Emperor], 2 vols. (Taipei, 1963 reprint), II, 1388.

[4] Chang Chih-tung's memorial of June 6, 1906, *Ch'ing-chi wai-chiao shih-liao* [Historical Materials on Foreign Relations in the Latter Part of the Ch'ing Dynasty], 243 *chüan* (Peiping, 1932–1935), 197. 2 ff.; *Nihon gaikō bunsho* [Documents of Japanese Diplomacy], 47 vols. in 76 books to date, covering the period through 1914 (Tokyo, 1936–   ), XL, Part 2, 564 ff.

greater administrative centralization. The Waiwupu, established in 1901, was headed by a grand councillor, and together with the Grand Council it functioned as the highest organ of foreign policy-making and had full authority over provincial governors on diplomatic issues. The Waiwupu functioned as the clearing-house of memorials and countermemorials on foreign issues. The establishment of telegraphic networks greatly accelerated the trend; governors and even lesser officials telegraphed the Waiwupu on every diplomatic matter, trying to solicit the latter's views or influence them. Selection of consular officials, if not diplomatic envoys, was made by the Waiwupu, and special missions sent abroad invariably reported to this office. Loans and concessions negotiated by the provinces with foreigners could be opposed by the Waiwupu; in 1903 it dissolved an Anhwei mining company for having negotiated with a British merchant, and in 1905 it opposed Chang Chih-tung's loan negotiation with British financiers for railway construction.[5]

Apart from the Waiwupu, the Peking government sought to centralize power by establishing offices to regulate railway, mining, and other matters in the provinces. The superintendents of various railways were appointed by the Peking government, and they took orders first from the Shangpu (Ministry of Trade) and after 1906 from the newly created Yuchuanpu (Ministry of Posts and Communications). The Shangpu, established in 1903, had far-reaching control over mines, as its officials drew up mining regulations and personally directed provincial mining activities.[6] The Shangpu also encouraged the establishment of chambers of commerce and the founding of trade schools. The essential ingredients of diplomacy—bureaucrats and military power—were likewise affected by centralization. The abolition of the examination system and the programs for establishing new armies under central control implied the government's determination to raise the level of efficiency as it conducted China's foreign affairs. It may be said that these two phenomena ex-

[5] This information on Waiwupu authority is gleaned from published and unpublished records of the Waiwupu.

[6] For a detailed study of Shangpu activities concerning mining, see Li En-han, *Wan-Ch'ing ti shou-hui k'uang-ch'üan yün-tung* [The Mining Rights Recovery Movement in Late Ch'ing China] (Taipei, 1963).

pressed the central government's interest in countering the centrifugal tendencies of the Chinese state, as traditionally manifested in gentry opposition to efficient government and in military decentralization through local armies. It is of particular significance that efforts were made to ensure that the central government was constantly apprised of provincial military affairs. The director of the provincial army was appointed by the Board of Army Training, founded in 1903 and later merged into the Luchünpu (Ministry of War). It is well to remember that by 1907 Yuan Shih-k'ai's Peiyang Army had been placed under the command of the Luchünpu.[7] In connection with the recruitment of new bureaucrats, the central government sought to obtain the services of students who had returned from abroad. Although there was no institutional framework for this, at least in theory Peking maintained control over students abroad through the legations as well as the provincial governments.[8]

A parallel phenomenon to administrative centralization was the emergence of self-conscious public opinion. To the extent that nonofficials had any views of their own, they had in the past been represented by the gentry and scholars. The local elites had made their views known by refusing to cooperate in executing a policy, as happened so often vis-à-vis missionaries.[9] Since the 1890's, scholars had begun to found schools and publish journals to promote ideas and influence policy. But it was only after the Boxer incident that a new concept of public opinion came to be widely accepted, and numerous bodies of people—merchants, students, and journalists, as well as gentry and scholars—began in earnest to demand a role in policy-making. Significant seg-

[7] See Hatano Yoshihiro's two studies: "Minkoku kakumei undō ni okeru shingun" [The New Army in the Republican Revolution], *Nagoya daigaku ronshū* [Nagoya University Essays], VIII (1954), 63–76; "Minkoku kakumei to shingun" [The Republican Revolution and the New Army], *ibid.*, XIV (1956), 33–58.

[8] Waiwupu archives at the Institute of Modern History, Academia Sinica, Taiwan (hereafter cited as Academia Sinica Archives), include a file entitled "Ch'u-shih Jih-pen" [Legation in Japan] which has basic material on the functions of the Chinese minister in Tokyo acting as superintendent over students.

[9] See Paul Cohen, *China and Christianity: The Missionary Movement and the Growth of Chinese Antiforeignism, 1860–1870* (Cambridge, Mass., 1963). The book illustrates the fact that the gentry's role was crucial, not in policy-making as such, but in the execution of policy.

ments of the nonofficial population became interested in influencing policy, and they developed techniques for doing so. A public opinion was developing for the first time in modern China.

A look at some of the publications will reveal what the Chinese were saying about this phenomenon at this time. An article in *Wai-chiao pao* (Diplomatic News) gave a very optimistic estimate of public consciousness; after several years of effort, it said, newspapers and journals had succeeded in arousing the people to interest themselves in political matters. Now everybody, even the lower classes, seemed to have stirred themselves up and accepted the principle that individual needs must be subordinated to public concerns and that they must strive to safeguard the country's interests and rights.[10] A more pessimistic note was echoed by an article in *Chung-wai jih-pao* (China and Abroad Daily). It said that in China the people were still not interested in national affairs. In the West, the people were the masters of their country, and the monarch and aristocracy were merely their representatives; in China the opposite was the case. Unless these differences were eliminated, there would be no true modernization of the country. "China first needs political reform before it can carry out new programs." [11]

These two contrary views in fact shared the same concern with political reform and the same assumptions about the nature of modern politics. Both took it for granted that people were the source of power and that their participation was imperative if there were to be effective government. It is these common assumptions rather than differences which most characterized Chinese thinking of the period. As a newspaper wrote in 1908, "A country's political affairs must reflect the people's will. The government must be derived from public opinion." [12] Liang Ch'i-ch'ao insisted again and again that people were the foundation of the state and that China's merits and shortcomings were their

[10] *Hsin-hai ko-ming ch'ien shih-nien chien shih-lun hsüan-chi* [Collected Essays Published during the Ten Years before the Revolution], eds. Chang Nan and Wang Jen-chih, 2 vols. in 4 books (Peking, 1960–1963; hereafter cited as *Shih-lun hsüan-chi*), II, Part 1, 7–9.

[11] *Tung-fang tsa-chih* [Eastern Miscellany], I (January, 1904), 10–13.

[12] *Ibid.,* V (April, 1908), 65–68.

merits and shortcomings. Only a people with a national ideology and capable of governing themselves could be called "citizens" (*kuo-min*); only through these *kuo-min,* Liang's "new people," could there emerge a renovated, vigorous, and independent China.[13] These ideas provided the basis not only of the constitutionalist movement but also of the general political agitation in late Ch'ing China. Liang's radical opponents, the *Min-pao* (The People) group, could not have agreed more with the thesis that a government owed its existence to the consensus of an enlightened citizenry. The revolutionaries, eager to combat the constitutionalists, tended to overemphasize their mutual differences. But the use of terms such as "people's rights," "people's psychology," and "nationalism" (*kuo-min chu-i*) in the *Min-pao* indicates that Liang's basic assumptions were never challenged but were taken for granted as a starting point by the revolutionaries.[14] Moreover, a cursory glance at the newspapers and periodicals then published in China makes it clear that similar ideas had become accepted by practically every interested Chinese. After all, the mushrooming of these publications, totalling several hundreds, was the best evidence that the active participation of people in political affairs was considered an essential basis of modern reform. This assumption was accompanied by suggestions for concrete methods of expressing public opinion. Most fundamental was organization. "If people express their individual views separately, they cannot be said to represent public opinion. We must have organized bodies as organs for expressing opinions," said the initial proclamation by the Cheng-wen She (Political Culture Association).[15] Since the 1890's, interest in organization had steadily grown. Initially only scholars were organizers, and their study groups were devoted to enchancing their own influence as new leaders of the country.[16] Now, with the passing of the exami-

[13] Liang's ideas were fully developed in his "Hsin-min shuo" [On the New People], which appeared as a series of articles in *Hsin-min ts'ung-pao* [New People's Miscellany] in 1902. See also Nomura Kōichi, *Kindai Chūgoku no seiji to shisō* [Politics and Ideas of Modern China] (Tokyo, 1964), pp. 167 ff.

[14] See *ibid.,* pp. 186 ff.

[15] *Hsin-hai ko-ming,* IV, 105–115.

[16] See John Schrecker, "The Pao-kuo Hui: A Reform Society of 1898," *Papers on China,* XIV (Harvard University, East Asian Research Center, 1960), 50–69.

nation system, even scholars such as Liang Ch'i-ch'ao talked of organizing the people, not simply educated men. Organizations were to serve as a link between the government and the populace. They would communicate the people's views to the government, and vice versa. All three—the government, organizations, and people—would be part of the organic whole, and the strengthening of one would result in the strengthening of the other two.

Once organizations were formed, it was but a step to trying to make use of them as active participants in decision-making. Propaganda, agitation, and petition were the three most commonly employed techniques. Organizations printed and distributed handbills, put up posters, and sang songs to promote a cause; and they sent out telegrams and letters to the Waiwupu and other agencies to press their views on the government.[17] This was organized and disciplined movement, to be distinguished from blind and ignorant xenophobia. That is why it was such a potent force in Chinese diplomacy, and why it proved such a challenge to the imperialist powers.

PUBLIC OPINION AND THE IMPERIALISTS

Chinese popular opposition to foreigners was, of course, no new phenomenon. What distinguished the years after the Boxer incident was the public's self-consciously disciplined and "civilized" way of confronting the foreign powers. Its basic concern was with the country's international status, and its ambition to elevate the nation once again to the position of a great power.

These points will become clearer if one examines the anti-American boycott of 1905, the first instance where public opinion became aware, as it were, of what it was doing. The boycott has been well documented as an early manifestation of modern Chinese nationalism. Not much attention, however, has been given to the way the boycott leaders and their supporters ex-

---

[17] Direct communication of the people with the highest organs of the government was a new phenomenon after the Boxers. This alone sufficiently distinguished post-Boxer public opinion from the *ch'ing-i* of the 1880's and degree candidates' petitioning of the 1890's. For an analysis of *ch'ing-i*, see Lloyd E. Eastman, "Ch'ing-i and Chinese Policy Formation during the Nineteenth Century," *Journal of Asian Studies,* XXIV, 4 (August, 1965), 595–611.

plained their thought and behavior. One would miss the essential significance of the movement unless it were recognized that for the principals the basic motive was political; they were to exhibit their influence in decision-making so as to support the government's effort to enhance national status. An article in the *Wai-chiao pao* best exemplified this attitude. The boycotters, it was pointed out, were employing "civilized words and acts" in order to unite and regain national rights. Specific grievances against the United States were not the fundamental issues. What was basic was the elevating of "people's wisdom" through political action so as to enhance the standing of China in the world. "All the world is watching us, and our success will determine our fate; if we succeed, foreigners will say we cannot be slighted." The article called on the boycotters to avoid extreme measures which would not only give the United States a pretext to refuse their demands, but would also embarrass the government's efforts. Finally, it was stressed that not all Americans supported the anti-Chinese policy regarding immigration. Actually it was only American labor that was stubborn; civilized Americans opposed labor's views. The implication was that as long as the Chinese conducted their movement in a restrained and disciplined manner, they would obtain the sympathy of enlightened foreigners, including Americans.[18]

The fundamental self-image of Chinese opinion leaders which emerges from this and other writings is one of responsible and public-spirited citizens resorting to nonviolent methods to obtain justice. As will be seen shortly, however, even obtaining justice was not an end in itself; a number of boycotters emphasized the educational significance of a national movement. But here it must be stressed that toward the government they expressed willingness to help. "We resort to the boycott in order to help our government," read an editorial in the *Hsin Chung-kuo pao* (New China Daily) of Honolulu, which had first advocated the boycott of American goods in 1903.[19] This kind of reasoning, an inevitable corollary of the general concept of public opinion noted earlier, was accepted without question by the leaders of the

[18] *Shih-lun hsüan-chi,* II, Part 1, 3–5.
[19] *Hsin-min ts'ung-pao.* Nos. 38–39 (October 4, 1903).

boycott movement. They wrote and telegraphed to the Waiwupu, kept in close touch with the provincial officials, and assured them all of their peaceful and civilized intentions. There were no overtly subversive, antigovernment thoughts and actions, except in a few localities where radical revolutionaries gained an upper hand, as happened briefly in Canton toward the end of 1905.[20] Actually, the majority of the boycotters self-consciously tried to distinguish themselves from ignorant xenophobes. As suggested in the above article, they attributed Chinese exclusion in the United States to the agitation of American labor, not to the American people or government as such. As a letter from Shanghai merchants to the Waiwupu pointed out, "Maltreatment of Chinese laborers derives from American labor's private views, while the boycott of American goods derives from the Chinese people's sense of public justice. Neither is what the two governments really want and [neither] has anything to do with friendly relations between the two countries." [21] Boycotters made sure that no blind attack would be made on Americans in China on account of the boycott, and that the Chinese should not give the impression of using force to prevent individuals from dealing in American goods.[22] When five American missionaries were killed in October in Lienchow, near Canton, the boycotting merchants in the latter city immediately disclaimed any connection between the two events.[23] It was most important that the boycott not be regarded as another outburst of blind antiforeignism.

The boycott lasted for only a few weeks, but the ideology and techniques of the movement remained. Actually, the boycott

[20] Ting Yu, "1905 nien Kuang-tung fan-Mei yün-tung" [The Anti-American Movement in Canton in 1905], *Chin-tai-shih tzu-liao* [Documents of Modern History], No. 5 (1958), pp. 42–50.

[21] Shanghai merchants to Waiwupu, September 13, 1905, Academia Sinica Archives.

[22] Shanghai merchants to Waiwupu, June 7, 1905, Academia Sinica Archives; see also Kikuchi Takaharu, "Tai-Bei boycott no igi ni tsuite" [The Significance of the Anti-American Boycott], *Rekishigaku kenkyū* [Historical Studies], No. 193 (March, 1956), pp. 13–22; and Chang Tsun-wu, *Kuang-hsü san-shih-i-nien Chung-Mei kung-yüeh feng-ch'ao* [The Chinese-American Labor Dispute of 1905] (Taipei, 1965), pp. 73–81.

[23] Edward J. M. Rhoads, "Nationalism and Xenophobia in Kwangtung (1905–1906): The Canton Anti-American Boycott and the Lienchow Anti-Missionary Uprising," *Papers on China*, XVI (Harvard University, East Asian Research Center, 1962), 178.

itself was considered far less significant than the experience it provided the Chinese people in asserting themselves and their right to influence policy-making. As an article in *Nü-tzu shih-chieh* (Women's World) wrote, the boycott movement was "the heralding voice of exercising our popular rights;" it was to be the beginning of the much more fundamental movement for political renovation.[24] Thus it was quite natural that many leaders and organizations behind the 1905 boycott should have turned their energy to domestic political channels. Beginning in 1906, the Ch'ing government made known its intention of effecting consti-tutional and political reform. The organizations that had agitated in 1905—chambers of commerce, schools, "self-government as-sociations"—now provided the framework and supplied man-power for the movement for constitutionalism. Tseng Shao-ch'ing, the Shanghai leader of the boycott, became a leader of the national movement demanding a speedy convening of a parlia-ment.[25] Liang Ch'i-ch'ao's Cheng-wen She, founded in 1907, started its activity in China by contacting the existing merchant organizations.[26] Canton's self-government association, also founded in 1907, was headed by those who had been active in 1905; its organ, *Kuo-shih pao* (National Affairs Daily), was edited by Ch'en I-k'an, the original spirit behind the anti-Ameri-can boycott, who had returned from Honolulu.[27] These instances illustrated the nature of public opinion at that time. It was concerned with both domestic and foreign issues, and sought to impress its views on policy-makers.

The duality of this phenomenon is illustrated by the *Tatsu Maru* incident of 1908. Again segments of Chinese public opin-ion were aroused when the Japanese imposed harsh terms on China as compensation for Chinese official seizure of a Japanese freighter with a consignment of arms obviously intended for

[24] *Shih-lun hsüan-chi*, II, Part 1, 29–30.

[25] Kojima Yoshio, "Hsin-hai kakumei ni okeru Shanghai dokuritsu to shō-shin-sō" [The Merchant-Gentry Class and the Independence of Shanghai in 1911], *Chūgoku kindaika no shakai kōzō* [The Social Structure of China's Modernization] (Tokyo, 1960), pp. 113–133.

[26] Ting Wen-chiang, ed., *Liang Jen-kung hsien-sheng nien-p'u* [A Chronology of Liang Ch'i-ch'ao] (Taipei, 1959), pp. 241 ff.

[27] Ueno to Hayashi, April 17, 1908, *Nihon gaikō bunsho*, XLI, Part 2, 69–70.

smuggling into China via Macao.[28] Canton's self-government association resolved to resort to a boycott of Japanese goods and services. Like Tseng Shao-ch'ing of Shanghai, the Canton leaders of the boycott such as Hsü Ch'in, Ch'en Hui-fu, and Lo Hsiao-ang had strong political views. Hsü was a member of the Cheng-wen She, and all were disciples of Liang Ch'i-ch'ao or of K'ang Yu-wei.[29] As in 1905, they made an effort to keep the movement within reasonable bounds. They tried to ensure that no illegal methods would be employed and drew a distinction between opposing Japanese policy and professing general friendship for Japan. The leaders again stressed that the boycott was a civilized method of protest and enjoined the people not to resort to uncivilized tactics.[30] A "song of national disgrace" exhorted the people to stir themselves up, assert their rights, enhance national reputation, and reach the level attained by civilized countries.[31]

There was thus an essential similarity between the inspiration behind and the techniques employed in the 1905 and the 1908 boycotts. But the latter was much narrower in scope, hardly extending beyond Kwangtung and Kwangsi. One obvious reason was that some student groups who had actively participated in the 1905 movement opposed the 1908 boycott. For the revolutionary students, opposition to arms smuggling could not be made an attractive cause, for they were the ones who were most anxious to obtain arms.[32] Apart from students, why was it that the Chinese outside of the Canton area, who had been universally clamoring for recovery of rights and trying to develop industries and railways on their own, failed to cooperate against Japan? The most plausible answer seems to be that public opinion in 1908 was concerned with other more pressing matters, and

---

[28] For documentation on the *Tatsu Maru* case, see *ibid.,* pp. 1 ff; and the Academia Sinica file entitled "Erh-ch'en-wan an" [The Second *Tatsu Maru* Incident].

[29] Uchida to Ishii, April 29, 1908, *Nihon gaikō bunsho,* XLI, Part 2, 73; Ueno to Hayashi, April 15, 1908, Japanese Foreign Ministry file entitled "Shinkoku ni okeru Nikka haiseki ikken" [Anti-Japanese Boycott in China].

[30] Kikuchi Takaharu, "Daini Tatsu Maru jiken no tai-Nichi boycott" [The Second *Tatsu Maru* Incident and the Anti-Japanese Boycott], *Rekishigaku kenkyū,* No. 209 (July, 1957), p. 1.

[31] Kubota to Hayashi, May 27, 1908, Japanese Foreign Ministry Archives.

[32] For student reaction, see Uchida to Ishii, April 29 and May 10, 1908, Japanese Foreign Ministry Archives.

outside of Canton it could not focus on anit-Japanese agitation. While it was outraged by Japanese action, its primary preoccupation was with domestic constitutional matters. The constitutionalist movement had reached a critical stage. While self-government associations continued to spring up in all provinces and constitutionalist groups in various cities prepared to organize a nationwide campaign, the Ch'ing court too was steadily moving toward the formation of a constitutional government. But the court was all the more determined to effect reform from above, and it could on occasion take harsh measures, as when in August, 1908 it ordered the dissolution of the Cheng-wen She. Under the circumstances, opinion leaders had to be extremely circumspect. Attack on the Waiwupu could be construed as an attack on Yuan Shih-k'ai, its President, as well as a symbol of the reform movement from above. Thus it is possible that many potential boycotters shied away from radical action in order not to embarrass the government and chose instead to concentrate their energies on demanding speedier constitutional reform.

No matter whether public opinion was directed internally or externally, foreign powers were now given notice that they could no longer treat Chinese opinion as if it were synonymous with traditional opinion or blind Boxerism. As American minister W. W. Rockhill wrote to the President, "There is now coming into existence in China a public opinion and a native press; both crude and usually misinformed, but nevertheless it is a public opinion and the Government knows it and recognizes that it must be counted with. This public opinion and press are at least developing a national spirit in China." [33] Foreign governments, it is true, never developed an adequate response to the new phenomenon; they often behaved as though they could continue to force their demands on the Chinese government. The United States and Japan, victims of the 1905 and 1908 boycotts, pursued a rigorous policy, demanding that stern measures be taken to suppress the boycotts. They insisted that by not controlling antiforeign movements the Peking government was giving the

---

[33] Rockhill to Roosevelt, July 7, 1905, quoted in Jessie A. Miller, "China in American Policy and Opinion, 1906–1909" (Ph.D. dissertation, Clark University, 1938), p. 15.

impression of tacit approval, which in turn would undermine the basis of Sino-foreign relations.[34] But in a more subtle sense, foreign governments were beginning to take note of the new situation in China. To illustrate by focusing on Japanese policy, beginning in 1904 dispatches from China were full of references to the rising tide of nationalism in that country. In a long report on railway construction in Fukien, the Japanese consul wrote in December, 1904:

> Everyone recognizes the most radical changes which have taken place in the Chinese people's ideas. The change has been especially noticeable in connection with the rights recovery question; Chinese have become nationalistic and everywhere they have been talking about rights recovery, railway redemption, and mining development without foreign intervention. . . . Nationalistic thought in connection with foreign rights has permeated the entire land of China, and all classes of people have been affected by the currents of the new thought.[35]

Similar expressions were found in numerous dispatches from other Japanese officials in China. During the boycott of 1908, the consul general in Canton frankly recognized the force of public opinion behind it; he realized, he said, that the movement had originated in the people and that it could not be suppressed merely by putting pressure on the governor or by trying to bribe a few newspapers.[36]

Undoubtedly the realization of what was happening in China raised serious problems for Japanese policy. It was no longer possible to deal only with a handful of high officials, taking advantage of their mutual suspicions and jealousies. It had become necessary to take account of aroused public opinion in China, which at that time was pictured by Japan as nationalistic vis-à-vis foreign rights and potentially antigovernment in domestic politics. Japan, as well as the rest of the imperialist pow-

---

[34] For American policy during the 1905 boycott, see *Papers Relating to the Foreign Relations of the United States, 1905* (Washington, 1906), pp. 204 ff; for Japanese policy in 1908, see *Nihon gaikō bunsho*, XLI, Part 2, 62 ff.

[35] Nakamura to Komura, December 24, 1904, *ibid.*, XXXVII, Part 2, 117–123.

[36] Segawa to Terauchi, July 31, 1908, *ibid.*, XLI, Part 2, 84–88.

ers, was confronted with the alternatives of either pursuing its rights and interests in China and risking not only the growth of anti-Japanese sentiment but possibly, also, a dangerous situation for the dynasty, or coming to terms with Chinese public opinion with a view towards consolidating essential Japanese interests and solidifying the power of the Peking government. Minister Hayashi Gonsuke, in Peking between 1906 and 1908, was strongly inclined to the second alternative. As he wrote in March, 1907, Chinese nationalism was a "natural phenomenon, expressing the people's self-awareness"; it was impossible to eradicate it by force. Japan should rather take advantage of such a sentiment with a view toward "supervising and guiding" Chinese nationalism. It was particularly urgent to form close ties with prominent officials in Peking and the provinces so as to prevent political upheaval. Both these objectives necessitated a conciliatory attitude and compromising spirit in dealing with less vital areas of Japanese rights in China.[37] Many, including Itō Hirobumi and the successive foreign ministers in Tokyo, agreed with such an approach.

The difficulty lay in distinguishing what was vital, which could never be conceded, from what might well be given up to conciliate Chinese public opinion. Japanese indecision on this question was costly. Even on such a relatively insignificant question as the right of Japanese Buddhist missionaries to proselytize in China, the Tokyo government and its representatives in China maintained an inflexible stand, presumably because they wanted equal rights with Christian missionaries; the result was alienation of Chinese officials and people who could not understand why Japan should be insistent on an issue of little apparent significance, belying the official protestation of friendship.[38] There is no doubt, as revealed in this and other episodes at this time, that Japanese policy failed to respond consistently and adequately to the emergence of public opinion in China. This inability, com-

[37] Hayashi to Hayashi, April 30, 1907, Japanese Foreign Ministry file entitled "Kakukoku naisei kankei zasshū, Shina no bu: Manshū" [Miscellaneous Items on Domestic Politics, China: Manchuria].

[38] Regarding the Buddhist missionary case, see my "Chūgoku ni okeru Nihon Bukkyō fukyō mondai" [Japanese Buddhist Missionary Activities in China], *Kokusai seiji* [International Politics], No. 28 (April, 1965), pp. 87–100.

mon to other imperialists, revealed more than anything else the dimension of the challenge posed by Chinese public opinion to the diplomacy of imperialism.

IMPERIALISM AND THE CHINESE GOVERNMENT

The situation, however, was by no means one-sided. The very existence of imperialist diplomacy limited the success and reduced the effectiveness of Chinese public opinion. Officials in China were uneasily aware of the country's real diplomatic position and were sometimes prevented from making full use of the support and encouragement given by the public. Officials were preoccupied not only with regaining the country's international status but also with its basic security, which could be jeopardized by too drastic a confrontation with the imperialist powers. It is also true that the Chinese government was worried lest popular movements grow out of hand and menace political stability. This is easy to understand, but it would be a mistake simply to talk of the officials' fear of the people as the factor inhibiting closer cooperation between the two. After all, Ch'ing officials themselves had done much to educate and organize the people, and, as will be seen, they recognized the legitimacy of moderate public opinion. It was rather their realistic appraisal of national security problems which made them cautious and hesitant, even though basically they shared the aspirations and ultimate goals of the people.

The thinking of all Chinese officials was conditioned by the cataclysmic experience of the Boxer affair, which was only a few years past. There was determination never to invite another such crisis. The image of what had happened in 1900, as seen in official writings during 1904–1908, was that of a foreign invasion of China, precipitated by the antiforeign uprising of ignorant mobs. Officials continued to talk of the latent danger of a similar catastrophe, given the still ignorant and potentially explosive masses and the ever ambitious and avaricious foreign powers.[39] No pretext must be given to either to repeat the events of

---

[39] See, for example, Chou Fu's long report to the Waiwupu in connection with the Buddhist missionary case, cited in *ibid.*, p. 91.

1900. Meanwhile, the government would strive to strengthen the country and regain the lost rights. How did the emergent public opinion fit into this picture? Most officials clearly recognized the possibility of using it not only to strengthen its hand in negotiation with foreigners but also to prevent nationalism from degenerating into xenophobia.

During the 1905 boycott, most high officials recognized that the boycotters had a legitimate cause for complaint. The Wai-wupu at first felt it could use popular indignation against the United States to obtain modification of its immigration policy. A Shansi censor suggested that the United States should be told of possible disturbances unless the immigration matter was remedied. Ts'en Ch'un-hsüan, the Liang-kuang governor-general, expressed sympathy with the boycott as a peaceful, civilized, public-spirited demonstration of the Cantonese people's anger with the American exclusionist policy. Since, however, there was a possibility that the movement might grow out of hand and disturb order, it was best to urge caution on the people while doing the utmost to modify the existing immigration regulations.[40]

Some officials, notably Yuan Shih-k'ai, stressed this last point almost exclusively and showed little sympathy with the agitation. He ordered officials in Chihli to control popular movement and exhorted merchants not to be swayed by "careless agitation." [41] But Yuan's case was exceptional, as the merchants in Tientsin, fearing market stagnation, were not enthusiastic about the boycott started in Shanghai. It would be difficult to say how he would have reacted if merchants under his jurisdiction had decided for the boycott. He would at least have found it necessary to pay lip service to their sentiment. Evidence for this possibility is supplied by the attitude of Chou Fu, governor-general of the Liang-chiang provinces and a close associate of Yuan's for many years. He thought the anti-American boycott originated in "public indignation" at the mistreatment of Chinese laborers, and it proved that Chinese were capable of unified and organized movement. However, Chou felt the boycott was actually more harmful to Chinese than to American merchants, and feared that unless it

[40] Chang Hsüeh-hua's memorial, June 29, 1905, Academia Sinica file entitled "Kung-yüeh an" [The Labor Treaty]; Ts'en Ch'un-hsüan to Waiwupu, August 21, 1905, *ibid.*

[41] Yuan Shih-k'ai to Waiwupu, July 14, 1905, *ibid.*

was brought under control "ignorant people, not knowing where the merchant association's true intentions lie, might resort to violent tactics, and make warlike speeches, while bandits may take advantage of the situation to confuse and agitate foolish people, create an incident, and complicate international relations." Since by the end of August, 1905 the United States government had promised to treat merchants, students, and travellers fairly, governor Chou saw no reason why the anti-American movement should continue. He thus ordered the taotai under his control to bring the movement to an end, prohibiting the pasting of posters advocating the boycott. There was no reason why public speeches should be prohibited, he instructed the taotai, but they should be peaceful and not aim at destructive purposes.[42]

By this time, the court, too, had become alarmed by the prospect of a xenophobic uprising. Pressed by the American minister W. W. Rockhill and prodded by Yuan Shih-k'ai, it issued a decree ordering strict control over all anti-American activities.[43] However, when Rockhill demanded the punishment of Tseng Shao-ch'ing and the Waiwupu complied, Chou Fu strongly protested. He wrote to Peking that such an act would infuriate the merchants, not only because Tseng was merely a spokesman for a popular movement, but also because the United States had been the guilty party to begin with. If stringent action were taken against the alleged ringleader, the matter would not end there but invite a storm of protest. "Even though our system of government is authoritarian," Chou wrote, "we cannot simply summon merchants and tell them they have to trade with so and so . . . or may not trade with so and so and will be punished if they do." Other officials supported this stand, and the matter was allowed to rest.[44]

As this episode revealed, most Chinese officials were willing to recognize the force of public opinion and even to use it to bolster their position while they dealt with foreigners. At the same time, they were extremely wary of irresponsible mass action which could be a prelude to foreign invasion. To this extent it would

[42] Chou Fu to Waiwupu, August 31, 1905, *ibid.*
[43] *Foreign Relations, 1905*, p. 225.
[44] Chou Fu to Waiwupu, September 7, 1905, Academia Sinica Archives.

seem that there was complete rapport between the majority of policy-makers and opinion leaders. This was on the whole true. To take two additional examples, Chang Chih-tung and influential bodies of men in Hupeh and Hunan cooperated successfully in 1904–1905 to bring about the cancellation of the Canton-Hankow railway contract which had been given to the American China Development Company. Chang knew that he could count on popular support as he pressed the government for the annulment of the concession. He wrote, "the determination of the gentry and people in the three provinces [Hupeh, Hunan, Kwangtung] is firm, their morale high, and their influence expanding." Unlike the immigration dispute, the Chinese authorities judged that the popular movement could be used without incurring strong American retaliation. The nationalism of officials and people coincided and brought about the annulment of the contract.[45] A second instance of this rapport can be seen in China's determined opposition to Japanese Buddhist missionary activities. Here not only nationalism but the fear of social disorder united the government and public opinion. It was felt that Japanese missionaries would infiltrate the "unemployed bandits" and "ignorant rogues" and disturb the peace; conversely, the latter might be aroused by the sight of foreign missionaries and precipitate another Boxer uprising. Since Japanese were indistinguishable from Chinese, and since it was much easier for Japanese than for Western missionaries to go to China, these risks seemed great. Chinese officials and reformers were especially incensed by the Japanese use of Chinese temples as missionary headquarters; this was the time when the educational reform movement in China was trying to use the existing temples as new school buildings. Here again, Peking authorities judged that Japan would not resort to force to settle the dispute, and they persistently refused to satisfy Japanese demands.[46]

There were cases, however, where officials sought to suppress public agitation. The Waiwupu's initial support of the 1905 boycott lasted for only a month; as soon as it realized the serious-

---

[45] Chang Chih-tung to Liao Ch'eng, March 24, 1905, in *Chang Wen-hsiang kung ch'üan-chi* [Collected Works of Chang Chih-tung], 6 vols. (Taipei, 1963 reprint), V, 3542; Chang Chih-tung to Grand Council and Waiwupu, August 12, 1905, *ibid.*, III, 1519–1521.

[46] Iriye, "Bukkyō fukyō mondai," pp. 91–94.

ness with which the United States took the matter, it changed its stand and ordered the suppression of the boycott. During the 1908 boycott, the Waiwupu was from the beginning opposed to public agitation. Yuan Shih-k'ai, its president, instructed the provincial governors to suppress the anti-Japanese movement, saying it had nothing to do with the legitimate constitutional movement. He would tolerate certain local movements for self-government, but they should not concern themselves with foreign affairs; to do so would only complicate Peking's negotiations.[47] Moreover, as it became clear that Canton was the only center of the anti-Japanese boycott and that the movement was strongly influenced by followers of K'ang and Liang, Peking redoubled its determination to crush it. In a telegram to governor-general Chang Jen-chün, the Waiwupu asked what was the nature of the "Canton self-government association" that was organizing the boycott; he was instructed to dissolve it.[48] But most fundamental was the Ch'ing officials' larger view of Sino-Japanese relations. The *Tatsu Maru* incident coincided with an aggressive Japanese policy in Manchuria, as revealed in the Chientao and the Hsin-mintun-Fakumen railway questions.[49] The Waiwupu needed to be extremely cautious lest any pretext be given to Japan to take forceful measures. Peking seems to have been especially concerned with the security of Manchuria; should an untoward incident occur in China as a result of the *Tatsu Maru* incident, Japan might use force in Manchuria in retaliation. The exchanges between governor-general Chang and the Waiwupu are revealing. Chang was convinced of the justice of the Chinese cause and insisted Japan be asked to express regrets as part of the settlement of the incident. He suggested that the Chinese officials directly involved in the seizure of the Japanese freighter be summoned to Peking to explain what had happened. The Waiwupu declined the suggestion, as it did Chang's offer of help. It told the governor-general that China had been partially at fault and that at any rate it did not want trouble with Japan. Under instruction,

[47] Waiwupu to Chang Jen-chün, March 12 and April 14, 1908, Academia Sinica Archives; Waiwupu to Tuan Fang, March 21, 1908, Academia Sinica Archives.
[48] Waiwupu to Chang Jen-chün and Chang Ming-ch'i, April 2, 1908, Academia Sinica Archives.
[49] For relevant documents, see *Nihon gaikō bunsho,* XLI, Part 2.

Chang reluctantly ordered his officials to prohibit anti-Japanese agitation, but he continued to voice opposition to what he thought were extremely one-sided terms of the settlement. In a revealing interview with Canton's merchants and gentry, he admonished them to forbear, since China had no choice but to succumb to Japanese pressure, given the fact that "our diplomatic effort is limited by our lack of power." [50]

A third and perhaps the most crucial example of official public differences was the railway nationalization controversy. At the base was the question of financing railway construction. Chinese officials, aware of the impossibility of raising funds at home, turned to foreign borrowing, which implied official control over the railways thus financed. In time this aroused gentry and merchant opposition, resulting in the Szechuan uprising of 1911. But it should be noted that Chinese officials had little choice in the matter. It was not that they initially refused to tap domestic sources of money. Chang Chih-tung tried desperately to raise funds to construct the Canton-Hankow railway after it was redeemed from the China Development Company. But the capital was not available. On the other hand, there were foreign financiers whose governments were ready to step in and offer loans; China could take advantage of their rivalries, but often they collaborated to obtain best terms for all concerned. The story of the Hukwang loan, the culmination of Chang Chih-tung's effort for railway construction, revealed what little freedom of choice the Chinese had in picking creditors. In the end, an enraged populace would revolt against the central government, not only because of the fear of increased control over provincial affairs, but most fundamentally because of opposition to foreign borrowing under duress. [51]

[50] Chang Jen-chün to Waiwupu, March 7, 13, and 19, 1908, Academia Sinica Archives; Waiwupu to Chang Jen-chün, March 4 and 7, 1908, Academia Sinica Archives.

[51] See Hatano Yoshihiro, "Shinmatsu ni okeru tetsudō kokuyū seisaku no haikei" [The Background of the Railway Nationalization Policy at the End of the Ch'ing Period], *Nagoya daigaku ronshū*, XVII (1957), 29–66; Sakurai Toshiaki, "Nichi-Ro sensō to Chūgoku no minzoku undō" [The Russo-Japanese War and the Nationalistic Movement in China], in Shinobu Seizaburō and Nakayama Jiichi, eds., *Nichi-Ro sensō shi no kenkyū* [A Historiographical Study of the Russo-Japanese War] (Tokyo, 1959), pp. 447–478.

CONCLUSION

Recent advances in the study of modern Chinese history and in the analysis of international relations have dramatized the need to bridge the gap between the two fields. There has been no significant dialogue between historians of modern China and analysts of international politics. This study has tried to remedy the situation by suggesting one approach and by raising questions so as to provoke further thought by specialists.

Many systems of schematization have been offered to analyze a country's foreign policy, and many variables have been identified in tracing developments in international power politics. Of the various alternative approaches, the most relevant to modern Far Eastern history would be to focus on the formulation of a given policy and on the specific international situation in which the formulation took place. The former would include the examination of such problems as the policy-makers' definition of national interest (security considerations, economic interests, national prestige, and moral considerations), as well as factors limiting the range of alternatives given to policy-makers (precedents, military and economic capabilities, administrative and constitutional obstacles, and public opinion). The second category of inquiry would be concerned with such questions as whether there was a gap between the international situation as perceived by policy-makers and the actual international situation, and the degree to which the policy conformed to, expanded, or modified the existing framework of international relations. What I have done in this study is to examine the functioning of Chinese diplomacy at a time when "imperialism" defined the Far Eastern international situation. It offered the framework within which China's policy-makers operated. At the same time, public opinion was emerging as one of the most significant elements, limiting the range of policy alternatives available to Chinese officials. Thus the Chinese state system and the international framework interacted through Chinese public opinion. This was because, on the one hand, the Ch'ing government was beginning to give weight to public opinion, and, on the other, public opinion had developed in response to imperialist diplomacy.

This tripartite relationship was never stable. The three elements failed to find an equilibrium with which they could rest satisfied. Chinese public opinion became bifurcated between the radically nationalistic but domestically moderate segment and the domestically revolutionary but externally moderate segment; Chinese officials never succeeded in catching up with the Hegelian gap between the practice and theory of public opinion; and the imperialist powers made no systematic response either to China's government or to public opinion. The imperialists too failed to incorporate a changing China into their scheme of international politics. In the end, if stability was to return to Sino-foreign relations, not only the Ch'ing state but also the diplomacy of imperialism had to go. Even so, decades would pass before a centralized Chinese state, a nationalized public opinion, and a revolutionized world would find at least a semblance of harmony.

ERNEST P. YOUNG

The Reformer as a Conspirator: Liang Ch'i-ch'ao and the 1911 Revolution

IN discussions of the background of the Chinese revolution of 1911, it has long been standard procedure to divide political activists who advocated radical institutional change into two groups. These modernizing intellectuals and agitators were either reformers or revolutionaries. Identification has been simple, at least for the period after 1905: reformers were followers of K'ang Yu-wei and Liang Ch'i-ch'ao; revolutionaries were attached in some way to Sun Yat-sen and the T'ung-meng Hui. Reformers were wedded to the monarchy and peaceful change. The revolutionaries would destroy the monarchy and pursue a course of violence in the form of military putsches and, in some cases, assassination. Once this dichotomy was established, further contrasts have been fed into it. The reformers were more traditional; the revolutionaries had a greater sense of "national consciousness." Sun Yat-sen's group were followers of Rousseau and French radicalism; Liang Ch'i-ch'ao was either a devotee of English liberalism or a disciple of the conservative Swiss constitutional scholar, J. K. Bluntschli. And so on, until the two groups seem to have inhabited different universes, and it would be incredible that they could share aims and programs or engage in similar sorts of political action.[1] The perpetuation of this view of a great contrast between reformer and revolutionary has been encouraged by the clear fact of personal antagonism between Liang Ch'i-ch'ao and some T'ung-meng Hui leaders, which became formidable after 1905 and was perhaps never abandoned.

Differences there were, including a greater degree of impatience and recklessness on the part of Sun's revolutionary colleagues. But concentration upon factional divisions and tactics has led to exaggerations of the contrast in overall outlook, ultimate goals, and methods. If we consider the enormity of the common problems facing both Liang and Sun in their desire to make China an equal of the West, it is perhaps not surprising that closer examination of their two groups reveals a greater identity of views than has commonly been supposed.[2]

In discussing Liang, we must not be trapped by any verbal system of antonyms, in which he is either reactionary or radical, conservative or liberal, reformer or revolutionary. Liang, who has so often been described as abhorring violence, actually called for a violent overthrow of the central government in the months before the 1911 revolution. He secretly planned a *coup d'état* which would have reduced the Manchu emperor to a figurehead. He was not shocked, therefore, when the revolution came. From his extensive correspondence at the time, it is clear that his associates were no more perturbed than he. A study of Liang in 1911 suggests how widespread radical sentiment was outside the specifically revolutionary organizations at the end of the Ch'ing.

[1] For examples of the use of the dichotomy, see: Ch'ien Tuan-sheng, *The Government and Politics of China* (Cambridge, Mass., 1961), pp. 56, 71; Li Chien-nung, *The Political History of China, 1840–1928*, trans. and ed. by Ssu-yu Teng and Jeremy Ingalls (Princeton, 1956), p. 274; Hsiao Kung-ch'üan in a preface to Chang P'eng-yüan, *Liang Ch'i-ch'ao yü Ch'ing-chi ko-ming* [Liang Ch'i-ch'ao and Revolution in the Late Ch'ing] (Taipei, 1964), pp. 2–3; Satoi Hikoshichirō, "Chin Ten-ka no seiji shisō" [Political Thought of Ch'en T'ien-hua], *Tōyōshi kenkyū*, XVII, No. 3 (December, 1958), 82.

[2] Robert A. Scalapino and Harold Schiffrin, "Early Socialist Currents in the Chinese Revolutionary Movement: Sun Yat-sen Versus Liang Ch'i-ch'ao," *Journal of Asian Studies*, XVIII, 3 (May, 1959), 321–342; Michael Gasster, "Currents of Thought in the T'ung-meng-hui" (Ph.D. dissertation, University of Washington, 1962), p. 137; Chang P'eng-yuan, pp. 327–331.

THE CALL TO REVOLUTION

In weighing any political or social system for adoption in China, Liang Ch'i-ch'ao was always much concerned with its relation to the social and political realities of China as he saw them. He valued China's unity and the cohesiveness of her people, and more than anything else he feared that Western intrusion would shatter or undermine these qualities. On such grounds he customarily rejected revolution, which he felt might invite outside intervention.

Yet on a few occasions before 1911 he wrote as if a revolution in China would not be uncongenial to him.[3] Although his concern with the danger of imperialism led him to defend stability and therefore the continuance of the Ch'ing dynasty, he was not immune to anti-Manchu feeling. Both K'ang Yu-wei and Liang were active in support of the Tzu-li Hui and its abortive uprising of 1900. This uprising, although ambiguous with respect to the dynasty, was directed against the existing government in Peking and made use of anti-Manchu propaganda.[4] In his debate with the T'ung-meng Hui, Liang admitted having advocated anti-Manchuism in the past.[5] In a private letter written less than three weeks after the Wuchang uprising, Liang asserted that he would not take second place to the T'ung-meng Hui in his hatred of the Manchus.[6] In 1909, he published a fictional account of China's future in which a republic is established.[7] Liang's commitment to the Ch'ing dynasty, such as it was, was complicated and conditional.

[3] Joseph R. Levenson, *Liang Ch'i-ch'ao and the Mind of Modern China* (Cambridge, Mass., 1953), p. 156.

[4] Joan E. Smythe, "The Tzu-li Hui: Some Chinese and their Rebellion," *Papers on China*, XII (Harvard University, East Asian Research Center, 1958), 51–68; Hao Yen-p'ing, "The Abortive Cooperation Between Reformers and Revolutionaries (1895–1900)," *Papers on China*, XV (1961), 106–107.

[5] Li Chien-nung, p. 207.

[6] Liang to Hsü Ch'in, October 29, 1911, in Ting Wen-chiang, ed., *Liang Jen-kung hsien-sheng nien-p'u ch'ang-pien ch'u-kao* [First Draft of a Chronological Biography and Sequentially Arranged Materials of Liang Ch'i-ch'ao; hereafter cited as *LCCNP*] (Taipei, 1958), p. 339.

[7] Levenson, p. 79.

Liang was not lacking in "national consciousness"; it was precisely his acute concern for national security that impelled him to argue against an anti-Manchu revolution. His view of the West was consistently more critical than that of his T'ung-meng Hui opponents, and his attitude toward imperialism, in this period, more apprehensive. Before 1905, fear of the foreign menace was a conspicuous part of revolutionary propaganda. With the founding of the *Min-pao,* however, the T'ung-meng Hui revolutionaries publicly discarded their previous emphasis on China's weakness in the face of the West or on dangers from that quarter.[8] In a manner suggesting Mao Tse-tung's notion of America as a paper tiger, Sun Yat-sen belittled the threat from imperialism, since emphasis on that threat served as an argument against revolution. Like Khrushchev, Liang saw this threat as a major consideration in the formulation of strategy.

Although Liang was consistent in his basic beliefs and attitudes towards politics, he was ever ready to adjust his strategy to changed conditions. After 1908, a series of changes took place both in Chinese politics and in his personal prospects which eventually induced a sharp break with the antirevolutionary positions he had taken in his debate from 1905 to 1907 with the T'ung-meng Hui.

Even though he was in Japan, Liang could not help but be influenced by the changing mood of politics in China. The Manchu mandate to rule China, long accepted as legitimate by the Chinese, was beginning to crumble under decades of assault by foreign powers. In response to these assaults, nationalist sentiment had emerged among the literate population and was rapidly spreading, through the writings of Liang among others. Dissatisfaction with the government's handling of its foreign relations was increasing in intensity far faster than the government could improve its performance. With the spread of nationalism went an interest in politics in general. The gentry fought to recover railroads and concessions granted to foreigners and at the same time demanded representative assemblies. Granted assemblies at the provincial level, they immediately demanded a national parliament. The increasing interest in politics of this

[8] Gasster, pp. 77–78.

segment of the population, which was far more important than its numbers, soon moved in a radical direction. The revolutionary party grew and inspired the country at large with its propaganda and its military sorties, even though they failed. Everything was reported, one way or another, in the expanding press. The Manchu court encouraged the growth of political concern and activity by its own reform program. It made the politicization more radical by its panicked retreat into a distrustful attitude toward Chinese in general.[9]

Against the background of the spread of political involvement among the people from whom Liang derived support, a number of events occurred which were of special interest to him and which contributed to his abandoning hope in the government.

The first event was the suppression in 1908 of a society of constitutionalists, the Cheng-wen She (Political Information Society), which he had organized the previous year. The purpose of the society was to petition and demonstrate on behalf of a responsible cabinet system of government, an independent judiciary, local self-government, and the achievement of diplomatic equality with the West. The society's aggressiveness in petitioning Peking and its organization of political meetings led the court to order the arrest of the entire membership, and the society was disbanded.[10]

Although a blow, the suppression of the Cheng-wen She was not really unexpected. But after the death of the empress dowager Tz'u-hsi in November, 1908, the expectations of the constitutionalists rose enormously. Even though the Kuang-hsü emperor, around whom many reformist hopes had been built, died almost simultaneously, the regent, the new child emperor's father, was a brother of the late emperor. He might have been expected to revive the spirit of 1898 and carry the reform pro-

[9] Interesting foreign analyses of this new politicization and nationalism can be found, for example, in: William J. Calhoun, Minister to China, to Philander C. Knox, Secretary of State, June 5, 1911, NA 893.00/530, Archives of the Department of State, Records Relating to the Internal Affairs of China, National Archives, Washington, D.C. [hereafter cited as NA 893.00/]; Sir John Jordan, Minister to China, to Sir Edward Grey, Foreign Secretary, March 5, 1911, Annual Report, Archives of the Foreign Office, Public Record Office, London [hereafter cited as FO], 405/201 (12149).

[10] Li Chien-nung, pp. 216–218.

gram much further and faster than had been the case under Tz'u-hsi's rule.

Reform did continue, but increasingly it was judged by reform-minded contemporaries as unsatisfactory. We do not yet have a thorough, detached evaluation of the reform effort of the Hsüan-t'ung period (1908–1912), which on several counts seems impressive. It is clear, however, that Liang and his group were disillusioned by the regent's handling of affairs. A close associate of Liang's during these years, Hsü Fo-su, writes in reminiscences that it was Liang who stimulated the more radical petition movement at the end of 1910, which insisted that 1913 was not soon enough for the opening of a parliament. When the court ordered the petitioners out of Peking, Hsü says, they decided to return to their provinces to organize a revolution.[11] Whether planning for revolution was in fact so general at the time or not, radical discontent was spreading rapidly. Hsü Ch'in, a follower of K'ang Yu-wei for over fourteen years, wrote to Liang in August, 1910 that the government was so rotten that he wished to resort to assassination.[12] Toward the end of 1910, it was apparent that Liang's group was gradually turning to a more radical program of action.

Added to the discontent with the government's performance was a more personal disappointment. After the death of Tz'u-hsi and until the early months of 1911, Liang retained a hope that he could return to China legally. The ban against him and K'ang Yu-wei, which was still in force, seemed in the eyes of its victims to have lost meaning and the last shred of justification. Indeed, Liang must have felt his first doubts about the new administration when the ban was not immediately lifted after Tz'u-hsi's death and the survivors of the 1898 reform movement were not invited home with honor.

In the latter part of 1910, a concerted campaign was mounted to exonerate K'ang and Liang. Liang's several agents in China hoped to influence certain Manchu princes presumed to be

---

[11] *LCCNP*, p. 314. Hsü's remarks must be taken with some caution, since he pursues the particular thesis that Liang more than anyone else brought on the 1911 revolution.

[12] Hsü Ch'in to Liang, August 27, 1910, *LCCNP*, p. 315.

sympathetic toward reform and the veterans of 1898, as well as to use the recently established National Consultative Assembly (*Tzu-cheng Yüan*).

A curious theme in Liang's activities during the last years of the Ch'ing dynasty was the hope that he placed in securing the cooperation of persons close to the court. Friends in Peking reported the tenor of thinking among prominent Manchus, and on this basis Liang selected a few to whom he addressed special appeals. In 1908 and early 1909, in an effort to destroy Yuan Shih-k'ai once and for all, Liang apparently hoped that Prince Su (Shan-ch'i), minister of internal affairs, and Tsai-tse, minister of finance, would be moved by his persuasiveness. By intermediary and by letter, he sought their help in a campaign to secure Yuan's political ruin.[13] By the end of 1910, Liang recognized that Tsai-tse was hostile, and his primary attention shifted to the brothers of the deceased Kuang-hsü emperor, especially Tsai-t'ao.

Although only in his twenties, Tsai-t'ao was one of the most influential Manchus in the government and was noted for his unusual honesty and liberal outlook.[14] At the end of 1908 he had been given the task of organizing the New Imperial Guard (*Chin-wei Chün*) on the same basis as a unit of the New Army. In 1909 he was put in charge of the General Staff Council (*Chün-tzu Ch'u*), designed to become an independent general staff on the model of Germany and Japan. Liang was told in the fall of 1910 by one of his agents in Peking that Tsai-t'ao was very keen on reform and had great respect for the talents of K'ang Yu-wei. Tsai-t'ao, it was said, wanted to plan for a new government on the model of the 1898 experiment. There was

---

[13] *LCCNP*, pp. 289–294.

[14] On his influence on appointments to important posts, see: Max Müller, Charge d'affaires in Peking, to Grey, August 31, 1910, FO 405/201 (33924). Jordan to Grey, March 5, 1911, Annual Report, FO 405/201 (12149), cites a case of Tsai-t'ao's refusal to accept traditional gifts from bureaucratic subordinates. The same source notes that Tsai-t'ao set ". . . an admirable example of integrity, zeal and industry, attending the Guards or General Staff offices daily." For his socially liberal attitude toward Chinese, see: Sao-ke Alfred Sze, *Reminiscences of His Early Years*, trans. Amy C. Wu (Washington, D. C., 1962), pp. 58–59.

even the suggestion that force might be used for this purpose.[15] This evidence of support from Tsai-t'ao induced in Liang's group a temporary optimism.

Meanwhile, Liang was told that resolutions had been proposed in the consultative assembly to rehabilitate K'ang and Liang and that his representatives had mounted a campaign to bring the pressure of public opinion to bear on the government. Ten to fifteen thousand dollars (Mexican) were allotted for bribes in high places, especially with the new empress dowager, Lung-yü.[16] Yang Tu, later famous as campaign manager for Yuan Shih-k'ai's movement to become emperor, memorialized from the ministry of education to request pardon for Liang on the grounds that the constitutionalism that Liang advocated had now become the policy of the court and that he was an enemy of the revolutionaries.[17]

In February, 1911, however, it became clear that this impressive effort had proved fruitless. At the beginning of the campaign, it was believed that Tsai-tse was working to block any lifting of bans.[18] After the battle was lost, one of Liang's emissaries reported that the failure was due to Yuan Shih-k'ai's use of money at court, to the revolutionary party's rumormongering, to the distortions of the daily newspapers in Shanghai, and to the covert opposition of certain prominent provincial figures.[19] Whatever the reasons for the failure, Liang must have been struck by the fact that the court, even after Tz'u-hsi's death, would neither welcome him back of its own accord nor be prodded into accepting his presence.

Liang's defense of the Manchu government had always been based on pragmatic arguments about the damaging consequences of the possible alternatives, and not on appeals to loyalty as a

[15] P'an Jo-hai to Mai Meng-hua, October or November, 1910, *LCCNP*, pp. 319–320. The other princes involved were Tsai-hsün, another brother of Kuang-hsü, and Shan-ch'i (Prince Su).
[16] P'an Jo-hai to Liang, December, 1910; Mai Meng-hua to Liang, October or November, 1910; P'an Jo-hai to Mai Meng-hua, October or November, 1910; Mai Meng-hua to Liang, December, 1910: *LCCNP*, pp. 319–322.
[17] *Shen-pao*, January 15, 1911; reprinted in *LCCNP*, pp. 323–324.
[18] Hsü Ch'in to Liang, August 27, 1910, *LCCNP*, p. 315.
[19] Ho T'ien-chu to Liang, February 17, 1911, *LCCNP*, pp. 324–325.

moral virtue or to the superiority of the Manchu administration. But whatever the ground, defending the legitimacy of a government which persists in rewarding you only with ostracism can eventually become an insupportable task. In March, 1911, with an article calling for the overthrow of the government, Liang took the first step in unburdening himself of this self-appointed responsibility.

The article was entitled "China's Hope for the Future and the Responsibility of Her People." [20] Liang began by an appeal for confidence in China's fate; he was annoyed with those who said the country was doomed. The major foreign powers, he argued, were tolerably balanced one against the other and would actually find it against their interests to divide the country into colonies. Only a war in Europe, which would bring to an end foreign competition and the stalemate over China, would make partition a grave and immediate danger. Although the hour was late, Liang argued, China still had time to meet the situation with strength. He asserted that a nation was destroyed only if its people willed it.[21]

Thus Liang, who had so often in the past used the threat of hungry foreign imperialism poised to pounce on a prostrate China as an argument against those who called for violent overthrow of the dynasty, now minimized that threat. Sun Yat-sen, when he came to Japan in 1905, had found it necessary to persuade some of the Hunanese revolutionaries that there was no need to worry about partition: revolution was possible despite imperialism.[22] Liang's new analysis of China's foreign relations, whether accurate or not, was also inspired by a desire to see radical change at home. If he was to argue that the situation required drastic political renovation, then he had to convince others (and perhaps himself) that this renovation would not

[20] "Chung-kuo ch'ien-t'u chih hsi-wang yü kuo-min tse-jen," *Yin-ping-shih wen-chi* [Collected Essays of the Ice-Drinkers' Studio], 45 *chüan* (Taipei, 1960), 26. 1–40. Original publication in *Kuo-feng pao* (Tokyo), II, Nos. 5–7 (March 21 to April 19, 1911).

[21] Liang, "Chung-kuo ch'ien-t'u," pp. 2–4, 11.

[22] Sung Chiao-jen, *Wo chih li-shih* [My History], 6 *chüan* (T'ao-yuan, Hunan, 1920), 2:27b–28.

cause the powers to assume greater authority in Chinese affairs and that in fact it would result in a government stronger in defense of China.

The change that Liang urged in this article, while vague as to specific measures, is nonetheless an unmistakable call to overthrow the existing government in Peking. The government, Liang wrote, was composed of "good-for-nothing, superfluous men," "the benighted and stupid," whose adherents were "joined together by sychophancy." The humiliating weakness of the Chinese in the world was due precisely to "the obstruction of the present bad government. If our people do not join their strength in planning the overthrow of this bad government and in reconstructing a good government, then no matter what policies or legal systems are established, they can only increase the government's corruption, and we shall just bring more misery on ourselves. . . . If the people of our country do not have this plan [of overthrowing the government], they are abandoning their responsibility and are hence accelerating the extinction of the nation." [23]

This article was Liang's last major political pronouncement before the 1911 revolution. The degree to which he adopted a full revolutionary position is remarkable. In the debate with the *Min-pao* writers, such as Wang Ching-wei, Liang had defended the dynasty and the notion of constitutional monarchy against the charge that reform was impossible under the Manchus. Without actually adopting the T'ung-meng Hui position vis-à-vis the dynasty, he nonetheless now accepted the highly revolutionary formulation that the "present government," whatever that might mean in precise terms, could not effect reforms. If it tried, the result could only be a worsening of the situation. He did not condemn the dynasty as such; nor, however, did he qualify his call to the overthrow of the government by references to the sanctity of the imperial line. From the article, it appeared that Liang was not much concerned about the dynasty's fate, either its preservation or its extinction.

Liang did not label himself a revolutionary, an epithet belonging to Sun Yat-sen's group, who were commonly referred to as

[23] Liang, "Chung-kuo ch'ien-t'u," p. 29.

the "revolutionary party" rather than by their formal name, the T'ung-meng Hui. But he was much more ready to risk disruption. It was as if the "new people" whom he had called for nine years previously had emerged. Perhaps he was influenced by the extraordinary energy shown in the struggle for the opening of a legislative assembly and the growing strength of the T'ung-meng Hui. In the course of calling for the overthow of the government, Liang declared his firm belief in the efficacy of popular action. The government, out of fear, was merely a servant of the foreigners, even to the point of anticipating their wishes. There was no point, Liang wrote, in remonstrating with such a government, which knew that its days were numbered. The government concerned itself only with gathering in loot from the people before China fell. "Therefore, if we wish our talk to have any effect, we can address ourselves only to the people. . . ." Then, even if the country fell to the foreigner, Liang asserted, the Chinese would never admit defeat but would fight until their sovereignty was recovered.[24] During the subsequent months, Liang planned for the implementation of his call to revolution.

THE NORTHERN PLOT

Liang's colleagues and followers refurbished their organization in China by founding the Hsien-yu Hui (Society of the Friends of Constitutionalism). This action, accomplished in June, 1911, seems to have had several purposes. The first national, partially elective body, the Tzu-cheng Yüan, a consultative rather than legislative assembly, had opened in late 1910. It was apparent that a political organization was necessary in order to work effectively with the factions that were forming.[25] A national assembly (legislative) had been promised for 1913, and it was time to begin marshalling forces for that day. The radicalization of the atmosphere was proceeding apace. The more aggressive constitutionalists, including those who later formed the Hsien-yu Hui, had been rebuffed and maltreated by the government in their campaign for an earlier opening of the national assembly.

[24] *Ibid.*, pp. 38–40.
[25] Hsü Fo-su to Liang, May 4, 1911, *LCCNP*, p. 335.

The central government in May, 1911 took two more steps which intensified Chinese distrust of Manchu rule and aroused the gentry in several provinces to the point of fury at Peking policy. A cabinet dominated by Manchus was instituted, and a plan to nationalize provincial railways was announced. The founding of the Hsien-yu Hui was an indication of this atmosphere of increasing tension.

Extravagant claims have been made retrospectively for the achievements of the Society and, by extension, of Liang Ch'i-ch'ao for their role in bringing about the revolution of 1911.[26] If events had developed in the way that Liang planned, the Hsien-yu Hui might indeed have become an important political instrument. Perhaps the most sensational new information revealed by the publication in 1958 of Liang's letters is the extent of his political plots in the year 1911.

Although we know his plans only as they were adapted for the situation after the Wuchang revolutionary outbreak, he had been working on a scheme to seize state power for "several months" and had been cultivating, by letter and emissaries, support for it. The purpose of the seizure, insofar as we can infer it from later evidence, was to overthrow the government of the current prime minister and his cohorts, establish a parliament with extensive powers, and make Tsai-t'ao, brother of the deceased Kuang-hsü emperor, prime minister. The vision seems to have been a more radical "1898," such as had been broached in reports to Liang in the autumn of 1910. Liang's hopes were based not on some spontaneous welling up of sentiment for his version of constitutional monarchy, but on the expectation of military backing. For this purpose, he looked to a Manchu prince and some military commanders of the New Army.

The Manchu princes, by now a familiar element in Liang's armory, had been asked much and had delivered little. In 1908 and 1909, Liang's Manchu friends had failed to accomplish Yuan Shih-k'ai's complete destruction, and in 1910 they failed to get Liang's banishment rescinded. Liang had correspondingly

---

[26] Hsü Fo-su, reminiscing about Liang in *LCCNP*, pp. 375–378. Some seem to accept this evaluation: for example, Nozawa Yutaka, *Son Bun* [Sun Yat-sen] (Tokyo, 1962), pp. 130–131.

diminished his reliance on this quarter. Tsai-tse, minister of finance, once thought to be an ally, was now known as an enemy. Tsai-hsün, younger brother to both the late emperor and the present regent, had proven himself "useless." [27] Another brother, Tsai-t'ao, was by this time the only Manchu prince upon whom Liang counted, although he realized that Tsai-t'ao's influence was limited. Still, Tsai-t'ao had agreed to make every effort to insure the loyalty of the New Imperial Guards to Liang's cause. This force could be crucial in any sudden military moves in the north.[28]

If Tsai-t'ao had been the crux of Liang's hopes, there would have been small chance for a successful seizure of power. A more substantial element in Liang's armory were three high-ranking officers in the New Army, who were stationed in the north in the fall of 1911. They were Wu Lu-chen, commander of the sixth division, Chang Shao-tseng, commander of the twentieth division, and Lan T'ien-wei, commander of the second mixed brigade. Their collective and individual actions in late October and early November, 1911—an ultimatum delivered on the court for radical constitutional reforms and an alliance with rebel forces in Shansi—did more than anything else, with the exception of the outbreak of the revolution itself, to destroy the self-confidence of the dynasty. Even in failure, these officers gravely weakened the position of the Peiyang army, which was shown to be untrustworthy. There have been several versions of what inspired their activities, although they have generally been considered revolutionaries or supporters of the T'ung-meng Hui cause. Liang Ch'i-ch'ao, however, has never been mentioned as an instigator of their mutinous behavior. For want of conclusive evidence, we cannot judge what were in fact the intentions of these men, who for a moment seemed to control the fate of the dynasty and the revolution. Their background, however, throws some light upon these obscurities.

All three of these New Army officers, who were in their early thirties in 1911, had been studying in Japan on government

[27] Sze, p. 58, remembers Tsai-hsün being "avaricious" and having a "bad reputation."
[28] Liang to Hsü Ch'in, October 29, 1911, *LCCNP*, pp. 339–340.

funds at the turn of the century.[29] Wu arrived in Japan in late 1898, Chang and Lan in early 1899, and all of them were in a special program in which Chinese officers entered various Konoe regiments for practical learning of the military arts. The program was in a sense preparatory for their year's training as students at the Japan Army Officers' Academy (Nihon Rikugun Shikan Gakkō), which all three entered. Wu and Chang were both in the first class (1901–1902) of Chinese who were so trained, and Lan graduated with the second (1902–1903). Thereupon they returned to duties in the modern New Army at home and rose rapidly in rank, as was expected of the small elite who had been trained at the Japanese officers' school.[30]

These officers, and other military men associated with Liang's schemes in 1911 and 1916, had been in Japan during the years of Liang's greatest popularity among the Chinese studying there. Wu Lu-chen, we know, had become personally acquainted with Liang at that time and had assisted him in arrangements for the Tzu-li Hui uprising of 1900.[31] Wu was also acquainted with Sun Yat-sen in 1900, and all three—Wu, Chang, and Lan— were later associated with the T'ung-meng Hui. But they were not in Japan when Liang emerged as one of the T'ung-meng Hui's chief antagonists and thus probably made no sharp distinctions between "reformer" and "revolutionary." Whatever his

[29] Wu Lu-chen and Lan T'ien-wei, both from Hupeh, had embarked upon military careers under the auspices of the military training programs sponsored by Chang Chih-tung while he was Hu-kuang governor-general (1889–1907). Chang Shao-tseng, a native of Chihli, was sent to Japan under the auspices of Yuan Shih-k'ai's Peiyang army.

[30] These facts have been culled from various sources: the biographies of these men as they appear in Gaimushō Jōhō-bu, ed., *Gendai Shina jimmei kan* [Biographical Dictionary of Contemporary China] (Tokyo, 1925) and Pekin Shina Kenkyū-kai, ed., *Saishin Shina kanshin roku* [Record of Contemporary Chinese Officials and Gentry] (Tokyo, 1918), Part I; the tables of Chinese graduates of the Rikugun Shikan Gakkō in *Saishin Shina kanshin roku*, Part II, pp. 392–405; Fang Chao-ying, compiler, *Ch'ing-mo min-ch'u yang-hsüeh hsüeh-sheng t'i-ming lu ch'u-chi* [First Collection of Lists of Names of Students Studying Abroad in the Late Ch'ing and Early Republic] (Taipei, 1962), pp. 1–53; and Sanetō Keishū, *Chūgokujin Nihon ryūgaku shi* [A History of Chinese Students in Japan] (Tokyo, 1960), footnote on page 65.

[31] Liang to Wu Lu-chen, 1911, *LCCNP*, p. 345; Chu Yen-chia, "Wu Lu-chen yü Chung-kuo ko-ming" [Wu Lu-chen and the Chinese Revolution], in Wu Hsiang-hsiang, ed., *Chung-kuo hsien-tai-shih ts'ung-k'an* [Selected Writings on Modern Chinese History], 6 vols. (Taipei, 1960–1964), VI, 165.

other loyalties, Wu was active as one of the small group working with Liang for Yuan Shih-k'ai's downfall in late 1908 and was in frequent correspondence with Liang on this matter.[32]

The act for which Chang Shao-tseng and Lan T'ien-wei are best known, the twelve demands on the court made on October 29, 1911, reflected a monarchical constitutionalist outlook.[33] Liang's intellectual influence on the document would seem probable from its contents, even if there were no evidence that he was wooing Chang and Lan. It called for a British-style polity, with the Manchu monarch reduced to a figurehead and with a cabinet responsible to a national assembly possessing budgetary powers. Moreover, it included a demand for a general pardon for all political offenders, which, when granted, lifted the ban on Liang's return—something his Manchu friends had never managed to accomplish.

Wu Lu-chen's behavior in October and early November, 1911 suggests the possibility that he, too, was seriously considering the notion of collaboration with Liang. He had recently been in communication with Liang through a mutual acquaintance, who travelled back and forth between Japan and Wu's residence.[34] Wu had lengthy meetings with Tsai-t'ao during late October, which would fit into the pattern of Liang's scheme, but which are difficult to explain if Wu is thought to be a revolutionary of the T'ung-meng Hui stamp. Indeed, a Chinese subordinate of Tsai-t'ao's at the time recalled later that Wu and Tsai-t'ao had hatched some mysterious plans and that Tsai-t'ao was greatly pained at their failure as a result of Wu's death.[35] Wu's one overt act which has been interpreted as revolutionary was his allying

[32] Liang to Chiang Kuan-yün, January 12, 1909, *LCCNP*, p. 291, in which Liang refers to receiving from Shou-ch'ing (Wu's *tzu*) "several letters" on Manchu opinion and mentions the expectation of more to come.

[33] Wu was not actually a signer but is generally described as participating in this matter from the beginning: e.g., Chang Kuo-kan, *Hsin-hai ko-ming shih-liao* [Historical Sources of the 1911 Revolution] (Shanghai, 1958), p. 200. At least one contemporary observer recalls that Chang Shao-tseng, privately as well as publicly, favored at the time a constitutional monarchy rather than republicanism. Cheng Ch'i-lu, "Kuan-wai ko-ming hui-i-lu" [Recollections of the Revolution in Manchuria], *Hsin-hai ko-ming hui-i-lu* [Recollections of the 1911 Revolution], 5 vols. (Peking, 1961–1963), V, 563.

[34] Liang to Wu Lu-chen, *LCCNP*, p. 345.

[35] Chang Kuo-kan, pp. 206–207.

with the rebel Shansi army, instead of suppressing it as he was ordered to do. According to a statement made within weeks of the event by an officer in the Shansi army who participated in negotiations with Wu Lu-chen, Wu's plan was to bring some of the Shansi troops to the junction of the Peking-Hankow railway which he held and to join them in presenting demands to Peking. The demands that Wu proposed did not include the abolition of the Manchu dynasty.[36] Until some means for a more intimate glimpse into Wu's attitude at the time is discovered, it is best to assume that Wu, like many others at this juncture, was neither fixed in his aims nor certain of the proper means to effect them. He had been associated in the past with the revolutionaries. At the same time, he was an admirer of Liang, Liang was offering funds, and they seemed to share a dislike of Yuan Shih-k'ai.[37]

This background of Liang's relations with the three commanders is necessary for an appreciation of his plot. Otherwise, Liang's schemes, when measured against the customary accounts of the events in the north during 1911, seem to be wild fantasies of an extraordinarily naïve political imagination. In the light of this background, it is conceivable that with better timing and better luck, this plot might have fundamentally altered the course of the revolution.

The notion of a *coup d'état* had been occupying Liang's mind at least since he published his call to overthrow the government in March of 1911. The essential arrangements were set in motion before the revolution broke out. But when the revolution erupted at Wuchang on October 10, 1911, it seems to have taken him by surprise, as it did nearly everyone else, including the revolutionary leadership. Liang had been planning to act about seven months later.[38] He frequently commented during

[36] Report by Capt. Otter-Barry, December 2, 1911, on the assassination of General Wu Lu-chen, as related by Shansi rebel Colonel Chiao, FO 371/1098. This version of the events is reinforced by an American report that the Shansi government was ready to accede to any reasonable terms, including a constitutional monarchy. Statement of Mr. K. McCoy, regarding the troubles in Shansi province, Calhoun to Knox, December 23, 1911, NA 893.00/942.

[37] On the funds, see Liang to Hsü Ch'in, October 29, 1911, *LCCNP*, p. 340; on Wu's attitude toward Yuan, as well as his cooperation with Liang in the effort to ruin Yuan in 1908 and 1909, mentioned above in the text, see Chang Kuo-kan, pp. 203 and 207.

[38] Liang to Hsü Ch'in, October 29, 1911, *LCCNP*, p. 340.

October and November that he was not fully ready. The Wu-chang uprising forced his hand.

Liang's plan for effecting a change in government, as it was adapted in the first three weeks after the Wuchang uprising, consisted of several elements. With the cooperation of the New Imperial Guards, there would be a *coup d'état* which would oust Prince Ch'ing, the prime minister, and Tsai-tse, minister of finance, from positions of power, and establish Tsai-t'ao as prime minister. In order to appease popular feeling, Sheng Hsüan-huai, considered the chief villain of recent despotic interference in the rights of the provincial gentry, would be killed as the National Consultative Assembly had requested (Liang, writing on October 29, apparently did not know that Sheng, impeached and dismissed on October 26, had proceeded on October 28 to Tientsin under the protection of foreign legation marines). A national legislative assembly would be convened immediately, and, while its members were being properly elected, the combined memberships of the present consultative assembly and the provincial assemblies would act as the legislative assembly. An imperial confession of error (*tsui-chi*) would be handed down. The government would abolish the Eight Banners, and the Manchus, including the emperor, would adopt Chinese surnames as a gesture to extirpate the hatred of Han for Manchu. The expeditionary force against the rebels would be recalled. Then, with a declaration that the times do not permit a civil war, the national assembly would negotiate with the revolutionaries. Since real power would already have been transferred to the national assembly, the revolutionaries would lose the support of the people if they persisted in resistance. This was the general outline of Liang's plan for a change of government in Peking and a reconciliation with the southern provinces—about five by this time—which had declared independence.[39]

The plan was based on the assumptions that Tsai-t'ao would prove equal to the leading role he was assigned and could control

[39] Liang to Hsü Ch'in, October 29, 1911, *LCCNP*, pp. 339–342, contains Liang's most detailed explanation of his program. It was written as an expansion of a telegram to Hsü appealing for immediate funds. The plan is repeated in abbreviated form in a letter from K'ang Yu-wei to Hsü Ch'in, November 9, 1911, *LCCNP*, p. 342.

the New Imperial Guard, and that Wu Lu-chen would be in a position militarily to dominate the capital area and would be cooperative. By the end of October, several weak points in this strategy had already emerged. Another Manchu prime minister, even if a reforming one, was a high price to pay for the control of the New Imperial Guard, particularly in view of the growing antipathy for the Manchus. Moreover, it was already unclear whether Tsai-t'ao was really able to perform his assigned function: Liang had received a report that one of Yuan Shih-k'ai's adherents, Chiang Kuei-t'i, had managed to get some of his soldiers into the New Imperial Guards.[40] Wu Lu-chen, who had been in command of the sixth division in Paoting lost one of his two brigades to Yin-ch'ang, the Manchu military leader, on October 30 and was instructed to leave Paoting and pacify the rebels in Shansi with his remaining brigade. On the favorable side, this transfer put Wu in a highly strategic position: Shih-chia-chuang, on the Peking-Hankow railway, which was the link between the northern forces and the front. Also, Chang Shao-tseng and Lan T'ien-wei, with a division and a half at Luanchow and Mukden, had put forth a program which, as we have noted, was remarkably similar to Liang's, and they could be expected to cooperate. Liang was greatly encouraged by the success of the demands of Chang, Lan, and other northern officers, which meant that he could return to China legally rather than in defiance of the ban against him. He was further encouraged by the apparently increasing power of the National Consultative Assembly whose members, Liang thought, were largely his supporters. He left Kobe for the Chinese mainland on November 4, believing that his "task was already halfway finished. . . ."[41]

Even before he left, Liang realized that his role had to be one of bargaining rather than dictation. He was anxious to cultivate the goodwill of both Yuan and the revolutionaries (not, however, of Prince Ch'ing and the existing government in Peking).

[40] Liang to Hsü Ch'in, October 29, 1911, *LCCNP*, p. 340. Perhaps the report was premature. Li Chien-nung, pp. 254–255, says that Yuan was able to check the threat to him from Tsai-t'ao and the Guards only later in November.

[41] Liang to Hsü Ch'in, November 3, 1911, and a postscript of November 9, 1911, to Liang's letter of October 29, 1911, to Hsü Ch'in, *LCCNP*, p. 342.

Yet by the time he arrived at Dairen on November 9, the assets upon which he had been depending to make bargains favorable to his cause had already begun to disappear. Wu Lu-chen, upon whom Liang had pinned so much of his hope, had been assassinated on November 6, probably on the orders of some faction of the government in Peking.[42] Chang Shao-tseng was reported to have left his post at Luanchow for Peking.[43] The political structure was on the point of collapse in the capital, and Liang feared that abdication might come about before he could execute his plans.

After he arrived in Dairen and learned of recent developments, he curtailed his aims. His purpose, he now said, was to establish a central government, whether it was dominated by his group or not, which could unify the country and prevent disintegration. He admitted that the plans spun in Japan had become largely inoperable and that action had to be in response to the situation as it developed from day to day. With the general plan of proceeding first to Mukden and then on to Luanchow and Peking, Liang began a series of consultations in Manchuria.[44]

At Mukden, Liang intended first to see the governor-general of Manchuria, the venerable Chao Erh-sun, who had held high posts in all parts of China and who later became the first military governor (*tu-tu*) of Fengtien under the republic. Chao, however,

---

[42] As Li Chien-nung in note 3, p. 512, referring to p. 254 of the text, points out, there are two versions of Wu Lu-chen's assassination. Li seems to prefer the conclusion that the murder was ordered by the court. Much has been written—although nothing based on contemporary evidence so far as I know—on the theory that Yuan Shih-k'ai was behind it, his first crime against the revolution. The *Min-li pao* [People's Independence] accepted the version which held the Manchus responsible, November 9, 1911, *et seq.* It was not until December 6, 1911, that it even printed the rumor that Yuan had been the perpetrator. The British army attaché heard from a revolutionary officer, who appeared at Shih-chia-chuang within a few hours of Wu's death, that the deed was done by some Manchu officers who had arrived in a special train from Peking, sent by the Peking government (report by Capt. Otter-Barry, December 2, 1911, FO 371/1098). Although the assassination served Yuan's interests, the evidence seems to support the theory that the court was responsible.

[43] *Min-li pao,* November 11, 1911, reported that Chang suddenly resigned and was instructed on November 8 to come to Peking.

[44] Liang to Liang Ling-hsien, two letters on November 9, 1911, and one letter on November 11, 1911, *LCCNP,* pp. 343–344. Postscript of November 9, 1911, to Liang's letter of October 29, 1911, to Hsü Ch'in, *LCCNP,* pp. 341–342.

was busy meeting with the local citizenry in a desperate effort to keep order in Mukden.[45] Liang did meet some of Chao's subordinates. Of particular interest was Chao's military chief of staff, Chiang Fang-chen (perhaps better known by his *tzu*, Po-li). Chiang, like Wu Lu-chen, Chang Shao-tseng, and Lan T'ien-wei, was an early graduate of the Japan Army Officers' Academy course for Chinese officers.[46] Although they had not met in Japan, Chiang was known throughout his life as a follower of Liang. According to the subsequent report of one of Liang's companions on this Manchurian trip, Liang and Chiang came to some agreement at this time on the use of troops.[47] These conversations may have been the inspiration for a move to use the army in Fengtien to declare the province's independence under Liang's leadership.[48] The import of these maneuvers was never known, since Liang did not stay long enough for them to materialize.

Within a short time after Liang arrived in Manchuria, it became apparent that his last hope lay with Lan T'ien-wei, the only one of the three northern commanders who had survived in his post into the middle of November. When Liang first arrived at Dairen, he heard that Lan was in Mukden and was extremely pleased that Liang was coming. Two days later, the very day that Liang actually arrived in Mukden, Lan withdrew from a complicated struggle for power with the governor-general, the provincial assembly, and Chang Tso-lin, and left the city without seeing Liang.[49] Although we cannot know what Lan's real intentions were at this time, it is possible that events were developing so fast that a two-day delay was crucial in Liang's final failure to establish a military base in the north.

On the evening of November 12, Liang was warned by an associate to waste no time in leaving Mukden.[50] The specific

[45] Liang to Liang Ling-hsien, two letters on November 11, 1911, *LCCNP*, pp. 344–345. Liang, cognizant of the unstable situation, had secured lodgings in the Japanese concession in Mukden.

[46] His was the third class, graduating in 1904. *Saishin Shina kanshin roku*, Part II, p. 393.

[47] Yang Wei-hsin to Ting Wen-chiang, undated, *LCCNP*, p. 345.

[48] Liang to Liang Ling-hsien, November 12, 1911, *LCCNP*, p. 345. This seems to be the meaning of Liang's somewhat obscure comment.

[49] Various Liang letters, *LCCNP*, pp. 343–344.

[50] Liang to Liang Ling-hsien, November 12, 1911, *LCCNP*, p. 345.

reason for the need to retreat is not clear. Perhaps, as one of Liang's companions on this trip later testified, there were intimations of a sudden move by Lan against Liang.[51] Perhaps, on the contrary, Lan's loss of a foothold in Mukden created a dangerous situation. In any case, after six hectic days in Manchuria, Liang boarded a Japanese ship on November 15 to return to Kobe, his conspiratorial failure complete.[52]

THE SOUTHERN SUBPLOT

When the military support upon which he had relied in his plans for the north dissolved over a period of two weeks in early November, Liang turned to the techniques of intellectual persuasion through articles and emissaries sent out from Japan. However, he had set in motion another plan to effect his views by force of arms, and it was several weeks before hopes in this quarter were completely abandoned by his agents. These hopes centered on the south, chiefly Kwangtung, and were more vague and complicated than his plans for the north. The tentative motions toward action in the south—one can hardly call them plans—never came as close to fruition as Liang's scheme for a *coup d'état* in Peking. But they indicate further the sort of scheme that Liang favored and the sort of people to whom he looked for cooperation.

Kwangtung, Liang's home province, was crucial to power arrangements in the south and southwest. It fell in early November to T'ung-meng Hui leadership (though there were many complications). One of Liang's colleagues, who was fully informed of the plots and was at the time raising money for them in the United States, wrote Liang in mid-November that power and influence under present conditions in China would come only with military strength and that Liang should work to establish a military training camp on Hainan Island, from which he could move on to central China.[53] Variations on this theme of establish-

---

[51] Yang Wei-hsin to Ting Wen-chiang, undated, *LCCNP*, p. 345.

[52] Shirani, Kwantung Governor, to Uchida, Foreign Minister, November 15, 1911, in Gaimushō, ed., *Shinkoku jihen (shingai kakumei)* [Uprising in China (the 1911 Revolution)], *Nihon gaikō bunsho* [Documents in Japanese Diplomacy], XLIV–XLV (Tokyo, 1961), 164; *Min-li pao*, November 21, 1911.

[53] Hsü Ch'in to Liang, November 14, 1911, *LCCNP*, pp. 366–367.

ing a foothold in Kwangtung occupied Liang's southern contingent until the end of the year.

The major figures in Liang's second attempt to change the course of the revolution were: Ts'en Ch'un-hsüan, a former governor-general; Chiang Tsun-kuei, a graduate of the Japan Army Officers' Academy; and Inukai Ki, the leader of a Japanese political party. The key person of this extraordinary trio was Ts'en. A native of Kwangsi and a *chü-jen* of 1884, Ts'en was approximately the same age as Yuan Shih-k'ai and for a time had enjoyed the same confidence of empress dowager Tz'u-hsi. During the Boxer rising, Ts'en had led troops as an escort for the court in its flight from Peking to Sian and thereby proved his loyalty and earned her gratitude. He was appointed in succession governor of Shensi, governor-general of Szechuan, and for four years governor-general of Kwangtung and Kwangsi. In 1907 he was briefly minister of posts and communications and then resigned under fire.[54] During this illustrious official career he gained a reputation for almost barbaric ferocity in suppressing disturbances within his jurisdiction and acquired some sort of following, particularly in his native area of Kwangsi and Kwangtung.[55] As one of the handful of eminent Chinese officials in 1911, he was, like Yuan Shih-k'ai, recalled from "retirement" to assist in saving the dynasty.[56] Ts'en never took up his post but remained in Shanghai to parley. The aura of authority and latent power

[54] Arthur W. Hummel, ed., *Eminent Chinese of the Ch'ing Period, 1644–1912*, 2 vols. (Washington, D.C., 1943–1944), II, 745–746; *Gendai Shina jimmei kan*, p. 1052.

[55] Ts'en had crushed the Kwangsi rebellion of 1905 with "merciless severity." Percy Horace Kent, *The Passing of the Manchus* (New York, 1912), pp. 88–89.

[56] Actually, Ts'en was first ordered to Szechuan on September 15, 1911, to advise Chao Erh-feng, the governor-general, on his suppression of the disturbance there. Ts'en raised questions about the job and stopped in Wuchang to confer with the governor-general there before proceeding. In Wuchang he decided to ask for leave on the pretext of poor health. He planned to return to Shanghai. He was still in Wuchang on October 10 but managed to catch a boat for Shanghai, in accordance with his original intention. On October 14 he was appointed Szechwan governor-general but declined on the grounds that communications were not open between Shanghai and Szechuan. Ts'en Ch'un-hsüan, *Lo-chai man-pi* [Rambling Notes from the Study of Lo], reprinted in Wu Hsiang-hsiang, ed., *Chung-kuo hsien-tai shih-liao ts'ung-shu* [Library of Chinese Contemporary Historical Materials], 4th Series (Taipei, 1962), pp. 18–19; Wu Hsiang-hsiang, "Ts'en Ch'un-hsüan," *ibid.*, p. 9.

which so many attributed to him led to his being wooed by different dissident groups at various times in the early republic. Occasionally he responded favorably.

The second figure in the plans for the south was Chiang Tsun-kuei. When Chang Ming-ch'i, the last Liang-kuang governor-general and a friend of Liang Ch'i-ch'ao, failed to appease the citizens of Canton by a break with Peking, he was succeeded by Chiang, who was also an admirer of Liang. Revolutionary forces gained control of Kwangtung's government on November 9, 1911. Chiang, a New Army brigade commander in Kwang-tung, was chosen chief of military affairs and, for one day, acting military governor, until Hu Han-min arrived from Hong Kong. It was Chiang who declared the province's adherence to republican forces.[57]

A native of Shao-hsing in Chekiang province, Chiang Tsun-kuei graduated from the Japan Army Officers' Academy in the third class for Chinese. Among his classmates were Chiang Fang-chen (Po-li), who, as we have noted, was chief of staff in Manchuria in 1911, and Ts'ai O, the famous leader of the independence movement in Yunnan—both of whom were identified with Liang Ch'i-ch'ao. Chiang Tsun-kuei, although active in the T'ung-meng Hui some years before, resigned his post as chief of military affairs in Kwangtung after only ten days. Not long after his resignation, he went to Shanghai and conferred with Liang's representative there.[58]

Inukai Ki, who appears prominently in all accounts of Japanese-Chinese relations from the 1890's until his assassination in 1931, was in 1911 leader of a newly-formed party, the Kai-

---

[57] *Ko-sheng kuang-fu* [Restoration in the Various Provinces], 3 vols. (Taipei, 1962), II, 428–430.

[58] T'ien T'ung, the revolutionary leader, recalled that Chiang Tsun-kuei was one of the authors of the T'ung-meng Hui charter in 1905, along with Huang Hsing, Wang Ching-wei, Ch'en T'ien-hua, and others. "T'ung-meng hui ch'eng-li chi" [Record of the Founding of the T'ung-meng Hui], *Ko-ming wen-hsien* [Documents of the Revolution], II (Taipei, 1953), 3. For his subsequent revolutionary activities in Chekiang, see *Ko-sheng kuang-fu*, II, 133. On the tenure of Chiang's position under the Kwangtung revolutionary government, see Segawa, Consul General in Canton, to Uchida, January 12, 1912, MT 1.6.1.50, reel 155, pp. 1989–1994, microfilmed archives of the Japanese Ministry of Foreign Affairs, Library of Congress, Washington, D.C. [hereafter cited as JMFA].

shintō. His relations with Sun Yat-sen are well-known: Inukai supported men like Miyazaki Torazō in their cultivation of Sun and interceded with the Japanese government more than once on Sun's behalf.[59] Soon after meeting Sun, Inukai became acquainted with K'ang Yu-wei and Liang Ch'i-ch'ao when they came as exiles to Japan in 1898. Liang lived for a time in a house adjacent to Inukai's home in Tokyo.[60] Even after bitterness developed between Sun and Liang, Inukai retained cordial relations with both and never quite gave up the hope of bringing them together in some united reform effort.

In December, 1911, Inukai came to Shanghai, ostensibly to recuperate from an illness, but it is obvious that he also hoped to participate in the events of the Chinese revolution. He and some of his followers stayed in China from December 19, 1911, until March 26 of the next year.[61] During the first weeks of his stay in Shanghai, Inukai met both with Ts'en Ch'un-hsüan and with Liang's men in Shanghai to discuss strategy.

The essence of the strategy proposed by Liang's advance agents was simple: Kwangtung or some part of it should be secured as a base of power for casting a deciding vote in the future organization of China, and Ts'en Ch'un-hsüan, they felt, was the one person who could at this date establish such a base. Inukai's role would be to obtain the revolutionaries' "understanding" of this action.[62]

Chiang Tsun-kuei, who had just come from Kwangtung, emphatically agreed on the importance of basing power on the support of the people in one's own area. He said that he was returning to Hangchow in his native Chekiang, where he probably would be made a military commander. Once he had secured a firm military foothold there, he promised, he would advocate rallying to Ts'en's banner.[63] This commitment could have been a powerful stimulus to the whole scheme: Chiang not only became

---

[59] Marius B. Jansen, *The Japanese and Sun Yat-sen* (Cambridge, Mass., 1954), pp. 64–68.

[60] Washio Yoshinao, ed., *Inukai Bokudō den* [Biography of Inukai Ki], 3 vols. (Tokyo, 1938–1939), II, 726.

[61] Washio, II, 735–736.

[62] Mai Meng-hua to Liang, letters #3 and #4, *LCCNP*, pp. 360–361.

[63] Mai Meng-hua to Liang, letter #1, *LCCNP*, p. 358. Mai Meng-hua's letters #1 and #2 in this series appear to be printed in reverse chronological order.

military commander in Chekiang, but on January 11, 1912, he was unanimously elected by the Chekiang provincial assembly to succeed the military governor, T'ang Shou-ch'ien, who had been appointed to Sun Yat-sen's cabinet in Nanking.[64]

Ts'en, meanwhile, was in touch with two of his former subordinates in the Liang-kuang, Lung Chi-kuang and Lu Jung-t'ing. Lung Chi-kuang, who had served under Ts'en in Kwangsi, was now commander of the twenty-fifth division in Kwangtung, and in November he had remained at his post when Hu Han-min's government came in. Ts'en would depend upon Lung's assistance if Kwangtung were approached from the sea. Lu Jung-t'ing had been a battalion commander under Ts'en in campaigns in Kwangsi and at the time of the revolution was provincial commander-in-chief (*t'i-tu*). Lu cooperated in the move for Kwangsi's declaration of independence under the leadership of the imperial governor and soon emerged as military governor of the province. His support would be instrumental in any march on Kwangtung from the interior. In the reports which Liang Ch'i-ch'ao received, Ts'en was described as very willing to act, since the action involved making a base out of his native area and using his old subordinates.[65]

For reasons that are not developed in detail in Liang's papers, the scheme petered out in early January. Some of the reasons may be surmised. There was from the beginning the question of Ts'en's reliability. Chiang Tsun-kuei, who was the first to see Ts'en, believed it possible that Ts'en had secret plans of his own.[66] A Liang aide who arrived in Shanghai in early January was impressed chiefly with the lack of substance in Ts'en's position and his haughtiness.[67] It is possible that the response that

[64] *Ko-sheng kuang-fu,* II, 171–172.

[65] Mai Meng-hua to Liang, letters #3 and #4, *LCCNP,* pp. 360–361. The account I have given of the participants in the conspiracy and their expectations is based largely on four letters from Mai Meng-hua to Liang, written apparently in late December and early January. It should be noted that I have not been able to decipher all the references to people. No one is referred to by his full name, and some of the references are in code. For example, Chiang Tsun-kuei is mentioned only by his *tzu,* Po-ch'i; Inukai by his *gō,* Bokudō; Ts'en Ch'un-hsüan by the code, Kung-hsiao or Shan-kung; and Yüan Shih-k'ai by the code, Kung-lu.

[66] Mai Meng-hua to Liang, letter #1, *LCCNP,* p. 358.

[67] Hsü Fo-su to Liang and T'ang Jui, January 2, 1912, *LCCNP,* p. 370.

Ts'en was receiving from Lung Chi-kuang and Lu Jung-t'ing was not as favorable as he had expected. Over the next few years, Ts'en would in fact find himself on the opposite side of the battle from them both at least once. As it turned out, Ts'en remained neutral and passive during the 1911 revolution.

Inukai Ki, it was soon discovered, would be useless as a mediator between Liang's group and the revolutionaries, since he interpreted the need for unity to read: join the new Nanking government of Sun Yat-sen. In an interview with Ts'en, Inukai urged that Ts'en go to Nanking; only the presence of a Liang agent prevented Ts'en from abandoning at that moment the notion of establishing a power base in Kwangtung.[68]

It is also clear that, as in the north, Liang had moved too slowly. By early January, 1912, the chaos in Kwangtung was coming under control. On December 23, 1911, the Japanese consul-general in Canton had heard that the Pao-huang Tang (Protect-the-Emperor Party, a name by which people persisted in calling Liang's group, despite the fact that the emperor for whom the slogan was designed was three years dead) was secretly storing arms and was planning to overthrow the new Kwangtung government. A thorough investigation of this report revealed that some agents of Liang's group had been in Kwangtung in December in a conspiratorial effort, but the crushing methods of suppression of the provincial government had left no room for maneuver. Consequently, Liang's group had departed by the end of December.[69] The American consul-general reported on January 5 that conditions were much improved in Kwangtung as a whole and that order was assured in Canton.[70] With the passage of time, an increasingly prodigious effort would have been necessary to seize Kwangtung from its T'ung-meng

[68] Mai Meng-hua to Liang, letter #4, *LCCNP*, p. 361.

[69] Segawa to Uchida, December 23, 1911, MT 1.6.1.50, reel 155, pp. 1859–1867, JMFA. Kunatsu, Acting Consul General in Hong Kong, to Uchida, January 13, 1912, *Shinkoku jihen,* p. 38. The Canton consul general's report is referred to in the Hong Kong telegram as having been made October 28, which, being quite impossible, must be a misprint. Segawa's report of December 23, 1911, is probably the document in question.

[70] Leo Bergholz, Consul General in Canton, to Knox, January 5, 1912, NA 893.00/1062.

Hui leadership, and the realization of this fact must have had an inhibiting effect on planning by early January.

Finally, it is possible that Liang himself called a halt to the conspiracy, because the national unity in which he placed so much store would, as conditions became less favorable to success, be badly damaged by renewed fighting in the extreme south. Even Liang's chief coordinator in Shanghai, as he was putting the final touches to the plan, expressed the fear that it could not be effected without results contrary to its aims, that is, without dividing the country.[71] If Liang were convinced that this was true —and the evidence for it seemed to be mounting—it is hard to imagine his continued approval.

The year 1911 brought to the surface qualities in Liang which had been dormant for several years. It revealed, or rather his private papers now show, that his network of contacts was extensive and that he was still a man to contend with on the political scene. It showed that not only the T'ung-meng Hui benefited from the flood tide of Chinese students who came to Japan in the first decade of the century. Graduates of the early Chinese classes at the Japan Army Officers' Academy formed an impressive group of potential allies for Liang near the top of the Chinese military establishment.

A detailed survey of his plots in 1911 underscores the fact that Liang, if a "conservative" or "moderate," was not content with the status quo, but rather was ready to take up arms for the sake of reform. It should be remembered of Liang that three times in seventeen years (1900, 1911, and 1915–1916) he stimulated and participated in plans to overthrow the established government by force. As a publicist he was innately political by the standards of Chinese culture. A scholar who pointed the way, he was, by implication, offering to lead as a power-holder. As in the 1898 reform movement, the abortive Hankow uprising of 1900, and in the succession of his political organizations, the underlying notion in 1911 was that he would assist directly in governing the country if the opportunity arose. The formulation

[71] Mai Meng-hua to Liang, letter #4, *LCCNP*, p. 361.

of concrete political plots was not, for Liang, an unnatural act.

Liang's monarchism in the decade before the revolution was theoretical, not specific. That is, he advocated a constitutional monarchy, and therefore the continuation of the Manchu dynasty, not out of loyalty, either Confucian or modern, but because he believed that retaining the monarchy would facilitate modernization and prevent political disintegration. At a time when Liang was still hoping to stage his *coup d'état,* he wrote that if the present imperial line could be used he would use it, and if not, then there were other ways of managing things.[72]

It was assumed by the T'ung-meng Hui that Liang's return to China in November, 1911 was directed against the revolutionaries. It is true that Liang was no friend, but they were wrong in thinking that he was primarily concerned with checking or destroying their organization. Indeed, in the early weeks, he was optimistic that the revolutionary leadership would drop its racial slogans and emphasize the political objectives of constitutional government and a national assembly with actual sovereignty. He went so far as to write that his "party" would stand aside if the revolutionary party could give the country "the basis of public peace and order." The reason that the revolution threatened disaster was that the T'ung-meng Hui could not in fact achieve this goal: they were at heart regionalists, he felt, and did not have the strength to launch an immediate attack on Peking. Thus the danger of foreign intervention on Peking's side, Liang believed, would grow greater with time.[73]

Liang had by no means come to like the revolutionaries and even sponsored activities designed to unseat a T'ung-meng Hui government in Kwangtung. Still, one feels that if some revolutionary leader with a sure political touch had, in the midst of this national crisis, issued a call to Liang to join the revolution on behalf of constitutional government, even if republican, Liang might have agreed. The reception accorded him by the T'ung-meng Hui, however, was of an entirely different order. For example, the major revolutionary organ, in reporting Liang's ar-

---

[72] Postscript of November 9, 1911, to Liang's letter of October 29, 1911, to Hsü Ch'in, *LCCNP,* p. 339.

[73] Liang to Hsü Ch'in, October 29, 1911, *LCCNP,* p. 339.

rival in Manchuria in November, stated that the headquarters of the revolutionary party in Shanghai had dispatched two assassins to follow him to Peking to kill him.[74] The revolutionaries had much more in common with Liang than with Yuan Shih-k'ai. A firm alliance with Liang and those whom he could have influenced would have been a major alternative—even if a limited one—to the other possibilities open to the revolution, such as fighting on or arranging a deal with Yuan. Liang did not have at his disposal power comparable to Yuan's, but, added to the revolution, his forces might have made an appreciable difference. It is a comment on the power of factionalism and the narrow vision of the revolutionary leadership that they seem never to have considered the Liang alternative but accepted so readily an arrangement with Yuan.

Liang, in spinning these plots in 1911, was motivated by two factors: first, he was concerned that the Peking government was inadequate to its job, especially in regard to the foreign danger; second, he desired that, in overthrowing it, the resulting government be an improvement and that the process not invite foreign intervention. In the later stages of the revolution, he resisted the advice of his colleagues and followers to declare for the republic and clung to the notion of a figurehead monarchy under a constitution. But no one who knew his activities and thoughts at this time could have imagined that his intellectual position reflected a conservative cast of mind, a personal devotion to traditional forms, or a reformer's abhorrence of violence.

[74] *Min-li pao,* November 12, 1911. The same newspaper called his eldest daughter a prostitute and punctuated his interviews with sarcastic editorial remarks (*Min-li pao,* November 16, 1911). Liang complained of T'ung-meng Hui spies infiltrating his meetings with local dignitaries in Manchuria. Liang to Liang Ling-hsien, November 12, 1911, *LCCNP,* p. 345.

JOSEPH R. LEVENSON

The Province, the Nation, and the World: The Problem of Chinese Identity[1]

ONCE, in the 1950's, I attended a conference on "Europa, Erbe und Aufgabe." "Europa" meant "West Europa," the inheritance was Hellenism and Christianity, the task (assumed with surprising aplomb, in a happy act of oblivion) was the preservation of sweetness and light through this David's-band in the middle distance, between the giants, the philistine materialists, America and Russia. There were other surprises. China received a passing (or failing) mention. It was paired, not with the Soviet Union, but with the United States: areas outside Europe which had been subject to the influence of Europe.

It was a nice conceit, rather like indexing, "J. S. Bach: composed the accompaniment to Gounod's 'Ave Maria' " (one can find it in "The Well-Tempered Clavichord"). And no one need be ill-tempered, for his country or his "field," because of a bit of deprecation—especially when it suggests a bit of truth. The United States and China (to trade on a famous title) may have been pasted together too casually in Mainz, but Europe did pose

[1] This is the only footnote, because what follows is an essay, not an article—an essay in the sense of first attempt, some theses thrown at the paper, a suggestion of a larger work in progress.

to them both, through all of American history and the latest part of China's, the problem of "Provincialism."

For generations, Americans have pondered the theme of innocence and experience. Christopher Newman was Henry James' *The American*. A nation of new men: perhaps it meant that America had it better, no ruined towers—or was it the callow land, gauche and timidly genteel, provincial? Yet, whatever it was doing, taking dictation or sending lessons back, America shared in a Western world. If America was provinces, its capital, in Europe, was really its own. But nineteenth-century China, which had plenty of ruined pagodas (or vanished, beyond ruin), was still a world itself. It had its own provincials within it while Confucian sophisticates ruled. It was when this world faded and a nation began to emerge that the old sophistication began to fail. Cosmopolitan in the Chinese imperial world, Confucianists struck a provincial note in the wider world of the nations. And consistently, provincialism as a literal, political fact dragged at the nationalists of the early twentieth century, post-Confucianists with a wide range, who figuratively, culturally, were changing the implications of "provincial."

Yet, when it came to establishing a Communist China, heir to the nationalist revolution and (some think) more essentially national in its fervor than ideological, a feeling for provinces was invited, not discouraged. Invited—in a way: the Communists were turning back the past, repelling it, not turning back to it. Modern history had not gone for nothing. They were exorcising the anti-national potential of the provinces. It was an act of killing the blooms (or certifying the deaths) of provincial selves, then not blowing them away, but pressing them into a national album. What blighted them was the cosmopolitan spirit—the same spirit (others think) that stamped the Chinese Communists as national all right, but national in an internationalist ideological sense.

PROVINCIALISM (LITERAL) AND RESISTANCE TO NATIONALISM

How nationalism became prominent in China is a story by itself. But if nationalism be taken as given, embroilment with provincialism will have to be there, too. French Revolutionaries, classic nationalists of that modern world which was now receiving China, had insisted that provinces be transcended, particularities smoothed away, to serve the sense of nation. Chinese history since the Opium War had seen the issue in many forms. There were the myriad examples of interest, sympathy, even conscious- ness cut off, and seen to be cut off, well below the level of any national integration. There were the observations, at home and abroad, that foreign conquest of the whole China would be easier to achieve while the inhabitants failed to see it as a whole. There was the running debate, in the context of shared nationalism, about the technical question of *administrative* provincialism, de- centralization. There were the streams of provincial sentiment, rising out of propinquity and expressed in separate organizations and areas of action, which flowed into the movement for revolu- tionary national union, even while they bedeviled it with divisive threats of faction. There was the "objectively" nationalist charac- ter of anti-Ch'ing provincialism in the last few years of the dynasty (or one could turn this around, to explain the chaos of the Republic, with its growing national feeling while the center could not hold)—Manchu centralizers (the conservative provin- cialists' targets), Manchu "usurpers" (the radical nationalists' targets), and Manchu purveyors of provincial plums to foreign- ers (the targets of both) were the same Manchus. There was the insinuating nationalist corruption of the atavistic rhetoric of pro- vincial xenophobia, and of provincial warlord slogans of political self-assertion.

So much for the political implications of provincialism, its capacity for inhibiting nationalism, aborting it, indirectly abet- ting it, or submitting to its solvent influence. But if these were all, no especially modern theme would have been sounded in Chinese history. The Chinese Empire, too—*t'ien-hsia,* the world of all- under-Heaven—knew tensions between the provinces and cen- ter, and the wholeness of China was certainly asserted. Yet it was not in the name of nationalism, but of Confucian universality. Why were such nineteenth-century officials as Tseng Kuo-fan and Chang Chih-tung loyal to the dynasty after the Taiping Re- bellion? Why did they not seize the chance, on late-T'ang lines, to be regional satraps? It was the Confucianism of a man like

Tseng that committed him to Empire, not region, even his own (really almost his own) beloved Hunan. For Confucianism was "high culture," above local ground. Tseng's literati language, the classical written style, had no provincial life; it was the language of no province, only of a past. This is part of what was meant when iconoclasts of the twentieth century called it, and wished it, dead.

Ironically, this was the language which had made the spoken forms *mere* speech, provincial, since none of them was the sole language of *t'ien-hsia,* the property of some men in all provinces. What all men in each province spoke was dialect, even the "mandarin" speech of Ch'ing Peking, supreme as speech—but speech was not supreme. Everywhere in the world dialect is a vehicle of restricted views on the world, compared to national languages, the media, translatable and translating, for world expression. And yet, by this criterion, in the cosmopolitan, revolutionary twentieth century, this same Chinese literary language, a very model of the more-than-provincial on its own historic ground, was arraigned as provincial: inadequate for world expression, when the world was not its own.

PROVINCIALISM (FIGURATIVE) AND NATIONALIST RESENTMENT

It was an aura, then, of cultural revolution which distinguished nationalists from Confucian universalists (whether as radicals the nationalists scored tradition, or as conservatives they showed in themselves the marks of its corrosion). They were still an elite, like the Confucianists—no distinction there—for the nationalism had to be preached first by men who knew the world, at least more of the world than "provincials" would ever know. Knowing this, they knew that provincial differences within China, compared to the foreign clash with China in general, paled in significance. And goaded by provincial unawareness, they were hortatory and lofty, to make the provincials *see* the nation which the elite could not but see. Where provincials would drone along the accustomed ways, nationalists would break with custom—by pondering foreign ways—to liberate creativity, to create a liberated nation. Like Nehru on Le Corbusier's Chandigarh ("The site chosen is free from the existing encumbrances of old towns and old traditions. Let it be the first large expression of our creative genius flowering on our newly earned freedom."), like Emerson repudiating "provincial culture" as "excessively deferential toward the past . . .," they made a connection between creativity and shaking free of tradition—or of provincialism.

This is provincialism in the figurative sense. If the Chinese past had congealed, resisting free and fresh intellectual probing, then China itself was provincial, together with the stale literati who organized the past, and whose cosmopolitan standing was now in the past itself. At least they should have been provincial and obsolete, and would be, when the avant-garde that saw it could expose it to the nation, and make the nation conscious. What new men saw was the "anachronization" of language that expressed traditional values. First it became inadequate, then sham —used to conceal a worldly interest, not just to explain the world. When Lu Hsün published what he saw between the lines of *jen, i,* and other classical terms, he was not quite ready to say that these grams of instant Confucianism no longer spoke to him; they did speak, and spoke deceitfully. Confucianists, that is, were not quite yet provincials, resting quietly, quaintly using vocabulary whose tone had slipped from universal range to local color. One does not fight a safely retired provincial, but smiles at him. Lu Hsün was not smiling.

The fully provincial is not only partial but really *passé*. Szechuan newspapers, for a year or two after 1919, gave a fine example of the provincializing process. They used the colloquial *pai-hua,* the language symbol of new thought and a post-Confucian world, and then abandoned it: "more space and less literary value than the literary language." And this took place in a context of Szechuan's retrogression from alignment with the nation. Thus, to go back to the literati's language, which was sophisticated, cosmopolitan, in the old world, was a provincial act, both literally and figuratively, in the new.

The modern historian Ku Chieh-kang, using a Chinese province literally as his reference point, shows what the metaphor "provincialism" implies. Discussing the work of two nineteenth-century Cantonese historians, he described their book as written "from the standpoint of that region—nevertheless, they show rather a lot of intelligent judgment." The expectation of limited views in "the provinces," the scientific historian's condescension, could hardly be more obvious. (Thus Matthew Arnold, wishing to "see life clearly and see it whole," dismissed the view of the Protestant sects as partial—and provincial.) Ku, like other post-Confucianists, saw China whole, and they prescribed for the nation's ills not Chinese medicine, but cosmopolitan science. The Confucian classics had etched out a Chinese "world" identity, above provincial identities in the past. But a Chinese *national* identity (which rendered the classics a purely national historical possession) involved a new "world" intellectual appeal—transcendence of nation to build a nation which itself transcended provinces.

The narrower the horizons, the more homogeneous the society; as Redfield noted in folk societies, by and large the country, "the provinces," shows local uniformity and regional diversity. But nationalism is the product of cities, and modern industrial cities, full of the *dépaysés,* reverse the pattern: it is local diversity—division of labor and a varied range of experience —with more and more international uniformity. Hence the paradox of the technological revolution, making nations more and more alike ("continents into provinces and countries," thought Yen Fu), while passions rise for national independence. Chinese nationalists' rejection of provincialism—in which they included, or to which they reduced, Confucian cosmopolitanism—was a fateful modern gesture; it launched China into modern cosmopolitanism, and into all the doubts, the search for roots, which the highly technological modern world is heir to.

THE COSMOPOLITAN WASTE LAND

The modern world is the culture of cities, with their connotation of rootlessness, the severing of bonds (in both the "good" and the "bad" sense: *"Stadtluft macht frei"* / "New York's a lonely town"). Another "bad" sense—Tagore: "Calcutta, Bombay, Hong Kong and other cities are more or less alike, wearing big masks which represent no country in particular." Another "good" sense—H. G. Wells: "Yet don't you think this very fact is an indication that we are reaching out for a new world-wide human order which refuses to be localized?" This recalls Michelet, who saw "the local spirit . . . disappearing every day . . . man's own power will uproot him from the earth . . . to the idea of the universal fatherland, to the city of Providence." But William Blake: "To Generalize is to be an Idiot, to particularize is the Alone Distinction of Merit"; and J. M. Synge, for the west of Ireland, deprecating "the modern literature of towns," clinging to the "springtime of the local life," before "the straw has turned into bricks"; and the composer Vaughan-Williams, ready for international audiences but not cosmopolitan art: "As our body politic becomes more unified, so do the duties of the individual members of that body become more, not less, defined and differentiated." This is organic theory, vitalism; and what is the city but artifice compared to the life of nature ("conquered," for Michelet, by his dear but dry abstractions, "society and liberty"), the organic life of the country, the provinces? But what if the provinces really are provincial, in the sense of Hume and Henry James: "provincial" meaning "barbarous and ignorant" (the Scottish preachers), "common and inelegant" (the Cambridge ladies)? What if the regional man's ignorance of the world is not what Allen Tate admires, "an intense and creative ignorance," "the only effective check upon the standardizing forces of the outside world . . ."? Whether the cosmopolitan city is the spoiler or creator, the anti-cosmopolitan note of duty, "the duties of the individual," is the note of desperation.

For time passes and "provincial" and "anachronistic" tend to coincide. Out from the center means backwards in time. Venice and Florence, "provincialized" by the unification of Italy (like the famous Greek cities under Roman centralization), became largely cities of museums, and museums as cities. "I was reminded of Nice or Biarritz in the time of Napoleon III," wrote Lévi-Strauss of the "Tristes Tropiques," provincial Brazil. Except for the occasional anti-nationalist, avowedly "provincial," only a rustic, a natural provincial, would be caught wearing the queue in China after the Ch'ing. The urban years of the Chinese Communist Party were the years of its unequivocally modern bias; it was in the nineteen-thirties, in back country, that the indigenous and the old (as in a measure of medical provincialism) recovered a certain standing with the Party. No wonder Trotsky, intransigently urban and explicitly cosmopolitan, arraigned the Party leadership for reducing revolution to "provincial peasant revolts"—provincial not merely in the categories of political geography, but in a deeper sense than that.

NATIONAL THEATER

Trotsky was wrong about the political prospects of the Party in the provinces. Culturally, too, the Communists, with their revolutionary nationalist and internationalist commitments, did not succumb to provincialism, whether temporal or spatial. They went neither "backwards in time" to the high culture of the Empire, nor "out from the center" to folk traditions. Their cosmopolitanism, both as an agent to kill provincialism and as a resource to fill its place, remained inviolate. In their early city days, as in Shanghai in the nineteen-twenties, they knew they ran afoul of provincial sentiment; the "rootless" class approach to combination was impeded by provincial guilds, which were trying by natural ties to humanize the vast nowhere city. And later, in the country, though provincials became their protégés after Liberation, the waste land was not re-sown, provincial traditions were not revived to any pre-nationalist, pre-cosmopolitan, vibrant historical reality. Peasants became actors, the Party was director, the revival was theater.

For traditions, authentic in the past on local ground, may survive in the mind, reenacted with all the kaleidoscopic variety and the ultimate detachment which an actor's roles (as distinct from his own *persona*) imply. One grows into oneself, but the actor has to contrive a role, and contriving means consciousness. Awareness of Eden was expulsion from Eden. Even if an actor's only role is to be himself—even if the repertoire, the kaleidoscope, is only the director's—consciousness is there: self-consciousness, the blight on the natural local idiom, the provincial's awareness that now he is "provincial," discovered by central casting for a city impresario. Is it only the true provincial who can, and can only, "be himself," without affectation: the boon, and the flaw, of a truly rooted identity? But the only provincials left are unauthentic, when their ways are being observed for conversion into "theater." When the bars are down and men are observed, their being observed affects them. We know the modern psychology of provincial and national dress; from the same cosmopolitan viewpoint that makes national dress "provincial," they both are called, significantly, "costume," and their wearers compelled to consciousness. It is as if they were characters in a historical novel of the anachronistic kind, where the issues, the sensibilities, are the author's, so that the "exactness" of the environment is a product of dead research, not living empathy, and the characters are a *cast* of characters, clad not in their own clothes but in costume.

Another type of consciousness: Ku Hung-ming, late Ch'ing and early Republican (in chronology, not in sentiment!), took pleasure in showing Europeans his knowledge of their culture so that no one should imagine that his Chinese affirmations were the fruits of a mere provincialism. But in the eyes of Chinese nationalists, Ku's last stand for the old cosmopolitanism made him precisely quaint and provincial. Unyielding apologist for practices like foot-binding—such a scandal to the moderns—he seemed to be striking attitudes all his life, playing a role, assuming theatrical poses. It was a special type of provincialism, divorced from spontaneity and becoming a performance, in the fullness of consciousness.

Consciousness, fatal to provincial authenticity, is essential to cosmopolitanism. All the world's a stage. It is appropriate, in the cosmopolitan world, that Marx and Freud, two of the most impressive contributors to the modern temper, suggest conversion to consciousness as the typical modern theme. Even the modern irrationalists, celebrants of the unconscious like Knut Hamsun or D. H. Lawrence, mean to bring it to conscious attention. They are primitivistic, not primitive. The Soil Grows, the Serpent Plumes for thee, *hypocrite lecteur,* provincial*istic* cosmopolitan. Just as for the Marxist the perennial class-struggle should issue forth in class-consciousness; just as for the Freudian the perennial subconscious should be dredged up to consciousness; so for the cosmopolitan in general (who may be wedded to nationality, which is also the product of consciousness—Renan called it, "a daily plebiscite"), the "natural" ways of the provinces are collected into a pick-and-choose amalgam. Things which have "just grown" from organic local roots—many things from many roots—are codified and selected in acts of conscious scrutiny.

Here, then, I wish to convey the idea of Chinese revolutionaries creating their own "theater." In another study I interpreted their action—against the world to join the world, against their past to keep it theirs, but past—as a long striving to make their museums themselves; it was to escape being exhibits, antiques preserved for foreign delectation. It amounted to this: let foreigners not be cosmopolitan *at Chinese expense* (as Japanese who prefer Brecht to kabuki—"for foreigners"—hold that the Western taste which the national must resist is the Western *schwärmerei* about the national traditional arts). "Gratitude" for the interest of foreigners in one's own past achievements would amount to accepting provincial status in the current cosmopolitan world, not vindicating the sufficiency, the sophistication, of one's own.

Perhaps that is one of the reasons why the work of Lin Shu, the prolific adapter of European novels into literary Chinese early in the twentieth century, left radical nationalists with a queasy feeling. The cosmopolitan aspect of the enterprise, the interest in Dickens and Dumas and the rest, was not the trouble; the provincialism was. It wasn't the feat but the humility: Lin was fond of the use of *hsiao* ("filial piety") in his titles, e.g. *Hsiao-nü Nai-erh chuan*, for *The Old Curiosity Shop*, with its superhumanly filial "Little Nell." Was Lin (who opposed the vernacular movement) just tactfully easing the traditional sort of Chinese reader into a foreign literature? Or was he defending ancient Chinese virtues by pointing out the *cachet* that came from enshrinement in foreign books? This would be the note of provincialism that vitiated the cosmopolitan effort.

And so autonomous Chinese "theater" and antonomous Chinese "museum" came in together. The only way to keep from being patronized for one's "ancient wisdom" or "local color"— the only way to avoid feeding the cosmopolitan appetites of others—was to patronize one's own, on one's own, in a spirit as modern and non-provincial as that of the West which would make China provincial. Hence, "theater," the mode in which provincial traditions, under Chinese Communist aegis, came to be rehabilitated. Such traditions, we know, had once been considered by early nationalists as inhibitors of national consciousness. But if they could be squeezed from the historical stage, they could be restored to just—"the stage." At last they could be regarded, in sophisticated spirit, as a diversified repertoire to which the nation gave attention, not as divisive single spectacles to which the provinces gave themselves. The provinces made an aggregation, and the attitude towards idiosyncrasy was not impatience any more but acceptance, even celebration, as in the loving revival (and *collection,* in every sense of the word) of provincial traditions in opera, lore, and legend. Communists might trip the Shensi light fantastic, the *yang-ko,* partly to get themselves into Shensi—and partly to get Shensi into China. Shantung should know and lay equal claim to what Szechuan had created. All provincials should share all provincialisms, patronize each provincial performance, and so diffuse the provincial spirit—the best way to depress it.

If we have time for a snack between the acts, let us turn, for another analogy, to cuisine. Provincial cuisines may be the delectation of the cosmopolitan. For these to have been created in the first place, there had to be limits, ingredients and combinations which were not locally known. But the cosmopolitan knows them all and may use them all, prizing the parts for making a perfect whole, and breaking down the wholeness which the creative limits formerly defined. A Jewish style of life, for example, may be more endangered when everyone eats bagels than when Jews eat hot cross buns. Such was the anti-provincial, cosmopolitan vision of the nationalist Michelet (if only he could have known!), who looked for the French provinces to flavor the national character while they yielded to the higher designs of nation, and then in the fullness of time, world state. To consciousness and homogenization, as characteristics of modern times, one should add specialization, the end of self-sufficiency. In the national collective, provincial characteristics are available

—simple contributions (how one can patronize the simple!) to a compound.

The "provincialism" of provinces, taken one by one, lies in their relative simplicity. They lend themselves—Chinese provinces certainly did, historically—to stereotyped identities, which are death to ambiguity. Writers with a sophisticated modern sensibility (Proust, or James, for whom "American innocence," an innocence of guile and ambiguity, was provincialism itself) thrive on ambiguity, rejecting single, simple lines in the coloring of characters. Just so, the nation is a sophisticated concept: not only is it farther along toward abstraction than the local, rooted province, but it seems, as an amalgam, inherently more ambiguous. The sum of many stereotypes—honest Shensi, greedy Kiangsi . . . —is not so easy to stereotype. The collector of many traditions is not so bound to tradition. And provincial traditions at last, as contributions to a repertoire of roles, not a congeries of identities, would no longer make a range of natural styles, dividing the nation or aborting the nation's birth.

How, then, could Communists preserve Confucius, whom once they had to attack? They put him in the museum (cf. Henry Ford, a new man for a new world, and his Dearborn "old America"). And how could Communists redeem provincials, whom once they had to deplore? They put them in the theater—less a provincial theater (victory of the old) than Old Vic in the capital. And the provinces go to pot, the common pot. The original anti-provincial aims were not gainsaid, but accomplished.

Accordingly, Chinese Communist economic indulgence of local expression, like cultural indulgence, has been really nationalist and centralizing. There is a difference between decentralization as a technical prescription and decentralization as a pre-nationalist "fact of nature." "Centralized decentralization" (ordained from the center, in the interests of the totality) is analogous to nationalist provincialism, whereby "provincial culture" may be patronized for central and modern, not provincial and pre-modern reasons. The question of degree of centralization, which fluctuates, is only a technical question; the whole is always the end concern.

"We no longer look on the past as a son looks on his father, from whom he may learn something, but as a grown man looks on a child. . . ." (Valéry, on modern civilization—"a machine . . . [which] will not tolerate less than world-wide rule.") From Confucianism to communism is a history like that, from reverence to condescension, and condescension sets the tone for the epithet, "provincial." This is the tone of the Chinese Communists' curious elitism, with its Heepish humility before "the people"— condescension, really, as the very term, "the people," "the (*little*) people," implies. "The people," in their several provincialisms, have created roles (*in the past*), and therefore they can be honored. But the Party, in the true spirit of elites, assembles and directs the repertoire, and the peasants, with their contributions from fine local cultures, are put on the stage. This is a fair specimen of modern "psychic tourism," joy in the "authentic" while the authenticity fades under the stare. But it is a Chinese stare at last, the revolutionary independence of making one's own theater (like one's own museum)—taking from the West not just certain values (in revolution against the "feudal-Confucian" past), but (in revolution against a "bourgeois-imperialist" presence) the license to condescend.

COMMUNIST PROVINCIALISM: CLASS AND NATION

The authenticity fades, the provincial becomes a part—a part of the nation, a part in theatrical repertoire. Is the actor, everywhere in the world, in danger of losing his own *persona,* Ortega y Gasset's "irrevocable 'I,'" menaced by the "mass man . . . mounted on a few poor abstractions . . ."? Is local ground paradise lost in the cosmopolitan present? "To us today" (the words of Richard McKeon), "the sense of tradition is not strong, not so much because we have no tradition but because we have mixed so many traditions." There are those who feel that art has lost its sting, since (given modern technology, the ground of cosmopolitan diffusion) we see or hear it, all different kinds of it, all the time. And so it is with provincialisms, collected and run by on the stage. What had cultural bite in the concentrated province becomes bland when gathered up in the nationalist's aggregate: the price of sophistication. This is what is meant by the sophisticate's envy of the simple(provincial) man, Yeats' ideal audience ("a simple Connemara man"), an audience he despaired of. Yeats, his personal culture ranging as far as the Upanishads and the Nō, was apparently far removed from the mass culture he hated, the culture he wished to spare the "Connemara man." But he was just as modern as the mass blight, "Calcutta, Bombay, Hong Kong," in their big impersonal masks. Yeats, like Tagore with his cosmopolitan culture, was as far from a lost Bengal or Connemara as any faceless victim of standardized mass society.

One of the things that has stripped provincial roots (and spread a non-provincial culture, in the variants "mass" and "sophisticated") is the universality won by science. Science used to be much more stylized, colored by local cultures, than today. Now it is cosmopolitan, "objectively": in modern times, nothing is more provincial than stylized science. (Psychiatry has been relatively slow to break away from national schools and styles: a way of saying that its standing as science is still not fully secure.) It is sophisticated to mourn the loss of stylization in art (the loss that makes the waste land) and to insist upon it in science. A "subjective" cosmopolitanism invades the provinces, as sophisticates, hopefully and blightingly, seek "the real thing" for their rootless miscellanies. But "the real thing" existed, the province was authentic, when sciences and arts were provincial together. When science was cosmopolitanized, reunion impended, at a level above the provinces, a level where (for the arts) the satisfaction of cosmopolitan taste brings, like a shadow, unappeasable regrets.

Is this a version of "Civilization (sophistication) and Its Discontents"—Freud and the nemesis of progress? Then it would not be by chance (comrades) that Communist China, unequivocally "progressive," should de-nature its local traditions by preserving them in the museum-theater way.

That is, the Communists were not reactionary, even when they seemed to be. Their provincialist excursions were neither primordially anti-nationalist (see above), nor in line with integral nationalism (see below). Provincial traditions, when collected into a national package, could be accommodated to communism because they added up, not to regional consciousness, which could splinter the nation, but to class consciousness. This is tantamount to saying, in response to another conundrum—is it really other? —that peasant passions could be properly channeled to Chinese nationalist communism in spite of the primal Marxist coolness to peasantries. The province is connected with "the people," since in Confucian China it was the mandarin literati, in or out of office, who had a trans-provincial identity. Not only their central-bureaucratic "world" standing but their normative high culture (and the language that enshrined it—a cosmopolitan language quite distinct from the local, living dialects, which were *heard* but not *read*) raised them above the barriers of provinces.

Literati had prized local connections and were ready enough, of course, to raise their local standing. But it was their "worldly" ties and identity that gave them the best lever. Intellectually, as Huang Tsung-hsi insisted in his early Ch'ing *Ming-ju hsüeh-an*, schools of thought might be tied to special localities. But these distinctions, these particular claims, often proudly asserted, for the significance of provinces, were felt to be claims to leadership in universal Confucian significance. Provincial *shu-yüan* (Confucian academies) inspired local pride, but the pride was for localities as centers of illumination for the whole intellectual world. It was not just pride in the province, but a fundamental assertion that the province—the *literati's* province—was not "provincial." It was a different case entirely with the sub-intellectual local popular forms. Indeed, the literati's well-developed sense of lofty eminence expressed itself in scorn for the merely local. When the Ch'ing scholar Chang Hsüeh-ch'eng criticized the Sung scholar Ou-yang Hsiu for niggling about choice of words, he called it "three-house village scholarship" (a rough equivalent of "provincial"). And if the Confucianists felt themselves so serenely above the provincial—both the literally provincial outsider, *sans* classical education and doomed to be of one time and one place, and the metaphorically provincial insider bruised in a polemic among the learned—then the Communists, in turning the tables on the "feudalist" literati, granting the low "provincials" a title to "People's China," were only stating the logic of revolution.

In the implications of local history objectively considered, one can see the grounds for a Marxist concern with provinces. As a field, local history tends to be social history, with an emphasis on way of life and impersonal trends within it; since the stage is remote and small, individual persons, even local notables, while they may "reflect" history, seem to have too narrow a scope to "make" it. What distinguishes "objective" local history (and Marxist scientism assumes objectivity) from "subjective" local history is that the latter implies what the Communist feel for the province helps to undo: a personal feeling for roots, a loving sense of place, vitality, and vividness instead of the scientist's abstractions. And what distinguishes "objective" local history from amateur "local antiquities" is that, in the latter, individuals, local notables, may well be the subject of discourse. But local (provincial) history, out of range of "the capital" with its levers of power on the grand scale, for the wide arena, is more in the anonymous vein, history of "the people"; and anonymity, with its veiled intimations of determinism, may suggest, to the suggestible, class analysis and dialectical materialism.

When attended to in a Marxist spirit, the contours of provincial life, the offerings of provincial culture, convey (as Lukacs puts it) the "concrete significance of time and place": they are the stuff of that Communist ideal, historical reality (or simply, in the aesthetic realm, *realism*). It has nothing to do with direct concern for the province, and everything to do with indirect concern for the class-conscious nation. Since intellectuals, with their famous lack of concreteness and their cosmopolitan view, wash off the smell of locality, they contrive "superstructure." It is this which releases "substructure," the materialist's realm of reality, to provinces.

But the provinces do not keep it for themselves; they make a nation, an aggregation, which claims the sum of provincial popular values. When high art and culture become international, as the province of cosmopolitans, the only popular art is national. And popular art (again, Lukacs) is anti-capitalist, in the sense that the proper art of advanced capitalist society, with its social division of labor, is a coterie art divorced from popular life. Then "the people" equal a nation—and an international class. That is why the Communists, assuming this, seem both anti-cosmopolitan and cosmopolitan. They counter the cosmopolitan with the provincial, in the interests of the nation—a leveling nation, with that egalitarian passion which led, in the classic example, from the "Marseillaise" to the "Internationale." Their provincialism being so ambiguous, it is hardly surprising that the same is true of their anti-cosmopolitanism. The anti-provincial provincialists are cosmopolitan anti-cosmopolites.

COMMUNIST PROVINCIALISM: CLASS AND WORLD

The benign attitude toward provincial identity, a Chinese nationalist version of provincialism, is the key to communism as a nationalist version of internationalism. For communism is by no means just a cover for Chinese nationalism, any more than the nationalism is just a cover (instead of a consumer) for provincialism.

As a Communist-nationalist version of provincialism, far removed from a pre-nationalist one, we must distinguish it from an integral-nationalist version. The Chinese provinces are not savored for some mystic one-ness of organic irreducibility. Here the Chinese Communist attitude differs from that of the nationalist provincialism of the proto-fascist Action Française or the Nazis, with their "Ich bin vom Saar . . . Ich bin vom Schwarzwald" choruses of Nuremberg Rally mystagogy. The Nazis conceived of a "Germanism" brooding in all the organic localities, which were archaistically praised. The spirit of the past was called from the vasty deep, in romantic Wagnerian old Nurembergs. But Chinese Communist "provincialism" (like Chinese Communist "Confucianism") conceived of making the provinces past by collecting bequests for the synthesizing nation. In romantic integral nationalism on Nazi lines, the locality is misrocosm, containing the nation; for Chinese Communists the nation is macrocosm, composed of local elements.

And when an integral nationalist like Barrès or Maurras sounded paeans to the provinces, he was appreciating their limiting (hence, their nationalist) potential as a counter to internationalism, which he attributed to class-conscious radicals. In this right-wing nationalism, nation confronted class, and the appeal to roots (peasant and provincial) was an appeal against an urban, cosmopolitan abstraction. This was just as modern an outlook as the Marxist: far from a conservative internationalism like Metternich's (" . . . Europe a pris pour moi la valeur d'une patrie"), and far from a conservative sub-nationalism, where provincial identity was self-sufficient and a natural endowment, with no need of deep angling to bring it up to consciousness. In wartime Vichy, with its Barrèsian, Maurrasian background, Pétain welcomed peasant groups parading (charading) in provincial costume. The provincialism was just as synthetic as the Chinese Communists': the two kinds of nationalists surely have much in common, as modern contrivers of consciousness. But if they belong together in the same world, they belong at opposite poles.

For while the Chinese Communists (and the Soviets), like integral nationalists, struck attitudes against "rootless cosmopolitans," the Communist attitude was hardly supposed to stifle class-consciousness—it assumed class-consciousness. "The people" (for the Chinese Communists), the provincials, were posed not only against "feudalists" (the Confucian-literati establishment, the supra-provincials in the *t'ien-hsia*), but against "bourgeois," and these would-be cosmopolitans in the new post-*t'ien-hsia* world. In the political sphere, this theme was adumbrated in the Opium War, when the conviction arose, to be revived by the Communists, that the Cantonese provincials had really defeated the British, only to see the officials and merchants of Canton city connive at yielding to the foreign will. And in the cultural sphere in Communist China, "bourgeois cosmopolitans" were indicted for holding, for example, that literature is independent of society. Society was taken to mean the real (not platonically), the phenomenal, the material conditions of life, "the concrete significance of time and place": the surroundings where writers are "at home." That is why Feng Hsüeh-feng was purged as a rightist in 1957—for advocating internationalization of "national form" (which was, usually on the folklore model, "people's").

Yet, if the Party was condemning cosmopolitanism not in order to stifle class-consciousness but to enhance it (thus winning abroad the title of "provincial" for the culture it supported), it was really opening the way for a sort of cosmopolitanism—as long as the class which absorbed it was not an enemy but a friend. What were "the people" whom the Communists found in the provinces, beneath the cosmopolitan culture (in *t'ien-hsia*, Confucian-world, terms) of yesterday's "feudalists" and the cosmopolitan culture (in *shih-chieh*, modern world, terms) of today's bourgeoisie? For some purposes "the people" were *min-tsu*, an organic community of integral nationality; not a cosmopolitan conception. An organism, while more than a cell, is less than an aggregation. It made, particularly in Kuomintang usage, for a conception of national essence—transcending individuals, but an individual itself, a folk, in its resistance to cosmopolitanism. For the Communists, however, "the people" were generally not *min-tsu* but *jen-min*, not organic, collective life but a collectivist abstraction—and not single and self-contained, but cosmopolitan.

As *jen-min*, provincials have supra-national not sub-national associations. "The people," located first at their most particular in the local earth of the provinces, then move into the abstract as the trans-national, trans-cultural, universal ground of a more-than-Chinese vision of the world. Province equals folk; nation equals the folk of province and province; folk equals "the people" of the world. Perhaps the claques for Cuban bongo-drummers were not convened in Peking just as a diplomatic tactic after all.

In short, Mao's peasant, one of his Hunan "folk" or of any other province, is quite distinct from the "Connemara man": Mao's constituency is a world-wide category, not the stubborn flesh and blood (though a poetic conceit) of a single provincial place. The industrialization which cosmopolitanizes the world is Mao's cause, Yeats' curse. Mao's provincial folk, as nationalized as the railroads, and the underpinning of international class society, are a futuristic fancy, not a phantom of nostalgia.

No wonder Liu Shao-ch'i could pay an even-handed tribute to "Nationalism and Internationalism." Nationalism, hostilities at an end with one seemingly natural foe, provincialism, could plausibly be at peace with another, internationalism—especially since provincialism, conceived in class, not classical terms, as aggregate and distillate informed the other two.

RECAPITULATION

The Ch'ing period was one of transition from *t'ien-hsia* to *kuo-chia,* empire and world to nation. Chinese nationalism involved a scaling up from a collection of provinces, a scaling down from a world. The Confucian *t'ien-hsia* had been its own cosmos, and the owners of the high culture embedded in classical language, transcending provincial speech, were culturally never provincial, though they had provincial ties. Such ties were part of, not rival to, ecumenical Confucianism, trans-provincial or *wordly* and cosmopolitan. These ties formed part of the personal-relationship ambiance of Confucianism, with its amateur's resistance to the impersonal-Legalist, specialist-cog variety of culture.

Industrialization, no Confucian value, has been conducive to uniformity in various ways—turning people into cogs (the critics say), erasing distinctions of provinces and obliterating the human, local ties. But it makes for diversity, too: the diversity of the many vocational types that come in with specialization. And specialization makes new elites, of professionals, not amateurs on the Confucian model. It is the professional field, not the fields of Flanders or Hunan, that more and more provides the "local" or particular identity.

Early Chinese nationalists, late Ch'ing and Republican, who were created by the rise of industrial nations and were seeking that kind of power for their own, strained against provincial ties politically, and scorned the self-sufficiency of literati-China, intellectually, as smothering and narrow. The Ch'ing's, the Empire's cosmopolitans became the Republic's, the nation's provincials. And the Ch'ing's provincials, the rustics whose culture was too "low" to release them from local ground, were moving toward a radical reassessment. In sum (in part) modern Chinese history is this: a history of movement from the politics of Confucian faction (deriving at times from provincial fellow-feeling, but in a world commanded, overall, by a common Confucian fellowship) to the politics of a new world, an international politics conceived in terms of class. The province, the nation, and the world, in sequence and combination, have all entered the Chinese view—provincial, nationalist, cosmopolitan—of "China, Erbe und Aufgabe," "China, its inheritance and task."

JOHN ISRAEL

Kuomintang Policy and Student Politics, 1927-1937

SINCE the early 1950's, scholars have debated whether the Chinese Communist regime can best be understood as a reassertion of traditional patterns of Chinese history or as a revolutionary break with the past. Similar questions might profitably be asked about its predecessor, the Nationalist Government that ruled from 1928 to 1949. It is a strangely neglected phase, for this relatively brief interlude is surely of critical importance, both in itself and as a prelude to the fundamental changes which have since overtaken China. The Kuomintang's effort to build a new China came, it might seem, tantalizingly close to the threshold of success. It is certainly arguable that, had it not been for the Japanese invasion, a stable and effective Nationalist regime might have met the various problems which confronted modern China adequately enough to remain in power and perhaps to retain and enhance its originally revolutionary program. On the other hand powerful elements in the Kuomintang consistently resisted fundamental change of the sort that was probably necessary for long-run political stability, and Chiang himself was clearly far more a traditionalist than a revolutionary. Nevertheless, it is conceivable that the political evolution of the Kuomintang might have gone either way, and this very ambivalence and inner contradiction needs further examination. Was the Kuomintang's rule revolutionary or reactionary? Was it a new stage in

China's modernization, a continuation of the warlord politics of a dynastic interregnum, or an anachronistic attempt to reestablish a neo-Confucianist order? Or was it, in fact, "the precursor of the Chinese Communist Party"? [1]

Before these questions can be answered, scholars must analyze and interpret the policies, personnel, and ideas of the inadequately studied decades of Nationalist rule. During its years of power, the Kuomintang was the subject of surprisingly little serious analysis. In the few scattered universities around the world where students of China existed, attention was focused either on the high periods of great tradition or on Sino-Western contact in the tragic era between 1840 and 1910. The spectacular development of communism in China over the past twenty-five years not only has drawn a growing number of specialists to the study of the current scene and some of its more obvious roots, but at the same time has reinforced scholarly as well as public interest in the history and institutions of the traditional civilization. The surge of new attention to the periods which preceded or followed the Kuomintang has tended to obscure this short but critical period. However, the brevity and ultimate failure of Nationalist rule does not rob the subject of interest or importance. The period, moreover, is still recent enough to give the historian appreciable advantages: the experience is over and one may begin to claim some degree of perspective on it; yet many of the primary materials, and indeed many of the principal actors, Western observers, and sometime participants, are still available.

This paper attempts to elucidate a critical aspect of the Kuomintang experience through an examination of Kuomintang educational policy in relation to the student movement. In the KMT's efforts to establish ideological orthodoxy in the school system we find a microcosm of the broader problem of factional politics among the party's civilian, military, and intellectual leaders—significant echoes of the reactionary-revolutionary ambivalence. No area of educational policy places these issues in sharper focus than that of the student movement. China's modern student group, socially and intellectually alienated and intensely

---

[1] John K. Fairbank, *The United States and China* (Cambridge, Mass., 1958), p. 308.

nationalistic, had matured during the decade following the abolition of the Confucian examination system in 1905. After the May 4 demonstration of 1919, both Nationalist and Communist leaders realized that this educated elite could be a powerful political weapon. In 1924, the KMT, which had just been reorganized under Soviet advisers, officially began to enlist students.[2]

Some of these recruits were simultaneously cadres in the Chinese Communist Party. Students rallied under both the KMT and CCP banners during the nationwide anti-imperialistic May 30th Movement of 1925. The following year, the Second Kuomintang Congress decided to make the student movement part of a broad, multi-class youth movement.[3]

In 1926–1927, students played a prominent political and military role during the first phase of the KMT's Northern Expedition to wrest control of China from the warlords. They were especially active in Wuhan, where the KMT's left wing established a government on January 1, 1927. However, on April 12, Chiang Kai-shek, supported by the party's right wing, began the anti-Communist purge known as the Party Purification Movement. Thousands of young suspects were executed; political measures were also used to rid schools of the "Red menace." Some were closed for several months, others completely reorganized. Teachers were dismissed; students who were not expelled were required to sign loyalty oaths or to secure guarantors. Student organizations were investigated, purged of alleged subversives, and placed under control of Central Party Headquarters. During the summer of 1927, the Wuhan government expelled its Communists, and some of its leaders moved toward alignment with Nanking. In June, 1928, Peking was captured and renamed Peiping. Nanking became the capital of China.

A major problem facing the new government was what to do about student and other mass movements. Could the Kuomintang as the ruling party continue to encourage student political activity? If it tried to do so, could the aspirations of a radical

---

[2] Chow Tse-tsung, *The May Fourth Movement* (Cambridge, Mass., 1960) p. 265.

[3] Pao Tsun-p'eng, *Chung-kuo ch'ing-nien yün-tung shih* [A History of the Chinese Youth Movement] (Taipei, 1954), p. 128.

younger generation be realized through the same party that had ruthlessly purged its ranks of Communist suspects? Further, would the KMT's Western-trained liberal educators accept a party-sponsored youth movement? But if an attempt were made to discourage student participation in national politics, might youth not fall prey to the blandishments of the schismatic Reorganization faction of the KMT or even to the Communists?

The student movement, subject of heated KMT debate while the Northern Expedition was still in progress, became a merely academic question during the party purification. However, the controversy flared up again following the establishment of the Nanking government. Many Wuhan figures who cast their lot with Wang Ching-wei (exiled leader of the Reorganizationist faction) argued that the revolution remained "unfinished." After the military and political victory, they anticipated an ongoing socio-economic revolution in which students would mobilize the masses. These arguments were forcefully presented by men such as Shih Ts'un-t'ung and Ch'en Kung-po (both Communist apostates) in Ch'en's short-lived periodical, *Ko-ming p'ing-lun* (Revolutionary Critic). However, Yeh Ch'u-ts'ang, who had recently urged students to devote eight hours a day to political work, now joined with Nanking conservatives and educators who contended that such student activity was incompatible with national reconstruction and social stability.[4] As president of the National Academy (education ministry) from October, 1927 to October, 1928, Ts'ai Yüan-p'ei remained the leading spokesman for this point of view. He said: "Now the responsibility for eradicating bad government lies with several hundred thousand party troops, and the administration of sixteen provinces is under the direction of party headquarters. There are men available for the task. Students should study diligently to equip themselves for great service at a future date."[5]

Ts'ai and his academic colleagues feared that an active stu-

[4] P'an Shih-hsüan, "Tui-yü hsüeh-sheng ju tang chih i-nan" [Doubts about Students Entering the Party], in Wang Chien-hsing, ed., *Hsüeh-sheng yü cheng-tang* [Students and Political Parties] (Shanghai, 1927), p. 7; *Chung-yang jih-pao* [Central Daily News], May 11, 1928.

[5] Chung-hua min-kuo ta-hsüeh-yüan (National Academy of the Republic of China), *Ch'üan-kuo chiao-yü hui-i pao-kao* [Report of the National Educational Conference] (Shanghai, 1928), Sec. D, p. 2.

dent movement would imply handing over control of education and of young minds to party functionaries. Therefore they insisted that student activities be limited by school walls and supervised by school administrators. Their fears were confirmed by the words and deeds of Ch'en Kuo-fu and his followers in the nascent Organization Clique or CC Clique (named after him and his brother Li-fu). Like the Reorganizationists, these men argued that youth should take the lead in carrying the unfinished revolution to success. They conceived of the youth movement in grandiose terms—as a weapon for fighting imperialists, warlords, political bosses, local riffraff, and oppressive gentry; as a force for renovating education, for enlightening the masses, and for leading "liberation movements" of peasants, workers, and women; and as a medium for military training. However the CC Clique insisted upon the need for centralized control and ideological conformity in the movement. The problem with student political activity, these men stated, was that it lacked discipline, leadership, and a guiding ideology, and that it was emotional and destructive, corrupted by individualism, heroism, liberalism, communism, and anarchism. The CC solution would have been a tightly regimented KMT student organization dedicated to the Three People's Principles.[6]

Ch'en Kuo-fu's plan provided for a national student union organized according to principles of democratic centralism, beginning on the lowest level with cells in every school, and leading upward through city, county, and provincial levels to a national congress, a central executive committee, and a standing committee. It was anticipated that this group would expand into a comprehensive union of youths from all classes, for, as Ch'en Kuo-fu said, only students had "the ability to enter farmer, worker, merchant, and other bodies and to serve as leaders."[7]

[6] Wang Tao-yü, Chin Chia-hsün, and Shang Hsi-fan, eds., *Min-chung yüntung yü hsün-lien* [Mass Movements and Training] (Peiping, 1928), pp. 26–28; Chung-kuo kuo-min-tang chung-yang chih-hsing wei-yüan-hui (Central Executive Committee of the Chinese Kuomintang), *Min-chung hsün-lien wei-yüan-hui kung-tso pao-kao* [Report on the Work of the Committee for Training the Masses] (Shanghai, 1929), Preface, p. 1.

[7] Wang Tao-yü, p. 205; Chung-yang mi-shu ch'u (Central Secretariat of the KMT CEC), *Chung-kuo kuo-ming-tang ti-erh-chieh chung-yang chih-hsing wei-yüan ti-wu-tz'u ch'üan-t'i hui-i chi-lu* [Record of the Fifth Plenum of the Members of the Chinese Kuomintang's Second Central Executive Committee] (Shanghai, 1928), pp. 139–140.

Other figures, older and more conservative than the Ch'en brothers, reacted with skepticism. They agreed that ideological uniformity was highly desirable but doubted that the youth movement was an effective vehicle for accomplishing this aim. Moreover, they feared that any attempt to encourage the movement would simply open the door to Communist infiltration. Even so, many of these men wanted students to continue to be active in the KMT, if only on an individual basis. As of October 31, 1929, students comprised 10.49 per cent of party membership; naturally, the party was reluctant to lose this elite element.[8] Tai Chi-t'ao's proposal that students continue their work at party headquarters, provided that their motives were "pure," was one attempt at a compromise solution.[9]

These divergent opinions clashed at a series of high-level meetings between early 1928 and late 1929, beginning with the Fourth Plenum of the KMT's Second Central Executive Committee (CEC), which opened on February 2, 1928. The question of the student movement arose in the context of a larger problem: what to do with mass movements in general. The plenum's decision to abolish the bureaus for peasants, workers, merchants, youths, and women) may be understood in part as an indication of the ascendency of party conservatives since April, 1927. Pichon P. Y. Loh suggests another reason: the decision was forced upon the party because the most active cadres had been purged during party purification.[10] The KMT's official explanation is that the existence of bureaus for various social classes had proved administratively unmanageable, incited class warfare, weakened party control over mass movements, caused "misunderstandings," and had become anachronistic since the Party Purification Movement.[11]

[8] Min-ch'ien T. Z. Tyau, *Two Years of Nationalist China* (Shanghai, 1930), facing p. 24.

[9] Tai Chi-t'ao, *Ch'ing-nien chih lu* [The Road of Youth], 2d ed. (Chungking, 1942), pp. 10–11.

[10] "The Popular Upsurge in China: Nationalism and Westernization, 1919–1927" (Ph.D. dissertation, University of Chicago, 1955), p. 317.

[11] Chung-yang hsüan-ch'uan pu (Central Ministry of Propaganda), *Chung-kuo kuo-min-tang ti-erh-chieh chung-yang chih-hsing wei-yüan ti-szu-tz'u ch'üan-t'i hui-i hsüan-yen ping i-chüeh-an hsüan-ch'uan ta-kang* [Outline for Propagandizing the Proclamations and Resolutions of the Fourth Plenum of the Members of the Chinese Kuomintang's Second Central Executive Committee] (Nanking, 1928), pp. 8–9; *Chung-yang jih-pao,* February 6, 1928.

In this new environment, declared the delegates, agitation would give way to constructive tasks: students would study, farmers farm, workers work.[12] The main task of the KMT vis-à-vis the masses would no longer be to rouse them to overthrow reactionary warlords, but to train them in the precepts of Sun Yat-sen. Hence the conference approved a resolution, presented by Chiang Kai-shek, Ting Wei-fen, and Ch'en Kuo-fu, which established a Committee for Training the Masses.[13] To reassure Ch'en Kuo-fu and his followers, who feared that the KMT would become alienated from its popular base, Ch'en was appointed chairman.

The Fourth Plenum's resolution on the student movement similarly attempted to reconcile opposing points of view within the party. A strong stand was taken against "the participation by immature students in our political and social conflict." Primary and secondary school students were to be barred from politics, and student unions would be reorganized as student self-governing associations with educational functions only. Students would no longer be permitted to participate in political activities through school organizations. However, this would not prevent individual students from joining the Kuomintang and working for local KMT headquarters or other approved organizations. Thus, a resolution calculated to mollify Ts'ai Yüan-p'ei was also designed to meet the minimal demands of Ch'en Kuo-fu. However, in reconciling factional differences, the plenum failed to make plans for the future. The debate had barely begun.

Following the plenum and while Ch'en Kuo-fu's Committee for Training the Masses was drawing up plans for a revitalized student movement, Ts'ai Yüan-p'ei convened the First National Educational Conference (May 15–30, 1928), which, he hoped, would place problems of educational policy in the hands of educators rather than in those of party officials.[14] In accordance with Ts'ai's proposals, the conference advocated limiting student organizations to the schools and forbidding students from assuming responsibilities at party headquarters. Thus the educators

---

[12] *Chung-yang jih-pao*, February 6, 1928.

[13] *Chung-yang jih-pao*, February 7, 1928.

[14] Allen B. Linden, "The Promising Years, 1924–1928" (draft of a chapter in a forthcoming Columbia University Ph.D. dissertation).

rejected the idea of a party-led movement isolated from the schools, as advocated by Kuomintang politicians of the CEC's February plenum. Instead, they proposed that students should remain under school control, insulated from the ruling party.[15]

The task of choosing between the irreconcilable views of Ts'ai and Ch'en fell to the Fifth Plenum of the KMT's CEC in August, 1928. No resolution evolved from this conference except for a subcommittee's observation that the masses had the legal right to organize under party sponsorship and government supervision. Ch'en Kuo-fu may have seen this as a green light; he quickly presented his plan for a party-controlled national student union to the CEC. However this body referred the proposal to the Standing Committee, which tabled it.[16] The failure of the KMT's top decision-making organ to accept Ch'en Kuo-fu's plan left little hope for a nationwide KMT-led student movement.

By the spring of 1929, the KMT's resolution of the student question had become identified with the career of Tai Chi-t'ao, once an intimate of Sun Yat-sen, subsequently a founder of and defector from the Chinese Communist Party, and then a close associate of Chiang Kai-shek. Such party notables as Chiang and Hu Han-min sympathized with Tai's opposition to the massive involvement of students in national politics. These cautious views gained further support after the Japanese occupation of Tsinan in May, 1928, when the KMT failed to keep student protest under control, and the persistence of leftist activities in Shanghai made a decision urgent. In October, 1928, Tai was appointed to the Committee for Training the Masses (following Ch'en Kuo-fu's retirement), and in April, 1929, he was named Minister of Training. Six months later, Tai disbanded the National Student Association when it violated his injuction by attempting to hold its Eleventh Annual Meeting. In January, 1930, the Ministry of Training announced two basic laws that dissolved all nonacademic student organizations and replaced the politically-oriented "student associations" with "self-governing associations," whose functions were confined to education.

In principle, therefore, the party had made its decision on

[15] *Ch'üan-kuo chiao-yü hui-i pao-kao*, Sec. A, pp. 71–72.
[16] Wang Tao-yü, p. 4.

student political activities by the beginning of 1930; in practice, however, its attitude remained highly ambiguous. Several months after the promulgation of the new regulations, Ch'en Li-fu continued publicly to urge students to carry on in the spirit of the Northern Expedition and the anti-Japanese movement.[17] Moreover, the KMT's response to student nationalism after the Mukden Incident of 1931 was much the same as it had been during the Tsinan Incident of 1928. In both instances students were aroused by vivid accounts in the official press of enemy brutality, and in the Kuomintang advocates of a positive movement seized the opportunity to mobilize youthful patriots. After the legislation of 1930, as before, party bureaus helped students organize anti-Japanese propaganda and boycott campaigns. On both occasions, indications that Communists had infiltrated the student movement provoked suppression by party officials and the police.

The Tsinan Incident of May, 1928 was settled through diplomacy; student activity was short-lived. But the Mukden outbreak was more than an "incident." From September to December, 1931, as Japanese troops occupied Manchuria, students by the thousands converged on the capital from all over China. They beseiged railroad stations, attacked station masters, and lay on the tracks to secure free transportation. After reaching the capital, they marched on government offices to implore China's leaders to declare war and to send troops to resist the aggressor. Authorities handled these unruly young patriots with finesse, housing them at government schools and sending high-level officials to receive and harangue them. Initially, these painstaking efforts met with success. Group after group departed, reassured that the government was preparing for war against Japan. However, as the more moderate elements retired to the sidelines, radicals came to the fore. Hundred of students from Peiping and Shanghai accused the KMT regime of following reactionary policies at home and of appeasing the foreign foe. Such treachery, they said, called for revolutionary opposition: students must act as the vanguard of a popular uprising aimed against the treachery of the Nanking government. These elements explicitly rejected the tactic of "petitioning" and called instead for "demon-

---

[17] *Chung-yang jih-pao*. May 4, 1930.

strations." It soon became clear what they had in mind. On December 15, they stormed government offices, seized Ts'ai Yüan-p'ei and Ch'en Ming-shu, and manhandled these two party notables before police could rescue them. Two days later they sacked the offices of the party organ, the *Chung-yang jih-pao* (Central Daily News). Once again the Kuomintang had to retreat from an attempt to manipulate student nationalism. Students from other cities were rounded up and sent home from the capital. Officials throughout the country were instructed to bar student groups from railway stations. Nanking warned that students who served as tools of subversive organizations would be treated severely.[18]

From 1932 to 1937, the government appeased Japanese imperialists by trading territory in Manchuria and north China for time to arm. Under such conditions it is remarkable that no major student uprisings occurred between January, 1932 and November, 1935. This phenomenon can be explained by the Sino-Japanese détente following the Tangku Truce of May, 1933, by the stabilization of educational administration under Wang Shih-chieh (Minister of Education from 1933 to 1938), and by the effective use of coercive techniques by the Kuomintang. Routine measures such as the regular payment of teachers' salaries eliminated sources of discontent that had kept the educational world in a state of turmoil. Steps were taken to reduce the percentage of politically obstreperous (and unemployable) liberal arts students and to increase the number of those in technological and scientific fields. Orthodoxy and diligence, tested by comprehensive examinations, were rewarded by scholarships. Government-appointed chancellors Chiang Monlin at Peita, Mei Yi-ch'i at Tsinghua, and Lo Chia-lun at National Central University restored order, raised academic standards, and won the respect of students. Simultaneously Kuomintang agents infiltrated student organizations, established party cells, and set up front groups on the Communist model. Suspected radicals were hunted down, arrested in predawn raids on student dormitories, and whisked off to jail, some never to reappear. This revival of the "White Terror," as leftist critics called it, was especially preva-

[18] *Chung-yang jih-pao*, December 20, 1931.

lent in Peiping, where the gendarmes of Chiang Kai-shek's nephew, Chiang Hsiao-hsien, led the antisubversive crusade. Police kept close surveillance over student organizations and arrested with impartiality members of anti-Japanese associations, as well as delegates to antiwar conferences. Even a YMCA club, which had held a commemorative service for Sung Dynasty patriot Wen T'ien-hsiang, was forced to disband.[19]

The most militant Kuomintang group was the Fu-hsing She (Regeneration Society), popularly known as the Blue Shirts. This quasi-secret body had been founded by a zealous group of Whampoa Military Academy graduates who felt that the KMT's civilian organization was undisciplined, bureaucratic, and too corrupt to guard the heritage of Sun Yat-sen. They visited Italy, Germany, and the Soviet Union to study Fascist and Communist techniques, which could be used, they hoped, to channel revolutionary youth in the right direction.[20] Blue Shirts served as military instructors on college and middle-school campuses, where they organized and indoctrinated progovernment activists. In middle schools, the military ethos was also perpetuated by the T'ung-tzu chün (Boys' Army), the Chinese branch of the Boy Scouts; membership was compulsory for all junior middle-school boys.

A more conventional program of extracurricular activities was sponsored by the KMT's Committee for the Direction of Mass Movements, the successor to the Committee for Training the Masses. The Kuomintang's most promising effort was to enroll students in a program to reconstruct rural areas from which the Communists had been expelled. Here, albeit on a very limited scale, was an appeal to youthful idealism and enthusiasm for social reform. Less dynamic was Chiang Kai-shek's New Life Movement, launched on February 19, 1934, which offered youth a Confucian puritanism as a sop for revolutionary zeal. The program reflected Chiang's personality—Chinese Confucian, Japa-

---

[19] *Chung-yang tang-wu yüeh-k'an* [Central Party Affairs Monthly], No. 52 (November, 1932), pp. 801–803; *Ta-kung pao* [L'Impartial], January 14, 1933; *The China Journal,* XVIII, 3 (September, 1933), 160; Dwight W. Edwards, "1934–1935 Annual Report" (Peiping, August 22, 1935), in the Historical Library of the Young Men's Christian Association, New York, New York.

[20] *New York Times,* May 22, 1934.

nese militarist, and Western Christian—in its promotion of punctuality, neatness, and discipline, along with the traditional virtues of *li* (propriety), *i* (right conduct), *lien* (integrity), and *ch'ih* (a sense of shame).

The New Life Movement and other Kuomintang programs were most successful among middle-school students of the lower Yangtze Valley. Little impact was made upon sophisticated college students or in those areas of the country where Nanking's influence was weak. The party still suffered from internal contradictions: organizational efforts of political activists thwarted pedagogical aims of liberal educators; the philosophic premises of the New Life Movement were antithetical to those of modern education; and militaristic Blue Shirts competed with the party's civilian authorities in the CC Clique. Although the KMT's many-faceted approach to the students had constructive as well as destructive aspects, the latter had the greater impact. The White Terror, immediately successful at ridding campuses of many insurrectionists and at frightening others into silence, was suicidal in the long run. The party had gained an unsavory reputation as a result of its oppressive techniques and was able to recruit few aside from the opportunistic, the indigent, and the frightened. An aura of fear clouded government-student relations and provided excellent propaganda material for Communists. Moreover, youth was only temporarily subdued. As early as January, 1933, a writer in *Ch'ing-hua chou-k'an* (The Tsinghua Weekly) observed that Kuomintang oppression was producing more student radicalism than it destroyed.[21]

After two years of relative inactivity, Japanese aggression in the spring of 1935 became the catalyst that precipitated a resurgence of radical nationalism. By forcing KMT party and military forces to evacuate the Peiping area, the Japanese created a vacuum; to fill it, they tried to create a five-province North China Autonomous Region. Young China's answer was the Peiping student demonstration of December 9, 1935, the beginning of the nationwide December 9th Movement. The thrust of this was twofold: (1) against the Japanese, their puppets such as Yin

[21] Ching Po, "K'ai-fang tang-chin yü chin-pa ch'ing-nien" [Cast Off Party Restraints and Rescue Youth], *Ch'ing-hua chou-k'an* [The Tsinghua Weekly], XXXVIII, 12 (January 14, 1933), 1225.

Ju-keng, and the autonomy movement; and (2) against the Nanking government's policy of appeasement. The youthful outburst exposed the fundamental inconsistency in the government's policies. The KMT was a prisoner of its own chauvinism. Having risen to power on slogans of national unity and having promoted a stridently nationalistic education through the school system, the ruling party had created a Frankenstein monster: a younger generation that demanded resistance at all costs. Given these facts, it is amazing that as of 1935, students, though critical of the Nanking government, still remained fundamentally loyal.

But the Kuomintang was too hidebound by old policies and attitudes and by the responsibilities of governing China to respond creatively to the new challenge. Its actions followed the familiar sequence of qualified encouragement, temporization, and finally repression. However, from the outset Nanking was determined to prevent a repetition of 1931. Though the Ministry of Education called the December 9th demonstration "patriotic," Wang Shih-chieh ordered local authorities to prohibit strikes, parades, and petitions.[22] When students attempted to seize trains to Nanking, rail service was halted. In Nanking and Wuhan, martial law was declared.[23] A recess was announced to disperse students to their homes. In the Yangtze Valley student activities came to a halt, but not in Peiping and Tientsin. The government's next move was to convene in Nanking a mid-January conference of educators and sympathetic students. Here it explained its policies and planned a counterattack through the formation of KMT groups to oppose leftist-dominated student organizations. When these moves failed to curb Peiping students, the government promulgated an Emergency Law to Maintain Public Order (February 20), followed by a directive outlawing the Peiping-Tientsin Student Union, which was labeled a Communist tool.[24] Subsequently, troops and police surrounded campuses and ferreted out left-wing leaders, but hard-core radicals

---

[22] *North China Star*, December 12 and 18, 1935; *I-erh chiu yün-tung* [The December Ninth Movement] (Peking, 1954), p. 84.

[23] *I-erh chiu yün-tung*, p. 88.

[24] [Helen F. Snow], "On the Student Front in Peiping," *China Weekly Review*, LXXVI, 1 (March 7, 1936), 35; quoted in Nym Wales (pseudonym for Helen F. Snow), "Notes on the Chinese Student Movement" (mimeographed, Madison, Conn., 1959), p. 49.

had received prior warning and escaped, while hapless followers and innocent bystanders were carted off to jail. Such heavy-handed police action silenced opposition for a few weeks but had the long-range effect of consolidating intellectual opinion against the oppressors.

The only move that could have won students over would have been for the KMT to adopt the Communists' slogan of a national united front against Japan. Such a policy was proposed by the editors of *Ch'ing-hua p'ing-lun* (Tsinghua Critic), a pro-KMT student newspaper, but the government was not prepared to make such a bold move and the advice went unheeded.[25] Consequently, no significant pro-Kuomintang student movement developed until December 25, 1936, when Chiang Kai-shek emerged from his captivity in Sian to lead the nation against Japan. However, by that time thousands of students were looking to Mao Tse-tung for leadership, not to Chiang Kai-shek; hundreds had already left to join the Communists in the northwest. Though outnumbered by those who followed the government to the southwest after the outbreak of war, they included many of the most active, vital, and idealistic elements of north China's student population. In the minds of many more, seeds of doubt about Kuomintang leadership were beginning to germinate, and under wartime conditions these bore bitter fruit for the party of Chiang Kai-shek.

KMT innovations in student policies during the war years reflected the government's militarization, the loss of its cosmopolitan base in the cities of the lower Yangtze, and the bankruptcy of its prewar policies. The Three People's Principles Youth Corps of the Whampoa Clique and the authoritarian regime of Minister of Education Ch'en Li-fu placed the control of China's youth in the hands of men who had been forced to operate clandestinely during the 1930's when official policy had been that of the liberal educators. But the failure of wartime policy is another story. Though it might be argued that the Three People's Principles Youth Corps, established in 1938, came ten years too late, we must ask whether a Kuomintang faced simultaneously with

[25] February 14, 1936, quoted in Wales, "Notes," pp. 50, 106.

radical nationalistic students, Japanese aggression, peasant revolt, civil war, intraparty turmoil, and natural disasters could have won over the younger generation regardless of its student policies.

Ideologically, the two decades of Kuomintang hegemony appear midway between China's Confucian past and its Maoist future. Politically, the Kuomintang government was a transitional stage in the interregnum between warlordism and communism. It staggered under the burdens of its predecessors and of its successor: while clumsily and ineffectually attempting to establish a one-party dictatorship, it was beset by residual problems of regionalism and militarism. These ambiguities were especially pronounced in the field of education. Party education was accepted in principle but frequently rejected in practice. A party-led youth movement was rejected by KMT liberals and traditionalists in principle but eventually put into practice by KMT militarists. Yet, these efforts at authoritarian control resulted only in a wider breach between students and the ruling party.

Had the Kuomintang been monolithic—consisting exclusively of Confucian gentry or Bolshevized revolutionaries, military zealots or industrial capitalists, Westernized educators or professional politicians, or a happy combination of two or three of these groups—it might have enforced consistent policies. But the presence of all these elements in a single party, harassed by enemies and loosely bound by diverse ties of power, idealism, self-interest, and personal relationships, was disastrous. Under less demanding circumstances, the KMT might have muddled through. But the breakneck pace of events in twentieth-century China allowed no time for gradual solutions.

ALBERT FEUERWERKER

Industrial Enterprise in Twentieth-Century China: The Chee Hsin Cement Co.

CEMENT is a dry and powdery substance, and its history perhaps an arid subject unless it is used to illuminate the fortunes and fate of industrial enterprise as a whole in the first half of the twentieth century in China. By many standards the Chee Hsin Cement Co. was a success. Its output and sales grew steadily from the time the firm was reorganized in 1906–1907 until the mid-1930's; during 1940–1945, under Japanese occupation, production recovered from the precipitous drop caused by the outbreak of the Sino-Japanese war. The company's plant and equipment were constantly augmented and modernized, and technically were probably the best in the industry. It had the largest rated capacity of any prewar Chinese cement company. Profits were large and steady for those who had invested in the firm. Management was capable and notably stable in its composition. At no point in its history did Chee Hsin come to depend upon foreign loans for capital equipment or operating funds. In all these respects, the experience of China's first and largest cement company contrasts sharply with that of two other Chinese industrial enterprises, each also the premier firm in its industry, whose histories I have examined elsewhere.[1]

[1] See Albert Feuerwerker, *China's Early Industrialization: Sheng Hsuan-huai (1844–1916) and Mandarin Enterprise* (Cambridge, Mass., 1958), pp. 96–188,

The student of China's modern economic history is faced with two sets of data which measure the development of modern industry from quite separate points of view. On the one hand, there is incomplete but convincing evidence that output of the modern industrial sector of China's economy increased at a very respectable rate throughout the period 1912–1949, notwithstanding the many obstacles to such a development. The often repeated epithet of stagnation has no merit when applied to this sector of the economy. A recent study of industrial production in China, including Manchuria, indicates that net value added in industry grew more or less continuously through 1936. The outbreak of the Sino-Japanese War in 1937 brought that growth to a halt and occasioned a marked decline. As Japanese industrialization efforts in Manchuria gained momentum, however, output expanded again and by 1941 exceeded the 1936 level. The peak year was 1942, followed by a sharp drop in 1945–1946, and a partial recovery in 1947–1948.[2]

Although the modern industrial sector grew rapidly during the

---

for the China Merchants' Steam Navigation Co.; and *idem,* "China's Nineteenth-Century Industrialization: The Case of the Hanyehping Coal and Iron Company, Limited," in C. D. Cowan, ed., *The Economic Development of China and Japan* (London, 1964), pp. 79–110. The source of much of the data in the present study is a recently published collection of documents from the archives of the Chee Hsin Co.: *Ch'i-hsin yang-hui kung-ssu shih-liao* [Historical Materials on the Chee Hsin Cement Co.], comp. by the Economic Research Center and the Department of Economics, Nankai University (Peking, 1963; cited hereafter as *CHSL*). The firm in its English-language correspondence and advertisements romanized its name as Chee Hsin. The author gratefully acknowledges the assistance of a Social Science Research Council Auxiliary Research Award in the preparation of this essay.

[2] John Chang, "Indexes of Industrial Production of Mainland China, 1912–1949" (Ph.D. dissertation, University of Michigan, 1965), has computed the following average annual rates of industrial growth, based on value added in 1935 prices, for 1912–1949 and sub-periods:

Periods	Growth Rate (%)
1912–1949	5.5
1912–1920	13.8
1912–1936	9.2
1912–1942	8.2
1923–1936	8.3
1923–1942	7.1
1928–1936	8.4
1928–1942	6.7
1931–1936	9.3
1931–1942	6.7
1936–1942	4.5

twentieth century, on the other hand its role within the economy as a whole remained a very limited one. In 1933, the combined output of all "industry" (factories, handicrafts, mining, and utilities) constituted only 10.5 percent of the net domestic product in current prices. If handicrafts were excluded, the "modern" industrial share was only 3.4 percent. Even if the output of construction, modern trade and finance, and modern transport and communications is included, the modern sector as a whole generated only 13 percent of the national product in current prices in 1933. Total employment in factory industry, mining, and utilities numbered no more than 2 million, or 4 percent of the nonagricultural labor force.[3]

China's pre-1949 economic experience was thus one in which some individual firms, or industries, developed rapidly, while the structure of the economy as a whole was not radically transformed. Modern industrial output as a whole expanded, but even after four or five decades was significantly inferior in quantity to handicraft production. And any increment in per capita output of modern industrial products was barely apparent in the face of a population which may have grown from 420,000,000 in 1912 to more than 500,000,000 in 1949. The gross question of the degree to which China had industrialized by 1949 is therefore not at issue. In looking at Chee Hsin as an example, our attention is directed rather to such matters as the nature of the small modern industrial sector which did develop, as well as its relation to the rest of the economy and to other parts of Chinese society, and to the factors which furthered such growth as did take place but restricted it to a relatively isolated portion of the economy. The Chee Hsin Cement Co. shared in the common experience of other pre-1949 manufacturing firms and in its uncommon individual success provides a valuable illustration of what the limits of possible economic development were.

CHEE HSIN PRODUCTION AND SALES, 1907–1949

In the immediate prewar period there were eight Chinese-owned cement plants in China proper, excluding the northeastern prov-

---

[3] Ta-chung Liu and Kung-chia Yeh, *The Economy of the Chinese Mainland: National Income and Economic Development, 1933–1959* (Princeton, 1965), pp. 66, 69, and 89 (Tables 8, 11, and 21).

inces.[4] The oldest was the Chee Hsin Cement Co. (Ch'i-hsin yang-hui kung-ssu) at T'ang-shan (Tangshan), Hopeh, which was a direct descendent of a small cement subsidiary undertaken by the Kaiping Mining Co. in 1889. In 1914 Chee Hsin acquired control of the Hua-feng Cement Co., which had been operated fitfully since 1910 by Shanghai investors at Shih-hui-yao, near Ta-yeh, in Hupeh. As a Chee Hsin subsidiary the Hupeh plant was known as the Hua-chi Hupeh Cement Co.[5] The Kwangtung provincial government operated two factories, opened in 1908 and 1932, on the eastern and northern outskirts of Canton.[6] Two new large firms began producing cement in 1923 and 1924 respectively: the Shanghai Portland Cement Co. (Shang-hai hua-sheng shui-ni kung-ssu), organized by the well-known Shanghai merchant Liu Hung-sheng (O. J. Lieu), with a plant at Lunghua, near Shanghai, between the Whangpoo River and the Shanghai-Hangchow-Ningpo railroad; and the China Portland Cement Co. (Chung-kuo shui-ni kung-ssu), founded by the Shanghai building contractor Yao Hsi-chou, the banker Ch'en Kuang-fu, and others, whose plant was located at Lung-tan, near Nanking, on the Shanghai-Nanking railroad. The Chih-ching Cement Co. at Tsinan, the capital of Shantung, a much smaller firm, was started at about the same time; the Taiyuan Cement Works of the Shansi provincial government, also a small plant, opened in 1935; and the Szechuan Portland Cement Co. completed its one-kiln plant at Chungking about 1935.[7] The

[4] For brief surveys of China's cement industry, see "Cement Industry in China," *Chinese Economic Journal*, X, 1 (January, 1932), 25–36; Fang Hsien-t'ing and Ku Yüan-t'ien, "Chung-kuo shui-ni kung-yeh chih niao-k'an" [A Bird's-Eye View of the Chinese Cement Industry], in Fang Hsien-t'ing, ed., *Chung-kuo ching-chi yen-chiu* [Studies on the Chinese Economy], 2 vols. (Shanghai, 1938), II, 652–663.

[5] "Cement factory in Tayeh, Hupeh," *Chinese Economic Bulletin*, VII, 248 (November 21, 1925), 294–295.

[6] "Cement Industry in Kuangtung," *Chinese Economic Bulletin*, XXVI, 7 (February 16, 1935), 99–101; "A New Cement Works in China," *Cement and Cement Manufacture*, VI, 7 (July, 1933), 223–232.

[7] Ch'en Chen, ed. *Chung-kuo chin-tai kung-yeh shih tzu-liao, ti-i-chi, min-tsu tzu-pen ch'uang-pan ho ching-ying ti kung-yeh* [Materials on the History of Chinese Modern Industry, First Collection, Enterprises Founded and Managed by Private Capital] (Peking, 1957), pp. 402–416, 559–563; M. H. Chou, "The Boom of Chinese Cement Industry," *Concrete*, XXII, 5 (May, 1923), 73–76; "Cement Industry of Lungtan," *Chinese Economic Bulletin*, XXII, 9 (March 4, 1933), 128–129; "Cement Industry in Kiangsu," *ibid.*, XXIII, 1 (July 1, 1933), 6–7; "The Northwest Cement Works in Shansi," *ibid.*, XXVII, 24 (December 14, 1935), 374–375.

rated capacity of these eight enterprises as of mid-1936 is shown in Table 1, but actual cement production was considerably less than these figures.

Before the major expansion of Japanese industry in Manchuria which began in 1932, there were two Japanese-owned cement works in China: a small plant at Ts'ang-k'ou, near Tsingtao, in Shantung, taken over from German interests in 1915;

Table 1

NOMINAL CAPACITIES OF CHINESE-OWNED
CEMENT PLANTS, 1936

Company	375-lb. barrels per year
Chee Hsin	1,650,000
Hua-chi	300,000
Kwangtung	1,000,000
Shanghai Portland	500,000
China Portland	1,300,000
Chih-ching	100,000
Taiyuan	150,000
Szechuan	270,000
Total	5,270,000

and the Onada Cement Co.'s much larger branch plant at Dairen, which began production in May, 1909 and grew rapidly thereafter.[8] New Japanese cement plants were established in Manchuria in the 1930's, and the output of the Onada works was greatly increased. The total annual capacity of the Manchurian cement industry in 1936 was approximately 4,000,000 barrels.

Both the number of plants and the output of cement in Manchuria grew after 1936, while in China proper, occupied and unoccupied, output dropped precipitously after the outbreak of the Sino-Japanese War. Production in occupied China, while still below the prewar level, picked up in 1939 and was fairly well

---

[8] On the Onada Dairen branch, see South Manchurian Railway, Tōa Keizai Chōsakyoku, "Shina cemento-gyō" [China's Cement Industry], *Keizai shiryō* [Economic Reports], III, 11 (November, 1918), 1380–1386.

maintained through 1945. Manchurian production increased greatly through 1943, after which it fell sharply. Total cement production at the end of the war, in 1946, dropped back to pre-1920 levels. Plans were announced for several new large cement plants and machinery was ordered.[9] Repairs and refurbishment at Chee Hsin and elsewhere resulted in higher output in 1947, but the ravages of inflation and civil war had brought the cement industry, like others, to a near standstill at the time of the Communist takeover.

Table 2 shows the output of cement in China including Manchuria from 1922 (the first year for which relatively reliable total data are available) through 1949, the respective shares of China proper and Manchuria in this total, and the relative position of the Chee Hsin Cement Co. Its position varied, but throughout these two decades Chee Hsin was a major producer, and before 1922 it had a near monopoly of production in China proper. An examination of the data available on major aspects of its history and operations can, therefore, not only indicate how this particular firm functioned, but also throw light on the parameters within which the small modern industrial sector as a whole operated.[10]

To begin with, Chee Hsin's rated capacity was increased significantly several times between 1907 and 1941. The reconstructed Tangshan plant had an initial capacity of 240,000 barrels a year in 1907. New machinery installed in 1911 raised the rated capacity to 630,000 barrels a year. Additions to the plant which went into operation in 1923, 1932, and 1941 increased its capacity to 1,410,000 barrels, 1,650,000 barrels, and 1,800,000 barrels respectively. The critical factor in the growth of capacity was the successive addition of ever larger rotary kilns, equipment that is central to the modern cement production process. Six of the seven kilns installed in the Tangshan plant were of Danish manufacture. Associated material-crushing

[9] See, for example, Philip Chen, "Hwa Hsin Cement Plant in Hankow Promises to be Largest in Far East," *Pit and Quarry*, XXX, 1 (July, 1946), 105–108, 112.

[10] Little information is available for the company's Hupeh subsidiary; the following account refers only to the Tangshan plant unless otherwise indicated.

Table 2

CEMENT PRODUCTION IN CHINA, 1922–1949
(375-lb. barrels)

	Total	China proper	Manchuria	Chee Hsin	China proper as percent of total	Manchuria as percent of total	Chee Hsin as percent of total	Chee Hsin as percent of China proper
1922	2,025,294	....	....	780,192	....	....	38.52	....
1923	2,307,084	....	....	1,390,692	....	....	60.28	....
1924	2,357,328	....	....	766,728	....	....	32.53	....
1925	2,408,856	....	....	766,710	....	....	31.83	....
1926	3,281,460	....	....	455,832	....	....	13.89	....
1927	3,295,746	....	....	1,146,654	....	....	34.79	....
1928	4,023,816	....	....	923,430	....	....	22.95	....
1929	4,993,176	....	....	1,402,878	....	....	28.10	....
1930	4,567,284	....	....	1,356,978	....	....	29.71	....
1931	4,550,970	....	....	1,590,780	....	....	34.95	....
1932	4,039,374	3,386,574	652,800	1,450,152	83.84	16.16	35.90	42.82
1933	4,701,270	3,591,870	1,109,400	1,476,486	76.40	23.60	31.40	41.11
1934	5,403,984	4,008,384	1,395,600	1,541,934	74.17	25.83	28.53	38.47
1935	6,565,500	4,300,500	2,268,000	1,424,622	65.50	34.50	21.70	33.13
1936	7,867,500	4,387,500	3,480,000	1,094,520	55.77	44.23	13.91	24.95

1937	6,600,000	1,800,000	4,800,000	1,127,772	27.27	72.73	17.09	62.65
1938	8,653,488	1,217,988	7,435,500	578,628	14.08	85.92	6.69	47.51
1939	7,905,552	1,694,880	6,210,672	919,350	21.44	78.56	11.63	54.24
1940	8,487,648	2,274,912	6,212,736	1,580,262	26.80	73.20	18.62	69.46
1941	8,876,664	1,894,464	6,982,200	1,286,622	21.34	78.66	14.49	67.91
1942	11,470,530	2,277,930	9,192,600	1,617,738	19.86	80.14	14.10	71.02
1943	10,981,374	1,963,374	9,018,000	1,418,514	17.88	82.12	12.91	72.25
1944	8,655,708	1,809,708	6,846,000	1,153,812	20.91	79.09	13.33	63.76
1945	7,021,224	1,819,224	5,202,000	643,926	25.91	74.08	9.17	35.40
1946	1,754,982	....	....	282,024	....	....	16.07	....
1947	4,494,000	....	....	957,708	....	....	21.31	....
1948	3,300,000	....	....	792,078	....	....	24.00	....
1949	3,966,000							

Source: Recalculated from John Chang, "Indexes of Industrial Production of Mainland China, 1912–1949" (Ph.D. dissertation, University of Michigan, 1965); and *Ch'i-hsin yang-hui kung-ssu shih-liao* [Historical Materials on the Chee Hsin Cement Co.; hereafter cited as *CHSL*] (Peking, 1963), pp. 151–152.

and handling equipment was either of Danish or German origin.[11] The technology of cement manufacturing is relatively simple. There were no innovations in the twentieth century of importance equal to the perfection of the rotary kiln in the United States in the 1890's; and the raw materials, lime and clay, are and were widely available. Most of the mechanical elaborations of the rotary kiln and other equipment were developed by the suppliers of machinery. A new firm entering the industry, therefore, was faced with minimal technological obstacles, provided it had adequate funds to purchase equipment on the world market. Chee Hsin was, in the manner we shall see, rather well supplied with funds for capital investment.

The European machinery installed by Chee Hsin in the first quarter of the century was in general up-to-date in relation to the contemporary technology of the cement industry. Rotary kilns in use in the United States before the 1920's were commonly between 60 and 250 feet in length; Chee Hsin's 100-foot and 200-foot kilns compare favorably. The installation of successively longer kilns made possible substantial savings in unit capital and fuel costs. However, from the 1920's and especially in the wartime decade, a period in which cement machinery in the United States and elsewhere improved greatly, Chee Hsin's equipment became progressively more obsolescent. Kilns over 400 feet long with heat-recuperating chain systems which considerably reduced fuel costs were coming into use when Chee Hsin purchased its 240-foot kiln in 1941. Even in 1948 the firm was still using a large part of the capital equipment which had been installed in 1908, 1911, and 1921–1924.[12] On the other hand, the sev-

[11] Capacity is calculated here on the basis of 300 operating days a year. When the firm was reorganized in 1906–1907, it purchased new equipment—the most important being two 100-foot rotary kilns—from F. L. Smidth & Co. of Copenhagen to replace the obsolete plant inherited from the Kaiping period. Two additional Smidth 150-foot rotary kilns were installed in 1911; and two 200-foot kilns were purchased from the same firm in 1922. In 1932 Chee Hsin's machine shop manufactured a 150-foot rotary kiln of its own design. An additional Smidth 240-foot rotary kiln was purchased in 1941. *CHSL*, pp. 135–138, 151–152. The Hupeh plant was equipped with two German-made rotary kilns and had an annual rated capacity of 300,000–360,000 barrels. Wang Tao, "China's Cement Goes to War," *Rock Products* (August, 1944), p. 110; *CHSL*, p. 148.

[12] *CHSL*, pp. 137–138; Samuel M. Loescher, *Imperfect Collusion in the Cement Industry* (Cambridge, Mass., 1959), pp. 33–36, 39–42; Paul H. Chang,

eral enlargements of the Tangshan plant's rated capacity were such as to keep its size steadily above the point considered necessary to achieve economies of scale in the cement industry. And the plant's location at Tangshan, on the Peking-Mukden railroad, was an excellent one both for the assembly of raw materials and for transporting cement to markets. Limestone, fire clay, and yellow clay were available in large quantities in the immediate vicinity. The nearby Kailan Mining Administration provided coal at a very low price and also electric power from its steam turbine plants. Manufactured cement was shipped by rail to Tangku and Chinwangtao and thence by steamer to ports in south and central China or, in smaller quantities, to Manchuria.[13]

These facts suggest that even those Chinese manufacturing firms which, like Chee Hsin, were initially able to equip themselves with technologically up-to-date machinery and were well located with reference either to raw materials or markets did not in the long run keep abreast of world developments in the technology of their industries. It is perhaps an exaggeration to state that the transfer of technology which provided the basis for modern industry in twentieth-century China was a single-shot affair, but it does appear that later infusions were slower and smaller than the initial dosage. In the cotton textile industry, for example, there was a clear trend in the 1930's for Chinese mills to spin rougher counts, while British and Japanese mills in China increasingly specialized in producing higher counts for which both the price and the profit margin were greater and which required somewhat more sophisticated machinery.[14] Chinese- and foreign-owned mills were thus in some degree supplying discrete markets, a larger portion of the yarn output of the Chinese mills than

---

"The Chinese Cement Industry—Past, Present and Future," *Pit and Quarry,* XXXIX, 4 (October, 1946), p. 68.

[13] *CHSL,* pp. 132–33; H. E. *Hsuehsi Chih-Chi Chow* (Tientsin: La Libraire Française, 1924), pp. 22–30; "Tangshan, An Industrial Town on Peking-Mukden Railway," *Chinese Economic Journal,* I (October, 1927), 888–889; "Growing Popularity of Chinese Cement in North Manchuria," *Chinese Economic Bulletin,* XVII, 26 (December 27, 1930), p. 330. Contrast the relatively poorer location of the Hanyehping iron and steel mill—at a site chosen as much for political as economic reasons. Feuerwerker, "China's Nineteenth-Century Industrialization," pp. 95–96.

[14] Leonard G. Ting, "Recent Development in China's Cotton Industry," *Nankai Social and Economic Quarterly,* IX, 2 (July, 1936), p. 435.

the foreign going to the handicraft weaving industry of the interior. Technological obsolescence in Chinese industry, however, was not merely a product of a demand structure which did not stimulate innovation, especially not in the case of cement which is a highly standardized product, the demand for which is price inelastic and cyclically unstable. The failure of Chinese industry to replace its first generation of capital equipment with newer machinery is above all attributable to the general weakness of demand throughout the period we are examining or, in other words, to the fact that the Chinese economy as a whole before 1949 was not radically affected by the beginnings of modern industry in the coastal cities.

Actual production of cement and cement sales were, of course, only roughly determined by the rated capacity of the Tangshan plant. Table 3 shows annual output, sales, gross value of output, and gross profit during the period 1912–1948. In 1912, 1922–1923, 1928, 1935, 1942, 1944, and 1947, production was significantly in excess of sales; and in 1918, 1920, 1929, 1931, 1936, 1939, and 1948 sales were noticeably greater than the output for the year. In general, however, the production and sales curves follow each other closely. Their joint profile was shaped in large part by domestic and international economic and political circumstances exogenous to the cement industry, as well as by intraindustry contingencies. It gives a remarkably accurate image of the development of modern industry as a whole in twentieth-century China.

Prior to the opening of the Tangshan plant in 1906–1907, almost all the cement used in China was imported from Japan or Hong Kong, but the total amount was small—200,000 to 300,-000 barrels a year. Imports for 1907–1910, still exclusively from these two sources, increased sharply, averaging about 610,000 barrels per annum for these four years.[15] In this same period Chee Hsin's new Tangshan plant was steadily increasing its output. Both streams of supply were directed largely to the same market, primarily the extensive railroad construction undertaken with foreign loans in the last years of the Manchu

[15] Cement import data from maritime customs records, *CHSL*, pp. 49–50.

Table 3

CHEE HSIN PRODUCTION, SALES, GROSS VALUE OF OUTPUT, AND GROSS PROFIT, 1912–1948

	(1)	(2)	(3)	(4)	(5)	(6)
	Production (375-lb. barrels)	Sales	Production as percent of rated capacity	Gross value of output (Ch. $, current prices)	Gross value of output (Ch. $, 1933 prices)	Gross profit (Ch. $, current prices)
1912	356,430	210,000	56.6	1,183,327	2,078,759	401,228
1913	290,682	355,998	46.1	1,646,985	1,695,257	433,161
1914	455,544	439,998	72.3	1,813,242	2,656,732	456,786
1915	450,510	436,002	71.5	2,178,079	2,627,374	472,907
1916	403,884	358,998	64.1	1,509,684	2,355,451	488,442
1917	525,738	553,002	83.5	2,201,130	3,066,104	501,704
1918	567,408	748,998	90.1	3,019,145	3,309,123	762,985
1919	638,868	640,002	101.4	2,939,528	3,725,878	928,443
1920	658,446	799,998	104.5	3,789,985	3,840,057	1,482,447
1921	728,514	730,002	115.6	4,247,801	4,248,693	2,020,640
1922	780,192	649,998	123.8	4,061,388	4,550,079	1,824,739
1923	1,390,692	1,183,710	98.6	6,086,444	8,110,515	2,005,106
1924	766,728	675,288	54.4	4,311,800	4,471,557	939,250
1925	766,710	806,604	54.4	3,995,865	4,471,452	1,077,692
1926	455,832	485,130	32.3	2,054,901	2,658,412	n.a.
1927	1,146,654	1,237,938	81.3	4,979,839	6,687,286	807,781
1928	923,430	763,074	65.5	4,214,087	5,385,443	833,286
1929	1,402,878	1,537,074	99.5	6,546,288	8,181,584	1,218,437

Table 3—(Continued)

	(1) Production (375-lb. barrels)	(2) Sales	(3) Production as percent of rated capacity	(4) Gross value of output (Ch. $, current prices)	(5) Gross value of output (Ch. $, 1933 prices)	(6) Gross profit (Ch. $, current prices)
1930	1,356,978	1,386,912	96.2	7,181,301	7,913,895	1,140,309
1931	1,590,780	1,749,984	112.8	9,058,287	9,277,428	1,544,356
1932	1,450,152	1,431,072	87.7	8,521,554	8,457,286	1,818,720
1933	1,476,486	1,409,310	89.5	8,611,048	8,610,866	2,288,302
1934	1,541,934	1,544,604	93.5	10,784,482	8,992,559	3,351,153
1935	1,424,622	1,169,178	86.3	7,266,753	8,308,395	1,490,081
1936	1,094,520	1,337,538	66.3	6,659,815	6,383,240	2,164,284
1937	1,127,772	1,143,852	68.3	6,218,143	6,577,166	717,305
1938	578,628	611,364	35.1	3,826,755	3,374,558	1,252,859
1939	919,350	1,121,040	55.7	6,091,348	5,361,649	2,042,570
1940	1,580,262	1,508,166	95.8	11,095,684	9,216,087	2,875,705
1941	1,286,622	1,256,958	71.5	15,544,589	7,503,579	600,000
1942	1,617,738	1,256,022 [a]	89.9	20,111,584	9,434,648	550,000
1943	1,418,514	1,354,998	78.8	24,997,639	8,272,773	1,500,000
1944	1,153,812	1,044,540	64.1	65,953,412	6,729,031	18,541,669
1945	643,926	637,134	35.8	789,501,157	3,755,376	96,604,746
1946	282,024	262,686	15.7	9,145,796,659	1,644,763	1,408,738,070
1947	957,708	790,620	53.2	n.a.	n.a.	11,230,611,850
1948	792,078	907,800	44.0	n.a.	n.a.	n.a.

SOURCE: *CHSL*, pp. 151–152, 155–156, 269–270, 289–291.
[a] The large discrepancy between production and sales in 1942 is not easily accounted for and suggests that the sales figure reported in *CHSL* is incorrect.

dynasty and the new factories and other buildings in the treaty ports financed by foreign investments.[16] Chee Hsin, for example, had long-term contracts to supply the Peking-Suiyuan, Peking-Hankow, Lunghai, Tientsin-Pukow and other railroads, which its management obtained initially with the assistance of Yuan Shih-k'ai.[17] In 1911, imports of cement began to decline; the annual average for 1911–1918, with small amounts from Indo-China and Macao supplementing imports from Japan and Hong Kong, was about 260,000 barrels. In part this decrease represented a weakening of total demand as World War I brought a temporary halt to foreign loans and investments in China. In part growing output from Chee Hsin, still the only Chinese-owned cement firm, and from the new Onada plant in Dairen, replaced imports.[18]

From 1919 imports of cement again increased significantly and averaged about 800,000 barrels per annum for the years 1919–1923. Chee Hsin output and sales also grew rapidly in this period, reaching a peak of 1,390,692 barrels produced and 1,183,710 sold in 1923. Sales to railroads were resumed as a new round of construction was undertaken, but this market was relatively weaker than it had been before World War I.[19] The concentration on war production by the European powers and the shipping shortages of the wartime and immediate postwar years reduced the flow of European exports to China and provided an opportunity for the establishment and growth of Chinese-owned industry. While orders for equipment were placed earlier, the opening of many of the new plants had to await the

---

[16] Out of a total railroad network of 24, 945 kilometers in existence in 1945, 9,618 kilometers were completed before 1912. Total foreign investment in China increased from an estimated $788 million in 1902 to $1,610 million in 1914; C. F. Remer, *Foreign Investment in China* (New York, 1933), p. 76. Wang Ching-yü, comp., *Chung-kuo chin-tai kung-yeh shih tzu-liao, ti-erh-chi, 1895–1914 nien* [Source Materials on the History of Modern Industry in China, Second Collection, 1895–1914] (Peking, 1957), pp. 1–25, 654, 657, 869–920, 1041–1042, records 136 foreign-owned and 549 Chinese-owned industrial firms inaugurated 1895–1913.

[17] *CHSL*, pp. 164–165; *H. E. Hsuehsi Chih-Chi Chow*, p. 21.

[18] Onada was producing 200,000–250,000 barrels a year during World War I. Tōa Dobunkai Chōsa Hensambu, *Shina kōgyō sōran* [A General View of Chinese Industry] (Tokyo, 1931), p. 375; "Shina cemento-gyō," pp. 1380–1384.

[19] 3,422 kilometers were completed in the years 1912–1917.

end of the war and the actual arrival of machinery from abroad. Between 1919 and 1924, for example, the number of Chinese-owned cotton spindles and looms approximately tripled.[20] Cement demand depends of course primarily on the construction market; the erection of a large number of new plants thus took up much of Chee Hsin's increased output and the additional imports as well. Private residential and commercial construction in Shanghai and elsewhere also experienced a boom, and from the early 1920's a growing part of Chee Hsin output was intended for the south China market.[21]

Among the new industrial plants established at the end of World War I were two large cement producers, the Shanghai Portland Cement Co. and the China Portland Cement Co., referred to earlier. Until 1923, Chee Hsin, with no serious competition within China except for the Onada plant in Dairen, had luxuriated in its monopoly position.[22] The entrance into the market of two competing firms at precisely the time when the postwar industrial boom was ending and when a prolonged period of civil war, which seriously disrupted the railroads' demand for cement, was beginning, accounts for the fall both in Chee Hsin production and sales and in imports of cement into China in 1924–1926.

Chee Hsin output and sales picked up again in 1927 and through 1934 reached new highs. Imports of cement into China also returned to approximately the 1919–1923 level and remained high until they were somewhat curbed by patriotic boycotts and increased duties on Japanese cement from 1933. In 1932, too, a fourth major Chinese-owned cement plant, the second unit of the Kwangtung government cement works, went into production. The return to relative domestic tranquility following

[20] Yen Chung-p'ing, ed., *Chung-kuo chin-tai ching-chi shih t'ung-chi tzu-liao hsüan-chi* [Selected Statistical Materials on China's Modern Economic History] (Peking, 1955), pp. 134–136.

[21] *CHSL*, p. 165.

[22] Cement was, however, produced in relatively small quantities in Canton, Hong Kong, and Macao. A third new large firm—the Ta Hu Cement Co.—was planned in the early 1920's by Shanghai and Wusih investors, a site chosen, and machinery ordered from Germany. It never went into operation; the plant and equipment were acquired by the China Portland Cement Co. in 1927. M. H. Chou, "The Boom of Chinese Cement Industry"; *CHSL*, pp. 225–226.

the establishment of the Kuomintang Nanking government in 1928 no doubt buoyed up the market for cement. Railroad construction and new industrial building were at least encouraged, if not greatly aided, by the new government.[23] The loss of the Manchurian market after 1931 affected only Chee Hsin among the Chinese producers, but was apparently compensated for in the early 1930's by a resistance to Japanese products in the all-important Shanghai market.[24] By 1934, however, the world depression, whose impact on China was delayed by a drop in silver prices which counterbalanced the deflationary effects of China's growing foreign trade deficit, began to be felt. In addition the United States Silver Purchase Act of 1934, by drawing silver out of China in large quantities, induced a severe credit stringency at a time when prices were falling. By June, 1935, for example, 24 out of 92 Chinese-owned textile mills had suspended operation and 12 others operated part-time only.[25] Industrial slowdown of course reduced the demand for cement. There was a consequent drop both in imports and in Chee Hsin's production and sales. Recovery had just begun when war with Japan came in July, 1937.

Some of the machinery of the Hupeh plant of the Chee Hsin Co. was dismantled and moved inland to Chenki in western Hunan, where it was incorporated into the newly organized Hwa Chung Cement Co. Nearly 94 percent of the cement capacity in China exclusive of Manchuria, however, was located in the provinces under Japanese occupation.[26] The initial effect on the Tang-

[23] Within China proper between 1918 and 1937, 3,400 kilometers of railroad were constructed. The extensive Japanese railroad building in Manchuria after 1931 mainly used Japanese cement.

[24] *CHSL*, p. 58. The Chinese Cement Producers Association in 1932 reported a new high in sales of Chinese-made cement after the "September 18 incident" as a consequence of strong anti-Japanese feeling. It complained, however, that Japanese firms had responded by "dumping" at prices Tls. 2 a barrel lower than Japanese domestic prices, and that Chinese firms were still operating at much less than capacity.

[25] See Albert Feuerwerker, "The Chinese Economy, 1912–1949," in H. L. Boorman, ed., *Republican China* (in preparation).

[26] Chang, "The Chinese Cement Industry—Past, Present, and Future," p. 66; Wang Tao, "China's Cement Goes to War," p. 110. Hwa Chung output never exceeded 500–600 barrels a day. Except for a small plant at Kunming, which amalgamated with Hwa Chung in 1942, other wartime efforts to produce cement in unoccupied China were even less successful.

shan plant of the outbreak of war, as Table 3 indicates, was a drastic fall in production and sales. By the end of 1938, both began to recover rapidly in response to increasing Japanese military purchases. Through 1942, perhaps a maximum of one-fifth of Chee Hsin's production was disposed of in the open market in China, the balance going directly to the Japanese army, to the Mitsui Co., which handled shipments to Japan, or to other Japanese-controlled purchasers. From 1943, the firm's total output was under the control of the Japanese embassy and no cement was available to Chinese civilian purchasers.[27]

Chee Hsin output reached an all-time peak of 1,617,738 barrels in 1942. Raw material shortages, transportation problems, and labor shortages, coupled with an increasingly obsolescent plant and inadequate repairs of the power-generating equipment led to a steady fall in output after 1942. Japanese demands for more cement were incessant, but the company was unable to meet them.[28]

The Japanese surrender in August, 1945 was accompanied by a nearly complete breakdown of the industrial structure throughout China. In the formerly occupied areas, Japanese technicians and managers were withdrawn and production came to a standstill. There was no adequate planning for the takeover of Japanese-controlled plants and the restoration of industrial output. Recovered factories were often treated like war booty as each civilian and military faction struggled to obtain a share of the loot. In the interior, the "hot-house" wartime industry was left to wither. Manchuria suffered large-scale looting of its industrial plant by the Russians. As a consequence, postwar manufacturing output was never restored to the peak prewar level of 1936; from 1948, it declined wearily.

[27] *CHSL,* pp. 84–85, 165–167.

[28] *CHSL,* pp. 76–87. While Chee Hsin's autonomy was formally guaranteed, Japanese dissatisfaction with output led to the appointment of "advisors" in August, 1944 who, in effect, controlled the firm. Other cement firms in occupied China also fared badly after 1942. The Shanghai Portland Cement Co. and the China Portland Cement Co. suffered severe shortages of coal; the power-generating equipment of the Lungtan plant of the China Portland Cement Co. deteriorated badly; the Kwangtung Cement Co.'s plant at Hsi-ts'un near Canton was nearly destroyed. Chang, "The Chinese Cement Industry—Past, Present and Future," p. 66.

Against this general picture, Chee Hsin initially fared rather well. Possibly because of close ties with the "Political Science Clique" of the Kuomintang, the company was easily cleared of charges of collaboration and remained in the control of its previous officers and management.[29] Output in 1946 was at an all-time low of 282,024 barrels, partly because the weakness of demand and large accumulated inventories forced a cut-back in production. The company complained about the slowness of economic reconstruction, the breakdown of transport which cut it off from the south China market, and the competition of cement imported from the United States at a time when the disrupted domestic market had not yet recovered.[30] In 1947, however, both Chee Hsin and total Chinese cement output increased sharply and reached a level roughly equal to that of the late 1920's. Imports were correspondingly reduced to a third of what they had been in 1946. As the civil war grew in intensity from mid-1946, an increasing proportion of the cement produced by Chee Hsin and other Chinese firms was disposed of through the Central Bank and the Central Trust Co. to supply military needs.

By late 1947, a serious deterioration in the military position of the Nationalist government and an accelerating inflation were increasingly evident. Chee Hsin and other north China industrial firms were forced to make large "contributions" for the defense of Tientsin and Peking and for relief of the civilian population.[31] Disruption of communications by the Communist forces threatened Chee Hsin's coal supply and its procurement of gypsum, much of which had formerly come from Shansi. Foreign-exchange shortages hampered the importation of paper for manufacturing cement sacks. The last desperate efforts by the Kuomintang to cope with runaway inflation—the issuing of new gold yüan notes in August, 1948–brought a momentary halt to the soaring price index, but at the cost of industrial stagnation. Chee Hsin sales dropped sharply in late summer and autumn of 1948.

[29] *CHSL,* pp. 114–115.
[30] *CHSL,* pp. 50, 115, 119–121. U.S. cement imported into China amounted to 167,000 barrels out of total imports of 275,000 barrels.
[31] *CHSL,* pp. 124–127.

By October prices were again rising, wildly out of control. The firm's income from sales of cement already produced could not keep up with its soaring costs of production. Throughout 1947 and 1948 it had been forced to rely upon 30-day loans at very high rates for operating capital. Its deficit on current account for the last three months of 1948 was G.Y. 60,759,935: [32]

	Receipts	Expenditures
October	G.Y. 785,034	G.Y. 737,625
November	G.Y. 1,297,437	G.Y. 2,767,317
December	G.Y. 1,324,841	G.Y. 60,410,382

With the total collapse of the Kuomintang military situation north of the Yangtze after the battle of Hsüchow (the "Hwai-Hai Campaign") of November, 1948-January, 1949, Chee Hsin was "liberated" and entered upon an entirely new phase of its history with which this account does not deal.

ECONOMIC FACTORS IN CHEE HSIN'S SUCCESS

This résumé of Chee Hsin's fortunes between 1907 and 1949 supports the conclusion that—after allowing for the always limited total market for cement in China and the adverse effects of war and civil war—the overall production performance of the firm was an impressive one. The total output of cement in China proper and Manchuria grew steadily through 1942, and except for periods of intense disorder resulting from military action, Chee Hsin's output trend was upward too. While the firm's relative position in the industry as a whole declined as Manchurian output increased after 1932, and its near monopoly of production in China exclusive of Manchuria ended in 1932, it continued to be the largest producer in China proper and after 1937 again overwhelmingly dominated the cement industry in that area. It was a profitable operation too. Chee Hsin's gross profits over the years 1908–1939 averaged 26.35 percent of gross revenues; payments to shareholders, 18.40 percent; and bonuses to management, 2.11 percent (see Table 4). Annual payments

[32] *CHSL,* pp. 117–119, 128–131.

to shareholders, as a percentage of the par value of shares out-standing, were never less than 4 percent, sometimes were as high as 17 percent, and averaged 8.45 percent for the years 1908–1939. A hypothetical shareholder who had invested Ch. $1,000 in 1908 would have received by 1947 dividends totalling $5,-493 (in 1936 prices), equal to a real annual return of almost 14 percent on his original investment, and would have realized impressive capital gains as well.[33]

Chee Hsin's success was made possible in part by the close political ties that its management enjoyed with the Yuan Shih-k'ai government and with Yuan's successors in the Peking government; this aspect of the firm's environment will be examined presently. Equally important was the relatively favorable cost structure which Chee Hsin enjoyed and its ability, because of its size and prior entry into the industry, to benefit from marketing agreements concluded with its competitors.

Table 4 shows, in an admittedly crude way, how the gross revenue of the Chee Hsin Co. was allocated among the several major items of cost and profit during the period 1908–1939.[34] Chee Hsin's favorable cost structure, as compared with a repre-sentative sample of cement firms in the United States, was largely a consequence of the fact that average variable costs (items 1, 2, 3, and 5 in Table 4) as a percentage of full costs (items 1–7) were higher in the Chinese case than the American—approxi-mately 78.5 percent and 58.5 percent respectively for the years 1924–1939.[35] Overhead costs broadly defined—that is, rela-tively constant costs regardless of the proportion of capacity utilized—were correspondingly a smaller proportion of total full costs in the Chinese case than in the American. The significance of this difference is that Chee Hsin could operate relatively more profitably at levels of operation substantially below rated capac-ity. Between 1908 and 1939, even in those years when Chee Hsin production was 60 percent or less of rated capacity (see

[33] *CHSL,* pp. 256–257, 260–262, 269–270.
[34] Available data do not, for example, permit a finer breakdown of item 4, Administration. Nor can this table reflect accurately what part of the changing proportion of items 1–4 is due to differential price changes of factors (probably little), and what part to altered composition of the firm's production function.
[35] Loescher, *Imperfect Collusion in the Cement Industry,* pp. 61–72.

Table 4

ALLOCATION OF GROSS REVENUE TO MAJOR ITEMS OF COST AND PROFIT: AVERAGE PERCENTAGES BY 4-YEAR PERIODS, 1908–1939

	1908–1911	1912–1915	1916–1919	1920–1923	1924–1927	1928–1931	1932–1935	1936–1939	Average 1908–1939
1. Wages [a]	12.01	9.72	9.65	7.56	7.78	6.76	6.35	5.11	8.20
2. Raw materials [b]	19.85	27.27	26.68	24.42	41.31	42.71	33.77	30.04	30.57
3. Transport [c]	4.81	6.19	6.05	5.56	9.40	9.70	7.65	6.90	6.99
4. Administration [d]	22.60	18.82	16.27	9.29	10.11	10.68	7.50	7.81	12.94
5. Interest [e]	7.95	6.25	7.26	4.61	5.74	6.00	2.93	1.85	5.33
6. Depreciation [f]	2.40	1.85	2.45	5.11	1.28	2.01	3.38	3.26	2.84
7. Taxes	4.77	3.13	3.64	2.32	2.66	4.30	13.56	17.49	6.46
8. Payments to shareholders [g]	19.91	21.51	18.94	22.32	17.83	13.29	15.75	17.68	18.40
9. Bonuses to management	2.39	1.82	1.82	3.36	0.83	0.87	3.22	2.54	2.11
10. Reserve and sinking funds [h]	3.71	3.29	7.12	15.58	3.14	3.62	5.79	7.41	5.84
	100.00 [i]	100.00	100.00	100.00	100.00	100.00	100.00	100.00	100.00

SOURCE: Computed from *CHSL*, pp. 128, 151–152, 264, 269–270, 289–291.
[a] Skilled and unskilled labor and immediate supervisors.
[b] Limestone, clay, coal, paper for sacks, etc.
[c] Railroad and water transportation of manufactured cement to markets.
[d] Including, presumably, selling costs and "gifts" to officials.
[e] Interest on short-term loans.
[f] As charged in annual accounts; not necessarily real depreciation costs.
[g] Regular and extra dividends, and interest on deposits.
[h] In part for retirement of "Industrial Bonds."
[i] Due to the rounding off of figures, columns do not exactly total 100.

Table 3), it made substantial profits and paid dividends ranging from 5 to 10 percent of shareholders' equity.[36] The total profits (average rates of net income after taxes to stockholders' equity— a much more inclusive figure than Chee Hsin's dividends just noted) of American firms during the period 1931–1940, when the percentage of capacity used was consistently less than 60 percent, varied from a loss of 5.6 percent in 1932 to a profit of 7.0 percent in 1940.[37]

Chee Hsin's lower overhead costs, it may be conjectured, were typical of Chinese manufacturing firms. In part they were the product of a strikingly low allowance for depreciation.[38] Over the period 1908–1939, Chee Hsin's average annual depreciation cost as a percentage of total costs was only 3.87 percent; this is the equivalent of an average of 2.84 percent of gross revenues. Abstractly, in a relatively capital-intensive industry such as the manufacture of cement, where moreover the entry of new firms is relatively easy, this would be a ridiculously inadequate figure. But in the circumstances of China in the first half of the twentieth century, it is not without a rationale. A low depreciation allowance is, of course, consistent with the observation already made that the firm in 1948 was still using much of the equipment installed at the beginning of the century. In a situation of abundant and cheap labor, the very concept of obsolescence may be largely neglected. While the availability of labor permits it, all equipment—old and new—can be used, and old equipment retained in operation until it literally wears out.

A continuously handsome return to investors combined with an increasingly obsolescent plant is also perhaps what one should expect in a total environment in which demand is limited and subject to fluctuations in the vital political context, as well as to "normal" variations in the construction cycle. It represents, from another point of view, an implicit recognition that while existing

[36] *CHSL*, pp. 281–282.

[37] Loescher, *Imperfect Collusion in the Cement Industry*, pp. 168–169, 173.

[38] The Hanyehping Co., for example, apparently made no provision for depreciation before 1908. The annual allowance of 5 percent on the value of the plant adopted in later years was neither an adequate measure of the obsolescence of the firm's equipment nor an actual depreciation reserve. See Feuerwerker, "China's Nineteenth-Century Industrialization," p. 104.

circumstances may permit one or a limited number of enterprises to grow and prosper up to a point and within a geographically limited sector of the economy, the likelihood is small that the environment will alter radically to present the prospect of unlimited expansion. Entrepreneurship becomes a matter of getting the largest possible share of a limited pie rather than continually seeking new ways to produce a bigger and better one.

The decline in the relative importance of "Administration," line 4 in Table 4, after 1919 accounts in part for Chee Hsin's lower constant costs noted above. This is a protean category and I am unable to decompose it accurately from the data available to me. It clearly includes, however, such special costs of doing business in a Chinese environment as *pao-hsiao* (to return [official] grace) payments to official patrons of the firm, and gifts or loans (in reality bribes) to other government agencies. The largest category of these exactions was the *pao-hsiao* which Chee Hsin remitted annually to the governor-general of Chihli (Hopeh province in the Republican period) under the Ch'ing dynasty as a sign of its semiofficial character and in return for the special privileges granted to it. While the company endeavored to keep the privileges, which are discussed below, it discontinued its payment of *pao-hsiao* after the death in 1916 of President Yuan Shih-k'ai, to whom, beginning in 1906 when as Chihli governor-general he had strongly supported the reopening of the firm, these payments had originally been made.[39] Yuan's warlord successors, in particular Wu P'ei-fu, demanded a resumption of *pao-hsiao* payments from Chee Hsin. In October, 1924, Wu threatened "extreme measures" unless Ch. $2,000,000 in alleged arrears were paid to the Hopeh treasury. The cement company, after lengthy negotiations, finally settled for Ch. $250,000 plus a small annual payment of Ch. $5,000.[40] While other occasional exactions later troubled Chee Hsin, they were in general small and the firm in this respect probably fared better than many others.

Chee Hsin labor costs per barrel of cement as a percentage of total costs declined steadily over the three decades after 1908. In

[39] *CHSL*, p. 269.
[40] *CHSL*, pp. 111–114.

the years 1924–1939, for which comparable data are available, they were less than half the proportion of labor costs to total costs in American cement mills, 8.42 percent and 22.57 percent respectively.[41] The smaller relative size of the Chinese labor costs reflects primarily the lower wages paid by Chee Hsin for roughly comparable work. This in turn is a product of the social context of Republican China, characterized in part by the absence of effective labor unions and the retention of ties with their villages by many who came to urban areas to work in factories. While there were a number of strikes at the Tangshan mill and apparently some activity by the Communist Party as well, except for a successful 22-day srike in 1922 these seem to have had little effect.[42] Most of the workers at Chee Hsin came from Tangshan *hsien* itself or from neighboring *hsien*. This was particularly true of the unskilled labor recruited by labor contractors during slack periods in the agricultural cycle to quarry limestone and clay. A high proportion of the more skilled workers, employed directly in production jobs by the cement mill, were from Shantung. Because of the greater distance and expense involved, workers from Shantung did not normally return to their villages in agricultural peak periods and thus made up the more stable part of the Chee Hsin labor force.[43]

Tangshan in the 1920's and 1930's directly employed approximately 2,000 workers in the cement mill itself and in such ancillary activities as the Chee Hsin Engineering Works; another 600–800 contract laborers were engaged seasonally through local labor bosses (*pao-kung t'ou*). There is evidence, though not conclusive, that their real wages showed a slight downward trend in the three decades before the Sino-Japanese War. In the 1940's wages as a proportion of total costs rose significantly, averaging 13.4 percent in the years 1940–1946 as compared with 8.42 percent for 1924–1939. This increase reflected a wartime labor supply problem, resulting from inflationary pressures, which Chee Hsin attempted to meet by various incentive plans, bonuses, and the payment of wages in grain rather than depreciating

[41] Loescher, *Imperfect Collusion in the Cement Industry*, p. 66.
[42] *CHSL*, pp. 316–339.
[43] *CHSL*, pp. 274–275.

currency. But after 1946, with inflation increasingly out of control, real wages dropped precipitously below the prewar level.[44]

The "cheap labor policy" followed at Chee Hsin and other Chinese- and foreign-owned industrial enterprises could, of course, counterbalance the high cost of other factors. Low wages are natural in the early stages of industrialization because of the inexperience of the labor force and its low productivity, if for no other reasons. Given a limited market and underemployment of labor in general, there was neither a pull to increase production very rapidly, which would have called for more efficient higher-priced labor, nor any effective wage pressure from the labor force itself. Chee Hsin, it may be suggested, was able to grow modestly with declining labor costs as a proportion of total costs—evidence of change in the combination of factors in the direction of greater capital intensity [45]—in part because the firm could minimize its wages bill.

Chee Hsin's tax burden before the Nanking government period was remarkably low. The firm was not subject, for example, to any taxation on output or profits. From its origin, through the intercession of Yuan Shih-k'ai, it was partially exempted from customs duties (paying only the 5 percent import duty, but no export duty or transit levies) on the cement it shipped by water from Chinwangtao.[46] From 1931, however, Chee Hsin cement was subject to a national commodity tax at the manufacturer's level (the so-called "consolidated tax" which was intended to displace the multifarious transit levies imposed by local governments). The commodity tax on cement began at a rate of Ch. $0.60 per barrel, increased to Ch. $1.20 in 1934, and was transformed into a 15 percent ad valorem levy in September, 1941 (roughly the equivalent of Ch. $1.80–2.00 in that year). While the firm's management was unhappy about the new tax, Chee Hsin's profit margin was on the whole only slightly affected. And in the absence of an effective income tax, management and

---

[44] *CHSL,* pp. 291–293.

[45] The new mill installed at Tangshan in 1922, for example, was more mechanized and required less labor per unit of output than the original equipment. *H. E. Hsuehsi Chih-Chi Chow,* pp. 22–30.

[46] *CHSL,* pp. 93–94.

shareholders continued to enjoy their respective revenues free for all practical purposes of any tax obligation.

While the commodity tax did not unduly burden the cement industry, in some other cases—for example the cigarette industry —the incidence of this levy favored foreign-owned factories in China which produced relatively lightly taxed higher-grade products as against Chinese-owned factories whose lower-grade output was taxed more heavily.[47] There were instances, too, of foreign-owned firms successfully evading this and other taxation. The cement industry in this respect was fortunate. Chee Hsin, as we shall see, faced competition from the two other large Chinese producers, and even after the import duty on cement was increased in 1933 the firm complained that Japanese cement was being "dumped" in Shanghai. But it did not have to compete also with foreign-owned firms physically located in China proper which were able to enjoy preferential tax treatment because of their extraterritorial status.

As an industry not dependent upon agricultural products, cement production was relatively free of the problem of raw material quality control which the Chinese tobacco and textile industries, for example, faced.[48] The Tangshan plant owned or had options upon sufficient high-grade limestone and clay deposits in its immediate vicinity to supply all its needs. The proportion of raw materials in total costs nevertheless varied considerably, increasing sharply in the 1920's and then falling again in the 1930's. I am not able from the data available to account adequately for these changes. They may, however, be linked to fuel cost and supply problems which arose after Chou Hsüeh-hsi, who headed both Chee Hsin and the Kailan mines, retired from active participation in these two enterprises. The cash cost of fuel for the kiln and of electric power to turn the kiln and operate fans and material-handling equipment is the highest of the vari-

[47] Shanghai Economic Research Institute, *Nan-yang hsiung-ti yen-ts'ao kung-ssu shih-liao* [Historical Materials of the Nanyang Brothers Tobacco Co.] (Shanghai, 1958), pp. 64, 159, 383–386, 420–421.

[48] See Y. C. Wang, "Free Enterprise in China: The Case of a Cigarette Concern, 1905–1953," *Pacific Historical Review*, XXIX, 4 (November, 1960), 400–401.

ous separate production operations in the manufacture of cement.

Further evidence of the limited demand for cement in China, and an example too of how a single firm might prosper even in these circumstances because of its priority of entry into the market and its relative size, is provided by an examination of Chee Hsin's relations with its competitors. The key fact here is the ability of Chee Hsin to maintain first a *de jure* and then a *de facto* monopoly of cement supply in north China, including the long-term contracts with the major government railroads already referred to, and from this secure base to expand steadily into the southern market. Both in 1908 and 1909 the Ministry of Agriculture, Industry, and Commerce affirmed Chee Hsin's "special right" (*t'e-ch'üan*) to the prior erection of branch plants in Manchuria and in the Yangtze Valley, as well as to a monopoly of cement production in Chihli.[49] While these privileges came to an end with the fall of the Manchu dynasty, the continuing political influence of Chee Hsin's management enabled the firm to block attempts to establish rival plants in Shantung in 1914, in Anhwei in 1916, and in Hopeh in 1922.[50] Chee Hsin's acquisitions of its Hupeh subsidiary in 1914, again facilitated by the political ties of its directors, eliminated its only rival in central China.[51] Before 1920, the output of the Tangshan plant had been sold primarily in north China, while the Hupeh plant supplied the Hankow market and west China. Southern sales however had grown steadily as evidenced by the establishment of a special Southern Wholesale Office in Shanghai in September, 1922, concurrent with the enlargement of the Tangshan plant which was undertaken in that year.[52] In 1923, 37 percent (520,-000 barrels) of the cement produced at Tangshan was sold through the Shanghai office. But in the following year southern

[49] *CHSL*, p. 90.

[50] *CHSL*, pp. 196–198. The 1922 scheme had Tuan Ch'i-jui's backing and was blocked by an agreement to purchase coal for Chee Hsin's Hupeh plant from mines controlled by Tuan. Chou Hsüeh-hsi's personal influence with Tuan was important here.

[51] *CHSL*, pp. 199–205.

[52] *CHSL*, p. 176.

sales dropped to 300,000 barrels as the Shanghai Portland Cement Co. and the China Portland Cement Co. came into production and, with lowered prices, attracted some of Chee Hsin's former customers.[53]

Chee Hsin responded by lowering its southern prices and making other concessions to buyers, but maintained its north China price level. By the latter part of 1924 the Shanghai Cement Co., unable to continue the price war, proposed to withdraw entirely from the Tientsin and Hankow markets if reasonable sales quotas in the south for the three competing firms could be negotiated. Chee Hsin, which would have its northern market secured as well as a guaranteed position in the south as a result of such an arrangement, agreed in principle, provided that the quotas were limited to the Shanghai market and there was no limit set on its total production. A five-year agreement between Chee Hsin and Shanghai Cement was subsequently signed and went into effect on July 1, 1925. It established a hypothetical annual sales quota of 700,000 barrels for the provinces of Kiangsu, Chekiang, Fukien, and Kwangtung, of which 45 percent was to be supplied by Chee Hsin and 55 percent by Shanghai Cement. Any sales above 700,000 barrels were to be divided equally between the two firms, except that Shanghai Cement's total sales could not exceed 400,000 barrels, and that company was not to increase its total production during the life of the agreement. The two firms would coordinate their prices closely for the purpose of maintaining the market proportions agreed upon, and would establish common prices in bidding for large contracts.[54]

The smaller China Cement Co., which planned a major expansion of capacity, declined to join the Chee Hsin-Shanghai Cement market agreement. It competed vigorously with Chee Hsin in north China. And, in spite of much talk on the part of Chinese cement producers, little check was offered to the importation of Japanese cement into Shanghai. The Chee Hsin-Shanghai Cement agreement, moreover, was not always faithfully observed. The Chee Hsin management, nevertheless, judged that the results

[53] *CHSL*, pp. 205–207.
[54] *CHSL*, pp. 207–215.

were decidedly positive: Shanghai Cement was kept out of north and west China and in 1929, for example, Chee Hsin was able to sell 700,000 barrels in the south and west at a satisfactory price.[55]

Negotiations at the beginning of 1930 to renew the agreement collapsed as a result of Shanghai Cement's demands that, as its productive capacity had been increased significantly, the area of joint marketing should be extended to west China, it should receive "preferential treatment" in Shanghai, and its quota should be increased to 600,000 barrels.[56] In late 1930 negotiations were reopened among the three firms—Chee Hsin, Shanghai Cement, and China Cement. The new talks were inspired by two facts: that even in 1929, the best year to date, their total sales (2,200,000 barrels) were only the equivalent of 70 percent of their combined capacity; and that the amount of imported cement, largely from Japan, sold in China was approximately equal to the difference between their combined capacity and their actual sales. In order to combat Japanese "dumping," the three Chinese firms sought to combine to agitate for adequate tariff protection and to coordinate their prices. A temporary accommodation was reached for the period July, 1931 through June, 1932, but as each of the three firms possessed considerable excess capacity and, therefore, rejected the quotas suggested by the others, and because Chee Hsin was adamant about preserving its special position in north China, no long-term market agreement could be negotiated. Further futile three-way talks were held in the winter of 1932, the spring of 1933, and again in 1935. By this time, a joint market agreement for south China had become a secondary issue for Chee Hsin, which now faced the prospect of increasing penetration of the north China market by cement from Japanese mills in Manchuria. With this hitherto secure base—which had permitted Chee Hsin considerable price flexibility and hence a competitive advantage in the southern market—threatened, the firm was not prepared to make any concessions in the Shanghai market. An arrangement which was favorable to Chee Hsin was reached in 1936 with the China

[55] *CHSL*, pp. 218–219.
[56] *CHSL*, p. 222.

Cement Co. alone, but with the outbreak of the war in the following year it became meaningless and was allowed to lapse.[57]

THE POLITICAL CONTEXT

Chee Hsin's expansion over the period we are examining was financed almost entirely by Chinese funds; no indication of borrowing from foreign lenders is to be found anywhere in the company's published documents. Nor was the firm successful in obtaining funds from foreign investors even after 1912 when 40 percent of its shares were transformed into anonymous bearer certificates which would have permitted their transfer to foreign holders.[58] Except for an initial loan of Tls. 400,000 from Chihli provincial funds which Yuan Shih-k'ai made available in 1906 and which was repaid in full in 1907, no government funds (as distinguished from private investment by officials) were ever invested in the firm. The land and buildings of the original Tangshan cement plant which Tong King-sing (T'ang T'ing-shu) had undertaken in 1889 were, however, turned over to the successor Chee Hsin firm by Yuan Shih-k'ai at somewhat less than their current value, and the acquisition of the land in particular was of substantial importance in getting Chee Hsin underway.[59] Except for the unusually chaotic civil war years of 1946–1949, Chee Hsin never found any serious difficulty in obtaining capital funds or funds for current operations. Here is one instance at least in modern Chinese economic history in which one cannot identify a problem of a shortage of capital.

Through 1948 there were twelve issues of Chee Hsin shares. Those of 1912, 1925, 1927, and 1930 were stock splits—in 1912 on a two for one basis, in the later years partial splits. New capital funds were raised in 1907, 1909–1911, 1915, 1921, 1924, 1940, 1944, and 1947. In this manner, the par value of the firm's paid-up capital increased from Ch. $1,-000,000 in 1907 to Ch. $13,081,980 in 1940.[60] In addition to equity shares, Chee Hsin from time to time issued "Industrial

[57] *CHSL*, pp. 237–255.
[58] *CHSL*, pp. 257–258.
[59] *CHSL*, pp. 38–41.
[60] *CHSL*, pp. 256–260.

Bonds" to finance expansion of its plant. Shareholders of record in the company were given an opportunity to purchase newly offered shares before they were made available to the public and, because of the excellent return noted above, generally took up the whole of the new issues.

Among Chee Hsin's largest shareholders were the men who, with Yuan Shih-k'ai's initial assistance, reestablished the firm in 1906–1907 and were its principal officers in the succeeding years. In 1920, for example, Chou Hsüeh-hsi, the managing director, held 4,800 shares; Wang Hsiao-ting, the assistant managing director, 3,300 shares; and the four senior directors owned 8,490, 4,864, 4,044, and 3,000 shares respectively.[61] Who were these men?

I have available some biographical data on twenty-nine of the thirty-nine persons who are known to have been the principal officers of the Chee Hsin Cement Co. and members of its Board of Directors between 1907 and 1948; more might be found by a diligent search. They were, first, overwhelmingly men from north China: ten were born in Anhwei and ten in Chihli (Hopeh), six in Honan, two in Kiangsu, and one in Kwangtung. Included in their number were four sons of Yuan Shih-k'ai, one or more of whom was a director of Chee Hsin in every year from 1927 to 1948. Twelve of the twenty-nine were minor officials, in at least five cases directly under Yuan Shih-k'ai, in the last years of the Ch'ing dynasty. Eight held high office during Yuan Shih-k'ai's presidency between 1912 and 1916, and among themselves furnished three ministers of finance, a minister of agriculture and commerce, a minister of war, a governor of the Bank of China, two vice-ministers, a provincial governor, and the director of several major government railroads.[62] Five of the twenty-nine, all

---

[61] *CHSL*, p. 42.

[62] Chou Hsüeh-hsi (Chou Chih-chi): see *H. E. Hsuehsi Chih-Chi Chow;* Chou Shu-chen, *Chou Chih-an hsien-sheng pieh-chuan* [Biography of Chou Hsueh-hsi] (Peking, 1948); *Ajiya rekishi jiten* [Encyclopedia of Asian History], 10 vols. (Tokyo, 1959–1962), IV, 282a; Tokyo University of Education, Research Seminar on Asian History, *Chūgoku kindaika no shakai kōzō* [The Social Framework of Chinese Modernization] (Tokyo, 1960), pp. 135–171. Sun To-shen (Sun Yin t'ing): see Intelligence Section, Japanese Foreign Office, *Gendai Shina jimmei kan* [Biographies of Contemporary Chinese] (Tokyo, 1928 ed.), pp. 570–571. Yen Tun-yüan (Yen Chung-yüan): see *Gendai Shina*

included in the previous eight, were high government officers between 1917 and 1927; among themselves they provided two acting prime ministers, a minister of war, a minister of interior, a minister of foreign affairs, a minister of agriculture and commerce, a vice-minister, and an important railroad official. Only one of the twenty-nine, who was also active in 1917–1927, continued in a relatively prominent political role under the Nationalist Government, serving in turn as minister to Washington, delegate to the League of Nations, and ambassador to the Soviet Union.[63] Collectively the twenty-nine had interests in at least twenty-five other industrial, commercial, or banking firms, principally in north China. Finally, the group of twenty-nine men for whom I have data includes one set of four brothers, one set of three brothers, and six sets of father and son.

These data support the suggestion already made of the initial importance of political support from Yuan Shih-k'ai both in getting the Chee Hsin Co. started and in consolidating its position in the years before World War I. It was less a matter of direct financial assistance from Yuan—this as we have seen was minimal—than the fact that from 1901 to 1907, as governor-general of Chihli, he was preeminent in north China, and from 1912 to 1916, as president of the Republic of China, he dominated the Peking government. Yuan's relationship with Chee Hsin, in effect, resolves itself into his relationship with Chou Hsüeh-hsi.

Chou Hsüeh-hsi (1869–1947), the principal figure in the organization of Chee Hsin, was associated with Yuan from the time that the latter was governor of Shantung in 1899–1901. When Yuan was promoted to Chihli governor-general, Chou was transferred with him and became his chief assistant in the pro-

---

jimmei kan, p. 123. Li Shih-wei (Li Po-chih): see *Who's Who in China,* 3rd ed. (Shanghai, 1926), pp. 477–478. Wang Shih-chen: see *Who's Who in China,* 3rd ed., pp. 824–825; *Ajiya rekishi jiten,* II, 22ab. Kung Hsin-chan: see *Ajiya rekishi jiten,* II, 408a. Sun To-yü (Sun Chang-fu): see *Who's Who in China,* 3rd ed., pp. 186–187. Yen Hui-ch'ing: see *Who's Who in China,* 1936 ed. (Shanghai, 1936), pp. 278–279; Japan, Foreign Office, *Gendai Chūgoku jimmei jiten* [Biographical Dictionary of Contemporary China] (Tokyo, 1962), p. 112. Yen Chih-i (Yen Tz'u-yüeh): see *Who's Who in China,* 3rd ed., pp. 928–929.

[63] This was Yen Hui-ch'ing.

gram of economic reconstruction and development which Yuan inaugurated in that province. Chou rose rapidly in the Chihli bureaucracy, becoming provincial judge in 1907. He played a leading role in the establishment of a modern mint in Tientsin and spent several months in Japan in 1903 investigating industrial conditions in that country before returning to organize the Peiyang Bureau of Industry, which coordinated industrial training and the promotion of model industrial enterprises in Chihli. It was while he was director of the Bureau of Industry that Chou negotiated the recovery of the old Tangshan cement plant from the British-controlled Chinese Engineering and Mining Co. and, with Yuan's backing, organized the Chee Hsin Cement Co., the first of many privately-owned industrial and financial enterprises in which he was to have an interest. While Chou came from a distinguished official family—his father Chou Fu had been governor of Shangtung, and governor-general of both Liang-chiang and Liang-kuang—it was not his family's wealth but his political position as a protégé of Yuan Shih-k'ai that provided the leverage for the beginning of his career as an industrial entrepreneur.

In 1908 Chou followed Yuan, who had been removed from his provincial post and "promoted" to membership in the Grand Council in September, 1907, to Peking. On Yuan's recommendation, he was authorized to organize a modern waterworks in the capital, the nucleus of the Peking Water Works Co., Ltd. In 1907 Chou had been one of the founders of the Lanchow Mining Co., which had the financial backing of the Tientsin Bank of which Chou was an officer and the political support of Yuan Shih-k'ai. The Lanchow Mining Co. had been established as a rival enterprise after repeated efforts to recover Chinese control of the Kaiping coal mines from the Chinese Engineering and Mining Co. failed. In 1908 Chou became managing director of Lanchow, a position that he retained for many years after Lanchow and Chinese Engineering and Mining amalgamated in 1912 to form the jointly operated Kailan Mining Administration. As the principal officer of both Lanchow and Chee Hsin (Chou was managing director of the latter from 1907 to 1925), he was in a position to insure that Chee Hsin purchased coal and electric power at favorable rates from Kailan. This contributed importantly to the early success of the cement company. The costs for raw materials including fuel, as we have seen, rose sharply after 1925, when Chou retired from the active management of Chee Hsin, Lanchow, and his other business enterprises. That there was a connection between these two occurrences is not definitely established, but it seems likely.

The formal monopoly which Yuan Shih-k'ai had obtained for Chee Hsin lapsed with the end of the dynasty. But the firm's partial exemption from customs duties continued, as well as its close ties with the government-owned railroads to which it was a major supplier of cement—a relationship that can be traced initially to Yuan's influence. A continuation of a favorable government attitude towards Chou's industrial undertakings was faciliated by he fact that during Yuan Shih-k'ai's presidency Chou served twice (from July, 1912 to May, 1913, and from January, 1915 to March, 1916) as minister of finance. He was an important member of the "Anhwei Clique," led by Yang Shih-ch'i, which throughout Yuan's regime battled for influence with the "Kwangtung Clique" (later known as the "Communications Clique"), whose leaders were Liang Shih-i and Yeh Kung-cho.

By the time of Yuan's death, Chou was already the most important financier and industrialist in north China. If one can speak of rival Anfu and Chihli militarists contending for power after 1916, it is equally important to identify the group of "Peiyang capitalists," among whom Chou was a central figure, who had close ties with both warlord cliques.[64] Chou's industrial and banking interests continued to expand after 1916 with the blessing of the successive warlord regimes which controlled Peking. His Hua Hsin (Wah Hsing) Cotton Spinning and Weaving Co. opened its first mill in Tientsin in 1916; and other plants were subsequently established at Tangshan, at Tsingtao in Shantung, and at Wei-hui in Honan. By the mid-1920's this firm operated some 200,000 spindles in north China. Chou founded and headed the National Industrial Bank of China (Chung-kuo shih-yeh yin-hang), which was established in Tientsin in 1919 with one-fifth of its initial capital provided by the Ministry of

[64] See, for example, Ch'en Chen, ed., *Chung-kuo chin-tai kung-yeh shih tzu-liao, ti-i-chi,* pp. 300–307.

Finance. In spite of its name, the bank invested very little in industry; serving as an agent for the issue of government bonds was more profitable. Chou was also a founder of the Hua Hsin Bank which opened in Tientsin in 1923; and of the Pu Yu Machinery Co. located near Tientsin which was established in 1921. He had extensive real estate investments at Peithaiho and elsewhere; and interests in gold mining in Manchuria and in a large glass manufacturing company in Wuchang. Chou's important political connections, the fact that many of the associates and investors in his enterprises were themselves civil or military officials, the broad scope of his economic "empire"—all these reinforced each other and before the demise of the Peking government provided a hospitable environment for the growth and prosperity of the Chee Hsin Cement Co.

After 1927 Chee Hsin had very few direct links with the central government. Five of the thirteen members of its board of directors in 1933, for example, had at some time served in the Peking government; only one of these had a post under the Nationalists, and in 1933 he was in Moscow as ambassador. By this time, too, Chee Hsin, as we have seen, was no longer the sole Chinese-owned cement producer. But it is also true that by the time of the Nanking government, Chee Hsin was already very solidly established, largely because of the conspicuous political influence of its founders and officers. The momentum of the earlier years carried the firm comfortably into the 1930's, and it needed little direct political patronage.

The ability of the firm to meet economic and political problems with the success I have indicated must in part be attributed to the stability of its leadership. The thirty-nine men known to have been directors between 1907 and 1948 had an average tenure on the board of ten years; seven of them served twenty years or more. While a larger than usual turnover in the membership of the board occured in the years 1927–1928, and probably in some fashion that I have not been able to determine was related to the important political changes of those years, four of the fourteen new directors who joined the board in the late 1920's and early 1930's were sons or other close relatives of the men whom they replaced; most of the others represented net additions to the size of the board. The technical and sales staff of Chee Hsin probably enjoyed a similar continuity although, apart from the firm's explicit policy of providing high salaries, bonuses, and other perquisites for its middle and upper managerial and technical personnel in order to defend itself against raiding from its competitors, the data on this point are scanty.[65]

CHEE HSIN AND CHINA'S MODERN INDUSTRY

How might one summarize the elements in Chee Hsin's success? It is perhaps first important to note that the firm produced cement and that it was the first, and for a long time the only, Chinese-owned cement manufacturer. Cement is a highly standardized product for which the required raw materials are widespread and the manufacturing technology relatively simple and generally accessible. In some degree, then, such technical decisions as the appropriate factor and product mixes required to operate profitably are less complex in the cement industry than in many others. Even the relatively inexperienced management characteristic of an early stage of industrialization is capable of producing at a profit cement generally free of major technical defects. Most of the industrial enterprises undertaken in China in the first half of the twentieth century were in fact, like Chee Hsin, appropriately of a kind that could be located toward the lower end of a scale measuring the technological sophistication required to manufacture their products. The technology employed, in the form of plans and machinery, was almost entirely imported. In this sense manufacturing firms like Chee Hsin were divorced from the society around them—neither held back by its scientific backwardness nor benefiting from the accumulated skills of its traditional technology. Cement manufacture, because the supply and quality of its raw materials were not dependent upon agricultural output (unlike textiles, flour, cigarettes, matches, and foodstuffs—China's principal pre-1949 industries), was on the side of supply

---

[65] *CHSL*, pp. 300–314; Negishi Tadashi, ed., *Chūkaminkoku jitsugyō meikan* [Directory of Business Firms in the Chinese Republic] (1934), pp. 673–674, lists Chee Hsin's staff as of 1933; some of these persons were with the company before World War I.

additionally and probably beneficially separated from the traditional economy.

The fact that Chee Hsin was the premier firm in the industry is
of major significance. Even when demand is absolutely limited,
the first supplier can both profit and expand so long as that limit
is not reached. Railroad construction in the last years of the
Manchu dynasty, the "rights-recovery movement" and tentative
Chinese industrialization efforts, foreign investment in the treaty
ports, the hiatus left by the temporary withdrawal of foreign
funds and commodities during World War I which Chinese industry rushed to fill—all these provided a potential market for
Chinese-made cement. While Japanese cement remained important in the Shanghai market until the 1930's, in north China
Chee Hsin had a distinct cost advantage over imported cement,
largely because of the high transport costs in relation to value
associated with this bulky, low-value product.

To its early near-monopoly position (enforced for more than a
decade with the aid of its political patrons) and this cost advantage in the north, the firm was able to add (again through the
political influence of its management) stable long-term contracts
to supply the government-owned railroads and the benefits of
substantial tariff concessions. By the time significant Chinese
competition appeared in the mid-1920's, Chee Hsin was already
soundly established with a secure market in the north and was
beginning to expand into south China. The point is that only one
firm can be the first on the scene. Even in the case of cement
where, as has been noted, it is relatively easy for new firms to
enter the industry, the fact that an early-comer has cornered a
large part of a limited market and developed considerable financial, managerial, and technical strength from that secure base
can be decisive in the ensuing competition.

The support of high government officials which contributed to
Chee Hsin's successful beginning and bolstered the firm at least
through the World War I period was paralleled by the financial
strength it enjoyed by being part of a complex of manufacturing
and financial firms controlled by Chou Hsüeh-hsi. Chou not only
lobbied successfully for preferential treatment by the Peking
government, but also obtained Kailan coal and electricity for

Chee Hsin at special rates, and was able to market Chee Hsin's equity shares and bonds among official cronies and his associates in his other enterprises—often the same persons. Chee Hsin, unlike many Chinese-owned firms, never lacked capital for expansion or operating funds until the runaway inflation of the late 1940's. There were other firms in twentieth-century China which were similarly placed; but while one in a handful might be especially privileged, it is of course impossible that all should be. In a sometimes radically unstable political context marked by civil war and foreign aggression, survival, profitability, and growth without some special favor, while not impossible, were always problematic.

As compared with other industries, textiles and tobacco for example, cement manufacture did not face competition from foreign-owned plants located within China and benefiting directly or indirectly from an extraterritorial status. Japanese cement in Manchuria was a possible exception, but very little of its product was marketed in China proper. Coupled with the substantial reduction of cement imports after China's recovery of tariff autonomy in the early 1930's, this favorable circumstance undoubtedly benefited Chee Hsin. Even when the firm operated at considerably below its rated capacity, in part because Japanese cement was allegedly "dumped" in Shanghai and other treaty ports, Chee Hsin was able to produce cement at a profit. Its relatively lower overhead costs (in relation to cement manufacture outside of China) and its low wages which resulted in a lower unit cost for labor in the unit cost of the product made this possible. Other Chinese cement mills probably shared a similar cost structure, though they may have lacked Chee Hsin's other advantages.

Finally, while the backward linkages resulting from Chee Hsin cement production were minimal (it procured most of its equipment abroad, its raw materials were mined by relatively primitive methods), even the substantial forward linkages (cement for China's railroads and the factories and other buildings of the treaty ports) were a mere drop in an oceanic society which boiled and stormed but which was not before 1949 directed to the colossal tasks of social change and economic growth.

Glossary

This selective list provides Chinese characters for some of the names and terms which appear in the text.

Arao Kiyoshi 荒尾精
Chang Chao-tung 張兆棟
Chang Ch'eng 張成
Chang Hsüeh-hua 張學華
Chang Jen-chün 張人駿
Chang Ming-ch'i 張鳴岐
Chang P'ei-lun 張佩綸
Chang Shao-tseng 張紹曾
Chang Shu-sheng 張樹聲
ch'ang-chu 廠主
ch'ang-t'ou 廠頭
ch'ang-yüan 廠員
Chao Erh-sun 趙爾巽
chao-mu sha-ting 招募砂丁
chao-shang 招商
Chee Hsin 啟新
Ch'en Hui-fu 陳惠甫
Ch'en I-k'an 陳儀侃
Ch'en Kuang-fu 陳光甫
Ch'en Kung-po 陳公博
Ch'en Kuo-fu 陳果夫
Ch'en Lan-pin 陳蘭彬
Ch'en Li-fu 陳立夫
Chen-kuan cheng-yao 貞觀政要
Cheng-wen She 政聞社

ch'i 器
chi-shih chih chün 繼世之君
Chiang Fang-chen (Po-li)
　蔣方震 (百里)
Chiang Hsiao-hsien 蔣孝先
Chiang Kuei-t'i 姜桂題
Chiang Monlin (Meng-lin)
　蔣夢麟
ch'iang 強
chiang-t'ou 匠頭
chieh-chang 街長
ch'in-ch'ai ta-ch'en 欽差大臣
Ch'in-cheng tien 勤政殿
ch'in-shen ti-hsiung 親身弟兄
Chin-wei Chün 禁衛軍
Ch'ing-i pao 清議報
Chou Fu 周馥
Chou Hsüeh-hsi 周學熙
Chu T'ing-piao 祝廷彪
Chün-tzu Ch'u 軍諮處
Ch'ung-hou 崇厚
Chung-kuo tzu yu ch'ang-tsun
　中國自有常尊
Chung-wai jih-pao 中外日報

Datsu-A ron 脱亞論

Enomoto Takeaki 榎本武揚
fu-chiang 副將
fu-ch'iang 富強
fu-shou i t'ing-ming
　　俯首以聽命
fu-t'ou 夫頭

Gotō Shimpei 後藤新平
Gotō Shōjirō 後藤象二郎

Hirayama Shū 平山周
Ho Ching 何璟
Ho Ju-chang 何如璋
hou-pu 候補
hsia 硤
hsiang-t'ou 鑲頭
hsiao-huo-chi 小伙計
hsiao-lieh 校獵
hsieh-hsiang 協餉
Hsien-yu Hui 憲友會
Hsin-min ts'ung-pao 新民叢報
Hsing-li ching-i 性理精義
Hsing-li ta ch'üan-shu
　　性理大全書
hsing-wei 行圍
Hsü T'ing-hsü 徐廷旭
Hsü Chi-yü 徐繼畬
Hsü Ch'in 徐勤
Hsü Fo-su 徐佛蘇
Hsü Hsi 徐熙
Hsü Jun 徐潤
hsü-huai na-chien 虛懷納諫
Hu-ch'iang ying 虎槍營

Hua-feng 華豐
huang 塃
Huang Ch'üan 黃筌
Huang Tsung-hsi 黃宗羲
huo-ch'i 火器
Huo-ch'i ying 火器營

I-hsin 奕訢
I-huan 奕譞
Inaba Iwakichi 稻葉岩吉
Inoue Kaoru 井上馨
Itagaki Taisuke 坂垣退助
Iwasaki Yatarō 岩崎彌太郎

jen-shih 人事
jen-ts'ai 人才
Jih-chih hui-shuo 日知薈説

Katsu Kaishū 勝海舟
Katsura Tarō 桂太郎
Kayano Chōchi 萱野長知
Kido Kōin 木戸孝允
Kim Ok-kiun 金玉均
Kishida Kinkō 岸田吟香
Kitamura Saburō 北村三郎
k'o-chang (tax man) 課長
k'o-chang (overseer) 客長
k'o-min 客民
Kokuryūkai 黑龍會
Konoe Atsumaro 近衛篤麿
Kōtoku Shūsui 幸德秋水
Ku Ch'eng-t'ien 顧成天
Ku Chieh-kang 顧頡剛
Ku-wen yüan-chien 古文淵鑑
kuan-shih 管事
kuan-tu shang-pan 官督商辦

Kuang Fang-yen Kuan 廣方言館

Kung Hsin-chan 龔心湛

K'ung chih tao jen tao yeh

孔之道人道也

kuo-min chu-i 國民主義

kuo-t'i 國體

kuo-t'ou 鍋頭

kuo-yün 國運

Lan T'ien-wei 藍天蔚

Li Feng-pao 李鳳苞

Li Han-chang 李瀚章

Li Ho-nien 李鶴年

Li Hung-tsao 李鴻藻

Li Shao-fang 李紹昉

Li Tsung-hsi 李宗羲

li (might) 力

li (profit) 利

li (right) 理

li-ch'üan 利權

Liang Ling-hsien 梁令嫻

lien-chün 練軍

Lin Ch'un 林椿

Lin Shu 林舒

Lin Wen-ho 林文和

Liu Chih-chi 劉知幾

Liu Hung-sheng 劉鴻生

Liu Ming-ch'uan 劉銘傳

Liu Sheng-tsao 劉盛藻

Lo Chia-lun 羅家倫

Lo Hsiao-ang 羅小昂

Lo Jung-kuang 羅榮光

Lo Ta-ch'un 羅大春

Lo-shan t'ang ch'üan-chi

樂善堂全集

Lo-shan t'ang wen-ch'ao

樂善堂文鈔

Lu Chih 陸贄

Lü Han 呂瀚

Lu Jung-t'ing 陸榮廷

lu-chang 鑪(爐)長

lu-t'ou 鑪(爐)頭

Lung Chi-kuang 龍濟光

Mai Meng-hua 麥孟華

Mei Yi-ch'i 梅貽琦

meishu 盟主

Miyazaki Torazō 宮崎寅藏

Miyazaki Tōten 宮崎滔天

Mo-hai shu-kuan 墨海書館

Mori Arinori 森有禮

Mu T'u-shan 穆圖善

Naitō Torajirō 內藤虎次郎

Nakae Chōmin 中江兆民

Nan shu-fang 南書房

niao-ch'iang 鳥鎗

Oda Yorozu 織田萬

Ōi Kentarō 大井憲太郎

Oka Senjin 岡千仞

Onada 小野田

pa-tao 霸道

Pan-li Miao-chiang shih-wu wang

ta-ch'en 辦理苗疆事務

王大臣

Pao Yüan-shen 鮑源深

pao-hsiao 報效

pao-kung t'ou 包工頭

Pao-yün 寶鋆

P'eng Yü-lin 彭玉麟

p'iao 票

Pien Luan 邊鸞

P'u-Fa chan-chi 普法戰紀

Saigō Takamori 西鄉隆盛

Saionji Kimmochi 西園寺公望

Sakamoto Ryōma 坂本龍馬

san-k'ou t'ung-shang ta-ch'en
三口通商大臣

Seng-k'o lin-ch'in 僧格林沁

Shan-ch'i 善耆

Shang shu-fang 上書房

Shao Chi 邵基

shao-lu 哨鹿

Shen Kuei-fen 沈桂芬

Shen Pao-chen 沈葆禎

Sheng Hsüan-huai 盛宣懷

Shiga Shigetaka 志賀重昂

Shih Lang 施琅

Shih Ts'un-t'ung 施存統

shu-yüan 書院

Soejima Taneomi 副島種臣

ssu-ch'eng yang-shui 四成洋稅

Su-pao 蘇報

Sun Chang-fu 孫章甫

Sun To-shen 孫多森

Sun To-yü 孫多鈺

Sun Yin-t'ing 孫蔭庭

Sung Ch'ing 宋慶

Ta-hsüeh yen-i 大學衍義

Tai Chi-t'ao 戴季陶

Takezoe Shin'ichirō 竹添進一郎

T'ang Shou-ch'ien 湯壽潛

T'ang Ting-k'uei 唐定奎

Tarui Tokichi 樽井藤吉

t'i 題

ti-hsiung 弟兄

t'i-tu 提督

t'ien-hsin 天心

t'ien-tao 天道

Ting Jih-ch'ang 丁日昌

Ting Wei-fen 丁惟汾

ting-pen 定本

t'ing-yen na-chien 聽言納諫

Tōa Dōbun Shoin
東亞同文書院

Tong King-sing 唐景星

t'ou-jen 頭人

Tsai-hsün 戴洵

Tsai-t'ao 戴濤

Tsai-tse 戴澤

Ts'ai O 蔡鍔

Ts'ai Yüan-ting 蔡元定

Ts'ao K'e-chung 曹克忠

Ts'en Ch'un-hsüan 岑春煊

Tseng Chi-tse 曾紀澤

Tseng Kuo-ch'üan 曾國荃

Tseng Shao-ch'ing 曾少卿

tsou-ch'ang-che 走廠者

Ts'ui Yu-fu 崔佑甫

Tsung-li shih-wu wang ta-ch'en
總理事務王大臣

tsung-ping 總兵

t'u-ssu 土司

tu-tu 都督

tung-chang 硐(洞)長

t'ung-ling 統領

Tzu-cheng Yuan 自政院
Tzu-li Hui 自立會

Uchida Ryōhei 内田良平
Ueki Emori 植木枝盛
Ura Eiichi 浦敬一

Wai-chiao pao 外交報
Wang Hsiao-ting 王筱汀
Wang K'ai-t'ai 王凱泰
Wang Shih-chen 王士珍
Wang Shih-chieh 王世杰
Wang T'ao 王韜
wang-tao 王道
Wei Han 魏瀚
Wei Yüan 魏源
Wen T'ien-hsiang 文天祥
wen-chiao 文教
Wu Ch'ang-ch'ing 吳長慶
Wu Ching 吳兢
Wu Lu-chen 吳祿貞

Wu Shih-chung 吳世忠
wu-tao (chih) hu-lang Ch'in
無道(之)虎狼秦
wu-yeh p'in-min 無業貧民

Yamagata Aritomo 山縣有朋
Yang Chi-sheng 楊繼盛
Yang Wei-hsin 楊維新
Yao Hsi-chou 姚錫舟
Yeh Ch'u-ts'ang 葉楚傖
Yeh Fu 葉富
Yen Chih-i 嚴智怡
Yen Chung-yüan 言仲远
Yen Tun-yüan 言敦源
Yen Tz'u-yüeh 嚴慈約
Yen Hui-ch'ing 顏惠慶
Yen-Li 顏李
Yin Ju-keng 殷汝耕
Yin-ch'ang 廕昌
yü-lun 輿論
yüan-chih chih chün 願治之君
vung 勇

Index